REORGANIZATION OF NORTH-EAST INDIA SINCE 1947

About the Editors

Dr. B. Datta Ray, (*b.*1925) a pioneer in promoting and popularising research in social sciences in the tribal areas of the North-Eastern India, is the founder-Secretary of the North-East India Council for Social Science Research. A veteran freedom fighter and a Tamrapatra holder, Dr. Datta Ray is a former Head of the Political Science Department of St. Edmund's College, Shillong, and has authored and edited a number of publications.

S. P. Agrawal (*b.*1929) was Director, National Social Science Documentation Centre, ICSSR, and Member-Secretary, Indian Association of Social Science Institution. He was also the Vice-Chairman of the Asia and Pacific Information Network in Social Sciences (APINESS). In 1988, he was awarded the degree of Philosophy in Education (Honoris Causa) by International University Foundation. Presently, he is a Member, Round Table on Research in Reading, IFLA and Member, International Committee for Social Science Information and Documentation. He is also Member of Board of Studies of National Archives of India and Hindi Advisory Committee, Ministry of Coal, Government of India. Born and brought up in the cradle of freedom movement which he joined at the tender age of twelve, he gained an insight into political problems and developed a sense of responsibility which bore fruit as an information scientist committed to Gandhiji's philosophy and action-plan in the field and its social concept. He has written extensively on various aspects of education, Indian polity and library and information Science.

REORGANIZATION
OF
NORTH-EAST INDIA SINCE 1947

Edited by
B. DATTA RAY
Secretary
North-East India Council for Social Science Research
SHILLONG

S. P. AGRAWAL
Former Director
National Social Science Documentation Centre, ICSSR,
NEW DELHI

CONCEPT PUBLISHING COMPANY, NEW DELHI-110059

ISBN 81-7022-577-9

First Published 1996

B.**Datta Ray** (*b*.1925)
S.P.**Agrawal** (*b*.1929)

Printed and Published by
Ashok Kumar Mittal
Concept Publishing Company
A/15-16, Commercial Block, Mohan Garden
New Delhi-110059 (India)

Phones: 5648039, 5649024
Fax: 091-(11)-5648053
E-mail: publishing@conceptpub.com

INTRODUCTION

The British took over Assam in 1826 to make the eastern frontier of the British possessions secure, although the architect of the British possession of the extended north-east frontier, David Scott, initially was against the permanent occupation of Assam. But the scene completely changed with the discovery that the tea plant was a native of Assam. The realisation that the plant was genuine tea and capable of manufacture into a marketable item and later discovery of open seams of coal and presence of petroleum and other minerals made Assam attractive to British capital investment in progressive measure. The initial hesitancy vanished and Assam was finally annexed in 1838. Assam underwent rapid transformation after this and British investment increased. With the final annexation of Assam, the Government of India assumed as successor government, the paramountcy over the north-east Hills. Like the Ahoms, the Supreme Government pursued a policy of non-interference tempered by conciliation and display of force. During the period of 1826 and 1874, the British authority extended over the hills bordering Assam and Barak valley.

During this period, relations with the hills had been handled on an adhoc basis by the officials in the neighbouring areas. The degree of authority exercised by the British on becoming the paramount power had varied in different areas and in reference to different races of hillmen. The object of British policy towards the hills had been conciliation and penetration giving the north-east India a new territorial and administrative unity.

The British inherited and continued the Inne Line policy from the Ahoms. This was assimilated and brought into line with their own political philosopy of broad non-intervention pursued elsewhere in India at that time. The Inner Line Regulation of 1873, the Scheduled Districts Act, 1874, the Government of India Act, 1919, the Government of India Act, 1935 broadly unfold the British tribal policy and administration of north-east India.

Under the Government of India Act, 1935, the administration of hill areas of the province of Assam were classified into Excluded and Partially Excluded Areas, Excluded Areas remaining with Governor of Assam exercising power in his discretion without ministerial advice. The initiative in all legislative and executive acts in the Partially Excluded Areas lay with the Provincial Ministers, but the Governor of Assam had a special responsibility acting in his individual judgement in this field.

With the coming of the Constitution of India in 1950, the tribal areas of north-east India were placed in two parts, A and B in the Table appended to the Sixth Schedule to the Constitution. In the part A, the United Khasi and Jaintia Hills District, the Garo Hills District, the Naga Hills District, the North-Cachar Hills and the Mikir Hills District were placed. The North-East frontier Tracts including Balipara Frontirer Tract, Tirap Frontier Tract, Abor Hill and Mishmi Hills and the Naga Hills Tribal Areas were categorised in Part B . Part A areas formed the Autonomous Districts and were administered by the Government of Assam with the Autonomous District Councils established in 1952 except in Naga Hills District. The Governor of Assam continued to administer at his discretion Part B areas as Agent to the President of India. The Naga Hills were restive and refused the scheme under the Sixth Schedule to the Constitution. In 1954, after minor territorial adjustments, the North-East Frontier Tracts with Abor Hills and Mishmi Hills Districts were transformed into North-East Frontier Agency, under Ministry of External Affairs. Subsequently in 1965, the Ministry of Home Affairs took charge of it. The Lushai Hills District became Mizo District in 1954.

The Tuensang Division of North-East Frontier Agency and the Naga Hills District became a new administrative unit under the Ministry of External Affairs in 1957. The Government of Assam lost its authority over the Naga Hills District and the rolling back process began. In December, 1963, the State of Nagaland was born. Nagaland became the trend-setter. The demands for separate political identities in the hills gathered momentum. A short lived experiment was made to stem the tide in the form of Autonomous State of Meghalaya in 1970. Meghalaya was made a full state in 1972. The North-Eastern Frontier Agency was transformed into Arunachal Pradesh and upgraded along with Mizoram into Union Territory. The Governor of Assam lost his administrative control over Arunachal Pradesh. The dream of greater Assam ended thus in 1972. The princely States of Manipur and Tripura which acceded to Union of India in 1949 under the Instrument of Accession were initially under respective Chief Commissioners and in 1972 they became full fledged states.

The Government of India Act, 1935 and the Constitution of India kindled the aspirations of middle class leadership of the Brahmaputra valley for an expanded Assam. The inner contradiction of the emerging society, the emergence of new middle classes in the Hills, ethnic and linguistic assertions, the lack of sensitivity for equitable economic development in the leadership led to the break up of Assam as it stood on the coming of Constitution of India which released new social forces all over the north-east. Insurgency for ethnic identity broke the fragile administrative unity believing that homelands would give better chance in the changing geopolitical scenario. History is a hard taskmaster. Like nature, it asserts itself. Reorganisation is a continuous process. So, further reorganisation of north-east, within the broad frame of the Union of India cannot be ruled out.

B. DUTTA ROY

ACKNOWLEDGEMENTS

The papers included in this volume were presented to a Seminar on Reorganization of North-East India since 1947 organised by North-East India Council for Social Science Research, Shillong, in February 1993. The basic perimeter of the seminar was framed by Professor Imdad Hussain of the Department of History, North Eastern Hill University. Professor B. Pakem, Vice-Chancellor, North Eastern Hill University not only inaugurated the seminar with an exposition of the basic issues of North-East India reorganisation but was a source of academic inspiration for this work.

We remain very grateful to the Indian Council of Historical Research, Indian Council of Social Science Research, New Delhi, North Eastern Council and Government of Mizoram for giving us generous support to undertake this study.

We wish to record our appreciation of the services of Mr. Rajarishi Roy, a journalist of Calcutta, who read the manuscript and of Mr. H.K.Gupta who gave me a strong secretarial support in the preparation of this volume.

To Mr. Ashok Kumar Mittal of the Concept Publishing Company, New Delhi, we owe a debt of gratitude for agreeing to publish this volume expeditiously.

B. DATTA RAY
S. P. AGRAWAL

CONTENTS

LIST OF CONTRIBUTORS

S. K. Agnihotri - Scholar, Meghalaya House, New Delhi
S. N. Ali - Deptt. of Political Science, Arunachal University, Itanagar
R. P. Athparia - Anthropological Survey of India, Shillong
Mrinmayi Banerjee - Anthropological Survey of India, Shillong
M. C. Behera - Zero, Arunachal Pradesh.
R. P. Bhattacharjee - Economic & Statistical Deptt., Arunachal Pradesh, Itanagar
Biman Kar - Deptt. of Economics, Gauhati University, Guwahati
P. C. Biswas - Scholar, Calcutta
Mahadev Chakravarti - Deptt. of History, Tripura University Agartala
Sucheta Sen Choudhuri - Anthropological Survey of India, Shillong
Sarit Choudhuri - Anthropological Survey of India, Shillong
J. N. Chowdhury - Scholar, Shillong
M. M. Das - Anthropological Survey of India, Shillong.
Nitendra Nath Das - Scholar, Sibsagar, Assam
Samir Kumar Das - Deptt. of Political Science, Calcutta University, Calcutta
P. S. Datta - Lal Bahadur Shastri National Academy of Administration, Mussurie, U.P.
L. S. Gassah - Deptt. of Political Science, North Eastern Hill University, Shillong
B. B. Goswami - Scholar, Lucknow
Imdad Hussain - Deptt. of History, North-Eastern Hill University, Shillong
Jagdish Kalita - Barama College, Barama, Assam
Sukhendu Mazumdar - Scholar, Assam Rifles, 99 A.P.O.
Prafulla Misra - Shillong Observer, Shillong
S. S. Mishra - Anthropological Survey of India, Ranchi, Bihar
S. K. Mukherjee - Anthropological Survey of India, Shillong
A. K. Neog - National Commission of Scheduled Castes and Scheduled Tribes, Shillong
R.N. Prasad - Deptt. of Public Administration, North Eastern Hill University, Aizawl, Mizoram
Asok Kumar Ray - Presidency College, Mothung, Manipur.
Jagat Jyoti Roy - Scholar, Tripura Darpan, Agartala
N.N. Sengupta - Anthropological Survey of India, Shillong
Archana Sharma - Deptt. of Economics, Gauhati University, Guwahati
R. P. Singh - Deptt. of Earth Science, Manipur University, Imphal
D. R. Syiemlieh - Deptt. of History, North-Eastern Hill University, Shillong
A. C. Talukdar - Deptt. of Political Science, Arunachal University, Itanagar

HISTORICAL BACKGROUND

1

ASSAM
Unification and Roots of Division

IMDAD HUSSAIN

Sir John Strachey's remark in an address to Cambridge undergraduates in 1884 that there "never was an India" of the kind that emerged under the British in the nineteenth century could well have been said of modern Assam. The province they bequeathed to an independent India in 1947 was never before a single political unit and the several states that have since emerged in the hill areas were not only independent of any valley based authority but also of one another. The Ahoms, the predecessors of the British in the Brahmaputra valley where they ruled for about six hundred years and after whom the kingdom and the modern province came to be known, never held the surrounding hills. Nor did the writ of the rulers of precolonial Cachar, themselves little in common with the Ahoms, run in the hills about the Barak valley.

The hill tribes however, did not remain as isolated as it is often but erroneously supposed. Apart from the more perceptible results of interaction in the marshlands there is evidence to suggest a continuous and close contact between the hills and the plains. This was a relationship that was later blurred by an overemphasis on the part of the British of the obvious physical and cultural differences. And with their love for the exotic, the British while conceding the connection of the two valleys with the rest of the country historical and cultural were less inclined to consider the hill peoples as part of India. Another distinguished member of the Indian Civil Service and a

Governor of the province, Sir Robert Reid, said of them in the early 'forties:

> they are not Indian in any sense of the word, neither in origin, nor in language, nor in appearance, nor in habits, nor in outlook, and it is only by historical accident that they have been tacked to an Indian province.

The historical accident in reality began a century and a half ago when after the first Anglo-Burmese War (1824-26) the East India Company occupied for the security of the Eastern-frontier as the British had declared, the western end of the Brahmaputra valley comprising roughly the districts of Kamrup, Nowgong and Darang, Cachar was brought Under British protection during the war and annexed in 1832. Eastern or Upper Assam corresponding to the district of Sibsagar and parts of Lakhimpur on the north bank of the Brahmputra which was restored to an Ahom prince in 1834, was resumed only four years later. The frontier areas further east occupied by the Khamti, Muttock and Singpho tribes, which began as a political agency, were brought under effective administrative and military control during 1839-43 in the interests of the tea industry. About the same time, the eastern Bhutan *duars* were annexed. The first hill area to come under the Company were the Khasi States, during 1829-33, where a determined resistance by the Khasi to colonial controls were overcome. The adjoining Jaintia Raj was annexed in the following year. The appointment of a British officer in Tura in 1856 led to the creation of the Garo Hills District which was made part of Assam. A similar appointment in the same year in Chumukedima the Samaguting, of British records, led to the formation of Naga Hills District.

These areas together with Goalpara and Sylhet were united in 1874 to become the province of Assam, administered by a Chief Commissioner directly under the Governor-General in Council. The old Commissionership of Assam associated with the names of Scott, Jenkins and Hopkinson consisted to Kamrup, Nowgong, Darrang, Sibsagar and Lakhimpur and the hill districts of the Garo, Naga and the Khasi & Jaintia Hills. The last was a political agency since 1835 and became a district of Assam only in 1854. Assam was one of the less important divisions under Bengal, the Commissioner however, dealing directly with the Government of India on frontier as Agent to the Governor-General. Goalpara was a part of Cooch Behar commissionership and Cachar since its annexaion of Dacca, though the North-Cachar Hills were transferred to Assam in 1839 for better defence against the troublesome Angamis. The new province as planned by Lord Mayo was to include the entire northern frontier of Bengal consisting of Darjeeling, Jalpaiguri and Cooch Behar but, It has been suggested, Bengali opposition allowed the transfer of only Goalpara. The Bengali *duar* of Buxa, vital for the defence of Bhutan frontier, was attached to Goalpara and was included in the Eastern Frontier of Assam Command.

It was in south-east Bengal where frontier problems had a more direct impact upon territorial adjustments. The Lushais who were a thorn at the side alike of Chittagong, Sylhet, Cachar and the native states of Manipur and Tipperah or Tripura called for a uniform policy and a single administration to deal with them. This, in the opinion of Government of India, could be provided if all these areas were placed under Assam, already experienced in frontier management. Once again, Bengali sentiments stood in the way of separation of Chittagong and its Hill tracts from the presidency. Only Cachar and Sylhet where tea interests were in favour of association with a name already famous for the quality of its tea became a part of Assam. The proposal for the transfer of Chittagong and the Hill Tacts was revived in the nineties, this time along with the newly annexed Lushai hills. One view was that the Chin Hills and the Arakan Hill Tracts of Burma should be attached to the Lushai Hills and placed under Assam. Sir Alexander Mackenzie, Burma's Chief Commissioner, who successfully opposed the move would have rather liked that:

> "Bengal should make over the Chittagong District, the Chittagong Hill Tracts District, and Hill Tipperah to Assam, and that a Commissionership should be formed under Assam embracing these tracts .... the North and South Lushai Districts and Cachar and Sylhet."

In the event Bengal gave up, only the South Lushai Hills which amalgamated with the Northern Hills already under Assam became the Lushai Hills District in 1898. By then Assam had further grown: the Naga Hills had extended and became settled district in 1881, though not before Naga resistance following the occupation of Kohima three years ago was crushed. Within a decade the Ao Naga territory was incorporated into the district as a sub-division. At the Simla Conference in 1913-14, the McMahon Line delineated the border with Tibet and the entire area became the North East Frontier Agency (NEFA) now Arunachal Pradesh and became a part of Assam.

For long Assam did not have its own civil service cadre and officers were 'loaned' from Bengal. They returned to their province in normal course after a five-year posting and Assam seldom was able to retain the services of senior civilians. "Covenented civilians from Bengal", Assam's Chief Commissioner Sir Joseph Bamfylde Fuller had protested, "offer the Bengal Government an irresistible temptation to plant upon (Assam) its undersirables". The solution of Assam's problems was the expansion of the commission, a point elaborated in a minute by the Government of India's Home Secretary, Sir Herbert Risley, in 1903:

> "It (Assam) requires territorial expansion in order to give its officers a wide and interesting field of work. It requires a maritime outlet in order to develop its industries in tea, oil and coal. The paying propositions of the Assam-Bengal Railway are in the south, and the whole if it is to be utilised in the interest of the ought to be under a single administration. Assam moreover will continue to be handicapped, so long as it is dependent for its service upon what it may be fortunate enough to borrow from Bengal. A province that only offer the prize of one Chief Commissionership that is remote in locality and backward in development and organisation will not attract the highest type of civilians to its employ. The Government of India regard it indeed incontestable that, with a service recruited as at present and confined within the present limits, Assam will find extreme difficulty in at-

> taining the level of a really efficient administration; and it is for this reason that, in considering the question of changes, they are impressed with the paramount necessity for making them on such a scale as will remove this fundamental source of weakness, and will, if possible, give Assam a service of its own, offering a career that will attract and retain men of ability and mark. No temporary opposition in the transferred towns or areas, no artificial agitation or interested outcry, should in their opinion be permitted to divert the efforts of Government from the main object, viz. creation of Assam into a vigourous and self-contained administration capable of playing the same part on the North-East Frontier that the Central Provinces have done in the centre, and the Punjab formerly did on the North West."

The proposed transfer of Chittagong would possibly have answered, even if partially, Assam's needs. But Lord Curzon's anxiety to reduce Bengal's size led to the inclusion of Dacca and Mymensing also. The Governor-General writing more on the basis of maps than on ground realities thus argued his case in a minute on 1 June 1903:

> "Geographically, Dacca and Mymensing are separated by a clear line of division, viz. the main channel of the Brahmaputra (though it is not here called the Brahmaputra) from Bengal. If they are joined to Assam, the latter will possess a definite and intelligible western boundary, whereas if the Chittagong division goes to Assam, and Dacca and Mymensing are left wisth Bengal, the two latter divisions will constitute a projection from the main body of Bengal obtruding itself into the heart of Assam, from which they will be separated by no ties of origion, language, region, or administration. Not only would the transfer enable Assam to obtain an independent service, but that service will possess three separate commissionerships, which would be its prized appointments. There would be: (1) the Brahmaputra Valley or Assam proper; (2) Dacca to which would be added Sylhet and Cachar, and (3) Chittagong."

The inclusion of the districts of Pabna, Bogra, Rangpur as well as Rajshahi, Dinajpur, Jalpaiguri, Malda and Cooch Behar went beyond Curzon's original scheme. As a single charge under a Lieutenant Governor, it was of the greatest benefit to the tea industry. Significantly, it was in their interests that the new province was named Eastern Bengal and Assam by the Secretary of State instead of 'North-Eastern Provinces' as proposed by the Government of India: "important commercial interests representing the tea industry would complain, 'India was told, if the name of Assams, now so widely known in world market as the chief source of Indian tea, was to disappear from the list of Indian provinces." To security concerns and administrative demands as factors in territorial organisation were other issues to be soon added.

The vast and diverse frontier brought under varying degrees of control and organised as district territorial units constitutionally within Assam were never administratively integrated. Rather Acts and Regulations and such measures as those in the northern frontier following the Expedition of 1912 though marking no dimunition of provincial territory, emphasised differences between the hills and the plains. It was this that the constitutional reforms after the First world was brought into sharper focus and perpetuated. Assam were never administratively integrated. Rather Acts and Regulations and such measures as those in the northern frontier following the Expedition of 1912 though marking no dimunition of provincial territory, emphasied differences between the hills and the plants. It was this that the constitutional reforms after the First World War brought into sharper focus and perpetuated.

The Montague-Chelmsford Reforms introduced albeit in a very limited form 'responsible' governments in the provinces based on an extended franchise and direct elections. But representation in the legislature was not territorial but based on religion and caste differentiation. Nevertheless they provided an apportunity and marked the beginning of mass involvement in Indian politics. The exclusion of hill districts and backward tracts from the reform scheme ensured their effective insulation from political developments in the rest of the country. Years later, the British could thus boast that "Gandhi cuts no ice with the hill people" and that his stock in these parts was not as high as in the provinces.

It was no coincidence that the Naga Clubs demand before the Simon Commission in 1928 for exclusion the constitutional reforms should also be the view of the Assam Government. In their memorandum to the Commission, Assam had stated:

> "The backward tracts should be excluded from the province of Assam in the new Constitution. These areas have nothing in common with the rest of the Province. There is no sympathy on either side and the union is an artificial one resented by both parties ......the Government of Assam is convinced that in the interests, both of the backward tracts and the rest of the Province, the present artificial union should be ended."

"The hills are an unprofitable possession," added the Naga Hills" John Hutton in a separate note. And "whatever solution to the problem is ultimately adopted, the administration of the hills should be entirely separated from that of the plains,with an entirely separated budget consisting of the receipts the 'backward tracts' plus an annual grant to cover the difference between receipts and expenditures. "The Superintendent of the Lushai Hills N. E. Parry's scheme at the same time for a separte" North Eastern Frontier Hills province to comprise as many of the backward tracts in Assam and Burma as could be conveniently included in it and its later development as the Coupland plan or Crown Colony scheme is now well documented.

Neither, however was the Assam Government nor its frontier officers singular in their advocacy of separation of hill districts from the plains. One member of the legislature from the Brahmaputra Valley, cited in Assam's *Memoranda* and later to be approvingly quoted by the leaders of the hill state movement, said on the floor of the House: "In our scheme it is submitted that the hill districts, with the exception of British portion of the Khasi Hills may be administered by his Excellency the Governor as Agent for the Government of India, and the whole expenditure also may be borne by the Government of

India". The remark of a member from Sylhet in the debate was even more emphatic:

> "If I read the signs and portents of the time correctly, I feel most sure that the hill districts will be separated sooner or later and I hope within about five or six year."

An Assamese Swarajist concurred; "Before long Assam Valley will have to see its own way to disjoin itself from the hill districts."

The British succeeded in excluding the Naga, Lushai and the North Cachar Hills and the Balipara and Sadiya Frontier Tracts from the Assam Legislature. As regards the other hill districts, J.J.M. Nichols–Roy says:

> "I wrote strongly against that exclusion. I was able to convince the Assam Governor Sir Lawrie Hammond to make the British portion of the Khasi and Jaintia Hills, the Garo Hills and the Mikir Hills to be partially excluded areas".

Nichols-Roys writings provide the tribal perception of the future of the hill areas in independent India. His *Hill Districts of Assam, Their Future in the New Constitution* submitted to the Cabinet Mission argued for greater autonomy for the tribal areas within Assam. But as he records in his *Memorandum of Personal Views supporting the Demand for a Separate Hill State,* disillusionment set in against the Assamese leadership during the debates in the Constituent Assembly and over the question of powers of the District Council and Shillongs future. By the time of the State Re-organisation (1954) the idea of a separate state was firmly entrenched in Garo and Khasi and Jaintia Hills.

The Memorandum submitted by the Highlander's Union to the States Reorganisation Commission in April 1954 envisaged a 'frontier Hill State' comprising the former excluded and partially excluded areas. But developments elsewhere had already eroded the unity move. The case of the Naga Hills and its elevation to a Union Territory finally to statehood is well known. By now the Government of India too appears to have come round to the hill leaders', way of thinking on the feasibility of small states. The fiction of NEFA as constitutional part of Assam, got undermined when the matter was placed in the hand of the External Affairs Ministry who decided to go away with it. The conclusion seems inevitable that in the tortuous process of reorganisation of Assam, the Government of Independent India proved to the true successors of the British.

2

THE FUTURE OF THE HILLS OF NORTH-EAST INDIA 1928-1947

Some British Views

DAVID R. SYIEMLIEH

I

Speaking at the annual prize distribution ceremony of the Welsh Mission Girls' High School in Shillong on 13 November 1941, the Governor of Assam, Sir Robert Neil Reid, told the audience of school children, their parents and guests that India was on the threshold of great many changes. "Where do you come in this picture?" he asked them. He then went on to say:[1]

> "It may be – it is no new thought, for it has been canvassed in the press often enough, that the destiny of these hills and other areas in Assam will follow another course than that of being linked with those of India proper. It may be otherwise. But sooner of later the question is going to be canvassed and the decision will depend in great measure on public support."

The Governor had only six days earlier completed a confidential twenty-two page pamphlet: *A Note on the Future of the Present Excluded, Partially Excluded and Tribal Areas of Assam* in which he suggested to Government the separation of the hill areas of North-East India and North-West Burma from their respective dominions and placed "perhaps under some appropriate department at Whitehall."[2] Reid was not the originator of the 'Crown Colony Scheme'. He had developed the ideas of N.E. Parry who had been Deputy Commissioner of the Garo Hills and later for many years served as Superintendent of the Lushai Hills District, and those of Dr. John H. Hutton who had served the Naga Hills District as its Deputy Commissioner. These two officers had each submitted separate memoranda to the Indian Statutory Commission (1928) on the future of the areas under their charge in a constitutionally reformed India. Hutton particularly showed how the hill people neither racially, historically, culturally, nor linguistically had any affinity with the people of the Assam plains, while their administration was wholly on different lines. He and Parry both suggested the formation of a North Eastern Frontier Province to comprise as many of the backward tracts of Assam and Burma as would be conveniently included in it.[3]

Hutton elaborated the plan in 1930[4] and 1935.[5] In all, the province would comprise 16 districts out of Assam and Burma. The advantages he believed were many but he stressed that it would enable people on both sides of the "so-called watershed", having common customs, languages and living under similar conditions to come under one administration. It would provide an opportunity for their political advance on corporate tribal lines. He saw of the opinion that the separation of India and Burma (1935) would permanently divorce portions of tribes which naturally should comprise a single unit. He saw the possibility of consolidation of a polyglot area into an uniform administrative unit with ultimately a common language as English for official purposes. As a separate province it would justify its own provincial cadre recruited for the province as a whole instead of borrowing civil servants from other provinces in India and Burma. Hutton also touched on the strategic importance of such a province should China "ever recover from her internal disorders, the question of the Chinese Frontier is likely to become more important than it is at present."[6]

The proposition for a North-East Frontier or some form of amalgamated administration had "great attraction" for

Government. However, when the constitutional changes took place, instead of the proposed province taking shape the backyard tracts in North-East India were redesignated Excluded and Partially Excluded Areas put under the special supervision of the Assam Governor. Sir Robert Reid said that the Act of 1935 had not given the hill people sufficient safeguards. As to their future, he argued that it would have to be decided by the British Parliament. "It cannot be left to Indian Political leaders", he believed, "with neither knowledge, interest nor feelings for these areas". He quoted the Secretary of State for India and Burma, L.S. Amery, who on 3 March 1941 said of Burma and its separation from India:[7]

> "That separation was the natural consequence of the introduction of self -government, for in her racial type and her culture, as well as in her geographical position Burma belongs not to India, But to the projection of the main bulk of Asia and the Indo-Chinese peninsula."

This, the Governor stressed, applied just as closely to the people of the Assam hills and that the "boundary between our hills and the Burma hills is as artificial as it is imperceptible."[8] Reid saw a way out of this situattion by reviving Hutton's idea of a North-East Province or Agency embracing all the hill fringe from the Lushai and Lakher land in the south in a crescent shape round to the hills of present day Arunachal Pradesh. Included in this scheme were the Chittagong Hill Tracts (to provide an outlet to the sea), the areas inhabited by the Nagas and Chins of Burma "and perhaps the Shan States to." He also included in this plan the 25 Khasi states and Manipur and the unadministered territory – the Naga Tribal Area of the Naga Hills District and the Tirap Frontier Tract further north. The proposed Agency would cover a large area of 68,985 square miles of administered and unadministered hill areas and 'native' states territories under India. Its population, he calculated, would be about 2.5 million. If the Burma areas were incorporated the area and population of the proposed scheme would increase considerably.[9]

The radical point of the *Note* under discussion is that Reid planned to remove the areas mentioned above from both the Indian and Burmese Government. He wrote:[10] "I would put this under a Chief Commissioner and he is turn would I imagine have to be divorced as is Burma from the control of the Government of India ..... and put perhaps under some appropriate department of Whitehall". This was the message Reid tried to convey to his audience that November day. He was convinced of the practicability of the scheme and wanted to change the destiny of the hill people and their future by this bold and rather controversial subject. Reid did admit that what he wanted was only a tentative proposal. Much detail would have to be filled in. But supposing it were decided, for whatever reason, that the plan he had attempted to outline were impracticable, he felt it was necessary to consider alternatives. He concludes the *Note* with these lines:[11]

> "I trust that sufficient has been said to prove that to place the hills under the control of the Ministry of an Assam as now constituted is utterly impossible and unworkable. A workable intermediate arrangement, though I would not myself advocate it, might be found in the formation of a Province of the Assam Valley only and in placing the hills under that, if they must be placed under a Provincial Government without any of the safeguards that at present exist."

He believed that at least the "old Assamese friendly methods of dealing with the hillmen .... might be in part revived ...... so that the hills would perhaps not get such a bad deal as they certainly would from the Bengali Politicians of the Surma Valley".[12]

II

The first person to have received a copy of the *Note* was the Viceroy, Lord Linlithgow. He thanked Reid for the "valuable Note" and informed that he would send a copy to L.S. Amery, the Secretary of State for India.[13] Amery had this to comment:[14]

> Supposing that Pakistan does come off, there will be possibly two Muslim areas, the whole of the states, Hindu British India.....and finally at least an important primitive hill tribe areas such as that which Reid has very interestingly outlined in the memorandum which reached me by the last mail.

He in turn passed the *Note* to the oxford Professor, Reginald Coupland who carefully succeeded in changing a private and confidential report into a scheme that took his name.[15] Burma found the plan "attractive and if other considerations are not involved would be worth pursuing".[16] By then the plan had caught the fancy of the Government of Burma, operating from Simla. The issue of amalgamating the hill areas of Burma and India was discussed at length at a series of meetings of the Committee on Scheduled Areas between 5 and 11 December 1942. Although the Committee in its meeting of 11 December voted not to resort to the amalgamation plans,[17] Governor Dorman Smith continued to flirt with the scheme well upto 1945.

That the plan was discussed in very high government circles, there was no doubt. Though it had its attractions to the last of the British administrators it came at a time when India was in the final phase of its struggle for independence. If implemented it would have added a new dimension to the partition of the subcontinent. The only difference would have been that the areas in the Agency or protectorate would still not have been independent but would have been:[18]

> "on lines of the High Commission territories in South Africa i.e that they should remain directly under the Crown representative until such time as His Majesty's Government, after the inhabitants have been consulted, feel justified in transferring them to an Indian Government."

III

Meanwhile serious discussions were in progress through 1943 to 1946 on the question of administrative amalgamation of the India and Burma tribal areas. It is not possible here to go into the details of the discussions and the decisions that were taken.[19] However, some of the developments need to be highlighted to see the trend of thinking on the future of the hill areas under study. The question of the readjustment of the frontier between Assam and Burma and Tribal Areas and the desirability of some system of coordination of administration was discussed at an informal meeting, held in Delhi on 10 March 1945. Attending the meeting apart from Sir Olaf Caroe, the Secretary of the External Affairs Department and Richardson, the Deputy Secretary, were J.P. Mills, Adviser to the Governor of Assam and R.E. McGuire of the Scheduled Areas Department of the Government of Burma. The Burmese Government official made it clear that his Government was not in favour of administrative amalgamation. It was viewed by the five members that distinct tribes should generally not be divided between two administrations and that boundaries should be drawn as to bring as far as possible the whole of a tribe under that Government which already had included in its territory the major population of a tribe. This meant that the Nagas in the adjacent hills in Burma would be brought within India except some Burmanised groups. Similarly, the Lakhers may be incorporated in Burma to enable them to be united with the majority of the tribe in the Chin hills. As to the future of the hill areas then administered under the Assam Province, Sir Andrew Clow, Reids successor as Governor of Assam, conveyed through his Adviser that he:[20]

> "preferred to envisage a future in which the Tribal Areas and Excluded Areas should be merged into the Province of Assam rather than cut off from it."

The meeting also ruled out the conversion of the Partially Excluded Areas (the Garo, Khasi, Jaintia and Mikir

Hills) to the status of Tribal Areas but left the question of the status of the Excluded Areas and Tribal Areas for future discussion. The solution to the problem of administrative adjustments, given Burma functioning as a separate province and Sylhet and some adjoining territories being tagged to Bengal was the formation of a province rather on the lines of Baluchistan, the same Official acting as Chief Commissioner for the Brahmaputra

Valley and the Partially Excluded Areas, as Resident for Manipur and the Khasi States and as Agent to the Governor-General for the remainder of the Province.[22] It was speculated that the Excluded and Tribal Areas would be brought under the Centre's administration but that it was essential to have a policy keeping in view the importance of the development of these areas away from paternal rule towards a system of Tribal Councils or bodies based on indigenous customs. The members admitted that these areas were not ready for Western democratic institutions and thus the eventual objective might be:[23]

> "That they should enter a Federal India of the future on the basis of their own institutions, no steam-roller of British Indian practice and procedure having been passed across them."

IV

Since the Centre was hoping that the charge of the Excluded Areas and the Tribal Areas would be given to the External Affairs Department the exact administrative and constitutional position had to be sought before the Indian Constituent Assembly could decide its future. Sir Andrew Clow's private and official correspondence makes it very clear that these areas were for all practical purposes not technically within the empire. He wrote to Sir Charles Pawsey, then the last Deputy Commissioner of the Naga Hills District that "the statutory Naga Hills tribal areas is completely independent and at liberty to negotiate on its own terms -or bid for time".[24] He also informed the Indian Constituent Assembly that the Naga Tribal areas and the

Tirap Frontier Tract were both technically and for practical purposes outside British India, for there was no statutory boundary between them and the adjoining districts of the province. He also informed that regarding the Tribal Areas of the Balipara and Sadiya Frontier Tracts and of Tirap Frontier Tract, "it can be held on a very strict interpretation of the flaw, that the fortuitous absence of an inner statutory boundary make them part of Assam and so of British India."[25] But he cautioned, "not only is this interpretation so entirely contrary to the administrative position that the Government of India have always treated the area as 'tribal', but it is also contrary to the position embodied in usage and treaty."[26]

Sir Andrew Clow wanted the Tribal Areas to be grouped together in a state-like structure to negotiate with the Government of India through their own representation"... it is only by giving the tribes the right to put them forward as their spokesmen that they can be heard. If unsuitable arrangements are imposed from above on tribesmen, who have not been heard, there will be bitter discontent and unrest on this frontier" he cautioned. Clow criticised Reid's administration that there was too much of a tendency to treat the tribals as subjects "for preservation and study rather than as objects of our help and guidance." "He made a criticism of British policy as being too chary of extending our administration and too slow in building up self–government institutions among them."[27]

Meanwhile J.P. Mills had been at work to compile a small but very useful pamphlet.[28] After reviewing the indigenous tribal administrative system, the historical background, the racial and cultural background and other related subjects, he put down his own view of the possible alternatives of the relationship between the hills and the plains of Assam. He ruled out that it was in the best interest of all the hill tribals to be included in Assam. Under the second alternative, the choice appeared to lie between the "two extremes of excluding only some of the present tribal areas and to including only the present partially excluded areas." The third alternative which he espoused was "that of temporarily extending all the hills from Assam and according to them special treatment designed, on the lines of indirect rule" to develop those indigenous institutions which still then survived, and to fit the tribes for eventual union with the province of Assam.[29] Chapter 15 and the remaining chapters of the monograph were devoted to working out how the Hill Districts, Frontier Tracts, Agencies and States in the region could be administered as either a Province or a Union of States; the composition of Council; their powers and functions, finance and indirect rule.

Similarly, at work was Sir Andrew Clow who between March and October 1945 worked on a draft treatise that when published[30] was to have much more of clout than the publication of his Adviser. Its significance was not so much the arguments in Chapter V which was devoted to demolish Reid's Crown Colony plan [31]--it was the suggestion he gave for administering the Hill tribes in an independent India. But briefly, his conclusions were that the northern hills (present day Arunachal Pradesh) and part of the Naga tribal areas should be treated as a federal agency. He viewed that for the rest of the Assam hills to be included in the Agency "would be one of the worst solutions". The choice was confined then two possibilities.

(a) A merger of the hills and plains of Assam in a manner which would conserve tribal rights and would recognize in an effective manner the different needs and outlook of the two areas;

(b) The constitution of separate provinces for the hills and the plains with some administrative links.

Clow informed the Victroy, Lord Wavell, soon after the draft was done that of the two possibilities "I have come down after some considerable hesitation in favour of (a)", as the arguments for it appeared to him stronger. Two of the arguments which in particular appealed to him were that it would keep the hill tribes and plains tribes together and that on the long term view there was no future for the Assam hills in separation from the plains. Both the Khasi states and Manipur could be fitte, into any scheme that were devised.[32]

The Governor concluded the *Memorandum* with these very befitting words:[33]

> "Assam is never likely to be as homogeneous as other provinces. The plains peoples are not so divided as those of the hills, but they are far from being a single people such as can be found in many equally large or larger areas in India. But this great collection of peoples, in hills and plains, have been set in a particularly well demarcated corner of the world and their welfare will depend on their proving able to live together. Assam should look to her diversity and to her capacity for toleration, which is greater than that of other provinces, to provide her strength."

It is a pity that we do not have sufficient time at hand to go into the details of all these plans, beginning with those of Hutton and Parry, down to Reid, Mills and Clow. It will appear apparent to many that some of these schemes were utopian, some very sincerely devised but impracticable and still others put into operation with minor modifications. Sadly much of what was suggested did not take shape, such as the well advances discussions to demarcate the Indo-Burma border on ethnic lines; or the decision to allow lakhars to join Burma. There was also no referendum or plebiscite given to the hill people to decide their own future. Neither were tribal leaders of the former 'Unadministered Areas', brought to the negotiating table. In fact, their future was decided not by themselves but by Delhi and Assam-and herein lay the seeds of discontent.

By early 1947, there was no illusion of British permanence in India, and they knew they had so little to say in these matters. Andrew Clow who completed his five year as the last British Governor of Assam on 4 May 1947 put his thoughts down rather pithily:[35]

> "The trouble of course is that we have not the time we would like, and that in the past we tended to

assume that we had much longer. The main thing now is to get the tribal people thinking within the limits of the practical, and my own profound conviction is that they should plump for cooperation and get the best bargain they can."

REFERENCES

1. (I)ndia (O)ffice (L)ibrary and (R)ecords, Reid Collection MSS Eur E/278/11(d).
2 IOLR , L/P&S/12/3115 A. The Note is dated 7 November,1941, See p.16.
3. Memorandum of the Government of Assam to the Indian Statutory Commissioner, Vol. XIV, pp. 111-122.
4. Assam State Archives, Note dated 6 July 1930, Assam Political Proceeding (Reform) A, December, 1930, Nos. 1-3.
5. *Ibid* Note dated 18 Sept. 1935. Assam Political Proceedings A, December 1936. Nos. 1-30.
6. R. Reid, *op.cit.* Note, pp-6-7.
7. *Ibid.* pp. 14-15.
8. *Ibid.*
9 *Ibid.*, p. 17.
10 *Ibid.*, p.16.
11. *Ibid.*, p.22.
12. *Ibid.*
13. IOLR, Reid Collection, MSS Eur E/278/4(9),Letter dated 5 January, 1942.
14 IOLR, Amery Collection, MSS Eur F/125/11, Amery to Linglithgow, 24 March, 1942.
15. IOLR, L/P&J/7/6789, Amery to Coupland, 30 July 1943; R.Coupland, the *Future of India,* London, 1943, p.164. Coupland wrote in his third and final volume on India..."the two areas might be united in a single territory, the administration of which would be separated in some way from the Government of India and Burma."
16. IOLR, M/4/2803, 'The Scheduled Areas of Burma', a confidential note signed by H.J. Mitchell, 26, November 1942.
17. IOLR, M/4/2803, Minutes of the Meeting on the Commission on Scheduled Areas; 5-11December 1942;M/4/2803, Dorman Smith to Pethick Lawrence, 13 August 1945.
18. ILOR, L/P&J/7/6787, Extract from a private and secret letter from Mr. Amery to Lord Wavell, dated 10 August 1944.
19. Also read H.K. Barpujari "New Light on the Proposed Crown Colony" paper read at the FiftyThird Session of the Indian Historical Records Commission, 4-5 February 1990, pp. 18-21.
20. IOLR, L/P&S/12/3115 a record of the Meeting of 10 March 1945.
21. *Ibid.*

22 *Ibid.*

23. *Ibid,* An official in the India Office, London, Initialed a note "If Government decide to implement a proposal to create a new Chief Commissioner's Province... one rather fears that the new proposal may have come to the fire too late to be worked out and brought into effect in time to anticipate other structural arrangement within British India (P.T.P.).

24. Cambridge South Asia Archive, Pawsey Papers, Box 1, No. 5 Clow to Pawsey, 24 April 1947.

25. Draft in *Ibid.*, Box 1.

26. *Ibid.*

27. *Ibid.*, Clow to Pawsey, 26 April 1947.

28. J.P. Mills, A Note on the Future Administration and Constitutional Position of the Present Excluded, Partially Excluded Areas and Tribal Areas in and on the border of Assam, 1945.

29 *Ibid.*, Chaper 14.

30. Andrew Clow, Memorandum on the Future Government of the Assam Tribal People. Shillong, 1945.

31. Clow also published a small pamphlet, The Excluded and Partially Excluded Areas of Assam, in which he argues against Reid's main thesis and calling for the hills ' union in Assam.

32. Andrew Clow, Memorandum, pp. 31-47; IOLR, L/P&J/7/6787, Clow to Wavell, 23, October 1945.

33. *Ibid.*, p. 47.

34. One more British Officer P.F.Adams published a small tract, Some Notes on a Policy for the Hill Tracts, Shillong (5.8.47.) which is referred in V.V. Rao, A Century of Tribal Politics in North East India, 1874-1974, Delhi, pp. 147-149. Note however, that Rao says Adam published his findings in 1945 whereas the tract mentioned above is dated 5.8.1947.

35. Cambridge South Asia Archive, Pawsey Papers, Clow to Pawsey, 26 April 1947.

PERSPECTIVE

3

THE ISSUES OF STATE REORGANISATION
Some Reflections

A. C. TALUKDAR

Although it was a foregone conclusion by the time India achieved freedom that independent India should be a federal state and although the Constitution of India provided for a federal structure, without of course using the word federation, the question of re-organisation of states remained a controversial issue till today. The Indian National Congress in its manifesto of 1945-46, assured the people that the provinces would be constituted on a linguistic and cultural basis. But the fusion of British India and the princely states, into the states of Indian Union under the new reorganisation of the federating units of the country on a rational basis.

The Dar Commission and the JVP (Jawaharlal Nehru, Vallabhbhai Patel and Pattabhi Sitaramaya) Commission that preceded the State Reorganisation Commission of 1953; opined that no new provinces should be formed as India was burdened with problems more urgent than the problem of redistribution of provinces. There was also an apprehension that creation of further provinces may retard the process of consolidation of nation's gains. However, the JVP Commission added that "if public sentiment was insistent and overwhelming, the practicability of satisfying public demands with its implications and consequences must be examined". A political compromise that helped in creating more and more demands and movements for newer and newer states even today. This led to the setting up of the state Reorganisation Commission in 1954 which submitted its report in 1955. The

Commission recommended that India should consist of states to be created on linguistic and cultural basis and union territiories. And the following year, the boundaries of the states in India were redrawn. But the linguistic reorganisation of the states generated more controversies than it solved.[1]

For, while it was successful in accommodating conflicts on the issue of language through the creation of new regional political areas, violent conflicts on the issues of caste, religion, ethnicity, sub-regional interest etc. continued to be at the forefront of Indian politics. They gave rise to fresh demands for more and more states. As a result a number of new states had to be created, most of them being in the North-East. But the rest of the country did not lag behind. As a result a number of States Reorganisation Acts had to be passed by the Parliament creating a new state or altering the boundary of some existing state during the last thirty odd years.[2] They too create more demand than they settled. Today, there are several ongoing demands for new states Jharkhand, Bodoland, Gurkhaland, Marathwada, Bidarbha, Chattisgarh, Uttarakhand, Banachal, Vindhayachal , Telengana and so on. Some of them are very active and others are not so active. But the success of one encourages others to press further their demands and give rise to some fresh demands. The situation has become so acute today that certain political parties have already started demanding another State Reorganisation Commission.[3] Others including certain scholars and academicians have advocated the cause of smaller states. We propose to examine here the efficacy of these suggestions in settling the question of state reorganisations in the light of our experiences so far.

It is true that the Indian federation is still in a process of formation. Given the historical background of the creation of our federation, it can hardly be argued that the shape and size of many of the Indian states will or should remain the same as it is today. No body can deny the fact that some of our linguistic states are so unwieldly , that sheer economic and administrative efficacy demand that they should be reorganised into smaller states. Many of the provinces inherited by India were arbitrarily created by the British and the hurriedly integrated 500 odd princely states often remained outside the mainstream of political process during the Indian Independence Movement.

It could, therefore, be hardly expected that the question of state reorganisation could be settled in one stroke. This fact was probably well recognised by the makers of our Constitution when they empowered the Parliament to create a new state, or alter the names or boundaries of the existing states by simple majority.[4]

Let us first examine the question of small states. The idea of small states is not new. In his dissenting note, appended below the report of the State Re-organisation Commission, 1953, K.M. Panikkar wrote: "I consider it essential for the successful working of a federation that the units be fairly evenly balanced". The Commission itself, in its report noted that in a small state, administration will be more accessible to the people. A closer link between the electorate and its representative may help to bring about a real unity of outlook and community of interest between the people and those charged with their governance. Recently, Prof. Rashiduddin Khan, while advocating the case of smaller states, wrote that a time has come now to go for more rational reorganisation of the states based on the principles of techno-economic viability, socio-cultural homogeneity and administrative and political manageability. He has even identified 59 sub-cultural regions which could form the basis of a federal system. Now the question is, given the prevailing political culture of the country, will it be possible to create so many states without opening a pandora's box? Will it be possible to identify the states with objectivity without yielding to all sorts of political pressures? Will it be possible to limit it to the 'sub-cultural regions' mentioned by Prof. Khan? Is it not likely that many such genuine 'sub-cultural regions' will get overlooked and many other sub-sub-cultural or pseudo-subcultural regions will gain recognition instead?

If we analyse the state demand movements of the country we shall find that while some of them are based on the principles mentioned by Prof. Khan, many others are based on consideration other than those. For example, if a Bodoland state is created tomorrow will it be a techno-economically viable unit? Or will it be a socio-culturally homogeneous unit? It is obvious that apart from the Bodos, the proposed Bodoland will include the Mishings and the Kocha Rajbangshis who are distinct ethno-cultural groups with all potentialities of a future state demand movement. The Karbi Movement is another potential state demand movement which includes the Karbis and Dimasas. In fact, almost all the North-Eastern States, although small in size include in them more than one sub-cultural groups, which may in turn stake their claims for a new state, and the process will be endless. This is so because the Indian nation is still in a process of formation, and the concept of sub-cultural region as a federating unit may thwart that process. Even if we accept that it is possible to do so whom shall we entrust the task to. Obviously, the political leadership. But the political elites today are not capable of undertaking such a gigantic task.

It is widely recognised fact that the great majority of political leadership in the county today are short sighted and guided by self-interest and immediate political gains. They lack the wisdom and vision to safeguard the long-term interest of the country. The average Indian political leader, no longer presents the image of a deliverer, a reformer, someone who would sacrifice his personal interest for the people.

Further, working of the Indian political system for the last 40 years have shown that greater democratisation of Indian politics, even as it brought into the arena people perviously excluded from political participation did not necessarily lead to fulfilment of popular aspirations or desirable socio-economic changes. Often it has revived collective memories of past conflicts, increased sense of deprivation and created new groups and communities aspiring for exclusive or substantial political power. This is well borne out by the experiences in the North-East. This has given rise to a crop of political elite who join politics just to gain power or enrich himself. And the people in India, simple and gullible as they are, place their blind faith or made to place their blind faith in them. In such a state of affairs a large scale reorganisation of the states on rational and logical lines will neither be possible nor desirable.

What is the attitude of the politician to the issue of creation of a new state in the country? If we closely scrutinise the approach of politicians whether it is in Bihar, Assam or Bengal or Uttar Pardesh we see a distinct pattern of politician's approach to the problem. Often the political leaders support such movements when they are out of power but strongly resist it once they are in power. The recent statement of the Chief

Ministers of Bihar, Bengal and Madhya Pradesh in connection with the question of Jharkhand State amply prove this. Another pattern of behaviour discernible in them is, once it affects their home states, political leaders of all hues join hands to resist it irrespective of their party affiliations. Even the less vocal among the political elites outside the movement show a remarkable reluctance to counlenance the need for creating a new state when it concerns their own state. This is often done not because of their genuine concern for the state but for short-term political gains in elections. Any attempt to create a large number of smaller states 'therefore' is bound to be resisted very strongly by the politicians, more so by the ones who are in power.[5]

Another aspect of the reluctance to create large number of smaller states is the argument that it will lead to further increase in the size of bureaucracy and governmental expenditure. This should however be no deterrant if it leads to better administration and effective socio-economic development. But the results of the last four decades are before us to show that, in the prevailing climate of self-seeking and corruption there is absolutely no guarantee that smaller states will necessarily lead to better economic growth and administrative efficiency. The performance of the smaller states in the North-Eastern Region is not very encouraging. None of the states of the region, except Arunachal Pradesh today are free from socio-political problems. All of them are special category state and are largely dependent on the Centre for their survival, a situation which negates the very concept of a genuine federation. According to a study conducted by N.N. Bhattacharya, the viability rating of as many as five (Meghalaya, Manipur, Nagaland, Arunachal, Mizoram) states in North-Eastern region is very low, while that of Tripura is low. Only Assam is placed in the medium level category by Bhattacharya.[6] In another study Archana Sharma, taking some ten relevant indices of economic development, has shown that the small North-Eastern states have a low level of development compared to other states of the country.[7]

Even Haryana which is often cited as a successful case of a small state is not free from problems. It is not able to settle yet the question of Chandigarh. So, small too is not always beautiful.

From the above discussion it is clear that reorganisation of states or creation of smaller states cannot be regarded as a sure cure of the ills of our political system. This is not to suggest that states should not be reorganised or new states should not be created. After all the Indian federation is not created out of independent sovereign states and the state boundaries are not treated as sacrosanct by our constitution. But since our nation and the federation is still in a process of formation, new states will have to be allowed to be evolved gradually and demand for the creation of a new state will have to be thrown up by the sub-region themselves. And before conceding , each such demand will have to be examined of what such region is being deprived of by being the part of a big state and what possible benefits will accrue to the people if separate state is created for them.

Meanwhile, we will have to study and understand the cause and nature of demands. It is seen that most of the state demand movements in the North-Eastern region started with a demand for socio-economic upliftment but long years of indifference to their grievances led them to demand for a separate state. The Bodoland Movement started with a demand for Autonomous Hill State.[8] If attended to in time, they probably would not have turned into a state demand movement.

Further, we should re-examine the development model adopted by us. The development model of the western democracies may not be suitable for us. It is alleged that the technological deterministic development model adopted by India is responsible for large scale depletion of resources of our rural and backward population[9] which has created discontent among them, and this in turn finds expression through movements for socio-economic upliftment. Further, we have adopted a development model evolved in a free market economy of liberal democracies. But in India, while economic development remained high on the agenda it was not placed effectively outside the political areas. Japan and South Korea achieved success because, developmental policy was made there the preserve of technocrates and financial elites working in close collaboration with the administrative elites and international capital. In India, not only the economic policy became involved in national and regional politics, but institutions such as Planning Commission and the adoption of mixed economy made it sure that it is not placed outside the domains of the politicians. So, our social goal and developmental strategies will have to be examined fully before we go for a large scale reorganisation of states.

REFERENCES

1. Quoted by P.I. Kaushish, Big Controversy over Smaller States, *The Arunachal Times*, September 29, 1992.
2. The following Acts passed between 1954 and 1987 have either created a new state or changed the boundaries of existing states.
   (i) Rajasthan and Madhya Pradesh (Transfer of Territories) Act, 1959.
   (ii) Andhra Pradesh and Madras (Alteration of Boundary) Act, 1959.
   (iii) Bombay Re-organisation Act, 1960.
   (iv) State of Nagaland Act, 1966.
   (v) Punjab Re-organisation Act, 1966.
   (vi) Andhara Pradesh and Mysore (Transfer of Territory) Act, 1968.
   (vii) Bihar and Uttar Pradesh Act, 1970.
   (viii) State of Himachal Pradesh Act, 1971.
   (ix) North-East Areas Re-organisation Act, 1971.
   (x) Haryana and Uttar Pradesh (Alterating Boundary) Act, 1979.
   (xi) Goa, Daman and Diu Re-organisation Act, 1987.
3. The erstwhile Jana Sangh in its Kanpur Conference in 1974 demanded the setting up of a new States Re-organisation Commission, and the BJP is after repeating this demand.
4. See Art. 2 and 3 of the Constitution of India.
5. See Bharat Bhusan, Need for Smaller States, *Indian Express*, 24.9.1992.
6. N. N. Bhattacharya, Viability of the State of North -East, *Journal of NEICSSR*, April 1989, p. 5.
7. Dr. Sharma, used the following socio-economic indicators to determine the level of economic development of the North-Eastern States.
   (i) Per capita Consumption of Electricity.
   (ii) Road Length per Lakh of Population.
   (iii) Vehicle per Lakh of Population.
   (iv) Number of bank offices per lakh of population.
   (v) Deposits of Scheduled Banks.
   (vi) Employment.
   (vii) Bank advances.
   (viii) Percentage of literacy.
   (ix) Density of Population to Total Population.
   (x) Percentage of urban Population to Total Population
   See Archana Sharma, Inter-State disparities in the levels of Development in India: With Particular Reference to North-Eastern Region, *Journal of NEICSSR*, April, 1,1991.
8 See Ajit K. Danda, Ethnicity and Social Transformation in North-East India, *Man in India* June 1992.
9. See Subrata Kr. Mitra, Development and Political Change in India, *The Journal of Commonwealth and Comparative Politics*, March 1992, p. 17.

4

CITIZEN'S PROBLEM, STATE RESPONSE
Crisis of Policy in North-East India

S. N. ALI

India's tryst with destiny since 1947, appears to have unfolded many paradoxes in the development process, making its evaluation difficult either in the positive or negative. The citizen of India, notwithstanding the philosophy of the Preamble, Fundamental Rights and Directive Principles of State Policy, often finds himself checkmated in a vicious game of patronage and power.[1] Over the years besides state, many intermediary structures have emerged competing with each other to ensure his prosperity. Motivated by Western paradigm of development, many functionlist correctives of legal-institutional nature have been applied in tackling the basic problems of diverse masses obviously without much success.[2] Any paradigm of development which claims neutrality of state, rational bargaining in decision making process, secular accommodation of interest, or say, impartial exercise of power for common good, misses out the class character of state and the governing elite substituting fiction in place of socio-political reality.[3] Thus such approaches fail to diagnose the disease and prescribe effective solutions worsening the fate of the common man.

The crisis in North-Eastern policy can be attributed to the blind adherence to an institutionalist strategy both by the protagonists and opponents of the demand for re-organisation. The impasse and confrontation on the issue excusively concentrate on political goal of autonomy/independence, relegating socio-economic concerns to the background.[4] The founding fathers of Indian Constitution accepted the principle of unity in diversity in preference to unity of diversity partially rejecting the bias equating state with nation[5] and melting pot model of integration. Parliamentary democracy, federalism, adult franchise, rule of law, fundamental rights and specific provisions for promotion of the interests of Scheduled castes, scheduled tribes and other weaker sections constituted basic ideological institutional framework of Indian model for development. Government of India from the very beginning displayed unusual mistrust and adherence towards emergent ethnic claims which demanded modification or rejection of the said framework.[6] The central hegemony was sought to be reinforced by the excessive use of coercive state apparatus, eventually to fail, and pave the ground for political settlement of conflicts. In the process, however, the centre has legitimised a feeling that it listens to only threats and violence, encouraging other aggrieved groups to resort to similar course of action aggravating the crisis in North-East and elsewhere.[7]

Centre's ambivalence towards problems in Assam was further confounded by the historical, parochial perceptions of the state political leadership. Assam had developed a deep sense of grievance against the official policies during colonial rule affecting its territorial, cultural and developmental interests.[8] Policies of partition, grouping plan and apparent surrender of Assamese interest by the Congress leadership further enhanced misgivings about their fate and future.[9] Thus, Gopinath Bordoli framed the constitutional proposals on tribal questions within the parameters of greater Assam, ignoring the ground realities and dynamics of ethnic politics.[10] Naturally, political leadership in Assam looked with disdain to any demand which violated her territorial integrity. All this exposed the limits of 'nationstate' in accommodating upcoming ethnic political formations seriously undermining its commitment to neutrality and socio-cultural federalism. Cracks in centre-state alliance, in such policy terms, appeared towards NEFA and Naga National question altogether on different grounds. In fact, in NEFA, external commissions like Chinese occupation of Tibet (1953), refusal to ractify McMahon Line, claim on land and other strategic, geopolitical considerations forced the centre to reverse the understanding of Bordoloi Committee, which expected the tracts to merge in Assam once the central government created the basic infrastructure for administration and development.[11] "Of course, official policy on NEFA had left little leverage with Assam to make an effective protest."

Naga National Council (NNC) emerged as the first ethnically mobilized and organized challenge against the establishment questioning the basic premise of the North-Eastern Policy. It opened its innings with demand for greater autonomy within Assam (1946-47), but soon after the takeover by extremists following the exit of government officials from membership as per government policy, it advocated complete independence from India. NNC capitalised on the fears of alien dominance after British departure on which enough ground had already been covered by Naga Club (1918), which had submitted a memorandum to this effect to the Simon Commission (1929) and shown positive disposition for Coupland's Crown Colony Plan.[12] Early contact with British Rule, experience of several Nagas in military service during First and Second World Wars, establishment of church and spread of Christianity, advancement in English language, health and education had caused the emergence of an articulate, vocal politically conscious local elite capable of mobilising several groups of Nagas under a common banner and ideology. British policy of exclusion of hills, inner line regulations, absence of influence of freedom struggle, etc. severely limited the charisma of Congress and its leaders like Bordoloi and Nehru in the Hills.

Thus, the central government in voice with the state, dismissed the whole issue as a mere law and order problem created by a handful of misguided extremists operating with the moral, material and military support of some of the hostile powers in the neighbourhood. It promptly rejected the arrangements suggested by NNC like a ten-year autonomous government of Nagas finally to decide whether the people wanted to stay within India or independence.[13] It took no cognizance of alleged support of 99 per cent people to indepenence claimed on the basis of a referendum held for the people, nor it cared to review total boycott of 1952 elections in

Naga Hills. Instead, several draconian laws were enacted to put down insurgency with an iron hand.[14] Subsequent developments, i.e. three meetings of Naga People's Convention, 1957, 1958, 1959, transfer of Tuensang area from NEFA to Naga Hills (1957) and announcement by Prime Minister of the proposal for the formation of the state of Nagaland (1960) despite non-fulfilment of the criteria laid down by the States Re-organization Commission (1956), clearly revealed the resilence of an ethnic community to assist its autonomy and identity in the face of massive challenge of state power. Birth of Nagaland delivered a death blow to the dominant ethno-centric concept of Greater Assam, legitimised ethnic politics and emboldened other latent aggrieved ethnic interest to pursue similar course of action in search of 'autonomy'.

It may not be a mere coincidence that since 1963 when Nagaland was formally inaugurated as a full-fledged state, Mizo rebels under the charismatic leadership of Laldenga demanded independence for Mizoram. It undermined the constructive advances made by Mizo Union and revived the secessionist activities initiated by groups like United Mizo Freedom Organisation (1946). The rebel leaders asserted that Mizos differed from Indians in religion and that Hindu Indian were against Christianity and not interested in the prosperity of Mizo Hills.[15] The widespread public discontent about slow pace of development and lack of adequate government relief to famine victims, paved the ground for popular sympathy for separatists. As in Nagaland here too, Government tried to suppress insugency by military means, but subsequently granted the status of Union Territory (1972) and finally statehood following two accords with moderates and MNF in 1976 and 1985, respectively.

Khasi, Jaintia and Garo tribes, though had the longest association and closest exposure to the plains of Assam, found serious fault with the provisions of 'district council' the moment grant of statehood to Nagaland was confirmed. Language Bill of state government (1960) among other things, making knowledge of Assamese compulsory for public empolyment acted as a catalyst to whip up demands for statehood as a protest against attempted assimilation and Assamization. Soon leaders of said tribes formed All Party Hill

Leader's Conference to make an organised move for autonomy.[16] in a similar move, plains tribal leaders who under the banner of Assam Plains Tribal League (1930-47)[17] Placed a crucial role in Assam politics, once again got organized under the name of PTCA (Plains Tribal Council of Assam, 1967) in order to press for autonomy which had been eluding them since independence. Similar demands surfaced from Cachar, North-Cachar Hills and Karbi Anglong and many other desperate groups within Assam.

An overburdened central government (war 1962, 1965, drought, political instability) favourably responded to these ideas with the offer of federal reorganization of Assam,[18] accommodating ethnic political aspirations in hills and plains. The formula envisaged a federation initially consisting two major valleys of Assam and four hills districts of Khasi-Jaintia Hills, Garo Hills, Mizo Hills, North-Cachar and Mikir Hills (Karbi Anglong). All these units were to have equal status, provision was made to enable NEFA (Arunachal), Nagaland, Tripura to join the federation subsequently. It provided for division of subjects between federal and constituent units ensuring autonomy in the form of separate Legislative Assembly and Council of Ministers in order to promote inter-ethnic cooperation and coordinated efforts for planned economic development of the entire region. Ironically, while several tribal leaders (APHLC, PTCA) favoured the idea, opposition by a section of Assamese leadership killed it in the bud. As a result, the centre initially created autonomous state of Meghalaya within Assam (1970) but subsequently enacted legislation to grant full-fledge statehood to Meghalaya and Union Territoryhood to Mizoram and Arunachal Pradesh (NE Reorganization Act, 1971). Some plains tribal groups were also given the option to join the new state of Meghalaya which they declined on the ground of religious differences and fear of similar ethnic suppression under the new set up. However, they were assured to suitable land legislation to tackle the problem of land alienation and rapid educational, economic development as was being done to solve the crisis in Telengana. Thus, besides unresolved problems like Purbanchal (1954), Udayachal (1967), a number of new ethnic movements have since surfaced demanding Scheduled Tribe State (Ahoms,

Koch, Rajbanshis, etc.) or Union Territory /Statehood (Karbis, Cacharis, Bodos) further intensifying ethnic strife and political fragmentation in Assam.

Several analytical explanations seeking to understand the full import of ethnic politics in the region, over-use ideological generalizations tend to neglect empirical, inter-disciplinary evidence available either from sentiment or prejudice leaving little room for scientific analysis. Definitional ambivalence[19] on the term 'ethnicity' shown contradictory perceptions on its meaning and nature. For instance, while Oxford English Dictionary viewed it as a negative value before 1972, of late even the worst detractors realise the need for a neutral use. The four dominant approaches on the theme, *i.e.* primordialist, cultural-pluralist, developmentalist neo-Marxist, indicate a similar confusion. Primordialist view stressess particularist, elements like descent, language, race, religion and holds that it constitutes roadblocks to national cohesion, disrupts social unity and dyefunctional on the developmental process of the civil society. Cultural pluralists go a step further and view ethnic politics in the framework of conflict/competition among culturally distinct ethnic groups held together in dominant-subordinate relation. Developmentalist looks at it as a passing sentiment to disappear with the establishment of industrial society. Whereas new-Marxists substituting 'nationality' for 'ethnicity' tend to see it as an aspect of class war as an inevitable product of uneven processes of capitalist development. Each one of these, if over-emphasized in isolation is sure to universalise conclusions at the cost of specific reality in a given context despite presence of formidable pointers to the contrary. Hence, an integration of these approaches at the micro and creative combinational applications at levels seems to yield better understanding of the phenomena. Viewed from this perspective, ethnic politics seeking territorial reorganisation in North-East appears to be dynamic tussle between the dominant ethnicity[20] (Assamese speech community) and non-dominant ethnicity (race, culture, religion) representing discrete tribal alliance within the ideological/institutional setting of the Indian state. The dominant community has been under pressure to accommodate both voluntarily or involuntarily due basically to its own internal weaknesses (political, social , psychological) and its failure[21] to remove the misgivings of non-dominant groups with regard to its will and intentions for balanced development of all free from political domination, economic expolitation, cultural discrimination and religious intolerance. Non-dominant groups, on the other hand, have benefited from colonial policy of isolation, historical insularity, territorial and demographic exclusiveness as well as a pattern of early modernization in which conversion to Christianity, English language, etc. prevented regional integration and accentuated historically inherited other differences in these sections. Hence, grant of partial autonomy (Sixth Schedule) within the overall socio-economic, political supervision of dominent group (Assamese) was unacceptable to them.[22] a Some of these, due to long exposure (co-existence) with plains culture, in fact, even preferred assimilation (acculturation, sankritization) before independence, but given drastic change in the rules of game attaching special premium to tribal identity following independence made them conscious of their apparent losses initiating the processes of retribalization[23] (Bodos, Ahoms, Mishings, Karbis, Rajbanshis), so that they can also reap the benefits as their counterparts in the hills.

So far, the Government of India has followed a policy of expediency frequently changing its perceptions and prescriptions on the problems, Initially, it had a negative approach. It condemned ethnic politics as parochial, against national interest and sought to curb it by military means. Failure of coercive means in Naga movement, geo-political compulsion, wars with China, Pakistan, erosion of strength of central leadership after death of Nehru, Shastri, threat of political instability since 1967, Mrs. Gandhi's bid to consolidate position in various groups and regions and finally absence of a strong regional political leadership in Assam, were some of the important factors which shaped Centre's politics towards the question of reorganisation. The pattern of central response and the selective basis in which certain demands have been fulfilled raises basic questions regarding Centre's commitment to universal welfare. It also renews interest in issues like class character of state, its distance from the actual problems of the people and its ability to intervene for public good.[24]

Unfortunately, while class character of the state, partisan

nature of the government and parochial outlook of the Assamese leadership have dominated the academic analysis of problems of North-East, very little has come to light explaining the processes of change in the new units. In fact, such negligence might have been caused by lack of adequate empirical data, value biases of more pragmatic local considerations. Condemnation of 'ethnicity' is as bad as its worship. Both tend to blow up its functions and dysfunctions out of proportions. Hence, an empirical view is more scientific than the imagined abstract properties. In this sense, the genesis and growth of ethnic formations in North-East impose certain constraints on its world-view and role performance.

The dawn of distinct ethnic consciousness among sections of Nagas, Mizos, Khasis, Garos and others was conditioned by development of administration, spread of Christianity Western education, communication and other infrastructural service, public empolyment, etc. during the colonial rule.[25] The same process was accentuated after independence. These early beneficiaries of change described variously as 'middle classes' or 'elite' articulated the political economic and cultural aspirations of the people and demanded independence/autonomy, etc. as sole representatives of their illiterate backward unconscious masses. They used ethnic mobilization as a means to establish their legitimacy. The problem of ethnic or sub-ethnic he terogenity was overcome by the elites by forging alliances on the basis of shared grievances and mutual advantages. Their concern and connection with the mases remained weak except on occasions when ethnic mobilization was necessary to demonstrate their strength to the adversaries. Their class character pushed them towards the goals of self aggrandisement, political power and economic privilege.[26] Once they captured power they become more indulgent in personal gain at times collaborating with those very forces against whom they had fought in the name of 'tribal identity' political domination and econmic exploitation. This has adversely affected the egalitarian character, cultural moorings, communitarian feelings in these groups. The scramble for status and power has brought new problems like, neo-feudal life-styles of leadership, elitist dominance, gross disparities in income, sectarian flow of benefits in land allotment, trade licences, contract works, forest permits, politico-administrative favours, developmental infrastructure, public employment so much so that sub-ethnic demands for autonomy and an equitable share in development in these units are becoming more pronounced day by day.[27]

Public disenchantment with the processes of development may be gauged from the remark of a student leader in Arunachal, "our ministers are like Maharajas, MLAs, the cheapest commodity on sale and the administrators like British Master want only power and profit, of course, in return, no service". This may look exaggerated, but it reflects the frustration of students and youth who face almost zero prospects of gainful employment with the degrees which are mostly irrelevant in the job market. Not only education, agriculture, industries, mineral resources remained neglected in all these new states for lack of political will, social commitment and sense of accountability of the leadership who by and large opted for the ideology and mode of capitalist development. Once again as is being done elsewhere, a heaven was promised but a hell was let loose on the common man.

It would be wrong to blame 're-organisation' and creation of new units in response to ethnic demands for all these development. In fact, re-organisation has once again upheld the principles of composite culture, unity in diversity leading to further homogenization of our federal system.[28] The causes of recurrent failure of functionalist therapies, certainly, lie somewhere else. Functionalists, in their defence may cite problems like illiteracy, backwardness, lack of vernacular press, absence of checks such as strong opposition parties, pressure groups, subject political culture, etc. but then, in America, too, they know the government is of the elites, by the elites and for the elites. Nehru's late realisation of the role of Panchayati Raj institutions as popular brakes against whims and caprices of the corrupt politico-bureaucratic machine, has not come upto the expectations as these too have fallen victim to the party politics and personal greed of the leaders.

Thus, problems created by class cannot be solved through identities like 'ethnicity' or 'caste'. 'Ethnicity' as a social formation has its own stratification and class contradictions. The class which causes under-development of the masses manipulates ethnic loyalty to project itself as their champion. The problems of average citizen of India emanates from the policies followed by the governments both at the Centre and States under the broad parameters of nature of class relations prevailing in the dominant capitalist mode of production. Thus, the fate of common man in Arunachal or Nagaland is intimately related to the fate of common man in other places except for differences. Dichotomous ideas like we vs. they. regional vs. national expressed in whatever terms (race, religion, language, culture, region, etc.) will further weaken the exploited ones. They, on the other hand, needs to organize both on horizontal/ vertical lines cutting across such small identities in order to assert their rightful share in the decision making and economic opportunities hitherto denied to them. Reorganisation has offered merely a few political rights but common man's struggle for social and economic justice in this region remains weak due to lack of an articulated, organised, broad based movement which defend their interests in village, block, district, state and nation without compromising on issue like traditions, culture and distinctive way of life.

REFERENCES

1. Atul Kohli, *The State and Poverty in India: The Politics of Reform,* Cambridge University Press, 1987, see Chapt. 2
2. For further details please see Michael Lipton, *Why Poor Stay Poor,* London, Temple Smith, 1977 and Indira Hirway, *Abolition of Poverty in India,* Delhi, Vikas, 1986
3. R. Francine, Frankel, *India's Political Economy, 1947-77: The Green Revolution,* Princeton, Princeton University Press 1978, Caps. 5, 6, & 7
4. Jyotirindra Dasgupta, "Ethnicity, Democracy and Development" in Atul Kohli (ed) *Indian Democracy,* Orient London 1991, pp. 144-168
5. Jagannath Pathy, "Nation Building in Multinational State" in *Man and Development,* Vol. XIII, No. 3, Sept. 1991, pp. 1-2
6. Tatu Vanhanen, *Politics of Ethnic Nepotism,* New Delhi, 1991, pp. 71-75
7. Tatu Vanhanen, *op. cit.* p. 80 also see Myren Weiner, *Politics of Scarcity.*
8. Amiya Kumar Das, *Assam's Agony–A Social Economic, Political Analysis,* New Delhi, 1982, pp 220-222
9. Tilottoma Mishra, Assam: A Colonial Hinterland, *EPW,* Vol. XV, No. 32. August 1980, pp. 1757-64
10. B. C. Bhuyan, 'On Udayachal Movement', in B. C. Bhuyan (ed) *Political Development in North-East,* New Delhi, 1989, p. 111
11. Venkat Rao and Niru Hazarika, *A Century of Tribal Politics in India,* New Delhi, 1983, pp. 28-30.

12. R. P Singh, 'Electoral Politics in Nagaland' in P. S. Datta (ed) *Electoral Politics in North-East India,* New Delhi, 1986, pp. 180-181
13. D. R. Mankekar, *On Slippery Slope in Nagaland* , Bombay, 1967 pp. 53-54.
14. Ghanshyam Shah, "Grass-Roots Mobilization" in Atul Kohli (ed), *India's Democracy : An Analysis of Changing State-Society Relations,* Orient Longman, Hyderabad, 1991, pp. 275-278.
15. Ghanshyam Shah, *op. cit.,* p. 278
16. P. S. Datta, 'Karbi-Dimasa Autonomy Movement' in P. S. Datta (ed), *Ethnic Movements in Polycultural Assam,* Vikas, New Delhi, 1990 p. 112.
17. Bhuyan, *op. cit.,* pp. 103-111
18. Bhuyan, *op. cit.,* p. 90
19. Urmila Phadnis, "Ethnic Conflicts in South Asian States" in Phadnis, Muni (ed), *Domestic Conflicts in South Asia,* Vol. II New Delhi, p. 101.
20. See Hiren Gohain's Views on the subject, *Economic and Political Weekly,* Feb, 28, 1981, p. 339.
21. P. T. Marwein, *Meghalaya Handbook,* Shillong, 1981, pp.1-111 also see B. M. Pugh, *The Story of a Tribal : An Autobiography,* Orient Longman, Calcutta, 1976, p.100.
22. For Details see Udayon Mishra, "The Naga Question", in *Economic and Political Weekly,* 8 April 1973, pp. 618-624.
23. P. S. Datta, "Koch-Rajbanshi Movement for Scheduled State" in P. S. Datta (ed) *Ethnic Movements in Polycultural Assam, op. cit.* pp. 160-181.
24. C. P. Bambri, "Marxist Concept of Political Economy and its Application to India," in Iqbal Narain (ed), *Development, Politics and Social Theory,* New Delhi, 1989, pp. 335-345.
25. See B. Datta Ray, Emergence of Middle Classes, North-East India.
26. B. Datta Ray, Tribal Identity and Tension in North-East India, *India Today,* Feb. 16-29, 1980.
27. These facts reflect the views of several articles/books published on various aspects of development in North-East India.
28. V. V. Rao and Niru Hazarika, *A Century of Tribal Politics in North-East India,* New Delhi, 1983, pp. 30-32.

5

CONSTITUTIONAL DEVELOPMENT IN NORTH-EAST INDIA SINCE 1947

S.K. AGNIHOTRI

North East India comprises seven states-Arunachal Pradesh, Assam, Manipur, Meghalaya, Mizoram, Nagaland and Tripura. These state form a compact geographical zone along the country's north-eastern borders. The region covers an area of 2,55,082 sq. kms. and had a population of 3,13,86,911 as per 1991 census. The region accounts for about 8 per cent of India's total geographical area and nearly 3.72 per cent of the country's total population. Arunachal Pradesh, Meghalaya, Mizoram and Nagaland all formed part of Assam at the time of independence so also Sylhet, the largest district at the time of independence. Sylhet was transferred to Pakistan (now Bangladesh) except for a few police stations of Karimganj sub-division in 1947. Another area of about 100 sq. kms., contiguous to Bhutan and claimed to be inhabited predominantly by the Bhutanese was ceded to Bhutan at the instance of the Government of India just after partition. Demands for reorganisation of the remaining state of Assam are still being made and will be discussed in the later part of this paper.

The Indian Council's Act, 1861; the Government of India Act, 1870; the Government of India Act, 1915 laid down the procedure for making laws and regulations and administration of the country. Under the Government of India Act, 1919, the Governor-General designated all the tribal areas of Assam as 'backward tracts'. These included (i) the Garo hills district; (ii) the British portion of the Khasi and Jaintia hills district other than the Shillong Municipality and Cantonment; (iii) the Mikir hills (in Nowgong and Sibsagars); (iv) the North Cachar hills (in Cachar district); (v) the Naga hills districts; (vi) the Lushai hills district; (vii) the Sadiya Frontier Tract; (viii) the Balipaura Frontier Tract; (ix) the Lakhimpur Frontier Tract. The Government of India Act, 1935 divided these tracts into 'excluded' and 'partially excluded areas'. The North-East Frontier (Sadiya, Balipara and Lakhimpur) tracts, the Naga hills district, the Lushai hills district and the North Cachar hills sub-division of Cachar district were specified as 'excluded areas,' and the Garo hills district, the Mikir hills (Nowgong and Sibsagar districts), the British portion of the Khasi and Jaintia hills district other than Shillong Municipality and Cantonment as 'partially excluded areas'. Where there was a definite tract of country inhabited by a compact aboriginal population, it was classified as an 'excluded area'. It was classified as 'partially excluded areas' if the aboriginal population was mixed with other communities. Both these areas were excluded from the competence of the Provincial and Federal legislatures. The administration of 'excluded areas' was vested in the Governor acting in his discretion while administration of the 'partially excluded areas' was vested in the Council of Ministers subject, however, to the Governor exercising his individual judgement. The areas which have seceded from the erstwhile Assam are these 'excluded' and 'partially excluded' areas mostly inhabited by hill tribals. This was the culmination of policies being followed by the British after occupation of these areas.

Indian Independence Act, 1947

With the transfer of power in 1947 , the Dominion of India was set up. The Indian Independence Act, 1947, provided that sall provinces and other parts thereof should be governed as nearly as might be in accordance with the Government of India Act, 1935 and the Order in Council, Rules and other Instruments, etc. However, extensive alternations and modifications were effected in the Government of India Act, 1935, which became the constitution of the Dominion of India till a new and permanent constitution was enacted. From 15th August 1947, the administrative jurisdiction of the excluded and partially excluded areas passed on to the Government of Assam which henceforth acted for the Government of India in the hill areas of Assam. The administration of these areas continued to be carried on by the Governor on the advice of the Chief Minister who was then called the Prime Minister.

Constitution of India, 1950

Special provisions were made under the Sixth Schedule to the Constitution for the administration of the tribal areas. The scheme of administration was almost wholly based on the recommendations of the North East Frontier Tribal and Excluded Areas Sub-Committee of the Constituent Assembly. The scheme was conceived with a view to building up an autonomous administration in these areas so that the tribal people may continue to follow their traditional way of life with such changes as they themselves may like to introduce.

In the Constitution, the tribal areas were no longer termed as Excluded and Partially Excluded areas but were specified in two parts, A and B, in the Table appended to the Sixth Schedule. The United Khasi Jaintia Hills district (which included 18 tiny Khasi states which acceded to India), the Garo Hills District, the Lushai Hills District, the Naga Hills District, the North Cachar Hills and the Mikir Hills were Placed in Part A and the North East Frontier Tract including Balipara Frontier Tract, Tirap Frontier Tract, Abor Hills District and Mishmi Hills District and Naga Tribal Area in Part B. While Part A areas formed the Autonomous Districts and their District Councils and were administered by the Government of Assam, the Part B areas were administered by the Governor of Assam acting at his discretion as Agent to the President. The Autonomous District had representation in the Assam Legislative Assembly and in the Parliament.

Barring such Functions as law making in certian specified fields, such management of any forest other than reserved forest, inheritance of property, marrage and social customs and certain judicial functions which are to be exercised by the District or Regional Councils, the authority of Parliament as well as that of the State Legislative extends over the Autonomous Districts under the general provisions of Article 245 (1) of the Constitution unless the Governor, by notification, directs to the contrary. All such laws made by the District Councils are to have no effect unless assented to by the Governor.The jurisdiction of the Supreme Court and High Court is not barred. Thus, the Constitution of India virtually re-enacted the provisions of the Government of India Act, 1935, as they applied to excluded and partially excluded areas and granted the partially excluded areas an even greater degree of autonomy.

In 1951, the plains portions of the Balipara Frontier Tract, the Tirap Frontier Tract, the Abor Hills District and Mishmi Hills District were transferred to the administrative jurisdiction of the Government of Assam, The remaining areas was renamed collectively as the North-East Frontier Agency by the North-East Frontier Areas (Administration) Regulation of 1954

In 1954, the name Lushai Hills District in Part A of the Table was changed to Mizo District by the Lushai Hills District (Change of Name) Act, 1954

Nagaland

The policy of non-interference in the internal affairs of the tribes living beyong the limits of effective British administration was laid down in 1851. Full British administration had by then extended to the five plains district of Kamrup, Darrang, Nowgang, Sibsagar, and Lakhimpur together with Sadiya and Balipara Frontier Tracts.

The British Administration discouraged communication between the hills and the plains. Though the tribal areas were shut out from the plains, the foreign missionaries were encouraged to carry on their proselytising activities even in the deep interiors of this regions to set up hospitals and educational institutions. This resulted in the emergence of an educated middle class capable and desirous of exercising self rule within their own territories, even if within the framework of the Indian Constitution.

After promulgation of the Constitution of India, the Autonomous District Councils were created in all the hills districts of Assam, namely; the United Khasi and Jaintia Hills, Mizo Hills, the Garo Hills and the United Mikir and North Cachar Hills. The Naga hills, however, the leaders rejected the concept and boycotted the elections scheduled to constituted the District

Council. Even before this the Naga Hills District Tribal Council was formed at Kohima in April 1945 under the initiative of a British official. Its main aim was to unite the Nagas and to repair some of the Second World Was damages. The name of the Council was changed to Naga National Council in March 1946. It was expected to foster the welfare and social aspirations of the Naga Tribes, to achieve local autonomy within the province of Assam and to train the people for self-government. In June 1947, the Naga National Council declared that the Naga hills would cease to be a part of India when the latter attained independence. A little letter, a Nine-Point Draft Agreement was drawn up between the Governor of Assam and the Naga National Council Leaders. This agreement was subject to endorsement by the Governor of Assam. However, this was not acceptable to the Naga National Council. Shri Phizo became its President and three deputations under the leadership of Shri Phizo visited Shillong and New Delhi to plead for sovereignty of the area. The Naga National Council organised a plebiscite involving entire Naga population during 1951 and administered an oath to all villages to fight for independence. The Nagas also boycotted the general election of 1954. On the other hand, the Naga National Council continued organising the Naga pupulation especially the youth to strengthen their movement. On March 22, 1956, the Naga National Council founded the Naga Federal Government and proclaimed inter alia 'Nagaland' as a people's sovereign republic.

During this period there was an armed rebellion in the territory. By the beginning of 1956, the rebels succeeded in building up an armed guerilla force. The Government of India had to engage the security forces to carry on operations against the armed hostiles in April 1956. During this period, the Naga hostiles also committed atrocities in the adjoining areas.

In the general elections of 1957 for Assam Assembly, three Naga candidates filed nomination pepers and there being no opposition or voting, they were returned to the Assam State Legislature. However, a strong section of the Naga Population relised that the campaign of violence was futile for paving the path for independence. This section subsequently began to assert themselves and hold discussion with the political leadership at Shillong and New Delhi. A Naga peace Organising

Committee was formed in 1956 which appealed to the hostiles to abandon the policy of armed rebellion. One of the resolutions passed in the first Naga problem. Another suggestion was that pending a final settlement, the Naga hills district of Assam and the tuensang Division of the North East Frontier Agency (a Naga populated area) to integrated into one political unit under the External Affairs Ministry of the Government of India. The second suggestion was accepted by the Government of India and a new administrative unit named as the Naga hills and Tuensang Area under the Ministry of External Affairs was formed on December 1, 1957. The area was to be administered by the Governor and it ceased to be under the administrative control of the Government of Assam.

The Nagaland (Transitional Provisions) Regulation of 1961 re-designated as "Nagaland" the areas hitherto known as the Naga hills-Tuensang Area and provided for the establishment of an interim body and an Executive Council on administrative matters involving general policy and development schemes. The Executive Council was to assist and advise the Governor in the exercise of his functions in relation to such matters (other than finance and maintenance of public order) as might be specified by the Governor in this behalf.

On December 1, 1963, the State of Nagaland Act, 1962, and the Constitution (Thirteenth Amendment) Act, 1962 came into force and from that date the Naga hills-Tuensang Area forming the State of Nagaland, ceased to be part of the State of Assam. Nagaland became the 16th State of Indian Union, with a Governor, a Legislative Assembly and a common High Court with Assam.

Meghalaya

In 1945, a memorandum by some Khasi leaders, pleaded for the creation of a hill province comprising the hill districts of Assam. It was argued that such an arrangement will bring about a more healthy atmosphere in the State. A conference was organised at Tura in October 1954. In this conference, the demand for an Eastern Hill State was mooted. The main reasons for this demand were two: land for a hydel project had been acquired without making any reference to the concerned District Council and secondly, the Government had withdrawn the license given to a District Council to operate its own tranport service. However, the conference also emphasized the difference of language and culture existing between the hills and the plains.

During the visit of the State Reorganisation Commission in 1955, the Hill State demand assumed the dimension of a mass movement. The demand drew considerable attention when in the second general election, the Eastern Indian Tribal Union spearheading the demand for a Hill State Swept the poll in most of the hill districts. With the introduction of the Assam Official Language Bill in July 1960, leaders of all political organisations in the hills including Congress converged at Shillong under the auspices of the Eastern Indian Tribal Union and formed the All Party Hill Leaders' Conference (APHLC). The meeting expressed unequivocally its strong and determined opposition to the move to declare Assamese as the language for all or any of the official purposes in the state of Assam. In August 1960, the APHLC held its second conference and authorised preparation of a plan or pattern of separation. Subsequently, the Mizo Union left APHLC and APHLC also lost its following in the Mikir and the North Cachar Hills. In the 3rd Conference in November 1960, the APHLC emphasised that the fulfilment of this demand was the only solution that could safeguard the interests and satisfy the legitimate aspirations of the hills people.

The 4th and 5th session of the APHLC rejected the Scottish Pattern - a loose federation with certain autonomy, offered by the Government of India on the basis of discussions during 1960-62. Under the Scottish Pattern, there was to be a regional Committee consisting of all the members of the Legislative Assembly from the Autonomous Districts with certain powers. There was a provision for a Statutory State Council for planning and allocation of funds sanctioned by the Government of India for the development of hill areas. There was also a provision for a committee under the Cabinet Minister incharge of the Hill Affairs comprising the members of Assam Legislative Assembly from the hill areas to scrutinise legislation before its extension to the hill areas. The plan included appointment of a representative from the hill areas in the Cabinet. The 6th session of the APHLC resolved to contest the elections wherever necessary. However, it reiterated the principle of boycotting the Assam Assembly, even if elected. The APHLC won 11 out of 15 Assembly seats allotted to the hill districts and also the only lok Sabha seat in the third general elections.

In 1963, the Government of India offered full autonomy to the hill areas in place of the "Scottish Pattern" and the 12th sessoin of APHLC at Tura in 1964 decided to give this a fair trial. The Pataskar Commission made certain recommendations in the meantime which were rejected by the APHLC in its 14th Session at Tura in May 1966. This session also rejected the 'full autonomy' plan offered in 1963 and decided to launch a non-voilent direct action by the end of 1966 unless the issue was settled.

In 1966, a regional autonomous system with separation at lower level and integration at a higher level was considered. However, this was not implemented. Subsequently, a 'Federal Plan' was considered (1967) which envisaged a federal structure of administration in Assam, composed of several units having equal status. According to this plan, a limited number of essential subjects of common interest were to be assigned to a regional federation leaving the rest of the state functions to the federating units which were to have their own legislature and council of ministers. At a later stage, other administrative units in the North Eastern Region may also join this federation. The 'Federal plan' even though welcomed by APHLC, was rejected in the plains. The Mizo District was, for the time being, kept outside the purview of this plan. The Mikir Hills and the North Cachar Hills District Council expressed their opposition to the scheme unless they were admitted to the set up as separate federating units and not made components of the proposed hills unit. A 12 member committee was appointed (1967) under the chairmanship of Shri A. Mehta to review the Federal Plan. The committee rejected the 'federal structure' to be the basis of the Assam reorganisation and proposed making a composite unit out of all the hill districts. It favoured voluntary amalgamation of two or more hills at a later stage. However, the report of the Committee was boycotted by the APHLC. The Government of India, therefore, referred the reorganisation issue to the national leaders belonging to all political parties.

After sometime, the demand for a separate political identity gathered momentum and the Government of India announced their decision to reorganise Assam by constituting an autonomous state within the state of Assam comprising the districts of Garo Hills and United Khasi and Jaintia Hills. Parliament enacted the Assam Re-organisation (Meghalaya) Act, 1969 which was brought into force on 2nd April, 1970. This Act provided, for a Governor (the Governor of Assam exercising his functions as Governor in relation to Meghalaya), a Council of Ministers and a Legislative Assembly and representation in Parliament. The provisions of the Sixth Schedule to the Constitution of India relating to District Councils were continued with some amendments.

The Government of India undertook a further reorganisation of the north-eastern region and no 21st January 1972, the North-Eastern Areas (Re-organisation) Act, 1971 was brought into force which led to the formation of the states of Meghalaya, Manipur and Tripura and the Union Territories of Mizoram and Arunachal Pradesh (hitherto known as NEFA). By this enactment, these areas ceased to be part of the Assam state and the administration of the North-East Frontier Agency by the Governor of Assam as agent to the President of India since 1950 came to an end.

Arunachal Pradesh

The area now forming part of Arunachal Pradesh was never before a politically compact area until it was re-organised in October 1951 and named 'North-East Frontier Agency'. The term North-East Frontier Agency had actually been coined and attached to the hilly North-Eastern Tribal area following an expedition to the Adi territory in 1911-12. The area was left by and large untouched by the British.

The first British law promulgated in the area was the Inner ine Regulation of 1873. An Assistant Political Officer was ppointed at Sadiya in 1882. A formal shape was given to the gion in 1914 under the Simla Convention. The area was vided into four or five divisions from time to time as an a ministrative expediency.

The Government of Assam was relieved of the responsibility for administration of the tribal areas when the Constitution of India came into force on 26th January 1950. Discretionary powers were reinvested in the Governor of Assam as an agent of the President under the provisions of para 18, Schdule VI of the Constitution pertaining to administration of these areas.

A portion of the North East Frontier Tract in the plains was transferred to the administrative jurisdiction of the Government of Assam in 1951. The remaining portions of the Tract were later grouped into a territorial entity called the 'North East Frontier Agency' under the North East Frontier Areas (Administration) Regulation, 1954. This came into effect on January 26, 1954. The areas falling within the Agency were constituted, with redefined boundaries into six division viz., Kameng, Subansiri, Tirap, Saing, Lohit and Tuensang. In 1957. Tuensang Frontier Division was separated from the North East Frontier Agency and attached to the Naga Hills district.

The North-East Frontier Agency, which was being administered by the Ministry of External Affairs was transferred to the Ministry of Home Affairs with effect from 1st August 1965. This brought about the changes in the nomenclature of the territories as well as the officers in charge of them

The North-East Frontier Agency, being constitutionally a part of the state of Assam, was directly administered till 1971 by the President of India through the Governor of Assam as its Agent, who was assisted by an Adviser. However, on 21st January , 1972, the North-East Frontier Agency was made into a Union Territory with the new name of Arunachal Pradesh and was placed under the charge of a Chief Commissioner.

A fullfledged Legislative Assembly with a council of Ministers was inaugurated for Arunachal Pradesh in August 1975 by an amendment to the Union Territories Act, 1963. The Chief Commissioner was re-designated as Lieutenant-Governor. Arunachal Pradesh became a full State as per Provisions of the State of Arunachal Pradesh Act, 1986.

Mizoram

Mizo Hills were brought under the administrative control of the British in 1890, when the territory was divided into North and South. The northern part was tagged with Assam whereas the southern part with Bengal. Subsequently, both the parts were merged into a district of Assam and put under a political officer or superintendent. The superintendent acted as a representative of the Viceroy and administered the district with the help of village chiefs.

After the promulgation of the Constitution of India, the Mizo District Council was set up in 1952 and the Pawi-Lakhar Regional Council in 1953 under the Sixth Schedule. General elections were held in 1951 and for the first time the territory was represented in the Assam State Legislature by three members. The Chieftainship was abolished in 1955 by an Act of the Government of Assam as a step towards democracy.

Two political organisations were active in Mizo Hills in the late forties. These were the Mizo Union and the United Mizo Freedom Organisation. The Mizo Union stood for the autonomous state in the Mizo Hills within India: whereas the United Mizo Freedom Organisation stood for sovereignty out of India. The Mizo Union was the stronger political organisation and it joined All Party Hills Leaders' Conference in its demand for a composite Eastern Hill State. In 1962, some leaders of the Mizo Union left All Party Hill Leaders' Conference and formed Hills People's Convention.

Great famine or 'mautam' engulfed the Mizo Hills during 1959-61 thereby causing a major responsiblity on the State Govenment for feeding of the population. Mizo National Famine Front, a voluntary organisation was formed in the district to collect and distribute the foodstuffs received from the Government. The organisation changed its name to Mizo National Front in 1961 after the famine was over with the objective of attaining independence and sovereignty for the Mizo Hills. Inspite of a conciliatory attitude of the Government of Assam, the Mizo National Front organised a revolt on February 28, 1966 and attacked the Government treasury and other establishments in the district. However, the disturbance were quelled with the help of security forces.

The Mizo revolt underlined the urgency of raising the political status of the Mizo district. With the implementation of the North-Eastern Areas (Reorganisation) Act of 1971 the Mizo Hills were renamed as Mizoram and made a Union Territory on January 21, 1972. It became a fullfledged State in 1986 with the passing of the state of Mizoram Act 1986.

Manipur

Manipur was a native state before Independence. However, it was different from other states as there were several constraints on the autonomy of the State. One of the main constraints was the agreement entered into by the king with the British Government in 1907, which made him subservient to the Government of Assam. The administration of hill tribes in Manipur was directly under the control of the Government of Assam. In 1931, the Maharaja expressed a desire to the Viceroy to have direct relationship with the Government of India.

There was a demand from the people of Manipur for a responsible Government after the close of the Second World War. On the basis of this demand, a constitution making body of 17 representatives, 12 of them elected by the people, was formed to suggest reforms. The Government of Manipur Act., 1947 was passed based on recommendations of this body. The Act envisaged the setting up of a legislature and a Ministry of 6 elected members headed by a nominee of the Maharaja.

On September 21, 1948, the Maharaja executed the instrument of accession following the Independence of India. The state was merged with the Indian Union on October 15, 1948. Manipur became a part 'C' State with the coming into force of the Constitution of India in 1950. A Council of Advisers under the 'part 'C' States Act' of 1951 was appointed to assist the Dominion Agent and the Chief Commissioner of the state. The States Reorganisation Commission recommended that Manipur should continue to have a separate existence as it was a border state and it was an independent territory for sometime. It was also considered that Manipur would become a burden, financially, on Assam if it was amalgamated with Assam. Therefore, Manipur was constituted into a Centrally administered Territory. It was given a substantial measure of local self Government under the provision of the Territorial Councils Act of 1956. However, it did not have the powers of legislation. A legislative body and council of ministers was created for Manipur under the Government of Union Territories Act, 1963. Manipur became a fullfledged State on January 20, 1972.

Tripura

Tripura enjoyed a special status among the princely States because it had no treaty obligations to the British Raj. Even though conquered by the British in 1761, no Political Agent was posted in the State until in 1871 when some Kuki depredators used the Raja's territory as their sanctuary. Tripura's accession to India after Independence was also voluntary. The last Maharaja who died in 1947 had expressed his intention to merge his kingdom with India after Independence. Partly, this was due to the movement for civil rights and responsible Government sponsored by two popular organisation *viz.*, Tripura Rajya Janamangal Samity and Tripura Rajya Ganaparishad. Tripura merged with the Indian Union on September 9, 1949 after the Regent Maharani signed the agreement of merger. The administration of Tripur was taken over by the Government of India on October 15, 1949. It became a Part 'C' State without legislature under the Part 'C' States Act of 1951. It then had a Council of Advisers to assist the Dominion Agent and the Chief Commissioner of the State like in Manipur. Tripura became a Union Territory with effect from November 1, 1956 under the provisions of the Territorial Council Act of 1956. Under the Government of Union Territories Act of 1963, Tripura was also given an elected legislature and a popular ministry. It became a ful-lfledged State on January 21, 1972.

Demand for Bodoland

For quite sometime population belonging to Bodo tribe have been demanding creation of a separate State (Bodoland) out of Assam. The main grievances of the Bodo are: lack of development, danger to language and culture, alienation of land, inadequate representation in Government sevices and feeling of non-participation in the management of their affairs. The main groups leading the Bodo agitation are: All Bodo Students Union (ABSU) and Bodo People Action Committee (BPAC). The agitation became violent in 1987. A dialogue had been initiated by the Government of India with the groups leading the agitation and the Government of Assam. An Expert Committee was appointed in February 1991 - (i) to determine the area of the

Bodo and other plains tribes to the north of the river Brahamaputra in Assam; and (ii) to make recommendations as to the legislative, administrative and financial powers that may be given to autonomous structures conceived of for these areas.

The main findings and recommendations of the Committee are at Annexure I.

The report of the Expert Committee was however rejected by the All Bodo Student's Union and Bodo People's Action Committee. After prolonged dicussions, a Memorandum of Settlement was signed on February 20, 1993 between the Government of Assam and representatives of the All Bodo Student's Union and the Bodo People's Action Committee. On the basis of this Memorandum of Settlement, the Assam Legislative Assembly passed a Bill in April, 1993 making provision for establishment of 'Bodoland Autonomous Council'. The Bill considered it expedient to provide for the establishment of Bodoland Autonomous Council within the State of Assam with maximum autonomy within the framework of the Constitution of India., for social, economic, educational, ethnic and cultural advancement of the Bodos residing therein. The Council shall have jurisdiction on contiguous geographical areas between the river Sankosh and Mazbat, the river Pasnoi. The Bill received the assent of the President of India in May, 1993. Interim Bodoland Executive Council took oath on 20th May, 1993 as per section 50 of the Bodoland Autonomous Council Act, 1993. Details on main provision of the Act are given to Annexure II. The Assam Government formally handed over charge of 38 departments to the newly constituted Bodoland Autonomous Council on 9th June 1993.

Demand for an Autonomous State in Assam

There is an ongoing demand since 1973 for constituting the two Hills Districts, namely, Karbi Anglong and North Cachar Hills in Assam into an autonomous hill state under the provision of Article 244-A of the Constitution. The Karbi Anglong North Cachar Hills Autonomous State Demand Committee (KANCHASDCOM) and the Autonomous State Demand Committee (ASDC) alongwith Karbi Students Association (KSA) and

North Cachar Hills Students Federation (NCHSF) representing the Hills tribals, have been spearheading this demand. The provisions of the Sixth Schedule of the Constitution extend to these districts, meaning thereby that management of land, forests and tribal affairs and local development is vested in the respective Autonomous District Council which is an elected body. The demand for converting this area into an Autonomous State has been considered on a number of occasions but the Government of India have been against any further division of Assam. However, the State Government has been advised to attend to the problems of the Hills tribals with sympathy and promptitude, take steps for speedy economic development of the area, reduce regional dispartities and create a sense of participation and the involvement among the people. The Government of Assam have discussed the matter with the representatives of the Karbi Anglong North Cachar Hills Autonomous State Demand Committee and have tentatively decided in May 1992 to transfer about 26 additional subjects covering various Departments for administration and development by the District Council Authorities. This is in addition to the 17 subjects already entrusted to the District Council Authorities as per earlier Government decisions in 1970 and 1976. Details on subjects proposed to be transferred to the District Councils are at Annexure III. This proposal was made as per 'tripartite' agreement on March 27th 1992 providing for greater autonomy to the districts, including the possibility of their being constituted into 'autonomous territories'. However, since then there has been much rancorous exchange of polemics between the leader of the agitation and the State Government, culminating in the dissolution of the Karbi Anglong District Council which was under the control of the ASDC on the 12th November 1992. The agitation which had by then resumed on a low, symbolic form, is new poised to return to the more sustained and organised pattern that was a notable feature of the agitation before the ASDC càptured the District Council.

ANNEXURE 1

THE MAIN FINDING AND RECOMMENDATIONS OF THE EXPERT COMMITTEE ON THE PLAINS TRIBES OF ASSAM

1. Determination of the areas of the Bodo tribes and other plains tribes in the north plain was done on the basis of the provisional 1991 census figures furnished by the Registrar General, India. The broad pattern of settlements in the plain north of the river Brahmaputra shows that the Bodo group is concentrated on its west central side with a total population of 11.07 lakhs and the Mishing with a population of 3.15 lakhs live mostly in the eastern sector. There is a big area in between in which none of the groups has any notable presence. The Tribe-wise district-wise distribution is roughy as follows:

	Bodo	Mishing	Sonowal	Rabba
	11.07 lakhs	3.15 lakhs	1.02 lakhs	0.80 lakhs
Kokrajhar	28.5%			13.1%
Darrang	16.8 %	–	–	37.8 %
Nalbari	12.4 %	–	24.3 %	19.5 %
Bongaigaon	12.0 %	–	–	7.3 %
Sonitpur	9.4 %	11.1 %	–	4.9 %
Barpeta	9.3 %	–	–	3.5 %
Kamrup north	5.1%	–	15.2%	2.8%
Dhemaji	–	45%	20.6%	–
Lakhimpur	–	43.3%	16.7%	–
Dhubri	–	–		10.8%

Certain other scheduled tribes like the Lalung are present in smaller numbers in the north bank areas but have larger presence south of the river Brahmaputra.

2. There has been a breakdown of communication, for

varying lengths of time at different periods, among the diverse ethnic groups that constitute the plural Assam polity. The resulting estrangement has created a socio-psychological gulf which has not been easily bridgeable. Among the factors which contributed to the breakdown have been dispossession of land, disappearance of forests, a slow pace of socio-economic development, low spead of education, persistent backlogs in reservation quotas in public services and posts, hegemonic attitudes in culture and language, intangible and tangible sources of discrimination and psychological alienation etc. Form where the communities could come together, interact with each other and sort out problems have been shrinking. Before the attitudes harden further, healthy intervention and promotion of interaction are necessary.

3. Two most important approaches could be firstly, better utilisation of existing socio-politico-administrative institutions or creation of new ones as are felt necessary and, secondly, devolution of maximum autonomy to such traditional and modern institutions.

4. "It is said that democracy is, in essence, majority rules and minority rights. The Legislative Assembly of the state does serve the purpose of enabling different socio-political entities to interact with each other, hammer out solutions to the public problems of the day and undertake legislation required for the entire society of the state. But the complaint of ethnic minorities has been that they have been neglected and discriminated against." The Committee therefore recommended creation of a second chamber in Assam i.e. a Legislative Council. In accordance with Article 171(3) of the Constitution and the present member of 126 in the Assam Legislative Assembly, the strength of MLCs would be around 42. The Council would enable adequate representation of scheduled tribes in the House. The additive is worked out as hereunder:

A. The ST population (1991) of 30.33 lakhs in the state bears a percentage of 14 of the total population of the state. This part of the additive could be 14 per cent of 126 seats of the Legislative Assembly *i.e.* 17.6 rounded off to 18.

B. According to Article 171 (3), there are five categories of constituencies which elect members to the Legislative Council. It is likely that out of the total of 42 MLCs seat up by the first four categories, some may belong to ST communities.

C. The Committee have postulated that there should be parity in this chamber as between ST and non-ST members. The total membership of the Assam Council would exceed the 42 prescribed on account of the additive in above. In case however, the ST membership does not enable parity to be achieved, the Committee suggested that "the Governor should exercise his power of nomination in accordance with clause (e) of Article 171(3) to bring the ST membership to parity level."

5. In the North Plain, there are two major tribes *i.e.* the Bodo with a population of about 11.07 lakhs and the Mishing with a population of about 3.15 lakhs. The Bodo are mostly concentrated in areas west of the Sonitpur district, though some pockets are found towards the east of the district. The Mishing are concentrated in the three districts of Dhamaji, Lakhimpur and Sonitpur. There are other similar scheduled tribe communities also which make up the balance of 2.09 lakhs out of a total ST population of about 16.31 lakhs in the north plain. Each of them like Sonowal (1.02 lakh), Rabba (0.8 lakh), Deorin (0.2 lakh), Lalung (0.05 lakh) and Mech (0.014 lakh) is a very small group and, according to Committees', proposals, would be represented in the three-tier socio-political structure that has been recommended. It is also possible that some may find a representation even in the second chamber, particularly if number is not the only criterion of representation.

6. Apart from the Bodo and the Mishing in the North plain, there are other scheduled tribes commities like Kachari-Sonowal (1,02,476), Rabha (80,097), Deori (20,128), Lalung (5133), Mech (1351), Hojai (29). The Committee considered that except a tribe like Hojai which has an extremely small population of 29, others should be able to find representation at the villege level in the Gami Jothums and Dolung Kebangs as well as at the regional level in Gudi Jothums and Banke Kabangs. If, for any reason,

they are missed out, special provision should be made therefor. Similarly, at the apex tier also, representation to the small tribes has to be ensured.

7. The Committee have carefully examined the framework of panchayati raj as ushered in the state by the Assam Government recently. Conscious of the fact that the statutory panchayati raj system has not performed conspicuously well in the other tribal areas of the country, the Committee suggested a structural framework, of autonomy which will be more suited to the North Plain.

8. Keeping in view the tradition and modern desiderata, the Committee conceived of a three-tier politico-administrative structure for both the west-central and eastern sectors of the north plain. At the bottom, the Committee envisaged a villege council, known as Gami Jothum in the Bodo west-central area and Dolung Kebang in the Mishing eastern sector. Above these village bodies, the Committee proposed regional councils, which may be called the Bodo Gudi Jothum and the Mishing Banke Kebang respectively in the two sectors. At the apex should be the Gojou Jothum and Bane Kebang.

9. For demarcating regional bodies, the Committee kept three criteria in view: (a) a region with normative population between 20,000 and 40,000; (b) to the extent possible retention of the existing administrative boundaries, say of revenue circles, sub-divisions and districts; and (c) physiographic features.

10. The Committee conceived of two apex Councils in the north plain, one for the west=central sector and the other for the eastern sector. Based on the traditional pattern, they should be capable of exercising both legislative and executive functions. The Committee also suggested an illustrative list of subjects (Appendix A) that could be considered for assignment to them. The membership of the Apex Councils should be related to the representatives of next lower tier *viz.* Gudi Jothum and Banke Kebang. For the west Central sector, the Committee have suggested 46 Gojou Jothum making in all 92

members for it. For the Mishing area, the Committee have suggested 18 Banke Kebangs in the three districts of Sonitpur, Lakhimpur and Dhemaji, each sending up three members and making, therefore, the apex Bane Kebang of 54 members.

11. The Committee have not made any specific recommendation in regard to the functions to be assigned to the Regional or Village Councils. This could be done by Apex Councils. However, the Committee felt that the devolution to the regional and village levels should be substantial, particularly in the executive field, so that each unit of the politico-administrative structure shares a sense of participation in self-governance.

12. There appear to be traditional procedures among scheduled tribes as per which representatives of the village community are chosen to constitute the village level Gami Jothums and Dolung Kebangs, the intermediate bodies Gudi Jothums and Banke Kebangs and the apex Gojou Jothum and Bane Kebang. In the interest of preservation of tribal ethos, the Committee suggested their continuance for formation of bodies at all the three tiers. However, if the leaders of the concerned tribes feel, on further consideration, that some change in the mode of choice of representatives is necessary, requisite modifications could be made.

13. The Committee considered the question as to the subjects and powers that should be assigned to the Apex Councils. These are indicated in the Annexure-I to this paper. In so far as devolutions in favour of Regional Councils are concerned, the Committee took note that they have been wielding such functions on the strength of tradition, custom and usage. On detailed examination, on the basis of customary usage and present day imperatives, functional lists can be prepared.

14. At the state level, the Committee recommended that there should be forging of linkage with the Legislative Assembly and the Legislative Council. Any legislative enactment proposed by the field formations should go through the Apex Councils, provided the subject falls within their jurisdiction, to

both the Legislative Assembly and the Legislative Council. The Legislative Council should have the benefit of the considered views of the Legislative Assembly on the particular legislative measure. The Legislative Council should make its own pronouncement on it. If it agrees with the bill of the Apex Council, it may ratify it. In the alternative, the ratification may be with amendments, modifications etc. That may be proposed by the Legislative Assembly and/or Legislative Council and accepted by the Legislative Council. However, in the event of a disagreement on substantive issue of a piece of legislation, the Legislative Council may send it back to the Apex Council for consideration of the objections. If the disagreement persists, the view of the Apex Council may prevail.

15. The Committee envisaged the Legislative Council Chamber to be a forum for discussion, debate and decision on ethnic matters as well as a guardian for the ethnic groups in the state. But the Upper Chamber may not be in session throughout the twelve months of the year. There may be need for a body to be created by the Upper Chamber which can oversee and act on its behalf, particularly during off-session periods. The Legislative Council may appoint such a body of five members out of its total membership. This body may have a small secretariat of its own. It may make its report and recommendations to the Legislative Council which might take up matters with the State Government. But it may not be precluded from inter-communication with the Government and Government departments. In the nature of things, it will have close interaction with Apex Councils in the North Plain. This body may be called the Council's Ombudsman. The Committee considered it a crucial administrative instrument.

16. The procedure for dissolution of the Apex Councils should be democratic in the sense that the decision should be arrived at by the Council of Ministers and be approved of by the State Legislature, including the Legislative Council. In the event of dissolution, the process of re-election and re-constitution should be completed within a period of six months from the date of dissolution. Similar remarks would apply to the question of dissolution of the bodies at the lower tiers.

17. For carrying out the purposes of legislative, executive and judicial functions, suitable administrative machinery is necessary. The higher echelons of this machinery may be contributed by the State cadres controlled by the State Government During their tenu of service with the new set-up in the North Plain, they should be recognised as sub-cadres and be under the full control of Apex Councils including matters of discipline. Clear lines of control demarcation should be drawn. The subordinate services *i.e.* belonging to Class III and Class IV should be recruited and controlled by the field formations as may be worked out.

18. Funds allotted by the State Government and the Central Government to the Apex Councils should be in the form of grants-in-aid implying non-lapseability. Further, funds allotted by the State Government to an Apex Councils should be shown in the State budget as a lump-sum under one separate head of account; their sectorwise utilisation should strictly be in accordance with the manner decided by an Apex Council. Similarly, funds allotted by the Central Government should be shown in the State Government's account under one separate head of account for each of the two Apex Councils and be utilisable in accordance with the sector-wise distribution of the Apex Council and not otherwise.

19. The accounts of the Councils should be in the form prescribed by the Comptroller and Auditor-General of India. The audit should also be conducted as per the directions of the Comptroller and Auditor-General of India. The Committee felt that the provisions of maintenance of accounts and audit are very important and should receive high priority attention from the concerned authorities in all the three-tiers.

APPENDIX – A

AN ILLUSTRATIVE LIST OF SUBJECTS THAT COULD BE ASSIGNED TO APEX COUNCILS (GOJOU JOTHUM AND BANE KEBANG) IN THE NORTH PLAINS

(i) Land and land revenue management;

(ii) Management of forest and environment not being a reserved forest;

(iii.) Use of any canal or watercouse for the purpose of agriculture;

(iv) Agriculture;

(v) Public health and sanitation, hospitals and dispensaries;

(vi) Tourism;

(vii) Vocational training;

(viii) Public works – development and plainning;

(ix) Construction and maintenance of all roads except national highways and state highways;

(x) Transport and development of transport;

(xi) Management of burials and burial grounds, cremations and cremation grounds;

(xii) Preservation, protection and improvement of livestock, prevention of animal diseases, veterinary training and practices;

(xiii) Pounds and the prevention of cattle trespass;

(xiv) Water, that is to say, water supplies, irrigation and canals, drainage and embankment, water storage;

(xv) Fisheries;

(xvi) Management of markets and fairs, not being already managed by municipal authorities, panchayat Samitis or Gram Panchayats;

(xvii) Education – primary, secondary and higher;

(xviii) Works, lanes and building vested in or in the possession of the General Council;

(xix) Small-scale and cottage industries;

(xx) All matters connected with customary law relating to

inheritance of property, marriage and divorce, social customs etc. of both tribal and non-tribal communities;

(xxi) Development of language, tribal/folk-culture in all aspects;

(xxii) Share of royalties from licenses or leases of minerals;

(xxiii) Any other matter connected with development.

ANNEXURE – II

MAIN PROVISIONS OF THE BODOLAND AUTONOMOUS COUNCIL ACT, 1993

The Bodoland Autonomous Council has been created within the State of Assam comprising the areas as may be specified by the Government by notification in the official gazette. The Assam Government has constituted an interim body of Council, although the territory under its jurisdiction is yet to be demarcated. The Council comprising eighteen members was sworn in on 20th May 1993. The interim body has five members representing the communities other than Bodos. These are from following communities : Adibasi, Koch Rajbansi, Rava, Bengali Hindu and Muslim.

In due course the Bodoland Autonomous Council shall have a General Council and an Executive Council. The General Council shall be a body corporate consisting of forty members of which thirty shall be from plains scheduled tribes. The Act provides details on delimitation of constituencies, qualifications etc. for membership of General Council, details of election procedure including powers of the State Government to make rules regulating the election of members, procedure for deciding disputes regarding election and procedure for removal of members. The elected members shall hold office for a period of five years from the date appointed by the Government.

The General Council shall meet for the conduct of business at least once in every three months. It shall have executive powers in the area, subject to the provisions of the Bodoland Autonomous Council Act, 1993 and any other law for the time being in force, relating to the thirty-eight subjects *viz:*

1. Cottage Industry
2. Animal Husbandry and Veterinary
3. Forests
4. Agriculture
5. P.W.D.
6. Sericulture

7. Education

   (a) Adult Education
   (b) Primary Education
   (c) Upto Higher Secondary including vocational training

8. Cultural Affairs
9. Soil Conservation
10. Co-operation
11. Fisheries
12. Panchayat and Rural Development
13. Handloom and Textiles
14. Health and Family Welfare
15. Public Health Engineering
16. Irrigation
17. Social Welfare
18. Flood Control Schemes for Protection of Villages (not of highly technical nature)
19. Sports and Youth Welfare
20. Weights and Measures
21. Library Services
22. Museums and Archeaology
23. Urban Development–Town and Country Planning
24. Tribal Research Institute
25. College Education (General)
26. Land, Land Revenue and Revenue
27. Publicity/Public Relation
28. Printing and Stationary
29. Tourism
30. Transport
31. Any other matter connected with development
32. Municipal Corporation, Improvement Trust, District Boards and other Local Self-Government or Village Administration
33. Tribal Welfare
34. Markets and Fairs
35. Lotteries, Theatres, Dramatic Performance and Cinemas
36. Vital Statistics including Registration of Births and Deaths

37. Food and Civil Supplies
38. Intoxicating Liquors, Opium and Derivatives etc.

Besides these subjects, State Government may entrust other functions to the Council after due consultation. The General council subject to the general policy of the Government, shall.

(i) formulate integrated development plans for the Council Area;
(ii) implement schemes and programmes for development of the Council Area;
(iii) have power to appoint class III and class IV staff within its jurisdiction;
(iv) have powers to regulate trade and commerce within its jurisdiction in accordance with the existing law including issue of permits and licenses to individuals within the Council Area;
(v) guide customs and traditions and social justice of the Bodos according to the traditional law;
(vi) organise special recruitment drive into army, paramilitary forces and police units for job appointment from the Council Areain consultation with the Central Government ;
(vii) allot permits for trade and commerce to the people residing in the Council Area, preference being given to the Bodos.

However, power to acquire, to hold and dispose of property etc. shall be subject to previous approval of the Governmen.The General Council shall have power to make by laws subject to certain conditions.

All public building s and public roads constructed and maintained by the Council Fund shall vest in the General Council so also lands and other properties transferred to the General Council by the State Government. The General Council has also been authorised to impose levy and collect taxes and fees subject to certain conditions and overall control of the State Government.

The Act provides for an elected office of the Chief of the

Bodoland Executive Council and a Deputy Chief and Vicee Chairman. The Chief of the Council shall,

(a) be responsible for the maintenance of the records of the General Council.;

(b) have general responsibility for the financial and executive administration;

(c) exercise administrative supervision and control over all officers and employees of the General Council., and the officers and employees whose services may be placed at the disposal of the General Council by the Government;

(d) for the transaction of business under this Act, exercise such powers, perform such functions and discharge such dutas may be exercised, performed or discharged by the General Council under this Act or the rules made thereunder; Provided that the Chief of the Bodoland Executive Councils shall not exercise such power, perform such functions or discharge such duties as may be required by the rules made under this Act to exercised, performed or discharged by the general Council at a meeting;

(e) exercise such other power, perform such other function and discharge such other duties as the General Council may by general or special resolution, direct or as the Government may, by rules made in this behalf, prescribe.

The Chief of the Council may delegate his function to his deputy.

Apart from General Council, the Act provides for establishment of a Bodoland Executive Council and Committees thereunder. The Bodoland Executive Council shall consist of its Chief and Deputy Chief, who shall be its ex-officio members, and seven elected members of the General Council to be nominated by the Chief of the Bodoland Executive Council. The executive functions of the General Council shall vest in the Executive Council. The Chief of the Executive Council shall exercise such powers and discharge such functions as are conferred on him by or under this Act. He may also allocate such business among its members in such manner as he thinks fit. The Executive Council may authorise its a Chief in writing to take certain action in anticipation of approval by the Executive Council.

The Secretariat of the Bodoland Council shall consist of a Principal Secretary who shall be the principal executive officer of the General Council. All other officers shall be subordinate to him. The Principal Secretary shall be appointed by the State Government in consultation with the Chief of the Bodoland Executive Council. In addition to the Principal Secretary, the Government may appoint other Secretaries and depute other officers in consultation with the Chief of the Bodoland Executive Council. The officers posted in the Council Area shall be accountable to the General Council for their performance and the assessment of their work shall be incorporated in their annual confidential reports by the Government.

The Act provides for the establishment of a 'Council Fund' and details on its management. The accounts of the Council shall be kept in such form as may be prescribed in consultation with the Accountant General. The audit of the accounts of the General Council shall be entrusted by the State Government to the Comptroller and Auditor-General of India. The Act also contains details on procedure for preparation of budget of the General Council and its approval by the Government. No expedition shall be incurred by the General Council till the budget is approved by the Government. The Act also contains provision for protection of rights of non -ribals, dissolution of the the General Council and the Executive Council, application of Acts of the legislature of the State reservation in services and jobs for Scheduled tribes, use of official language etc. Under the Act special courts shall be set up in consultation with the Guwahati High Court to try suit and cases between parties all of whom belong to Scheduled Tribe or Tribes in accordance with the tribal customary laws and procedures as follow

(a) Village Courts;

(b) Subordinate District Customary Law Courts within Civil sub-divisional territory; and

(c) District Customary Law Courts.

There is special provision for the Council Area with regard to religious and social practices of the Bodos. Bodo customary laws and procedures and ownership and transfer of land within the Council Area. The State Government shall consult and give due regards to the views of the General Council before any law is made and implemented in the Council Area on the aforesaid three subjects.

ANNEXURE – III

SUBJECTS PROPOSED TO BE TRANSFERRED TO THE KARBI ANGLONG AND NORTH CACHAR DISTRICT COUNCILS

Sector	Schemes
	State Plan
(1) Cottage Industry	(i) Exhibition
	(ii) Subsidies as per New Industrial Policy
	(iii) Seed Money of EMIS including stipend
	(iv) Knitting, Tailoring, Embroidery Training Centres
	(v) Training Programmes
	(vi) Industiral Loan
	(vii) Industrial Estate/Growth Centre/Commercial Estate
	(viii) Promotional Schemes
	(ix) Training Centres for Handicrafts
(2) Animal Husbandry and Veterinary	**State Plan**
	(i) Veterinary Service and Animal Husbandry:
	(a) Establishment of R. P. Check post.
	(ii) Cattle Development:
	(a) R.A.I. Centre/Mini I.C.D.P
	(iii) Sheep and Wool Development:
	(a) Establishment of sheep breeding farm .
	(iv) Other expenditure:
	(a) Zeliangrong Naga Development
	(v) Dairy Development Project:

1	2
	(a) Rural Dairy Creamery Centre. (b) Dairy Extension Service. (vi) Education and Training: **Additive Plan** (i) Animal Husbandry and Veterinary Service: (ii) Cattle Development: (a) I.C.D.P. (b) Buffalo Breeding Project (c) Cattle Breeding Project (d) R.A.I. Centre (iii) Poultry Development (iv) Sheep and Wool Development (v) Dairy Development (vi) Dairy Development Project
(3) Forest	**State Plan** (i) Planning Cell (ii) Working Plan Officer (iii) Forest Resources and Survey (iv) Social Forestry **Additive Plan** (i) Silvicultural Works (ii) Consolidation of Forest (iii) Plantation of Quick-growing Species. (iv) Buildings (v) Public Garden
(4) Agriculture	**State Plan** (i) Extension and Training (ii) Agricultural Research

1	2
	(iii) Agricultural Economics and Statistics (iv) Development of Banana Progeny Orchard
	Additive Plan
	(i) Horticulture (Entrusted & Non-Entrusted (ii) Agricultural (Entrusted & Non-Entrusted) Engineering (iii) Agricultural Research and Education (Non- entrusted)
(5) P.W.D.	**State Plan**
	(i) New Roads (ii) Expansion of P.W.D: (a) Tools and Plants.
	Additive Plan
	(i) Tools & Plants (Machinery & Equipment) (ii) Accommodation
	Grant-in-id (State Plan)
	(i) Grants-in-aid (District Council roads) (ii) Rural road (Small Schemes)
(6) Sericulture	**State Plan**
	(i) Eri Silk Industry (ii) Mulberry Silk Industry (iii) Publicity and Propaganda (iv) Strengthening of Supervisory Technical Staff

1	2
	(v) Training
	Additive Plan
	(i) Eri Silk Industry
	(ii) Mulberry Silk Industry
	(iii) Muga Silk Industry
	(iv) Tussore Silk Industry
(7) Education :	
Adult Education	Only State Programme
	State Plan
Primary Education	(i) Primary Education
	Additive Plan
	(i) Primary Education
	Grants-in-Aids (State Plans)
	(i) Primary Education
(8) Cultural Affairs	Grants-in-aid to Voluntary Cultural Organisations
(9) Soil Conservation	**State Plan**
	(i) Soil Survey and Testing
	(ii) Nature Conservation
	(iii) Building and approach roads
	(iv) Watershed Management Plan
	(v) Education and Training
(10) Co-operation	**State Plan**
	(i) Training and Education
	(ii) Construction of Office Building
	(iii) Grants for Credit Stabilization
	(iv) Share Capital Contribution to Longpi Danangi Rural Bank Ltd.

1	2
(11) Fisheries	**State Plan** (i) Other Fisheries - Collection of Statistics (ii) Fisheries Extension Service **Additive Plan** (i) Direction and Administration
(12) Panchayat and Rural Development	**State Plan** (i) Construction of Senior B.D.O.'s Quarters (ii) Construction of E.O. (W&C) Quarters (iii) Nutrition Pre-School & School Feeding Programme **Additive Plan** (i) Construction of Building in New Blocks
(13) Handloom & Textiles	**State Plan** (i) Strengthening of Supervisory and Technical Staff (ii) Publicity and Propaganda **Additive Plan** (i) Strengthening of Supervisory Staff.
(14) Health & Family Welfare	**State Plan** (i) Establishment of District Medical Stores (ii) Expansion of District and Sub-Divisional Hospitals

1	2
	(iii) Malaria Eradication Programme.
	(iv) T.B. Control Programme
	Additive Plan
	(i) Expansion of District and Sub Divisional Hospitals
(15) Public Health Engineering	**Additive Plan**
	(i) Direction and Administration.
	Grant-in Aid (State Plan)
	(i) Rural Water Supply
(16) Minor Irrigation	**State Plan**
	(i) Ground Water Resources
	(ii) Building
(17)	Social Welfare Children in need of care/protection
(18)	Flood Control Schemes for Protection of Villages (Not of highly technical nature)
(19)	Sports & Youth Welfare
(20)	Weight & Measures
(21)	Library Services
(22)	District Museum & Archaeology
(23)	Urban Development-Town & Country Planning
(24)	Tribal Research Institutes
(25)	College Education (General)
(26)	Land Reforms

6

ISSUES OF REORGANISATION IN NORTH-EAST INDIA

SUCHETA SEN CHOUDHURI
AND
SARIT CHOUDHURI

At the time of independence the national leaders as well as administrators did not have a clear perception about the variegated communities of North East India. As a result they deliberately tried to bring all the communities under the rule of thethen Assam province and at the same time they provided autonomous hill district council for a few communities. Naturally, as an approach it corroborated the same by the British ruleers. Probably, here lies the root of the concept of reorganisation. An attempt is made here to underscore the various issues of reorganisation in the North-East India, on the basis of analysis of structural strains. One important aspect not taken into consideration is the problem of ethnic minoriteis in North-East India.

Nationalism in India

Political nationalism in India is the outcome of British domination which gave birth to various political movements. The movements had for their objectives an increasing share in political power and subsequently, dominion status, Home rule and even complete independence. The political movements embodied the striving of the Indian people and it's various sections to secure political power which they could use to serve their respective social , economic and other interests.

The industiral bourgeoisie found in the absolute control of

India by Britain an obstacle to carry through it's programme of unfettered industrial development. The educated classes found in the monopoly of key posts in the state machinery by the British, an obstacle to their just ambition to secure jobs. The sons of the soil, the pesesantry found in the new land and revenue systems introduced by Britain, the basic cause for their progressive impoverishment. Thr proletariat found in the British rule a foreign undemocratic agency, preventing it from developing class struggles for improving their conditions of life and labour and finally for ending the wage system itself under which they were exploited.

Further, the Indian people, as a whoel recornised in the British rule an alien rule which barred their normal social, economic and cultural development. The national sentiment almost spontaneously arises among the people who are ruled by foreign nation since this rule imposes basic handicaps on the free development of the subject nation.[1]

The British established a uniform reign of law in the country. Such a uniformity was unknown in pre-British India in establishing a new system of law and tribunals. The British had to suppress the customary law which prevailed in pre-British India and expropriate village and caste communities of their power to enforce the customary law which further varied from place to place in the absence of a uniform system of law.[2]

But in the case of North-East the above uniformity regarding law was not imposed by the British. The following reasons may be responsible:

(i) Difficult geo-morphological nature of the North-East;
(ii) Unawareness about the resource potentiality of the North-East India:
(iii) Existence of small communities with variegated social organisations and custemary laws and very unstable political relationship among themselves made them reluctant.

It is true that a conception of unity of India existed and flourished in pre-British India. But that was predominantly geographical and religious cultural unity.

British and North East India

The East India Company on the eve of the march of the British troops into Assam, proclaimed to the people: "We are led into your country by the thirst of conquest but are forced in our defence to deprive our enemy of the means of annoying us." The Burmese were deprived of the causes of annoyance and were compelled to cede Assam to the Company, but the question of restoration of the administration of Assam to her former rulers, the Ahoms, could not be solved immediately and the country was retained under British authority for the time being. In the year 1765, after getting Dewani from Mughal, Assam came under British control. But before 1826, they were not so much interested about this region.

However, the fertility of the Brahmaputra valley was a possible source of income, but in the opinion of the Bengal Government it was an 'area of doubtful value' on account of frequent subjugation to the raids of the surrounding hill tribes – the hill tribes were identified by British as identical with Burmese towards the people of Brahmaputra valley. So to keep them away from further aid to the Burmese, adoption of a policy of recognition and friendship between the Company and these savages was thought to be expedient instead of securing their allegiance at the point of gun. With these in view, the Company had established a station at Sadia under an European officer with political authority over the neighbouring chiefs.[3]

Under the policy of recognition, Scoot involved himself in a process of agreements with the chiefs of the Eastern Hill Tribes. And for making friendship they had introduced different policies. One of these policies adopted by the British towards hill tribes was the suspension of land revenue. The British policy at that time was to extend the area of British sovereignty by compelling more chiefs to pay nominal tributes.[4] Assam tribal areas beyond the eastern border of Bhutan (only finally delimited by the Tawang expedition of 1938) and upto the point of issue of Brahmaputra and it's great tributaries from the Himalayas, then round to the South along the new Indian-Burma border lies a great belt of tribal territory. The tribes to the North of the valley, eg. the Akas , Miris, Daflas Abor and Mishmis are interposed between India and Tibet. In 1914, Henry Mcmahon as British representative and Lhasa authorities specified and agreed on a frontier line which has come to be known as red line or the Mcmahon line between India and Tibet. But after 1914 came the great war of which a minor result was that no action was taken by the Indian Government to exert it's authority upto the new frontier. Actually the local Government of Assam which was chiefly concerned, was not even made aware of the allocation of the frontier until some years later.

According to Elwin (1960), the British Government was inclined, on the whole to leave the tribesmen alone, partly because the task of administration, specially in the border areas, was difficult and unrewarding.[5]

According to Ghurye (1963), the main purpose of the British policy was to secure peace and not necessarily to help the people to advance on the road to progress either by integration with the plain Hindus or otherwise. Consistently with keeping the peace, gradual survey settlement was carried out, and by slow stages regular land revenue was levied, wherever and whenever possible.[6]

Independence and North-East India

It is generally agreed upon that the very concept of tribal development which emerged in our country after the attainment of national independence is some what paradoxical when it is compared with the previous tribal policy of the British Government. While the approach adopted by the British was purely guided by their colonial interest, the present Government's attitude is prompted by a desire of welfare and socio-economic upliftment. The report of Gopinath Bordoloi Committee recommended autonomy in the administration of the hill areas. Accordingly autonomous hill district councils were set up under Assam in 1952.

Prior to the enforcement of the Constitution of India, the Khasi and Jayantia hills and other areas had been administered by Deputy Commissioners who acted on the advice of Governor of Assam. This was because the hill areas were never brought under the direct administrative control of the State Government.[7]

After independence, the old pattern of district administration as prevailing during the British period continued to be maintained under the overall control of the Deputy Commissioner. Supervision of law and order problem also vested with him. Later, the post of a superintendent of police and other posts in village and Mouza level were created.[8]

After independence with the implementation of the Sixth Schedule, a number of Autonomous District Hill Councils were formed. As regards the form and functions of the District Council, it resembles a miniature State Government, having legislative, executive and judicial organs of it's own in the framework of responsible State Government. This Council consists of members elected from different territorial constituencies on the basis of adult franchise and a few members nominated by the Governor.

The District Council is both an administrative and legislative body and it has also powers to legislate. Some of the salient provisions of the Sixth Schedule are as follows:

1. There shall be a District Council for each autonomous district, consisting of not more than 24 members, of whom not less than three- fourths shall be elected on the basis of adult suffrage.
2. There shall be a separate Regional Council for each area constituted as autonomous regions under sub-paragraph (2) of paragraph 1 of this schdule.
3. The Regional Council for an autonomous region in respect of all areas within such region and the District Council for an autonomous district in respect of all areas within the district except those which are under the authority of Regional Councils, if any, within the district shall have power to make laws with respect to certain aspects, a few of which are:

(i) The management of any forest not being a reserved forest;
(ii) The use of any canal or water-course for the purpose of agriculture;
(iii) The regulation of the practice of Jhum or other forms of shifting cultivation;

(iv) The appointment or succession of chiefs or headmen;
(v) The inheritance of property;
(vi) Marriage;
(vii) Social customs;

4. The District Council of an autonomous district may make regulations for the regulation and control of money lending or trading within the district by person other than Scheduled Tribes resident in the district.

Reaction to the New System

Implementation of the Sixth Schedule in the hill areas of Assam was subjected to several strains from the very beginning:

(i) The Nagas of Naga Hills, which till 1958, constituted part of Assam, were demanding separation from the state of Assam since the very beginning. As a protest they boycotted the first election of Assembly and Parliament in 1955.
(ii) The demand for creation of a separate state comprising hill areas of Assam is cancelled by State Reorganisation Commission in 1954-55.
(iii) Eastern Indian Tribal Union with the demand of separate tribal state was interested to propose several amendments to the Sixth Schedule. A careful observation upon this proposal reveals that they were in favour of more power for district council than state legislature.
(iv) Most of the communities were not in favour of staying under the Government of Assam, as a sense of insecurity prevailed among themselves.[9]

Conclusion

From the previous discussion it is evident that 'patriotism'. of different ethnic groups and feeling of exploitation of different classes against British colonialism had given birth to Indian political nationalism. At the same time, boundary of nation was not decided smoothly. As a consequence of that Pakistan and East Pakistan (Bangladesh) were separated from India on the basis of religion.. After that though the formation of states pivoted round the basis of language but still there were some inconsistencies in that respect. As an example Telengana dominated by Telugu language was included within the state dominated by Tamil language. Accordingly there was plan to include Hindi dominated Bihar with West Bengal. But this question of language had not emerged as an important issue in case of North East India probably due to unique ethnic mosaic and lack of common language. Here, according to Bordoloi Committee report Autonomous Hill District Council were formed with the power to form as well as implement certain rules and regulations, within its own jurisdiction. In this regard we agree with Prof. J.B. Ganguly's statement that a review of the functioning of the District Councils in the early year of their existance indicates that even as they suffered from inadequate financial resources particularly as the grants provided by the State Government, which itself was handicapped by lack of resources and was unable to carry out its own development programmes for overcoming its economic backwardness, were far less than was needed. The tribal people earnestly endeavoured to build up and run a modern form of government to discharge whatever legislature, executive and judicial functions they were entrusted with by the Constitution. This development represents a unique constitutional innovation of involving the tribal people in bringing about peaceful transformation of the traditional tribal policy into a legally elected form of Government.[10]

Perhaps Indian nationalism is consistent with the old saying "my cousin and me against the stranger, and my brother and me against my cousin." Once independence from the colonial power is attained through co-operation among ethnically different groups, tensions turn inward over the distribution of power and resources in the newly created state.[11] But with the formation of seven tiny sister states that inward tension is not yet dissolved. Spirit of reorganisation still persisting not only through the demand for further division of some of the North Eastern State but also through the emergence of anti-national movements in various parts.

REFERENCES

1. A. R. Desai, 1959 : *Social Background of Indian Nationalism,* 3rd edn.; Bombay, Popular Book Depot, p. 281.
2. *Ibid.* p. 153
3. M. S. Barkataki, 1985 : *British Administration in North East India.1826-74.,* Delhi, Mittal Pub. p. 204
4. J. N. Das, 1980 : *A Study of the Land system of Meghalaya,* Gowahati, Law Research Instt. Gawahati High Court.
5. Varrier, Elwin, 1960 : *A Philosophy of NEFA,* Shillong.
6 G. S. Ghurye, 1963 : *The Scheduled Tribes,* Bombay, Popular Prakashan.
7. P. R. G. Mathur, 1979 : *The Khasis of Meghalaya* : New Delhi Cosmo
8. P. C. Kar, ed. 1975 : *The Garo Code of Law,* Meghalaya Catholic Church, p. 3.
9. B. K. Roy Burman and Thukral 1961 : *Census of India,* Demographic and Socio Economic Profiles of the Hill Areas of North-East India. New Delhi. Pub. by Office of the Registrar General, India, Ministry of Home Affairs. p. 114
10. J. B. Ganguly, 1992 : *The Sixth Schedule to the Constitution of India and the North East* : Paper presented in I.C.S.S.R. Guwahati.
11. Saad Nagi, 1992 : *Ethnic Identification and Nationalist Movements. Human Organization* Vol-51 No.4 Winter.p.309.

7

SOME REFLECTIONS ON THE REORGANIZATION OF NORTH-EAST INDIA

SIKNENDU MAZUMDER

It is rather disturbing to note that the process of reorganisation which had started right after independence in this north-east part of the country, is continuing unabated even till today. There would hardly be a day without an incident either for separate statehood or for autonomous status. However, such bizarre trend is a global phenomenon today. And painfully so, the same has swept the Indian sub-continent too. There have been mounting pressures and problems in Punjab and Jammu & Kashmir and similar issues are erupting in West Bengal and Bihar also. It is indeed a pity that even after such a pathetic fragmentation in the N.E. zone, there has been constant demand for the Bodoland and the autonomy for the Karbis. In addition, those hilly areas where statehood has been granted with the hope of all round development and peace, disruptive force have been playing havoc ! States like Manipur, Mizoram and Nagaland are often seen troubled by the insurgent forces.

Since times immemorial, this exquisite piece of land of flora and fauna coupled with natural richness has not only attracted people from all walks of life from within and out side the country, but has also served as the eastern gateway of India. It has attracted scholars form various fields, – including travellers, missionaries, traders, invaders etc. The inland mountain routes and the Brahmaputra and its tributaries have served infiltration into this part of the country since 3000 B.C. The ancient Assam has been described at length by the Greeks, Romans, Chinese travellers and others. From the writings of Yuan Chwang, who had visited Assam in A.D. 642 one may find that Assam attracted people of talents both for education as well as livelihood. This makes it amply clear that the region has constantly been enriched by the give -and -take process. From the descriptions of Ibn Batuta, who had visited the region in A.D. 1345, there is a vivid account of commercial production, geographical distribution, ethnic conditions etc. Last but not the least, is the account of European travellers who had penetrated deep into the territory from the sixteenth century to the end of British rules. Besides, travellers, British military and civilian officers were often been to the region for discharging their duties and they too have left many valuable accounts of this region for the historian and researchers. Virtually all of them carry the same message. They relate to geography history, land its people or political, economic and ethnic problems. Yet one cannot depend much on their findings since they do not help to draw any conclusions, nor lead one to settle problems in any judicious manner.

What then are the reasons that lead to the divisive forces getting stronger and stronger? It is shocking that the very British that had existed for two centuries at a stretch did not pay heed to the needs of the people. They resorted to naked exploitation of the resources and left the ill-fated people and the land in a forlorn state. Truly speaking, they kept the entire area almost unadministered. This resulted in communication gap between the people and the administration. And the process did not end here. It has continued to haunt the minds of the hill-people and the tribals till today that they do not get their due and that they are neglected and being exploited also. Even after the pathetic fragmentation, the people of Assam and the 'seven sisters' feel that they are still neglected by the Centre and the economic development has not been up to the mark. There is probably some truth in this. But does it mean that one should allow and accept such fragmentation, again?

One must also consider other connected issues to arrive at a conclusion as they too have contributed a lot to pave the way for reorganisation of states. These are ethnic difference, difference of region, languages and topographical featues of the hills.

These are facts and need consideration. It is in the nature of human beings to be fond of their tradition and culture and obviously fond of preserving them too. The identity crisis exerts that pressure and the people tend to stick to that. Sometime, it is the political aspirants who create an artificial climate for their political goals and sometimes it is the fear in the minds of the people of losing their ethnic values that give rise to these pressures.

The issues concerned may be political or economic, there is no denying the fact that ultimately it is the deprivation at all levels that makes man desperate. The post-independence era has witnessed a number of marked changes and measures in the NE region. The introduction of Panchayati Raj system and setting up of District Councils have considerably curbed the authority of the chiefs and tribal leaders. So this dissatisfied lot ever remains hungry to fulfil their motives. Even the District Councils have shown leniency towards particular tribes leading to conflict and distrust in other tribes. But this is only one side of the coin! The tribes have always gone for the interest of their respective tribes only. They have never shown tolerance for other tribes. One would notice ethnic difference in Mizoram, in Nagaland. Such problems coupled with economic backwardness of the entire zone and unbalanced growth have contributed a lot to the re-organisation of states.

Along with the above, problem of immigration in the pre-independence and post-independence period in Assam has added fuel to the fire. In the words of Acharya Vinoba Bhave, "It is not a regional problem, but a national problem." Mr. C.S. Millan, the Census Commissioner, in the Census Report of 1931 said, "In fact the way in which they have seized upon the vacant area in the Assam Valley seems almost uncanny, without tumult, without fuss, without undue trouble to the district revenue staff, a population which must account to over a half a million has transplanted itself from the Bengal to the Assam Valley during the last 25 years... an event which seems likely to alter permanently the whole future of Assam and destroy more fully than did the Burmese invaders of 1820, the whole structure of Assamese culture and civilisation." For the Hindu Bengalee settlers in Assam it is reported that they maintain separate identity and are rather keen to establish their linguistic and cultural supermacy. These are mind boggling and complicated issues which have acted as gangrene and bred many problems. Perhaps people have become more conscious of their group interest and have shown inclination to live in clusters.

Take a look at the recent developments that have taken place in different parts of the world. The German Wall has been removed and the people of two Germanys are rejoicing their unification. But that is a dream for the people of this country and nothing more. However, recent happenings in the U.S.S.R. and other European countries are rather contradictory compared to the German issue. There has been one dissection after another taking place in a natural fashion! It is also well recognised that smallness in size is not considered as an obstacle towards smooth functioning and economic growth. Even as one tries to forget the present upheaval boiling around, the very map of Europe remainds one that many smaller countries are several times more advanced than many larger countries! Again, looking at the two giant countries or say, the two super powers, it is natural to come to the conclusion that it is neither the shape and size nor the thickness or the thinness of population that matters much to determine the growth of the economy anyway. Here, one has to coordinate all the relevant factors that play a crucial and decisive role in the all-round development of the nations; otherwise it would be very difficult to comprehend the situation.

To draw a conclusion, it can be said without much doubt that if division of land serves the purpose of the people and helps in the rapid economic development of the concerned states, it is of course most welcome. The statesmen should recognise the reality and help in shaping such popular demand in a peaceful manner. But, before acceding to a demand it must be ensured seriously that it is the crying need of the hour and has not been motivated by any selfish opportunists for achieving their political ends. While looking close at the developments in the country one cannot say the same of the North-Eastern states which have received many jolts on various accounts. Truly speaking, the 'seven sisters' have already reached a point after which any further disintegration will be suicidal for the integrity of the country. Further, if you allow such divisions and accept the demand of the agitators, it will not help the nation to progress towards the path of peace, economic growth and political stability. This will certainly be detrimental to national integration and economic development to a great extent. However, sometimes the veil of a popular demand under the guidance of political leaders, forces situations to turn voilent and often they go beyond control also. Sometimes, it is observed that the agitated youth fall victims to the trap set by selfish political leaders and quite unwittingly resort to violence over issues such as unemployment and many other asssociated and created problems. Naturally it is not proper to give room to such demands. The pros and cons of everything should be studied. The Government should, however, adopt sympathetic attitude and solve the related issue in a judicious manner.

In conclusion, it may be stated that, further fragmentation of the NE zone states can not be advocated at any cost. This will certainly weaken the nation as a whole. And similar demands in other parts of the country will also be strengthened leading to chaos in national life. However, it is a hard fact that region of the country in particular has received less attention this organisation like NEC should 'therefore' be given opportunity to serve better and to help the zone to come out of this vicious circle of poverty. The Central Government should ensure that there is no further infiltration in the territory and the borders are sealed in an effective manner. This is, however a real problem since 98% of the borders are international border. The Government has to be vigilant and deal with it firmly.

8

ETHNIC ASSERTION AND REORGANIZATION OF ASSAM

PRAFULLA MISRA

Inter-ethnic problems are no longer confined to any particular country or region. It has become a world-wide phenomenon. It is attracting a great deal of attention from the media, academicians and political thinkers especially after the recent spurt of inter-ethnic conflicts in Caucasus, Baltic region, and Central Asian region of the former Soviet Union and its disintegration as also the conflicts in the former Yugoslavia.

These problems are bequeathed by history, while at times baffle solution because of certain stereotyped ideas and dogmas. Engels once said that everyone would have to admit to himself that he had no idea what the future would be. This is difficult for us as we are used to regard any spontaneous growth of new ideas,concept or movement, not keeping with our set notions, not only disturbing, even at times consider to be heresies.

There is a widespread view that the genie of national conflicts have been released by prestroika not only in the former Soviet Union but also in the East European countries. But it is wrong to project the effect as the cause and *vice versa.* Turning to history is the best way to argue with those who would like to portray the present problems and conflicts of today something entirely new, that had sprung from nowhere.

In the course of our freedom struggle various ethnic groups, which were earlier disunited or at logger heads with one another, joined the national movement under the leadership of Mahatma Gandhi and the party he led, the Indian National Congress, which also embraced in its fold different shades of political opinion from conservatives to radicals, to free the country from the British yoke and to have a just society and order in its place. Similarly, in the erstwhile Russian Empire, under the leadership of V.I. Lenin and the party he built and led, the Russian Social Democratic Labour Party (Bolshevik), various ethnic groups, in various stages of social development joined the revolution to have a just order to free themselves from all types of subjugation and injustices. With the success of the October Socialist Revolution and also attainment of independence of India, the people in general believed that their dreams would be realised. But the concept of freedom or just order were understood by various ethnic groups in their own way according to their own perspective.

It may be noted that ethnic interests are not invariable, but always in the process of development. It is also not easy to establish a state structure which could become the foundation of harmonious and equal relations, more so in a multi-national country. It would be worthwhile to discuss the problems of the Baltic regions of the erstwhile Soviet Union, before discussing the ethnic problems, identity crisis of the people of North-East Region and reorganisation of the composite State of Assam.

There is no denying of the fact that the October Revolution liberated non-Russian people of the erstwhile Tsarist empire termed by Lenin as the "prison house of nations". Along with industrialisation, cent per cent literacy was achieved in the backward outlying regions of Central Asia, where more than 90 per cent were illiterate before the revolution. But in course of time, apart from too much centralisation of administration, bureaucratisation, the rulers of USSR took a simplified view and believed that national question had been solved for good. They did not give due regard to the sensitivity or otherwise of the ethnic relations and Tridtity of the small ethnic groups. They allowed unrestricted migration of Russians and Ukranians to these republics, which were in the process of industrialisation. At present the migrants are about 40 per cent of the population of Estonia. In Lithuania, 20 per cent are migrants, mostly Russians, total population of the state being 3.6 million. Out of the total population of 2.6 million in Latvia, the Latvians number a little more than 1.3 million. In Kazakhstan, Kazakhs are only 38 per cent. Majority of the migrants are Russians. Now three Baltic Republics have become independent republics. But the moot question is had the process of migration been not restricted, these nationalities would in no time would have become minority in their historically evolved homeland. This is the cause of the identity crisis. Nor the Baltic Republics are going to take measures to introduce residential qualification for the migrants as far as the voting rights are concerned.

It may be noted that when Lithuania declared Lithuanian as official language, the Russian migrants opposed it. When Moldavia declared moldavian as the official language, it was opposed not only by the Russian migrants, but also by Gagauz, a small ethnic group, who felt that the declaration of Moldavian as the official language would be a threat to their language, culture and identity. It may be recalled that when Assamese was declared as the official language in Assam, it was opposed not only by the Bengali speaking Barak Valley, but also by the people of the hills who considered it to be a threat to their language, culture and identity.

The disintegration of the USSR and Yugoslavia, however, has not resolved the ethnic problems. As is known, armed clashes between various ethnic groups are still continuing. For Russians, the experience is distressing and at times humiliating, because as big brothers they enjoyed the privileges of the majority every where before the disintegration of USSR.

Even in the advanced countries like the United Kingdom, the Irish question, the Scottish question, in Canada the French speaking Quebec question and in Belgium the Wollens questions are very much alive.

The only country which has to a great extent solved the ethnic problems, notwithstanding some minor irritants now and then, is Switzerland or the Swiss Confederation, having peaceful co-existence of three ethnic groups: German, French and Italian. One of the interesting features of the Swiss education system is its federalism. All matters relating to education are controlled by the 26 cantons. There is no federal ministry of education.

Till the annexaion of Assam or the Ahom kingdom by the East

India Company, Assam meant the Brahmaputra Valley. With the extension of colonial rule various hill areas were brought under their control and merged with Assam proper as districts. Cachar and Sylhet districts known as Surma Valley were also tagged to Assam for the administrative conveniences of the colonial rulers. Prior to the annexation of Assam by the British East India Company and extension of British occupation of the hill areas, these areas were ruled by independent kings or chieftains. They were never part of the Ahom kingdom. The Ahom rulers of Brahmaputra Valley never directly ruled these areas. When the hill tribes carried on raids in the plains there were hostilities between the Ahoms and tribes concerned. But there were also friendship treaties. Even the tribes in the Brahmaputra Valley had self-rule or autonomy. The Ahom King can loosely be termed as Suzerein. Ahom Kings had officials to maintain relations with the frontier tribes, which now-a-days termed as Frontier Service.

Looking back, the reorganisation of Assam is a historical process. There is nothing surprising about it. The Indian National Congress supported the formation of linguistic states. That is why Surma Valley Congress Committee was affiliated to Bengal Provincial Congress Committee (BPCC). Had their been no partition, Surma Valley would have been a part of Bengal. Because of partition of the Country, Cachar, now-a-days called Barak Valley is still with Assam.

Whatever might be the weakness of the Constitution of India, it has one great merit, that is its flexibility. That is why the founding fathers of the Constitution incorporated the Sixth Schedule to the Constitution of India so that the hill tribes of the composite State of Assam can develop according to their own genius. Sixth Schedule means self-rule or autonomy. But the Sixth Schedule could not fulfil their aspirations. They wanted more power. The demand became more strident with the rise of the hill intelligentsia. They demanded a separate state and got it. But many well-meaning people could not understand that demand for separate State is the outcome of the introduction of Sixth Schedule to the Constitution and termed the demand as divisive or separatist.

The demand for Jharkhand, Uttarakhand State or Baster State reflected the ethnic assertion of the people even though at times the expression may be distorted. Notwithstanding its distortions one should be sympathetic to these demands and should not be guided by fossilized dogmas or ideas as some of the Marxists, because of mechanical understanding believed that economic development would solve the national or ethnic question. One should understand that national question or ethnic question by itself is an important question. That is why Lenin in his wisdom considered national question by itself an important problem and incorporated it in the programme of Russian Social Democratic Labour Party as early as 1904.

In North East region, the ethnic assertion is taking verious shapes, the Karbis rare demanding an Autonomous State within Assam. The Bodos are demanding a separate State – Bodoland, the Hmars are demanding a separate autonomous district. The Lanungs or Tisas are also demanding a separate district. Now the autonomous district councils of Manipur are demanding the application of Sixth Schedule, while those who are governed by the Sixth Schedule are either demanding more power or separate state, according to the stages of development.

When in the early 'eighties the hill states of the North East region where the tribals are in majority, demanded reservation of assembly and parliamentary seats to safeguard their identity, it was considered a new issue by some particularly those belonging to major ethnic groups. The argument was: when tribals are in majority in these states why should their seats be reserved. But they were oblivious of the fact that small ethnic groups whose population is few lakhs could be outnumbered if influx of outsiders continue unabated, ultimately losing their political power to the migrants. Nearer home Tripura is an example.

According to 1981 Census, the population of Meghalaya is 1.4 million of which around 15 per cent are non-tribals. (At that time the Koch and Rabhas were not included in the S.T. list). The population of Nagaland is 7,74,930 and Mizoram 4,93,757. Thus the migration of few lakhs of people from outside can change the present demographic pattern. One cannot dismiss their fear of being outnumbered and losing their political power and identity as groundless. Of course, the provision of Sixth Schedule helped to stop the alienation of land in these states. But the tribals of other parts of India including Assam plains had no such safeguards and as a result over the year land alienation took place and they have been reduced to minority in areas where they were in majority even in 1947.

But what was considered to be a non-issue is no longer a controversy. It has become part of life when the Constitution was amended to give reservation of seats to tribal people of the hill states.

During the period of freedom movement, the Indian National Congress gave the call for an independent India where the constituent units (linguistic states) would be autonomous and residuary powers would be vested in the states. But the way the constitution was drafted it became more unitary than federal. So, the demand has come from various quarters for restructuring the centre-states relations. Under the blows of insurgency in Nagaland and Mizoram and the unprecedented mass upsurge in Assam, the Union Government was forced to become objective, rather pragmatic. And the accords were signed to diffuse the situation and accept some of the demands raised by those movements. The signing of the accords means handing over more power to the states by the Centre by agreement and which contributes to the development of the federal character of the administration. How far the accords were successful in implementation under the present set-up is quite a different matter. But many well-meaning people, being unable to overcome ossified ideas failed to appreciate the significance of these accords.

As stated earlier, the Constitution of India has its inherent strength in its flexibility. Take for example the incorporation of the Sixth Schedule to the Constitution. In Sikkim, after its merger, the provision of equal representation of indigenous Bhutia-Lepchas who are 27 per cent was kept. There are 12 reserved seats for Bhutia-Lepchas and for the majority 12 general seats.

As per TNV accord, now the number of reserved seats has been raised from 17 to 20 in Tripura. Earlier, TNV demanded 30 seats. When a TNV leader was asked why they accepted reservation of 20 seats in the assembly he told that it was accepted only as a first step. Some are of the opinion that if fifty per cent seats are not reserved in the Assembly for the tribals the demand for an Union Territory in place of the present autonomous district council of Tripura may gain momentum.

It may be noted that in Kazakhastan Republic of former USSR, as a result of certain historical causes the Kazakhs became minority that is about 38 per cent. But in Republican constitution it was incorporated that Kazakhastan is the homeland of the Kazakh people, not of the Russians and other migrants who are in majority. The migrants of course used to get all the privileges of citizens.

In Malaysia, the indigenous Malaya people retains the political power, not the huge Chinese and Indian migrants. That is why that country is free from any major ethnic strife for a long time. If the indigeneous people lose their political power in their homeland, the breeding ground of ethnic strife cannot be eliminated. Ethnic conflicts flared up in Fiji, when the indigenous Melanesians to their dismay found that their political power had been taken away by the migrant Indians dominated Labour Party. These Indians were the descendents of indented labour taken by the British for plantation work. In the new constitution of Fiji, 37 seats are reserved for ethnic Fijians and 27 seats for Fijians of Indian origin. The ethnic Fijians make up less than half of the country's population. It seems, the Indian dominated Labour Party has become realistic and given up the path of confrontation and extended support to the former General Rabuka to become the Prime Minister.

There are two major points in the Assam accord signed on 15th August, 1985. These are detection and deleting of names of foreigners from the voters list and their deportation and the other being "Constitutional, legislative and administrative safeguards as may be appropriate, shall be provided to protect, preserve and promote the culture, social, linguistic identity and heritage of Assamese people". One view is that the identity of the ethnic Assamese can only be safeguarded by making provision of reservation of seats in the assembly and parliament, which can help it to retain its political power, whatever might be the population complex. Even if, foreigners are detected, their names deleted from the voters list, how far deportation would be practicable is any body's guess.

Nobody can wish away the identity crisis of the Assamese, which is the result of unrestricted migration for almost a century. Question may arise that according to the 1971 Census when ethnic Assamese are in majority in the State, why should they be given reservation. One need not answer this question because the majority status of the Assamese is very often challenged by a section of the people of the State. In a memorandum submitted to the Home Minister dated 22nd December 1989 by All Assam Minority Students Union (AMSU), a front organisation of the United Minority Front, which by and large represents the interest of migrants of Bengal origin and opposed to the Assam accord, puts the figure of the ethnic Assamese at 27 per cent making a statistical jugglery, forgetting for a moment that this jugglery only strengthens the demand for reservation of seats for the ethnic Assamese.

Interaction and process of assimilation is a long historical process and the formation of Assamese nationality is no exception. But it is also to be noted that some of the plains tribals of Assam like the Bodos, Mishings, Rabhas, Tiwas etc., even though bi-lingual have retained their ethnic identity and are fighting for safeguarding their identity like the Assamese. This is a natural urge and it should be sympathetically considered and they should be given autonomy or self-rule in their homeland, so that they can feel assured that they are masters of their land. Any delay in recognition of their rights and aspirations will only create ethnic tension and strife. The causes of the present ethnic tension should be objectively analysed and as far as practicable without any preconceived notions, instead of being carried away by the belief that the effect is the cause.

9

THE STATE AND THE MIDDLE CLASS
The Case of Assam (1979-90)

SAMIR KUMAR DAS

Introduction

This study intends to assess the impact of states reorganisation on what may be called the style of middle-class politics in Assam. The main features of the style of middle-class politics in Assam (Das,1991 A:113-33) are discussed elsewhere at length. Two of these features that deserve reconsideration may briefly be noted at the very outset: First, everywhere the phenomenon of middle-class politics is characterized by a certain universalist ethos. What we mean by this ethos is that the fact of being a middle-class becomes far more important in shaping the style of its politics than anything else (like its being affiliated to a *particular* ethnic community). Viewed in this light, middle-class politics is seen to cut across the particularistic ethnic affiliations and loyalties. It seems that the middle-class politics in Assam is not infused with such a universalist ethos. When we refer to the middle class in Assam, we invariably refer to an ethnically affiliated middle-class: an Assamese middle class, a Bodo middle class or a Bengali one at that. It is one of those occasions in history when the emergence of classes does not result in the obsolescence of ethnic communities. The ethnic differences amongst these *middle classes* are so pronounced that they are found to be at the 'root of separatism' in the North-East in general. As Hiren Gohain observes:

> "A rising middle class, with a sprinkling of rich businessmen and contractors, with educated youths and students as militant cadres, leads the rural masses in such movements."

In other words, middle class in Assam is hardly a homogeneous quantity it is seen to be *ethnically fragmented* in character.

Secondly, coming to Assam. What stares at one's face is the *movemental nature,* of its middle-class politics and the Assamese middle class perhaps not without reason, is commonly designated as 'agitationist' and sometimes less charitably as 'xenophobic' (Das, 1991 A:115-7). According to a rather recent estimate made available, there are as many as 19 ethnic movements (of which 10 happen to be only in Assam) having in some way or the other to do with a demand for further reorganization (Chattopadhyay, 1990:206-7).

That the region in general and Assam in particular have undergone frequent reorganization and restructuring reflects the institutionally fluid character of the Indian state. A state that is unable to act as a *stable* institutional contrivance is a contradiction in terms and may be considered to be one of the principal indicators of a minimal state (Das, 1991 B: 1-40;1992 A: 58-72).

The term 'stability' is used here in any of the three relatively distinguishable senses or in any of their combination : First of all, take chronological stability :

> "The older an organisation (*read,* institution, SKD) the more it is likely to continue to exist through any specified future time period. The probability that an organisation is one hundred years old will survive one additional year it is to be hypothesized, is perhaps one hundred times greater than the probability that an organisation that is one year old will survive one additional year." (Huntington 1968 : Ch. 1).

Viewed thus, the reorganised units of the North-East are comparatively new and have really not been put on trial.

Next one may refer to the ability on the part of the institutions to withstand the succession of one generation of leaders by another. The days of Gopinath Bardoloi and Bimala Prasad Chaliha are now over. With the assumption of power by Asom Gana Parishad in 1985, a relatively inexperienced but highly educated youthful band of legislators took over the political scenario of Assam. With an average age of little over 30 years, it is India's youngest-ever legislative party to occupy the treasury benches in state assembly. Prafulla Kumar Mahanta at the age of 32 becomes the youngest Chief Minister of India. In fact, only 4 of the 109 AGP candidates in the fray had ever contested an election earlier and the only one whose father was once a minister, Atul Bora, lost narrowly from Marigaon. The legislative party included 56 with a bachelor's degree or more, with just two members without any formal degrees, this was the most educated legislature party in the country. By contrast, the AGP members for Lok Sabha constituted a kind of senior team headed by veteran parliamentarian Dinesh Goswami. The youngest of the MP's, Gokul Saikia at 34 also just fall short of becoming the youngest-ever MP from Assam, falling behind the venerable Dev Kant Barooah who first went to Lok Sabha at the age of 33 (Gupta, 1986:26). The high hopes raised by this youthful takeover however faded into a whimper by the close of the, eighties. AGP's disastrous non-rule was mostly evident in two ways: in its failure to hold divergent sections of the people of Assam together and there by, maintaining her composite identity and also, to implement the basic provisions of the Accord of 1985 (Das, 1992 B:53-7). The tenure of the AGP- government was cut short by the imposition of President's Rule and it suffered an ignominious electoral debacle in 1990. A relatively senior team of legislators under the stewardship of Hiteswar Saikia, a seasoned Congress (I) campaigner, came to power in the same year.

Finally, stability also depends upon an institutions ability to 'find out' and also effectively discharge newer functions. An institution unable to 'find out' newer functions once the older ones are exhausted, faces what Huntington would call, 'a lingering death'. What is at issue here is the symmetry between the institutions and their functions. Such a symmetry, as the States Reorganisation Commission feels, can be maintained if, and only if, Assam remains a 'compact unit'. Proliferation of states in the region would only make "co-ordination of policies and programmes between State of Assam and the hill areas on the one hand and between the hill districts themselves on the other difficult" (Report, 1955:187). Sometimes, as the Commission points out, powers delegated to the newly created bodies are not undertaken by them. As a result, "the local government is saddled with an unnecessarily heavy burden of expenditure" (Report, 1955: 189). By contrast, it should also be noted that sometimes necessary institutions are not created and reorganisations not being made to cope up with the ever-expanding functions of the government. For one thing, the communal massacres of February-March, 1983 have amply exposed the un-governability of the erstwhile district of Darrang. As Arun Shourie comments.

> "Darrang district, for instance, stretches across a distance longer by far than the distance from Delhi to Chandigarh. And in normal times, the distirct has just 1,000 to 1,200 policemen to maintain the peace. Thus, whether law and order will in fact prevail depends primarily on the temper of the people themselves" (Shourie, 1983: 60).

In all these senses-chronological, generational and functional, the institutional stability of the Indian state insofar as the North-East is concerned, is definitely put at stake. But, why do one argue that a state that is unable to act as a stable institutional contrivance approximates a minimal state and is only a contradiction in terms? Broadly, for two reasons: On the one hand, stability of institutions enables them to contain the rapidly growing social mobilization that left to itself, threatens to sweep them away. On the other hand, and more importantly, stability is what lends to the governments an element of credibility. Frequent regime changes in France (remember only the quick succession of Republics since 1789) or nearer home, in Bangladesh especially during 1971-85 have resulted in an enormous credibility gap (Sen, 1988: 1-39,56-126) whereas persistence of an "old patrician structure of England's political system, inspite of tremendous revolutionary changes has given to itself, consummative political stability at home" (Nairn, 1977: 21-3). It is no wonder then that the States Reorganisation Commission in its report (that has certainly been undone as Assam was made subject to frequent amputations) sought to be guided by the Principal objective of stabilizing states' institutions in the region rather than anything else (like, mindlessly subjecting them to reorganizations for placating regional feelings).

In simple terms, the question is : How are ethnic fragmentation and movemental nature of middle-class politics in Assam affected among other things, by the functioning of a minimal states: ? It is, therefore, worthwhile to evaluate the impact of the functioning of a minimal state on the style of middle-class politics. Thus, it is proposed to shift the focus of inquiry from the formative history of the middle-class and consequently its leading role not only in the arena of 'governmental politics' but also in the "struggles launched by the Assamese people on economic issues and for the protection of the identity of Assam" (Sharma, 1990: X) to the minimal state in asmuch as it affects, among other things, the style of middle-class politics in Assam. It may be reminded that this shift in the focus of inquiry is in tune with the recent researches in political sociology that view the state as 'a potent and autonomous factor' in 'shaping the society' (Skocpol, 1985: 6) and bring it to the centre stage of inquiry.

Before making any further headway, it is necessary to point out some of the major limitations of this study: First, this analysis concentrates on states reorganisation to the extent that it affects, *among other things,* the politics and that too, the style of middle-class politics in Assam. This is not to say that politics in Assam is synonymous with middle-class politics. Nor is it to say that the style of middle-class politics has no role whatsoever to play in states reorganization. Secondly, by the middle class in Assam it does not exclusively refer to the *Assamese* middle-class. The middle-class in Assam is an inclusive category drawn from various ethnic communities living in Assam and the Assamese middle-class is only one of them. Thirdly, unless otherwise stated, this study restricts itself to an analysis of the Assamese situation during 1979-90. Everyone knows that 1979, marks the beginning of the Assam movement, while 1990, the exit of the AGP-government. It is also recognized that this period cannot be properly understood unless it is placed against the broader historical perspective.

The Dominant Assamese Nationalism

The process of reorganization was expected to produce ethnically homogeneous units and thereby drastically reduce inter-ethnic tensions. But due to the peculiar demography of the region (where even an ethnic majority hangs on thin air and is constantly under the threat of begin swept away by almost unlimited immigration from across the borders and ethnic minority is too culturally distinct to be politically discounted), such an expectation has been completely belied. The reorganisation has on the one hand led to an entrenchment of what is called, dominant Assamese nationalism (Baruah & Sharma, 1991: 20). It, on the other hand, creates disaffection amongst the ethnic minorities living in the state. They are in disarray in the sense that their disaffection poses no organized challenge to the domination of the ethnic majority. How?

As Assam was made subject to surgical operations, the claims of the ethnic minorities could be effectively eliminated and the Assamese middle-class, in effect, could tighten its control over the state power and more particularly, the law-and-order machinery. It was possible for it then to use this power against the minorities and it *reportedly* did it in that manner on countless occasions. Pradosh Chaudhury, Secretary of the Committee for the Protection of Linguistic Minorities, asserted that "the stepmotherly attitude of the state administration has further imperilled the Bengalis of Assam" (quoted in Chaudhury, 1973:52). It now appears that the Bodos have very little faith in the efficacy of the Assamese-dominated administration. The depreciation of the state administration in the eyes of the ethnic minorities was most eloquently expressed when during the worst-ever communal riots at Gohpur in August 1989, the Bodos refused not only to approach Assam Police to come to their rescue but also to take shelter in the relief camps run by the Government of Assam.

The rising disenchantment with the Assamese dominated administration was further aggravated by the partisan responses of the state to the varieties of ethnic demands. Thus to cite an instance, the Assam Accord of 1985: according to Citizens' Rights Preservation Committee, is 'a pious fraud on Indian democracy' for in the name of detecting and deporting the 'foreigners', the administration would now purge Assam of outsiders (*Bahiragatas*), an euphemism for the Bengalis who have been living in Assam for generations together (Chowdhury, 1990: 182-293). The All-Bodo Students, Union (ABSU) in the same vein, regretted that the Accord denied the existence of the aboriginal tribal people and reorgnized only the Assamese-speaking people by including clauses for special safeguards to Assamese language, culture and heritage. The ABSU said that the Accord threatened the very existence of the tribal people in their own land (Chowdhury, 1990: 210). In other words, the cultural policy underlying the Accord of 1985 was meant to entrench the dominant Assamese nationalism to the detriment of the minorities. This of course is not new. That the minorities are in the process of being deprived of state patronage did not escape the notice of States Reorganization Commission way back in 1955 (that is to say, long before Assam was dismembered) that in its report did not fail to mention: "The Bengali-speaking people have cited for instance the fact that the number of government primary schools in Goalpara district with Bengali as the medium of instruction has fallen from 252 in 1947-48 to at the present time" (*Report*, 1955: 191).

Morover, as dominant Assamese nationalism asserts itself, the contribution of ethnic minorities to the composition of the political elite of the state being gradually to dwindle almost to the point of insignificance. Table-gives us an index of Muslim representative Assam Legistative Assembly

TABLE 9.1 : Muslim Reprentation

Year	Total No. of Seats in the Assembly	No. of Muslim Members	Total Muslim Population (In Lakhs)
1947	71	16	18.66
1952	105	15	20.72
1957	108	15	24.57
1962	98	13	28.48
1967	112	20	31.79
1972	126	20	35.94
1978	126	28	N.A.

Source: (Dev & Lahiri, 1985:165)

While Muslim representation in the Legislative Assembly has been rather crratic, their representation, it may safely be concluded, falls far short of the rate of increase of Muslim population over the years. But it is true that the number of ministers drawn from the Muslim registers only a marginal increase during 1978-83: 'In the Janata Ministry installed on 12 march, 1978, under the stewardship of Galap Borbora, 3 Muslims were inducted to the Ministry. The downfall of Borbora Ministry was followed by the emergence of a defectors' Ministry under the leadership of Jogendra Nath Hazarika which too had 3 Muslim members. In quick succession this was followed by Anwara Taimur Ministry which came to power on 6 December, 1980.... Taimur Ministry which continued till 28 June, 1981 included two from each Valley. In the Gogoi Ministry that was installed after a spell of President's Rule, the number of Muslim representation in the Cabinet went up to five. In the.... Hiteswar Saikia Ministry, the importance of Muslim community has been amply acknowledged by including as many as eight of the Congress (I) MLA's (Dev & Lahiri, 1985: 166). It must be admitted that a high representation of the minorities in state administration and Legislative Assembly is no guarantee that their interests will be preserved and protected. But still, their thinking representation *vis-a-vis* the increase in the population certainly makes the situation bleak and desparate.

Finally, the Assamese middle-class, in the name of Assamese nationalism is seen to usher in a process of economic development that only helps in creating and exacerbating intra-state inequality. Thus, it is no surprise that the enclaves where the minorities are found in number (whether in Kokrajhar of Assam or Telangana of Andhra Pradesh) seem to lag behind the remaining parts of the state. Kokrajhar, for instance, is mostly inhabited by the Bodo (30 per cent, roughly). It also happens to be one of the most backward districts of Assam. That is why, it also serves as the breeding ground of ethnic unrest: "... uneven development at the state level may lead to the emergence of powerful dissident forces within the regional system. The Bodo agitation is perhaps an instance of the emergence of such forces within Assam" (Ghosh, 1990). States Reorganization, in simple terms, remains oblivious to the problems of intra-state disparity and consequent resentments voiced by the ethnic minorities against it: "Structural, economic and cultural imbalance led to the problem of intra regional integration" (Azam, 1981: 109). Perhaps that was inevitable for no amount of states reorganization could make the states absolutely free from traces of ethnic minorities in a country of civilization magnitude.

The Demostration Effect

The much-expected de-ethnicization of political demads in linguistically organized states remains an elusive dream. For what it does is to open up pandora's box. This is due to what may be called demostration effect. Even a small concession to the demand for statehood acts as a source of active encouragement to those yet to lay hold of a state. If the Nagas and the Mizos can get away with their respective states why not Tai-Ahoms? In other words, it has a demonstration effect on them and subsequently sets the ball rolling. Middle-class politics has hence, a built-in tendency towards further radicalization. In fact, a seemingly sympathetic commentator on the movement launched by UARP (Ujain Asom Rajya Parishad) reiterates the same argument:

> "The Central Government did not concede the demand of the UARP although it fulfilled the demand of the Naga Nationalist Organization, Mizo National Front, All-Party Hill Leaders' Conference by creating Nagaland, Mizoram and Meghalaya respectively. Even Arunachal Pradesh has now been made a separate state" (Lahon, 1990:50).

Is it because those who have been granted with statehood could make their demands felt at the nerve-centre of the political system by taking resort to violence? This is how violence becomes the order of the day. The above point bears out two-fold implications: On the one hand, under all normal circumstances, the state shall not listen to the demands for statehood unless it is made to listen. This only gives credence to what Bayley calls, an increasingly 'deaf' state in India (Bayley, 1969) and as the state becomes more and more 'deaf' ever-higher levels of violence are required to make the state listen to ethnic demands. Violence thereby acquires a self-spiralling character. On the other hand, this involves a downright devaluation of regular institutional channels of putting up demands before the political system. Increasing resort to violence only knocks such regular channels out of currency: "Agitational politics becomes a substitute for institutionalized participation. Protests not only supplement them but supplant them and render them irrelevant" (Bayley, 1969). We have already noted how the Bodo faith in the Assamese-dominated adminstration has received a severe jolt in recent years. The regular institutions of the state suffer from what we have called, a credibility gap.

The Disenchantment

The process of reorganization is what lends to the middle class its movemental character. When no conceivable scheme of reorganization can satisfy all, it is bound to poduce disillusionment in the minds of a section of people and also a sense of disenchantment with the state itself. This is what pushes the middle-class to the extreme path of self-reliance, that is to say, of doing without the state. Besides, it so happens that in times of relative full, the state comes up with proposals for reorganization (some of which are nevertheless implemented) that satisfy none of the parties involved. Things get immediately out of hands. In all such cases, the state plays its rόle in *inventing* a movement almost from out of nothing.

Thus even if Nagaland became a separate state there remained many places inside Manipur where Nagas like Meos and Ukhruls still live: "Was it not necessary to tag the area inhabited by the Nagas with Nagaland and thereby reorganizing the state and making Manipur a distinctive and concentrated area?" (Ray Chaudhury, 1986: 125, trans. mine). In other words, the reorganization of states of Nagaland and Manipur was ill-conceived and justly angered both the Meiteis and the Nagas. To take another instance, the proposals for shifting the capital of Assam from Dispur to Chandrapur was of course ill-time. At a time when there was a general mood against the Indian state and acrimonious communal battles were fought (1983) the state could have done well not to float the proposal. Obviously, it was received as yet another conspiracy of the Indian state to evict autochthonous people of Assam for the construction of the capital. Similarly, the idea of changing the name of Goalpara to Kaziranga about the same time was both preposterous and uncalled for. It only added to their alienation.

All this has led the Assamese middle class to come gradually to realize the ultimate futility of states reorganization and has subsequently driven them to chart out a self-reliant coursre- that is to say, to secede from the Indian Union by establishing what is designated as 'Sovereign and Socialist Assam'. As an ULFA-spokesman puts it:

> " . . . establishment of a separate state has given nothing to the Khasi people. Meghalay is still a backward state.

> So, creation of a Bodoland is no real solution to the problems of the Bodo people. Within this system, some Bodo ministers and bureaucrates will replace the Assamese ones. In one word, this will give birth to a Bodo ruling class and rampant corruption....So, establishing Bodoland without transforming the system is no real solution" (ULFA-R-Sathe..1991): 70-1, *trams. mine.).*

This to one's mind is a recognition of the ultimate futility of the experimentation with states reorganization in the region and ULFA perhaps takes this recognition to the extreme of demanding secession from the Indian Union with the hope of transfoming the system.

NOTES

1. Cf. It is also important that with the creation of linguistic states, the salience of language demands tends to decline and the energies of these states are channelled to more productive competition and cooperation. Within each state, language competition tends to be replaced by other modes of competition (Das Gupta, 1975).

2. As a *Sunday*-report poits out:

   Significantly, the Bodos,did not seek any help from three Assam Police out-posts in the area. Instead, they all run towards the hills of Arunachal Pradesh. Not a single Bodo family can be found among the 20,000- odd refugees who have been put up in nine relief camps in Gohpur. Only a handful of them have continued to stay behind in the seven relief camps set up for about 10,000 affected people in Lakhimpur. However, about 20,000 Bodos are living in almost sub-human conditions in four make-shift camps at Sonajuli, Kukila, Holangi and Magoni in Arunachal (Ramaseshan, 1989:10).

3. It is true that the rate of increase recorded by Muslim population during 1951-61 has been greater than that of Hindu population; it became the lowest during 1961-71. The author is thankful to Prof. Biplab Dasgupta for drawing his attention to the necessity of looking into comparative rates of increase recorded by respective religious communities. This is borne out by the following Table:

TABLE-9.2 : Population by Religion

Religion	Population 1951	Population 1961	Population 1971	Decadal Variation (51 -61)	Decadal Variation (61-71)
Hindus	57,81,974	77,30,698	10,604,618	+ 33.70	+ 37.18
Muslims	19,81,859	27,42,287	35,92,124	+ 38.37	+ 30.99
Christians	1,62,932	2,63,132	3,81,010	+ 61.50	+ 44.80
Buddhists	9,854	16,782	22,565	+ 70.31	+ 34.46
Jains	4,121	9,310	12,914	+ 125.92	+ 38.71
Sikhs	2,983	8,345	11,920	+ 179.75	+ 42.84
Tribal Religions	76,819	52,234	..	- 32.00	..
Other Religions	8,314	14,541	..	+ 74.90	..

Source: *Statistical Handbook* 1982. Gauhati: Govt. of Assam. pp. 40-43.

4. Prof. A .K. Neog draws the attention of the author to the formulation of tribal subplans. The representatives of the Bodo community, according to him, are free to draw them and thereby determine the course of the economy of this region. So, economic underdevelopment of this region is more due to their fault rather than anything else. The Assamese are not to be blamed for the economic underdevelopment of the Bodos. As a matter of fact, it is not the intention of the author to argue that the dominant Assamese nationalism is the only responsible factor. The Bodo middle-class, for instance, is squarely responsible. In his view, it is not so much a question of apportioning blame. It must be admitted that the tribal sub-plans are to operate within the constraints and requisites set forth by the state plans. In no case, can they violate them.

REFERENCES

Azam, Kousar 1981, *Political Aspects of National Integration,* Meerut, Meenakshi.

Baruah, Apurba Kumar and Manorama Sharma 1991, "Nationality question in Assam : Some Conceptual Issue" in *Nation-Building and Development in North-East India.* ed. by Udayon Misra, Guwahati: Purbanchal Prakash.

Bayley, David 1969, 'Public Protest and the Political Process in India' *Pacific Affairs,* 42, Spring.

Chattopadhyay, Dilip Kumar 1990, *History of the Assamese Movement*

Since 1947, Calcutta, Minerva.

Chaudhury, Narayan 1973, *Asamer Bhasha Danga (in Bengali),* Calcutta, Moni Prakashan.

Chawdhury, Rabijit 1990, 'Minority Movement : Emergence of the United Minorities Front' in *Ethnic Movement in Poly-cultural Assam,* ed. by P.S. Datta, New Delhi, Vikas.

Das, Samir Kumar 1991, A, On the Style of Middle-Class Politics, The case of Assam (1979-83), *The Calcutta Journal of Political Studies, X (1&2).*

Das, Samir Kumar 1991 B, *State Ethnicity and the Assam Movement,* Calcutta, University of Calcutta.

Das, Samir Kumar 1992 A, 'State against Nation' : Regional Movements in Contemporary India' in *Regional Movements in India,* ed. by G. Palanithurai and R. Thandavan, Delhi, Kanishka.

Das, Samir Kumar 1992 B, *ULFA : A Political Analysis* (unpublished).

Das Gupta , Jyotirindra 1975, 'Ethnicity, Language Demands and National Development in India' in *Ethnicity : Theory and Experience,* ed. by Nathan Glazer and Daniel P. Moynihan., Mass, Harvard University Press.

Dev, B.J. and D.K. Lahiri 1985, *Assam Muslims, Politics and Cohesion,* Delhi, Mittal

Ghosh ,Sravani 1990, 'Regional Conflicts in India : The Pattern of Crisis Management–Study of the Bodo Movement', paper presented to the National Seminar on Emerging Trends During the Nineties, held in Calcutta University during 14-5 April, 1990.

Gohain, Hiren 1988 "Roots of Separatism" *The Telegraph,* 2 January.

Gupta, Shekar 1986, "Assam : A Youthful Take-over", *India Today,* 15 January

Huntington, Samuel P. 1968, *Political Order in Changing Socities,* New York, Yale University Press.

Lahon, T. 1990, 'Ujani Asom Rajya Parishad : A Phase in Ahom Aspirations, in *Ethnic Movements in Poly cultural Assam,* ed. P.S. Datta, New Delhi, Vikas.

Nairn Tom 1977, '*The Breakup of Britain.* London, NLB.

Ramaseshan, Radhika 1989, 'Carnage in Gohpur', *Sunday,* 27 August-2 September.

Ray Chaudhury, 1986, *Uttar-Pub Seemanta : Ashantir Mul Karan Samuha (in Assamese),* Pathsala, Bani Prakash.

Report of the State Reorganisation Commission 1955, Delhi, Manager of Publications

Sen, Anupam 1988, *Bangladesh : Rashtra O Samaj.* (*in Bengali*) Dhaka Sahitya Samabaya

Sharma, Manorama 1990, *Social and Economic Change in Assam : Middle Class Hegemony,* Delhi, Ajanta.

Shourie, Arun 1983, Assam Elections : Come What May', *India Today,* 15 May.

Skoepol, Theda 1985, 'Bringing the State Back in Strategies of Analysis in Current Research' in *Bringing the State Back In.* ed. by Peter B. Evans, Districh Rueschmey and Theda Skoepol, Cambridge, CUP.

ULFA 'Sathe Kichhu Katha' 1991, in *Communist Chintav Bharate Jati Prasna (in Bengali)* ed. by Amit Roy Calcutta, Radical Impression.

10

PROSPECTS FOR ETHNIC REORGANISATION

B.B. GOSWAMI

I

Since the British Rule, the land and the people of the area comprising North-East India had for administrative purposes been organised on the basis of factors such as comparative backwardness, ecology, geo-political location, homogeneous territory, culture, language, ethnic identity and political demands.

During the British period, the region was organised in various ways at different points of time. Most important administrative decision was taken under the Government of India Act, 1935 whereby the tribal areas were divided into 'Excluded' and 'Partially Excluded Areas'. This was enforced in the North-East India in addition to a Regulation promulgated 120 years ago called Bengal Eastern Frontier Regulation, 1873. The Regulation gave the authority to enforce Inner Line Regulation which is even now operating in three states of North-East region (Mizoram, Nagaland and Arunachal Pradesh) ostensibly to protect the tribesmen from exploitation by the plainsmen.

When India became independent in 1947, the area was administratively divided into 'state' 'region' 'division' 'area' and 'princely' 'state' but for practical purposes, most of the territory was federated with Assam and administered from its capital, Shillong. At that time some people of the hills and plains were happy and some were unhappy for shedding land and people to a newly created country, the East Pakistan.

Ethnic Factor of Division

A number of autonomous districts/regions in Assam were carved out after 1947 under Part A of the Sixth Schedule of Constitution of India, which in turn was based on the recommendation of the North-Eastern Frontier Tribal and Excluded Areas Sub-Committee of the Constituent Assembly known as the Bordoloi Committee. The areas incorporated in Part A of the said Sixth Schedule became autonomous districts by virtue of the provisions of the constitution within the State of Assam *viz.*, the United Khasi - Jantia Hills District, the North Cachar Hills District, the Mikkir Hills District, the Garo Hills District and the Lushai Hill District. Since then the fragmentation of the North-East India is a continuous process, as an example, look at such process in *Mizoram.*

In 1890 (erstwhile), the Lushai Hills (now Mizoram) came under the British rule. At first the South Lushai Hills was tagged with Chittagong Hills tract (East Bengal) and the North Lushai Hills with Assam. In 1898, the two areas, North and South Lushai Hills, were forged and administered under a political officer called Superintendent. The Zawngling area of Myanmar was subsequently added to the area. In 1936, the Lushai Hills was declared as Partially Excluded Area. Subsequently, it was named as the Mizo Hills district by the Mizo Union party during its tensure in the first District Council. The Mizo Hills district was divided into a District Council area and a Pawi-Lakher Autonomous Regional Council area, under the Sixth Schedule of the Constitution of India. The former was inaugurated on 25th April 1952 and the latter on 23rd April 1953. The Pawi-Lakher Regional Council was entrusted to look after the interests of the Lakher, Pawi and Chakma tribesmen. It was further fragmented into three autonomous Regions for three above stated ethnic groups for the professed diversity in social and cultural traits. But fragmentation did not end here. The recent agitation for the creation of Hmar Autonomous District by the Hmar and the autonomous Subregion for the Pangs tribesmen of Mizoram indicates the possibility of further administrative division of the state.

Since the Hmar have taken up disjunctive techniques they have enlarge their area of action and follow the techniques used by the Mizo National Front in 1966 (Goswami 1974). They are violent in the contiguous areas of Mizoram *viz,* Assam, Manipur and Meghalaya. They have also taken shelter under the umbrella of the Nationalist Social Council of Nagaland (NSCN) to strengthen their bargaining power. As a result of this, their demands for creating administrative district by incorporating areas of neighbouring states and preserving ethnic identity based on the fact of compact settlements are under consideration by the Central and the Mizo Governments. As a result of reorganisation of the area in 1972, Union Territory of Mizoram was created. It became twenty-third state of India in February 1987.

Non-Ethnic Factors for Division

In the North-East India, the divide of hills and plains has come as a relief to the life of the people. Dry farming and wet cultivation are the dominant mode of activities of the hills and plains. This has been internalised by the people as one of the dividing line. The British kept the backwardness and low productivity of the hills is mind, and ruled the hills to protect the plains from plunder. This benefited them economically. By 1972, the hills people wanted this protection extensively and demanded new states. The 1972 reorganization of states was mainly to provide honourable facilities to control the way of life of the hill people as distinctively separate from the dominant people of the plains. Incidentally, at that time the people of the North Cachar Hills District and the Mikir Hills District refrained from joining Meghalaya. With the numerical and political dominance of three matrilineal tribes the state of Meghalaya was ireated. Thus Meghalaya has its own unique identity in India in socio-cultural terms. The socio-cultural uniqueness permeates in the economic activities of the tribesmen of Meghalaya.

The backward region of hills once called as a 'Tract' then 'Division' and 'Agency' has been turned into a state in 1972 as Arunachal Pradesh, separating it from Assam, neither as a sequal to any political demand nor due to any administrative reasons. It is a geo-political frontier inhabited by nascent, colourful, diverse ethnic groups. It is the administration which decided to create the hill state of Arunachal Pradesh by separating the plains of Assam for initiating development and preserving cultural identity of the people.

The Mizo Hills District became a union territory and then attained statehood for they demanded separation from Assam because of administrative callousness, linguistic chauvanism, exploitation and inequality. There was the Mizo unrest of 1966 demanding separation from India and political parties demanding statehood. The statehood demand was acceded to accelarate development and safeguard cultural identity of the tribesmen. (Goswami,1979).

Nagaland the sixteenth state of Indian union got statehood much earlier than the above mentioned three states. The state was inaugurated on the Ist December 1963 purely to satisfy the political demand for self-rule, safeguarding the cultural identities of the inhabitants and to counteract the upsurge for secession. (Goswami1992).

II

It may thus be seen that alongwith other factors the maintenance of ethnic identity is the common denominator in all the political demands. The underlying process can be seen through a perusal of the different memorandum submitted to the Government by the tribesmen and non-tribesman. The exercise gives one the impression that a group of people in a territory demarcate themselves as numerically, dominant, separate and unique, in contrast to the others. They feel that their way of living, behaving thinking are unsafe. They also feel that in their own territory they are constantly at a loss, and highlight this for socio-political separation. They urge to control the social, political and natural resources without sharing the same with others.

As a consequence to this, ethnic solidarity is intensified, traditions glorified, and the feeling of 'we' and 'they' (ingroup and outgroup) reassessed (Goswami 1975). New generic terms are coined, cognative notions are given new meaning, even new ethnic groups emerge on the basis of tradition and folklore. Integration and disintegration both emerge. This has been seen in the North-East India since Independence. In Mizoram, the word 'Lushai' was replaced by the word Mizo as a symbol of unity and solidarity for most of the ethnic groups. Today, the ethnic groups such as the Pang, Paite and Hmar deny that they are Mizo. They clanour for separate identities; but their way are different. The Paite of the Mizoram want to get recognition as a separate scheduled tribe only; the Pang want a sub-autonomous region; and the Hmar an autonomous region.

We can also observe this phenomenon in the Brahmaputra Valley. The main divide between the people of Assam is based on language, one of the important ethnic traits. Those who speak Assamese language are considered as 'we' in contrast to 'they' *i.e.* those who do not speak the language. 'They' are infiltrators and thus unwanted. This sort of divide resulted in the language riots in 1960 between Assamese and Bengali speakers. As a matter of fact, just before every decenneal census enumeration this issue gets uniformally raked up leading to language related riots, between Bengalis and Assamese. Cognitions are shaken. The meaning of Assamese word 'bongal' is misused (*ef vai* of the Mizo, Goswami 1975, 1991).

The 'we' category of the Assamese people, however, was not very clear at any point of time. It is influx. When in 1967, the Plains Tribal Council demanded a Union Territory called Udayachal to be carved out of area from North of Brahmaputra of Assam for 4.5 million Bodos, the Assamese speaking 'we' were shocked. The peaceful movement of the Bodos took a violent turn when the youth adopted aggressive attitude towards the Assam Government under the banner of All Bodo Student Union (ABSU) and demanded Bodoland. A former editor of the daily newspaper *Assam Tribune* described the situation (Kakati 1989) from the Assamese point of view by stating, "presently the ABSU is ruling the roast in the tribal areas as the AASU (All Assam Studnent Union) did in the Brahmaputra Valley during 1979-85". He further stated, "A striking feature of the Bodo movement is that, in stressing its goal of a Bodoland the ABSU interprets it as search for an identity as a distinct ethnic group with a proud historical past. There the ABSU is playing the AASU card which enabled the Asom Gana Parishad (AGP) the political outfit born out of the erstwhile AASU-AGSP combine, to capture power in 1985 in its maiden bid in parliamentry politics. This was undoubtedly an extraordinary achievement for even a more closely Unit regional party..." 'We' of 1960, thus got divided into further 'we' and 'they' with changed perception and perspective.

The Bodo wants to divide Assam almost into a half. As in Mizoram, the tactics followed by MNF being followed by the Hmar people's convention and its militant wing, the Bodo are playing the cards of the AASU. In the hills of Assam, the autonomous state demand committee of Karbi Anglong eclipsed the Asom Gana Parishad in 1989 District Council electio, rejected the Budget and intensified the agitational demand for creating autonomous state for the people of Karbi Anglong.

The hardliners of the AASU formed banned United Liberation Front of Assam (ULFA) and encouraged violence demanding secession of the valley from India. The ULFA asks, 'outsider' to leave the valley. The militant party issues threats, collects 'taxes', kidnaps people and rebels against administration. It is held that most of the people especially, "*the youth and the middle class,* (emphasis mine), none of the actions of ULFA beginning with the kidnapping is being viewed as especially offensive or gruesome" (Kamroopi ; 1991).

III

Ethnic Cleaning

Due to this, with the help of political activists, in the post-Independence period, ethnic cleansing is becoming a regular feature. To execute ethnic cleansing first outgroup is identified and then the member of the outgroup are deported by violent agitation and threat. It is a consequence of ethnicity. Through ethnic cleansing the desire is to bring about 'we' feeling into relief. Ethnic cleansing can be in relation to two or more generic ethnic groups; it can be in terms of hills and plains,in terms of religions or linguistic groups etc. In short by this process cognitive categorisations are created and misinterpreted; or if it is in existence it is reinforced. The typolisation of relationships is stratified in terms of benefits and values, assuming the ingroup's approach as the best. An intensified cleansing movement generates negative consequences not only among the outgroup living in the territory but also among the ethnic groups living in the immediate hinterland, which is detrimental for constitutional integration. Ethnic cleansing has positive consequences among the ingroups for deriving benefits out of it. In the demands for separate states, districts, autonomous regions and seccession, latent arguments are prepared. For the militants this is one of the manifest demand and overt wish. Which group is to be cleansed, when, why and how, differ over space and time. The extreme situation is again in Mizoram where Inner Line Regulation is in force. There the earlier migrant tribes have been cornered. The immediate later migrants, who are still having trans border marriage and kinship relationship are questioning the earlier migrants. The vexed question is a hornet's nest.

Three types of consequences are emerging as a result of ethnicity. One is the role of the people (they) who at one time asserted that 'they' only can run the administration and will forever rule over the educational development and business arena, as enlightened and specified group of people, are challenged, with the agitional approach. Thus the 'outsider's' monopoly is getting weaker 'Outsiders' are being dispossessed and are forced to leave the arena of their activities. Second type of consequence relates to those who were marginal to interethnic conflict. They distancing themsalves from playing any role in the scenario. And thirdly, the ethnic groups who have achieved their partial goal by attaining statehood, high percentage of reservation in acquiring occupation, right over land and forest, etc. have reversed their ranked position in political hierarchy. The erstwhile privileged 'they' are now at the mercy of erstwhile under-privileged.' The whole process is 'dialectic'. Universalising and homogenising trends exist along with parochial and discriminatory tendencies. The dominant ethnic groups having 'we' reeling on the one hand want to draw the maximum from modernising and developmental activities On the other hand, they want to be different by retaining some important cultural traits and even using them in the unrest (Goswami 1979).

IV

In understanding the patterns of ethnic and reorganisation of linkages between ethnic groups, there are various frame works such as culture as barrier for development, culture as stimulus for development, culture as mystifying ideology, culture as forceful trapping and culture as collective illusion concealing the mechanics of power and exploitation. Earlier feeling of ethnic groups (ethnicity being culture oriented) did not receive the centre stage importance by the economics oriented political administrators, for either it was thought that the persistence of tradition would hamper the process of modernisation or inevitability it of history that is transformation of traditional society into modern. But now in the North-East India, the ethnic groups and their culture are occupying the centre stage.

Indian constitutional experts gave jural importance, to certain communities by calling them as scheduled tribes. Constitutional provisions were provided for their welfare and progress leading to ethnic consciousness and higher degree of solidarity in controlling all the resources of their territory. The point regarding ethnic i.e. cultural autonomy has come into relief devising effective tactics and strategies to overcome the designs and advantages of outgroup. In the context of intergroup competitions, ethnic groups are divising 'a conviction of status and prerogatives' through ethnicity, and by following antagonistic devices to prove that they are not the people 'wretched on earth'. If solidarity is intensified in war, present day ethnic shocks in the North-East India are intensification of the age old custom.

Interplay of ethnic, centrifugal and centripetal forces leads to fission and fusion of groups and territories. It may be observed that reorganigation of territories on the basis of ethnicity is a global phenomenon. The crucible of North-East India will also go through many such processes to attain relative equilibrium in persuance of aspirations and organisation and balance of interethnic relationship. Changing mood of the people should be viewed in a new way. Tambiah has rightly cautioned by stating, "In the late 20th century a surprising number of militant and seemingly irrational" eruptions have occurred. "They challenge the confident post Enlightment prophecies that the decline of religion was inevitable or that at best it could only survive in a demytholized form; that primordial loyalties and sentiments would fade into a oblivion as national integration took effect, or be carried away as flotsam by the currents of wourld historical process. These violent and ubiquitous explosions also challenge and strain our conventional social science explanations of order, disorder and conflict". (1989: 346).

NOTES

1. More than ninety per cent of the government jobs are reserved for scheduled tribes in the hill states. The business in the hill towns, where Inner Line Regulation Act is not in force, are in the hands of tribesmen and non-tribesmen. There is latent dislike for this situation by the tribesmen. In Mizoram, where Inner Line Regulation Act is in force the situations is extremely bright for the tribesmen. Lalrimawia, a Mizo author writes, "Most of the rich business people and big contractors belong to Mizo community themselves." Even, in these states, if any consitutional facilities are Considered for non-tribal permanent settlers, these are stopped by initiating agitation.
2. The demand for the imposition of Inner Line Regulation Act in the areas where it is not in existence is a constitutional technique for maintaing ethnic homogeneity.
3. Those who are called scheduled tribes (a jurnal category) under the provision of the Constitution of India were first grouped under Tribal religion in 1891, as Animist in 1901, as Hill and Forest tribes in 1921, as Primitive tribes in 1931 and as Tribe in 1941. A few communities of India were enumerated in some of the censuses as Criminal tribes.

REFERENCES

Goswami, B.B. 1975, Outgoup from the point of view of Ingroup, *Man in India,* Vol. 55, No. 4. Ranchi. 1979 *Mizo Unrest – a study in Politicisation of Culture,* Aalekh Publishers, Jaipur, 1991 Ethnic Cognition in North-East India (*In*) *Ethnonationalism-Indian Experiences,* Chatterjee Publishers, Calcutta, (In Press)

Factor of Debilitation in North-East India *(In) Man and Life,* Bidisha.

Goswami, B.B., Somaro, G and Vigorelli L. Origins and History *(In) The Nagas,* Bergamo, and Italy.

Kakati, Satish C. 1989 Portents in Assam. *The Statesman,* April 11, 1989 Calcutta

Kamroopi, 1991, Enigma of ULFA, *Economic and Political Weekly* July, 27, Bombay

Lalvilmawia 1992, Inner Line (Mizoram) *(In)* Seminar Papers, Higher & Technical Education Deptt, Govt, of Mizoram, Aizawl.

Tanbiah, S.J. 1989, Ethnic Conflict in the World Today, American Anthropologist, Vol. 16, No.1, Washington

11

REORGANIZATION OF NORTH EAST INDIA
A Point of Economic Viability

R.P. BHATTACHARJEE

I

The North-Eastern region is strategically located and is characterised by political instability and economic backwardness. The region has been constantly threatened by escalation of tensions and conflicts, which are now assuming geo-political dimensions. These problems are due to, among others, alienation of land, raising resource requirements and so on. These are also indicative of incompatibility between the statist imperatives and planned transition.[1]

As we know that the planning process in our country started in 1951 after the attainment of independence (1947) and already we have completed seven Five -Year Plans and six Annual Plans and second year of Eighth Five Year Plan (1992-97) is in progress. Majority of the N.E. States are facing problem of resource mobilisation for their plans and its investment alongwith the country. "The country's debt service payments (principal and interest) will reach over 38 billion dollers in the five-year period 1992-96 as against an estimated gross disbursement of 22 billion dollers, the latest World Bank projections indicated. It will be a period of net aid outflows."[2] In this context, one may as well take a look at the financial position of the seven N.E. States *vis-a-vis* the economic viability of these States after the re-organisation specially in terms of central-aid and grants.

II

Ten of the twenty-five States of India are categorised as Special-Category States in respect of allocation of grants-in-aid for their respective plan-allocation. These Special Category States get about 90 per cent of their plan allocations as grants-in-aid and meet the remaining 10 per cent from their own resources or by raising loans and advances from Central Government or financial institutions. Many scholars have recently pointed out that these States are nothing but a liability on the Central Government.

The pattern of the revenue receipts[3] of the North-Eastern States during 1990-91 (Budget Estimate), is given in Table 11.1. It may be seen from this table that central grants and contribution of all the N.E. States are between 59 % to 68% except Assam (38.97 %). Similarly, the tax revenue and non-tax revenue of all the States except Assam are less than 8% while the share in central taxes is between 23-30% including Assam. It shows that the main sources of revenues of all the N.E. States are mainly central grants and contributions and share in central taxes. If the revenue receipts of preceding years of these N.E. States are analysed one with find more or less the same pattern. This explains that the States own resources are very much limited. The per capita revenue receipt[4] of N.E. States during 1990-91 (B.E.) are shown in Table-11.2.

TABLE 11.I : Revenue Receipts of N.E. States During 1990-91 (B.E)

(Rs. in crores)

Sl. No.	States	Tax Revinue	Non-tax Revene	Share in Central tax	Central Grants & Contributions	Total Revenue
1	2	3	4	5	6	7
1.	Arunachal Pradesh	2.50	28.34	81.85	240.67	353.36
2.	Assam	377.78	150.03	430.39	611.74	1569.94
3.	Manipur	16.58	26.03	112.02	242.24	396.87
4.	Meghalaya	27.93	16.32	88.37	239.69	372.31
5.	Mizoram	5.35	15.83	82.27	203.69	307.14
6.	Nagaland	16.47	24.08	121.88	238.15	400.58
7.	Tripura	20.16	18.61	150.94	317.68	507.84
8.	All India State	29026.90	9006.08	14199.36	12226.69	64459.03

TABLE 11.1 *(contd.)*

No.		Percentage of Total Revenue				
		Tax Revenue	Non-Tax Revenue	Share in Central Taxes	Central Grant &Contributions	Total Revenue
1	2	8	9	10	11	12
1.	Arunachal Pradesh	0.71	8.02	23.16	68.11	100
2.	Assam	24.06	9.56	27.41	38.97	100
3.	Manipur	4.18	6.56	28.22	61.04	100
4.	Meghalaya	7.50	4.38	23.74	64.38	100
5.	Mizoram	1.74	5.15	26.79	66.32	100
6.	Nagaland	4.11	6.01	30.43	59.45	100
7.	Tripura	4.06	3.66	29.72	62.56	100
8.	All India (States)	45.03	13.97	22.03	18.97	100

TABLE-11.2: Per Capita Revenue Receipts of N.E. States During 1990-91 (B.E.)

Sl No.	State	Population ('00)	Tax Revenue	Non-tax Revnue	share in Central Taxes	Central Grants & Cont-ribution.	Total Revenue
1	2	3	4	5	6	7	8
1.	Arunachal Pradesh	8185	30.54	346.24	1000	2940.38	4317.16
2.	Assam	247804	152.45	60.54	173.68	246.87	633.54
3.	Manipur	17833	92.97	145.97	628.16	1358.38	2225.48
4.	Meghalaya	17157	162.79	95.12	515.07	1397.04	2170.02
5.	Mizoram	7016	76.25	225.63	1172.61	2903.22	4377.71
6.	Nagaland	11205	146.99	214.90	1087.73	2125.39	3575.01
7.	Tripura	25590	80.54	72.72	589.84	1241.42	1984.52
8.	All States (India)	8197967	354.07	109.86	173.21	149.14	786.28

Note: Source of population, C.S.O.,GOI, New Delhi (as on Ist Oct. '90)

During 1990-91, the per capita Central Grants & Contribution was highest in Arunachal Pradesh (Rs. 2,940.38) and lowest in Assam. (Rs. 246.87) in the N.E. State compared to Rs 149.14 for all-states per head Central-aid As Table-2 shows all the N.E. States except Assam are perhaps liabilities of the Central Government in respect of financial position. Now, imagine if the Central Government discontinues the special grants to these N.E. States, perhaps the administrative machinery would collapse. Therefore, unless and until the N.E.S tates mobilise their own resources sufficiently, it would not be possible to maintain economic stability of the respective States. It will therefore be difficult to justify the economic viability of the reorganisation of the N.E. States from the above simple example. It is perhaps true to some extent that the economic stability is the cousin of political stability and it is seen that political stability of the small States are very much vulnerable due to more scope of defection etc. Therefore, except political and social consideration, it is difficult to justify the reorganisation of the N.E. Staes especially in regard to economic viability of the States. In this respect, it is imperative that the backward N.E. States pay increased attention to economic development and related matters.

III

There are some who view the process of economic development in the Third World countries purely in terms of an increase in per capita income. Even the highly controversial World Bank, as evidenced in the various speeches of Robert Mcnamara, its former President, has adopted a broader definition. The overall consensus now seems to be for a definition of economic development of the type proposed by Prof. Amulya Reddy. To quote from a report he prepared for the United Nation Enviornment Programme (UNEP):[5]

"According to this restatement, development must be directed primarily towards:

(a) the satisfaction of basic needs (material and Non-material), starting with the needs of the neediest, in order to achieve a reduction of inequalities between and within countries; (b) endogenous self-reliance in order to promote social participation and control; and (c) ecological soundness in order to attain harmony with the environment and make development sustainable over the long term.

"This view of development is focused on human beings, rather than only on goods and services. It is principally concerned with the quality of life, and not merely with the quality of goods and services. It is deliberately directed towards the neediest instead of hoping that the benefits of growth will automatically and spontaneously trickle down to the underprivileged. Not merely growth (and the magnitude of GNP) but also the structure and benefits of growth (and the composition and distribution of the GNP) are of central importance."

Similarly, in the case of a State, it is not merely the growth of State Domestic Product (SDP) but the distribution of SDP among all walks of life. The growth of macro-economy does not clearly explain the development of the economy but the growth of micro-level economy, shows the actual development of the economy at the State. The growth of SDP only shows the trend of the economy but does not explains the existing inequalities among its inhabitants. But there is lack of sufficient study at the micro-level, even the rural-urban distribution of the economy is not available for the North Eastern States. In the absence of this, the percentage contribution of the SDP in the total revenue receipts of the State as shown in Table 11.3 needs to be examined.

The revenue receipts as percentage of respective Net State Domestic Product in N.E. States are shown in the above stated table.

The percentage of Central-grants and contribution of NSDP of the N.E States are higher than the all-India average but these are note-worthy for all the States except Assam. This shows in macro-perspective how the N.E. States economy *vis-a-vis* the NSDP demands on central-grants and contribution.

TABLE-11.3 : Revenue Receipts as Percentage of Respective Net State Domestic Product in Different States.

Sl. No.	State	Revenue Receipt during 1990-91 as % of SDP during 1989-90					
		NSDP (Rs. in) Crores (1989-90) (Q)	Tax Revenue	Non-Tax Revenue	Share in Central Taxes	Cental Grants &Cont-ribution	Total
1	2	3	4	5	6	7	8
1.	Arunachal Pradesh	342	0.73	8.29	23.93	70.37	103.32
2.	Assam	7699	4.91	1.95	5.59	7.94	20.39
3.	Manipur	618	2.68	4.21	18.13	39.20	64.22
4.	Meghalaya	551	5.07	2.96	16.04	43.50	67.57
5.	Mizoram	258	2.07	6.14	31.89	78.95	119.05
6.	Nagaland	361	4.56	6.67	33.76	65.97	110.96
7.	Tripura	716	2.88	2.60	21.08	44.37	70.93
8.	All India (P)	349613	8.30	2.58	4.06	3.50	18.44

(P) = Provisional, Q = Quick-estimate.
Note: (I) NSDP of Nagaland relates to 1988-89 (Q) & NSDP of Mizoram relates to the year 1987-88.

The correlation -co-efficient ('r) of NSDP,1989-90 (col-3, Table-11.3) and the Central-grants and contributions (col.6 Table-1) of all the seven N.E. States together is 0.88 which shows the NSDP and Central grants and contributions are highly related and 'R' (the Co-efficient of determination) of these two variables is 0.77 which explains that the variation in NSDP for that particular period depends on the variations of Central grants and contributions by about 77 per cent. It means that the macro-economy of N.E. States mainly depends on Central-grants and contribution and not on their own resources.

Therefore, it may be stated that the growth of NSDP in the N.E. States based on their own resources is hardly about 23 per cent of whatever recorded. So to sustain development of the N.E. States need Central-grants and contributions.

REFERENCES

1. R. Gopalakrishnan, (1990): "Ideology, *Autonomy and Integration in the North-East India,"* Guwahati, (p. 6).
2. *The Shillong Times,* December 29, 1992 (p. 4).
3. Economic & Statistical Organisation, Planning Deptt., Haryana, Chandigarh: *An Analysis of State Revenue,* 1990-91", (pp. 8-9).
4. *ibid* (p,10).
5. Vinod Vyasulu, 1987 : *Development of Backward Areas,* Yatan Publicaitons, New Delhi, (p. 1).
6.
   (i) *An Analysis..... ibid,* (pp. 8,9,11).
   (ii) CSO, Deptt. of Statistics, GOI, New Delhi, *Estimates of States Domestic Product and Gross Fixed Capital Formation,* 1991, (p. 3).

12

REORGANIZATION OF ASSAM AFTER INDEPENDENCE

NITENDRA NATH DAS

People are endowed with remarkable natural gift-consciousness, the ability to feel and think. The consciousness of people differs depending on its exponent as well as the level and depth of its reflection of reality. The history of deorganisation of the state of Assam is more or less the reflection of those realities *viz.* reality of facts and circumstances. Assam was a poliglot state consisting of diverse ethnic groups and culture. It was assimilation of multilingual, multi-caste, and tribals and multi-religious in character, based on historical identity. The separation and formation of independent political units was inevitable under the circumstances. In a federal secular democratic republic, it is not proper to resist the recognition of the legitimate aspiration of each unit of the states. If one believes in unity and realises that unity could be made stronger and firmer. Then people living in each unit must feel that they are an integeral part of India. Therefore, it must be admitted that local language, culture and identity must be preserved and allowed to prosper in order to retain the unique cultural mosaic.

Deorganisation of Assam

Just after independence of India, the first step towards the reduction of Assam was Eastern Duars consisting of 32 sq. miles of territory in the Devangiri Hills. It was annexed in 1866, by the British rulers after the conclusion of Bhutan war, and in 1874 transfered to the Chief Commissioner of Assam who transfered it to Bhutan Government on their demand. This was followed by the people of Hill District demanding separate Hill State. The people of Cachar district also raised their voice for a Purbanchal State comprising the Hill Districts, Cachar, Manipur, Tripura and Goalpara. While Cachar wanted separation on linguistic issue, those of the Hill districts talked about culture, custom, social systems language etc. in favour of their demand. The Nagas sought independence from Assam as well as India. They alleged that the Asamese dominated Government was not looking to the interest of these minority groups. The move to declare Assamese as the state language has once again brought the demand for a separate Hill State or a Purbanchal State to the forefront. Then there was the demand for formation of Kamtapur State comprising of Goalpara, Garo Hills, Cooch Behar, Darjeeling and Jalpaiguri. The Government of Assam was in favour of merger if possible of Cooch-Behar, Manipur and Tripura alongwith NEFA, though it was constitutionally a part of Assam. According the State Reorganisation Commission was appointed with Sir Saiyad Fazal Ali, Hriday Nath Kunzru and K.M. Panikkar as members. With the setting up of the Commission, the perspective altogether changed. The S.R.C. did not accept any of these demands and thought of an integrated North East India in the form of an enlarged Assam. It suggested the merger of Tripura with Assam on the ground that it would be desirable to bring the entire region between Pakistan and India under one administration - the Government of Assam. But the Commission did not suggest the Assam. But the Commission did not suggest the merger of NEFA and Manipur on the ground that NEFA being the frontier area required special attention and manipur had an individual characteristic of its own.

The Government of India accepted the recommendation of the Commission and the Constitution (Seventh Amendment) Act, 1956 came into being. The scheme of state reorganisation involved change of boundaries of different states except Assam. The scheme also abolished the previous classification of states into those of Part A, Part B and Pact C. The states of Part A and Part B were places on an equal footing while the states of part C were now designated as Union Territories.

The recommendations made by S.R.C. were not all acceptable to the people of hill districts. While Nagas continued their demand for independence from Assam and India, other Hill people continued their pressure for separation from Assam. Ultimately, Nagaland Bill received the President's assent on 4 September 1962, and thus Nagaland became the sixteenth State of India.

Other Hill Districts of Assam have been agitating for separate Hill States, the formation of Nagaland further strengthened their demand. The Mizo continued to press their demand forcefully on the lines of Nagas. Their demand was based on the ground that the political and socio-economic policy followed by the erstwhile Assam Government was not acceptable to them. They also complained that they did not get full scope to develop their language and culture and were forced to live in penury. On the implementation of Assamese Language Act, 1960, the people of Hill Districts vehemently opposed making Assamese the State Language. However the Language Act was not the only cause for demanding separate Hill State. The Hill leaders made it clear, that their agitation for separate Hill State would continue even if the Language Act was withdrawn. The demand for independent states of Nagas or Mizos are not of recent origin. They had the tendency of secession even before independence *i.e.* during the transitional period of transfer of power in India. This is evident from the invitation extended by Naga National Council leader, Sakhrie in 1946 and Phizo in 1947 urging the Mizos to join hands with Naga and fight for political independence. But Mizo union was not impressed and politely rejected the offer.

However, instead of demanding independent Mizo State, they demanded in 1971 a referendum over the question of statehood for the Mizo. In order to satisfy their demand the Central Government through Constitution (Twenty-seventh Amendment) Act, 1971 made the Mizo Hills a Union Territory there by seceding from Assam.

Apart from the Nagas and the Mizos, the tribal people living in the area of Garo, Khasi-Jayntia, Mikir and North Cachar formed the All Party Hill leader conference (APHLC) and demanded separate hill states, The Khasi expressed their concern over the danger posed to their tribal heritage, culture and traditional way of life by foreigners specially from Bangladesh and Nepal and also 'Dakhar' from other states of India. The Government of India agreed to recognise Assam on federal basis and a limited number of essential subjects of common interest were to be assigned to the regional federation and functioning of the rest of the subjects was to be left to the federating units. The APHLC agreed to accept this proposal and set 18th January 1967 as the last date for its implementation. As the federation did not come into being they continued their agitation and on 9 September 1968 a complete hartal was observed at Shillong. As a result the Union Government passed the Assam Reorganisation (Meghalaya) Act, 1969, by setting up the State of Meghalaya as autonomous hill state within the state of Assam. This was a new experiment to meet the regional aspirations within a state.

This being an autonomous state within Assam the people of Meghalaya were not satisfied and on 30 September 1970, the Meghalaya Assembly unanimously resolved to request the Union Government to convert the autonomous state into a full-fladged state. This demand was ultimately considered by the Union Government in January 1972 and accordingly Meghalaya became another full-fledged state.

The deorganisation of Assam, however, did not ended there. Bengali people of Cachar Hill of Assam demanded separate state of their own because their interest was not safe in the hands of Assam Government. But their demands were turned down by the Union Government. There may be further deorganisation of Assam, which is not at all absurd as the Bodos and other tribes are still agitating for a separate Bodo Land.

Causes of Separation

Assam has undergone changes so fast after independence that it is difficult to ascertain the specific causes as to why such dynamic change had taken place. Different sections of people assign different reasons. A section of people advocates a separate state due to dominating influence of the Assamese people over the rest. While advocates of Cachar wanted separation mainly on the linguistic issue, those of the hill district mention culture, custom, social system etc. alongwith language. There was a feeling among almost all ethnic groups that they did not get full scope to develop their language and culture and were prone to annihilation by other culture. Economic, political and all round development of tribal people seemed to be very bleak.

They demanded a separate statehood on the ground that in the erstwhile Assam they were denied proper place in the scheme of economic development and economic welfare. Plans were framed and executed with broad national perspective ignoring the factors of tribal integration and without proper consideration of their sociological, ethnic and historical background.

Further, they were aggrieved on the report of the State Reorganisation Commission. They expressed that the Sixth Schedule did not adequately safguard the interest of the hill people. The political elite tried to manipulate things by diverting public attention from their various lapses and failures to ameliorate the lot of the masses and give the much needed sense of belonging.

However, if the facts are examined in detail it would be found that the process that led to separation of Assam after independence has not been brought about by accident or single mistake. It is the result of series of acts and mistakes committed both by the Central and State administration. And when any untoward incident takes place they try to shift the responsibility on to one another.

One thing that sowed the seed of separation among the Hill Districts was the Sixth Schedule of the Constitution. By this Schedule the tribal people of India were discriminated against those of Assam by according separate status. India has a population of 298 lakh tribals out of which only about 8 lakh live in Assam hill districts. Whereas the tribal people of other states of India are governed by the Fifth Schedule, the tribals of Assam hill districts have been given autonomous administration under the Sixth Schedule.

The second mistake was the creation of new administration machinery *viz.* Tribal Area Department. The function of this department was primarily to look after the people of the Hill districts as well as the tribals of the plains. But in order to satisfy some. hill leaders, artificial division were created that led to administrative inconvenience. As a result the Government was treating the Hill tribals as a separate entity different from the plains people.

The concept of community development and democratic decentralisation under the Panchayati Raj failed to alleviate the socio-economic and political problems of the tribals. In tribal area panchayats are controlled by the tribal people and non-tribal live there peacefully, District Councils are quite different and they exercise their right in their own authority and not under the authority of the state government. Thus there arises the feeling among the tribal people that they are being separated from the plains people. Besides, it appears that the existence of Sixth Schedule and administrative reorganisation cause the development of separatist movement.

Lastely, the most important factors that give rise to the separatist movement are the personal and narrow selfish end of the politician for power.

Post Partition Achievement

After partition of Assam, seven-sister states came into being having their own characteristic geographical contiguity and historical traditions. There lie the dissimilarities of socio-economic lives of the people. It may even be found that in one state itself there are two or more distinct parts having different culture and language or dialect. Hence these are some real obstacles to development of these states for even after attainment of statehood these places have not been able to make any significant agricultural, economic and industrial progress.

Agriculture is the mainstay of the people of these seven states. about 80 per cent of the people depend on agriculture. But major portion of these are, being hilly adequate land is available for agriculture. In most of the hill areas the age-old farming system known as shifting cultivation still predominate. The increased in population also poses serious problem of shifting cultivation. The farmers have less incentive to use inputs like improved machinery, seeds, fertilizers pesticide, etc. The net cultivated area in North-East Region is only 15.6 per cent against the corresponding all India average of 46 per cent. Within the seven states itself the percentage of cultivated area varies from state to state. In Assam, it is 34.1 per cent, in Tripura 23.5 per cent, in Meghalaya it is 7.9 per cent, in Nagaland it is 11.0 per cent, Manipur 8.3 per cent and Mizoram 3.7 per cent.

The economic condition of an average person in these states is distressingly low. Though North East India has one of the highest per capita ability of national resources, it is one of the economically most backward regions of the country. There is a large disparity between the rich and the poor. In the hill state, there are some affluent people who earned money either through contract or by supply of goods. Entire business in this region is under the control of Marwari and other communities. The pace of industrialisation is also very slow in the region. The standard of consumption is poor as the large section of population of these states are underpriviledged. Price levels in these states are much higher than all India average. The chief beneficiaries of these states are a few urban elites and politicians thus keeping the vast majority of population distressingly backward.

Whether the People of Assam Wanted Separation?

The people of Assam was not in favour of separation. It was the Union Government who by ignoring these people and flouting their opinion, *i.e.* without following the procedure laid down in article 3 of the Constitution of India, brought into existance these separate state though they were not economically viable. Since independence the rulers of India have all the time found it difficult to deal with many situations in the country and had a constant fear of Assam seceding from India territorially as well as functionally. This fear was deep-rooted in the minds of the rulers because of its geographical situation. As such the divide and rule policy was adopted to control this region.

Since independence, the pace of development of Assam itself has been very slow. Even the rate of progress of the hill people in all respects was much faster than that of the plains people. This is evident from the Pataskar Commission Report according to which during 1951 to 1961, the percentage of literacy in the Hills area rose from 16.29 to 20.36 against 18.49 and 27.23 in the plains. The number of hospitals during 1951 to 1964, increased from 4.21 to 11.51 per lakh of population. The corresponding figures in the plains are 4.69 and 5.93. The per capita income in 1950-51 was 196 and in 1962-63 was 299. The per capita contribution to the State revenue from the hills in 1951-52 was only 2.56 per cent and in 1964-65 it was 4.14 per cent against 12.12 and 32 per cent in plains. Thus it appears that since independence the hills have been developing at a much faster rate than the plains while contributing much less to the state revenue.

The Official Language Act was also misunderstood by the people. The Assam Official Language Act is clear on the point that regional language to be used in hills has been left to be decided by the respective District Councils.

Towards Integration

The people living in the hill areas have developed their own social, economic and political system having less similarity with plains people. During the pre-colonial period, through trade contact development between plain people and hill people, political and economic relations had increased.

They intercepted the earlier political and economic contact through Inner Line Regulation, the Excluded and Partially Excluded Areas. As a result, social, economic and political interaction stopped which still continues to prevail. Though after independence the Government of India made an attempt to revive the lost contact between the hills and plains people yet they were left isolated with very little interaction by the same Inner Line Regulation. Because of this long dissociation with each other, it took time for the people of the region to come forward to like each other. Each of them felt that they were different from one another. But all of them know that economically they are to depend on each other. Though they may demand political separation, the need for economic unification is essential. As such unlike other parts of the country, the North Eastern Region is yet to be emotionally integrated with the national fabrics and the varied ethnic groups are to be psychologically prepared to share the concept of planning and development like the rest of India.

The North-Eastern Council (NEC) which was inaugurated in 1971 provided the necessary organisational set up for coordinated development of the region. The Council initiated steps towards a new era of integration. The Council has frequently discussed matters in which the constituent units had common interest and advised the Union and the State governments to take action in such matters, particularly relating to economic and social planning. The Council also occasionally reviewed various measures taken by the constituents for maintenance of security and public order and recommended measures whenever necessary. Thus NEC has made an attempt to turn the region into a single economic unit for proper economic development.

North-East India Council for Social Science Research is another social organisation established in 1974, at Shillong making an attempt to interact between the people of North East India through organising different seminars/ workshop since its inception.

Conclusion

Every person of North-East India is under heavy pressure of adjusting himself between two coroillaries *viz.* political separation and economic unification. One is the demand from various quarters for economic unification. Thus the people are placed in a dilemma to choose the best solution and to reach the correct answer. They are placed in such a situation that they can neither go here not there. Further the present developments cannot guarantee any political stability. As a result of political unrest, the youth of these states have unwittingly stepped into the movement whether secessionist or insurgent.

While referring to the political or economic unification one must take into consideration the common sentiment of the people of each of these tiny states. Their language, territory, culture, way of life, belief, tradition, psychology shaped by the geographical environments prevailing in tribes, must all be preserved and allowed to flourish along with the political and economic development. There is no sovereign remedy to eliminate such ethnicity and difference in order to have a uniform pattern of thinking and behaviour. Nation will have to exist with these differences so that they do not lead to disintegration. National integration is thus an experiment in peaceful co-existence.

REFERENCES

1. ALAP 1951, the Legislative Assembly transferred to the Bhutan Government 32 sq. miles of territory in the Devengri Hills quoted in *A Century of Government and Politics in North-East India* by Rao, V.V. and Niru Hazarika, Vol. I, p- 29.
2. M.P. Tain, *India Constitutional Law,* 3rd edn. (p. 720).
3. D.C. Gupta, *India Government and Politics* 6th edn. p. 586.
4. K.C. Baruah, *Critical Days of Assam,* p. 23.

13

REORGANIZATION OF NORTH-EAST INDIA

P.C. BISWAS

Introduction

The North-Eastern Region of India presents a unique picture of its own without any semblance or similarity to any other part of the country, whether in respect of geographical position (bordering with foreign countries in the north, south and east), composition of heterogeneous population, stages of economic, social and political development etc. This region could not be brought under control by the East India Company or by the Raj in the later period, at a sweep. Manipur and Tripura remained separate from direct British administration as they were Princely States.

So, the different parts of the North-East Region remaind under different stages of administrative control, without the prospect of any common binding thread so as to bring them within a unified political entity. However, the Assamese-speaking people, who were comparatively more developed and comprised the major population in the Brahmaputra Valley, occupied the centre stage in the whole region. But for a long time, the Bengalee-speaking population who were in majority in the District of Sylhet and Cachar, and formed a good chunk of the population in the districts of Goalpara, Nowgong and parts of Kamrup and Darrang had exercised a dominating influence over the Assamese people till as late as 1930, which gave ground to the emergence of the Assamese national consciousness and the gradual rise of the theory of assimilation and the eventual formation of a greater Assam, including the tribal areas, which were actually undergoing the process of gradual assimilation with the Assamese people in the upper and central parts of Assam. But this process was halted when education spread amongst the tribal people, rousing in them, the sense of separate tribal identity. The passing of the Assam State Language Act in 1960, with a view to developing a composite Assam, further drove away the tribal and other non-Assamese linguistic groups in the opposite direction. Thus the process of gradual natural assimilation was halted and instead of facilitating integration. It unleashed the forces of disintegration. The resultant picture of the changed and changing administrative maps of the region, on the assumed basis of nationality or ethnic identity, offers a challenging task for serious study.

Background

The British rulers, in pursuit of their imperialist policy, kept the different linguistic and tribal people, distributed in different districts (Nagas were scattered in Nagaland, Manipur and Burma; Mizos in Lushai Hills, Tripura, Cachar etc.) keeping them in constant feuds, to serve their administrative convenience. The tribal peoples in general were kept segregated from the mainstream of national life and the more advanced Assamese and Bengalee people also did pretty little to fraternize with the 'backward' tribal people and looked down on them. The tribal areas were kept completely untouched by the national movement and these were left in the 'safe custody' of the foreign benefactors.

In Assam Valley itself, the Congress organisation was formed as late as 1921, and its activities were confined to Assam Valley, while Sylhet and Cachar districts (administratively in Assam) remained under the Bengal Provincial Congress Committee, on the basis of linguistic political entity. The British, when faced with the compulsion of transferring power, conspired to keep the tribal areas (as the princely states) under their sphere of influence through devious plans like the formation of a Crown Colony or a Christian-dominated state (as most of the tribal districts had a dominant Christian population) which could provide a foothold to exercise constant pressure on independent India in this most sensitive frontier region. Coupland Plan was designed with this end in view.

In the later period the American also came into the field and in the garb of scientists, tourists and bird watchers etc. were very active in penetrating the tribal areas and formenting separatist tendencies.

As regards the Muslim living in Assam, some of them opted for Assamese as their mother tongue in 1950 census as a trick to avoid eviction from their lands. But in the pre-independence period, the Muslim League demanded the inclusion of the whole of Assam in Pakistan. There was a strong movement in Assam to keep the territory in tact, while allowing Sylhet district to be tagged to Pakistan through a referendum. The idea was, with Sylhet district separated, the integration of Assam might be facilitated. The rising tribal consciousness about their separate identity, was not taken into account. Following the separation of Sylhet, many Bengalees (Hindu refugees and also Muslim) entered Assam, complicating the demographic picture all the more. This eventually led to a strong movement for driving out the foreigners and 'outsiders'. As a result, conflicts between the Assamese and non-Assamese (Bengalee people and also the tribals and non-tribals engulfed the whole region. Thus the aim of developing a uniform linguistic state, with Assamese as the State language got a setback and the demands for separate states or autonomous states within Assam were raised, which presented a very difficult problem to be solved to the satisfaction of all concerned.

The Concept of Linguistic State Formation

There can be no dispute about the salutory principle of State formation on the basis of language. The National

Congress was committed to the formation of linguistic states after independence and its organisational framework was designed on that basis. Following this principle, Sylhet, which was tagged by the British to the Assam State, for administrative purpose, was kept under the Bengali Provincial Congress Committee. This principle was followed in cases of other provinces of the country. Though the Bengalees considered Goalpara district as the Bengalee dominated area (which was supported by the zamindars of Goalpara, the Assamese opposed it and they claimed Cooch Behar (Kamtapur) to be included in Assam. The Rajbanshis and the Kochs who comprised the major population of Goalpara, as also the Plain Tribals to some extent (who had their own distinct features) were generally called Goalparians, as apart from the Assamese and Bengalees.

It was in that light that a movement was unleashed in Goalpara district, demanding district autonomy for the district of Goalpara and even the district committees of Goalpara, Dhubri and Kokrajhar supported this movements, as there was a strong feeling amongst the people that they were being neglected by the Assamese dominated State Government. But when the Bengal Congress leaders claimed inlusion of Goalpara in Bengal, during the hearing of the Commission for the Reorganisation of the State, instead of being carried forward further it was transformed into a movement for remaining in Assam. There was no movement as such, in the Hill district for separate states at that time but there was enough indications amongst the educated tribal youths of the rising sense of separate tribal identity and aspirations for some sort of autonomy within the Assam state. But neither the State Government nor the Central government paid any heed to the undercurrent of the feeling of dissatisfaction of the tribal peoples.

So after independence in 1947 the North-East Region remained mostly as it was during the British Raj except that the district of Sylhet (leaving a part of Karimganj subdivision) was cut off from India. The North-Eastern Frontier Agency was formed into a Union Territory under the Ministry of Foreign Affairs. It was enigmatic that a part of India was virtually treated as a foreign country. Perhaps the underlying idea was, just like the British rulers, that this region inhabited by the different primitive tribes, could not be administered as any other part of the country, because of its special position. The growth of anti-India feelings amongst sections of the Hill tribal peoples in the later period, could not be prevented by such tricky measures. The fact remained that the Assamese dominated ruling class was not favourably inclined to properly appreciate the rising consciouness among the Hills and the Plain tribal people about their respective languages, ethnic character, their customary right and the growing trend to move forward from a primitive tribal stage towards a sub-national status and the Government followed a 'carrot and stick' policy *i.e.* doing out some benefits and ad hoc grants and pursuing a strong-arm administrative policy, to supress their growing national aspirations and demand for autonomy. The Nagas and the Mizo hill tribes claimed to have all the respective Naga and Mizo inhabited areas which were distributed in different districts, to be incorporated into their respective districts. This seemed quite justified from the principles of linguistic state formation, but this was not countenance by the State and the Central Government. Nehru himself, supposed to be a tribal lover even refused to meet a delegation of the Naga National Council when it went to Delhi in 1950 to meet him with a memorandum. Consequently, the movement took a violent turn under the leadership of A. Z. Phizo. Peace Mission of Dr. Aram and Jaiprakash Nargain proved futile and ultimately Nagaland has to be made a separate state under the Act of 1962. This fact exposes the lack of farsight amongst the national and state leaders in dealing with the tribal people.

In 1951 United Mikir and North Cachar Hills district was formed with one subdivision of Cachar and some parts of K & J Hills, Nowgong and Sibsagar, without looking into the linguistic homogeneity of the respective people concerned and as a consequence, even now claims and counter-claims are continuing and the Mikirs are now demanding greater autonomy.

Outcome of the State Reorganisation Commission

The State Reorganisation Commission which was found in 1955 ruled out reorganisation of Assam on linguistic or ethnic basis, neither it held Assam to be a unilingual state on the ground that the Assamese speaking people did not comprise more than 70% of the population. According to it, if there was 30% linguistic minority people in a state, it should be considered bi-lingual, In 1931 Census, the Assamese-speaking people were 1,61,000 and Bengalee speaking people were 4,76,000. There was no Census in 1941. In 1951, the number of the Assamese went up to 6,87,000 and Bengalee came down to 1,93,000 (because of the separation of Sylhet and many Bengalee immigrant Muslims entering Assamese as their mother tongue). This trend continued in the subsequent censuses, yet the Assamese population did not form 70% and Assam could not be considered a unlingual state. However, this position could not be entertained as a fact of life by the Assamese people, spedially by the middle class youths and they thought that the presence of sizable number of non-Assamese people and the influx of the 'outsiders', stood as a stumbling block on the way of forming a unified and composite Assam on the basis of Assamese language and the question of assimilation came on the agenda as the only solution. But this was found, by experience, to be counterproductive. Besides, the Bengalee, the tribal people (who claimed to be the original sons of the soil) began to move in the reverse way and the movement for separate Hills State and 'Udayachal' and later on 'Bodo State' began to gather monentum.

Impact of the Passing of the Assam Language Act, 1960

The Assam Language Act was passed with the ostensible purpose of ensuring a composite and integrated Assam and Assamese was made the State Language with provision for getting it accepted as such in the Bengalee-speaking district of Cachar. The Hills districts were allowed to use English for their official purpose. The result was quite the reverse. Resentment in the district of Cachar was uncontrolable and then Home Minister, Lal Bahadur Shastri had to intervene to work out a compromise, but the Hills tribal people came out with stronger voice for the formation of a separate Hill State under the leadership of All Parties Hills Leader Council (APHLC) and they were not to be silenced by the statement of the Education Minister (Deva Kanta Barua) that there was no intention of imposing Assamese in the Hill districts. Though there were socio-economic factors behind the demand for a separate Hill State, Language and culture were the more dominant factors and the language Act acted as the accelerating force. Ultimately Nehru came out with the proposal of 'the scottish Pattern of Autonomy' but it was not acceptable to the APHLC leaders.

Then the proposal for an autonomous state within Assam was mooted and the Congress Committee, which was a constituent of the APHLC readily accepted it and came out of the APHLC. The APHLC agreed to give it a fair trial, but minority section did not agree to it and came out of the APHLC and formed a separate party HSPDP. It wanted to carry on its struggle till the achievement of a full-fledged state. Within one year of its functioning, the APHLC also became dissatisfied with the limited autonomy given under the provisions of the Assam Reorganisation (Meghalaya) Act, 1969 and it again started the movement for a full state in a non-voilent way and the Central government with the support of all the political parties conceded the demand for a full-fledged state and passed the North-East Areas (Reorganisation) Act in 1971, which covered other Hill districts also. While the APHLC wanted a Hill state compriseing K & J Hills, Garo Hills, Mizo Hills, Mikir Hills and North Cachar Hills, it was found to be incompatible for lack of geographical contiguity and linguistic and ethnic variations and neither the APHLC nor the leaders of the Mizo Hills, Mikir Hills or North Cachar Hills insisted on their original claim. By the Act, a full-fledged state (Meghalaya, an anachronism in view of the creation of a Hill State) was formed with K & J Hills, Jaintia Hills and the Garo Hills. The Principle of linguistic state formation was not followed by this, as the languages of the Khasis and the Garos and their culture were quiet different from each other and did not provide for any common ground for composition of one state. Apart from being tribals, as opposed to the non-tribals, there was no stable binding force between the Garos and the khasis. By the above Act the Union Territory of Manipur was made into a full-fledged state. Tripura, Mizoram and Arunachal were made into Union Territories.

All these reorganisations proved that the founding fathers of our Constitution could not in their wisdom. visualise that the provisions of the District Council as provided in the Sixth Schedule could not contain the emerging aspirations of the Hill tribal people. It is to be remembered that even the limited provisions of the Sixth Schedule were opposed by some of the Assam leaders and it was only due to the effort of Gopınath Bordoloi that the said provisions could be incorporated in the Constitution. But the framers of the Constitution did never contemplate the continuance of the Sixth Schedule for the Hills districts, when these could be eventually formed into a separate state (as one witnesses now in the state of Meghalaya). It is also enigmatic that the framers of the Constitution did not provide the limited provisions of the Fifth Schedule (no question providing the Sixth Schedule) to the Plains tribal areas of Assam as was provided to the Plains tribals of other states and now the question of the formation of separate state itself is being raised by the Plains tribal people. After the formation of separate states for the Nagas and Mizos, cry is being heard in some hill areas for going out of India, which is being aided and abetted by some foreign powers. So the very concept of integrating different linguistic and ethnic groups living in the North-Eastern region is being challenged by different types of disintegrating forces, which have to be faced with sober political acumen.

As far as the demand for the formation of Bodoland (with much more dimension than Udayachal) there is no way out but to concede some autonomy to the Plains tribals and the state government seems to be ready to provide them some autonomous status within Assam. But the dispute has arisen on the area to be included in the autonomous Council. While the All Bodo Students Council (ABSU) demands 4,655 villages, the Chief Minister is not agreeable to it as some of these villages do not have 50% or more of the tribal population and 109 tea gardens where non-Bodos form the majority, also pose a problem. but these points of contention should not be allowed to stand in the way of finding out an agreeable solution.

As regards the demands of the Karbi Anglong and the North Cachar Hills people, for greater autonomy under Article 244, the State Government has come out with the proposal for larger powers to the District Council, but they are not satisfied with this. The demand for a separate state might be raised in near future, if genuine autonomy is not granted to them as early as possible.

It could be appreciated that this region has been reorganised so many times weakening the process of forming a composite Assam and achieving unity and integrity of the whole region, there was good reason that the majority people (*i.e.* the Assamese people) could feel frustrated and leading them to think that a composite state with Assamese as the base even with a smaller size is the only way out. The whole problem however has to be viewed with a wider national outlook, satisfying the aspirations of the tribal and other non-Assamese people living in the region from pre-independence days. Reorganisation of the region could not perhaps be prevented by a dealing with the tribal and other linguistic groups by pursuing a policy of suppression or by any sort of palliatives. We shall have to accept the reorganisations of this region which had started in 1875 as fact of life, born out of the failures of the national leaders to foresee the future position events, and try to check disintegration and fragmentations. Way should be found to work out some sort of a federal structure for the whole region on the basis of common interest to develop the backward region with mutual understanding and cooperation and recognition of the distinctive linguistic, culture and ethnic characteristics of the different units of the federal structure.

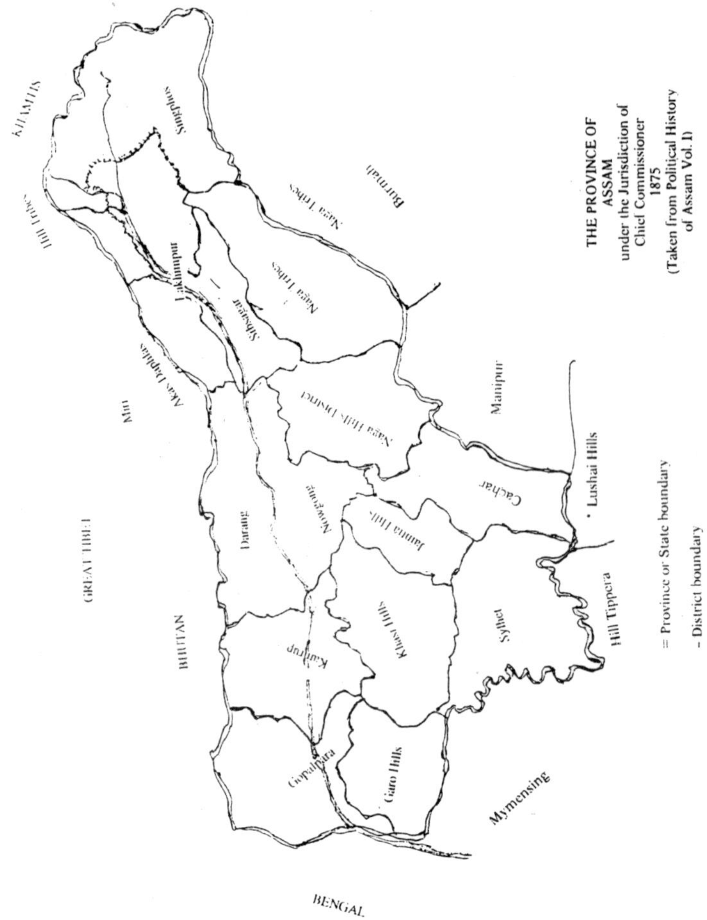

THE PROVINCE OF ASSAM
under the Jurisdiction of Chief Commissioner
1875
(Taken from Political History of Assam Vol. I)

THE PROVINCE
OF
EASTERN BENGAL
AND
ASSAM
1906
(Taken from Political
History of Assam. Vol I)
Burmah
Lakhimpur
Naga Hills
Sibsagar
Manipur
Darrang
Nowgong
Cachar
Lushai Hills
Khasi & Jaintia Hills
Sylhet
Chittagong Hill Tract
Hill Tippera
Kamrup
Goalpara
Garo Hills
Mymensing
Dacca
Tippera
Backr Gunge
Faridpur
Bhutan
Jalpaiguri
Rangpur
Bogra
Rajshahe
Dinajpur
Malda
Bengal
Mouth of Ganges

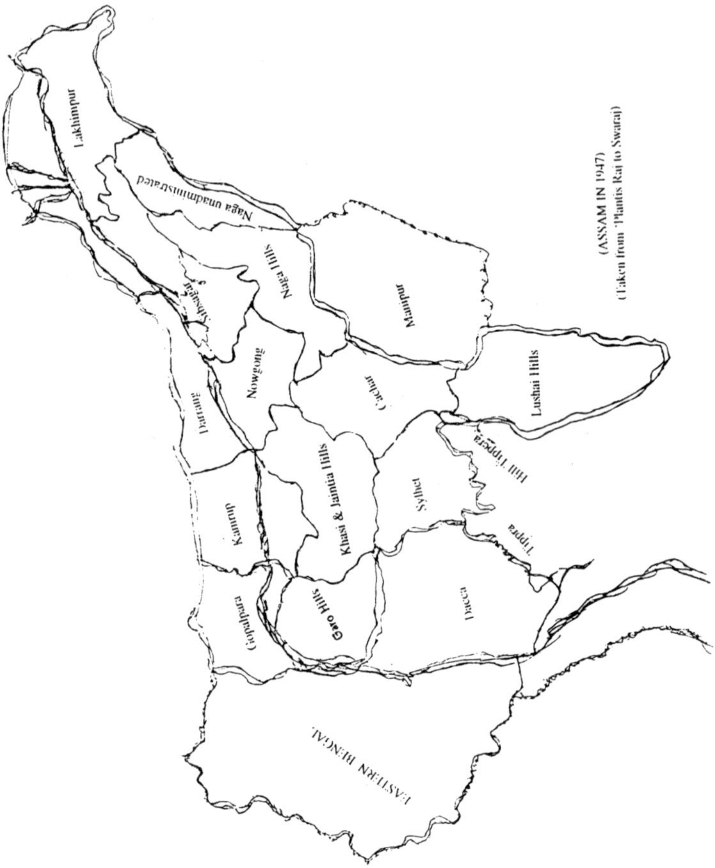

(ASSAM IN 1947)
(Taken from 'Plantis Rai to Swaraj')

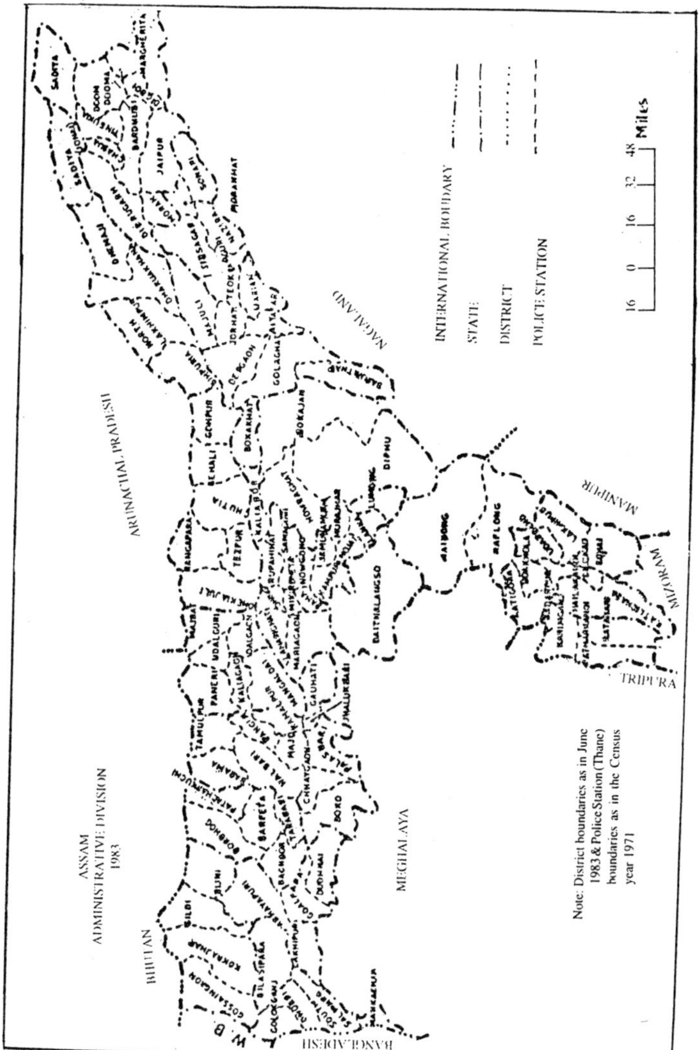
ASSAM
ADMINISTRATIVE DIVISION
1983
ARUNACHAL PRADESH
NAGALAND
MANIPUR
MIZORAM
TRIPURA
MEGHALAYA
BANGLADESH
BHUTAN
W. B.
INTERNATIONAL BOUNDARY
STATE
DISTRICT
POLICE STATION
16 0 16 32 48 Miles
Note: District boundaries as in June 1983 & Police Station (Thane) boundaries as in the Census year 1971

14

BALKANISATION OF THE NORTH EAST INDIA
A Tentative Hypothesis

BIMAN KAR

Wayback in the, twenties Congress Party resolved in favour of formation of provinces on the basis of language. It was an opportunistic step since linguistic sub-nationalism was already a strong force to reckon with in many parts of the country. After independence came States' reorganisation in the late fifties. North-East remained unaffected by these developments. Trouble started in Assam after the adoption of Official Language Bill. The famous and protracted Assam Movement, even though its declared objectives were correct, deepened the sense of alienation among a section of the tribals in the plains, as well as in the hills. On the other hand, the Bengali assumption of Bengali speaking Tipras as a subsect of Bengali people, considering the state a hinterland of Calcutta not only in commercial (until recently Tripura's purchase point was Calcutta and the State was described by air distance from Calcutta), but also in cultural sense, neglect of the tribals in traditional moorings, continuous population inflow from adjoining Bengal eventually led to tribal non-tribal rift there.

In the 'fifties and definitely not earlier the Khasis or Garos or the Mizos did not think of separation from Assam. Assam was considered a land of composite language and culture. The tendency of Assam people to make it a defactor unilingual state and growing rhetoric about other linguistic sects to immerse themselves in the Assamese linguistic cultural mosaic had its inevitable result. On the other hand, Bengali chauvanism hurt the sentiments of those among the middle class Bengali speaking Tripuris who capitalised on the growing misery of the Jumias and others engaged in subsistence and sub-subsistence level occupation which has resulted in this present situation. What defies commonsense is that Tripura did not learn from this experience of Assam in the, sixties and refused to implement even that part of land reform mearures which makes it incumbent on the State machinery not only to prevent any further alienation of tribal land, but also to reinstate the already alienated land.

Now administrative delimitations within India never followed logic of either physical geography or economics and instead of seeking its roots in the past (say glorious days of Asoka or Akbar) drew inspiration from Europe. Europe fought many bloody battles in search of ethno-linguistic homogeneity. This, as we all know, added to, instead of solving any problem. Language based spirit or nationalism, a by-product of the ashes of Roman Empire, may finally resolve itself in the emerging European community. Economic compulsions may bury a vain issue. May we not take a lesson? Reason of physical geography and economics would recommend an integrated North-East. This would have benefited the Assamese and Benagali people most. What baffles one is why should the swelling of number of linguistic stock precede the considerations of material advancement of the existing people.

The Balkanisation of the North-East is pathetic. Each one of the constituent State is non-viable. The biggest State, Assam, earning less that 70 % of its revenue expenses from its own sources rejoices being on the list of special category States who receive plan funds as 90:10 grant-loan ratio. The bargaining capacity of each State is too weak. Each State is financially incapable of having adequate supply of efficient and skilled manpower for development purposes. The formation of North Eastern Council has not solved any problem and the State view it only as an additional funding agency. Lack of inter-State understanding not only creates territorial disputes but also hinders formulation and implementation of projects requiring Inter-State cooperation and collaboration.

In the light of the above it may be valid to propose the central hypothesis to explain the post-Independent Reorganisation of North-East as follows myopia and vanity of the Assamese and Bengalee people instead of playing a positive role in bringing about an integration of north-east India had helped its Balkanisation.

The above were definitely not the only causes. Some of the other causative factors have also been indicated. But they are exiguous to the region and can not be framed as hypotheses. However, the wrong and half-hearted policies and steps taken by the Centre, lack of implementation of programmes, whatever might have been their suitability, lack of concern for the poor and deprived must be added to the vested personal interest of those who lead movements for fresh delimitation of various sorts. All these may be bunched into a set of hypotheses. But even then the central hypothesis would remain the one suggested above. Being the most advanced among all the ethnic stocks, the Assamese and Bengali people have historic mission to fulfil integrating the region for its transformation into a modern vibrant economy.

15

COSTS AND BENEFITS OF REORGANIZATION
The Case of North-East India Since Independence

ARCHANA SHARMA

The North-East India represents a region which is characterised by its spectacular scenic beauty, rich natural resources, peculiar topographical features and variegated populationn composition. In addition to the people from various religious and linguistic groups, the region is inhabited by a large number of tribes, in the hills and the plains alike. It has been estimated that 10 per cent of the total scheduled tribes population in the country resides in this region alone.[1]

With this heterogeneity in the population composition, it is but natural that conflicts and confusions between various sections of the population prevail. This happened to be true and as a result of all these, the region had to undergo reorganisation a number of times both before and after independence. Particularly the independence of the country created enthusiasm amongst all sections of the people for representative government by the local people for the administration of each socio-cultural region. The Constitution of India also provided for formulation of District Councils in the Hill Districts. But this did not satisfy the local aspirations. By 1972, the whole of North-East India was divided into five states *e.g.* Assam, Nagaland, Meghalaya, Manipur and Tripura and two Union Territories

(Mizoram and Arunachal Pradesh). In 1987, these two also attained the statehood.[2]

Now that two decades have elapsed since the complete division of the region, the costs and benefits of the reorganisation can well be evaluated

To do this, it is necessary to know, first of all, what were the main reasons for the creation of these states:

1. One apparent reason for this was the growing discontent among the tribes. "In the past, energy and enthusiasm, were concentrated in maintaining law and order in studying socio-economic conditions of the people in the tribal areas. Therefore, the attitude of the government towards the tribals was negative -- preserving and protecting the tribes. Little thought was bestowed in the possible means of progress of the tribal areas. There was no recognition of the fact that in a rapidly changing world, the tribes should not stand still. The result of the negative policy of the government resulted in keeping the tribes as a human museum. There was little regard for their future. They had no connection with the outside world. There might have been justification of this policy in the past but certainly not in the present century. The effect of this policy was to encourage the feeling for isolation and independence."[3]

2. Another reason was the conflict between the various parts of the region over the language issue.[4] It was believed that 'contentment lies in the satisfaction of the political aspirations of the people'.[5]

3. It was also argued that 'small states were able to make good progress than big states'.[6]

But soon after the creation of the five states and two Union Territories, the problem of co-ordination of the development programmes arose. To solve this problem the North Eastern Council was established.

Thus, the necessity for establishing the North Eastern Council was the outcome of the fact that although small states may be politically imperative, 'economically it is an accepted fact that small units would not be viable'.[7] It has been estimated that about 80 per cent of Rs. 1,800 crore invested during the last 20 years of NEC service had been confined to Power, Transport and Communication which had pumped back more than half of the investment in the form of capital investment and payment of service cost to experts and skilled personnel from outside the region'.[8] This gives a glimpse of the cost of reorganisation.

In order to measure the benefits of reorganisation in comparison to the increased cost off administration one can also look at the rate of development of the region over the period. But unfortunately, the region still figures among the least developed states in the country.[9] To cite a single example, according to the Health Information of India, 1986, none of the North-Eastern State except Manipur (1:2750) had acquired the ideal Doctor-population ratio, (Assam 1 : 11,879, Meghalaya 1 : 5891, Nagaland 1 : 3713, Tripura 1 : 4543, Mizoram 1: 4718, Arunachal Pradesh 1 : 3613), the ideal being 1: 3500,"[11] whereas in 1971 it was found to be in a much better position in terms of the same ratio.

The benefits or otherwise of reorganisation can be known also by comparing the state of affairs in the region at the time of reorganisation and at present. For example, the problem of immigration had only worsened over time.. So is the problem of insurgency. The burning problem of insurgency in the North-Eastern States only proves that even the reorganisation had not been able to satisfy the political aspirations of the people and hence discontentment and the sense of alienation still prevails among them, one of the basic reasons for which may be founding the problem of increasing unemployment. All these prove nothing but the fact that the costs of reorganisation have been higher than the benefits accrued from it.

The region can boast of being at a better level than the rest of the country in terms of literacy rate. But what will only a higher literacy level do if the people cannot acquire the knowledge necessary for facing the challenge thrown by technological developments and commercialisation all around, particularly in the face of the globlisation of the economy. One important benefit that has been awarded to the people through reorganisation is that administration has come much nearer to the people of the various parts of the region. This is giving the people the benefit of decentralisation of power. If a proper programme for decentralised planning which can encourage people's participation in the planning process can be added to it, then only the full benefits of reorganisation can be derived. To quote Prof. Pakem, "decisions made so far by national planners and national bureaucracy have failed to seriously take note of the consequences that their decisions may have on the people of North-East India" and "while Sectoral planning at the National and State levels are welcomed there should be disaggregated or special planning at the district or block level. This is particularly needed in the tribal hill areas of the north-eastern region so that responsible development is the end result of the entire planning process in the country".[12]

REFERENCES

1. V.V. Rao, and Hazarika, N. 1983, *A Century of Government and Politics in North-East India,* Vol. I, p. 3.
2. P.C. Goswami, 1989, Evolution of Development Strategy in North East India. In *Assam Economic Review,* Vol. No. I, Jan. 1989, p. 21.
3. V.V. Rao, *et. al., A Century of Government and Politics in North East India,* Vol. III, p. 34.
4. V.V. Rao, *et al.,* 1984, *A Century of Government and Politics in North-East India* , Vol. II, pp. 36-43.
5. *Ibid.,* p. 37
6. *Ibid.,* p. 43
7. B. Pakem, 1992. North-East India.: The Need for Responsible Development in Understanding Society and Politics, Deptt. of Political Science, Gauhati University, p. 44.
8. *Ibid.* p. 44
9. A. Sharma, 1991. Inter-State Disparities in the Levels of Development in India: With particular Reference to the North-Eastern Region in *Journal of NEICSSR,* April, 1991, pp. 11-17.
10. NEC Secretariat : *Basic Statistics of North-Eastern Region,* p. 92
11. Rao, V.V. *et at., op. cit.* p. 7.
12. B. Pakem, *op. cit.* pp. 45-46.

MICRO STUDIES

16

REORGANIZATION AND THE ECONOMIC PROBLEMS OF THE BORDER AREA OF JAINTIA HILL

L.S. GASSAH

I

Way back in the' eighties one of the senior and retired ICS officers who had worked among the tribals of North-East India for a long time and seen them at a very close range, wrote thus:

> "Despite the carefully planned scheme to create a climate of confidence between the people of the hills and plains, Assam found herself bereft, . . . of all but a bare handful of her hill tribal population. The Assamese had looked forward to the departure of the British as the opportunity for the creation and consolidation of the 'Greater Assam' which they envisaged as the union of plainsmen of the province with the entire hill tribal population extending to the international frontier with China, Burma (Now Myanmer) and East Pakistan (now Bangladesh). Hydari and Bardoloi could never have fore seen that their plans for bringing the hill people closer to Assam had precisely the opposite effect and were in part responsible for Assam's final disintegration. For the hill tribals apprehended that all this talk of integration was nothing but the prelude to a wider and fiercer cultural campaign in the future".[1]

This attitude of indifference towards the hill tribes by the Assam leaders led to an ill-feeling between the two. It soon became abundantly clear to the tribal people and their leaders that they have to react against this indifferent attitude as their interest dictated. The tribal leaders of the tribal districts of Khasi-Jaintia Hills and Garo Hills who had experienced longer and closer association with the latter. Even some of the representatives from these districts were accommodated in the Assam ministry and harboured hopes of better treatment through progressive increase in their political weightage. But this was shortlived as they soon found that they might not succeed in holding their own against Assamese pressure. Thus, it was not long before even the tribal districts which had originally agreed to a tribal co-existence with the Assamese within a single State found disillusionment.[2] To top it all, in 1962, the Assam Legislative Assembly passed a bill prescribing Assamese as the official language for the entire State. This, for the tribals, in short, was the point of no return, for with Assamese as the official language, the tribal minority would at once be placed at an unfair disadvantage. "It was Assamese chauvinism, ironically enough, that diminished Assam and lost her tribal population. It is anomalous that the Assamese failed to anticipate the reactions of the tribal people to the imposition of Assamese when they themselves were so sensitive over the issue of language..... It is an attitude which the tribal people have suffered in the past with a patience beyond belief but are not prepared to endure much longer".[3]

The Government of India could not have been more generous than when they eventually agreed to separate the Nagas from Assam and grants them a State of their own, which came into existence from the lst of December 1963. As expected, there was violent and bitter opposition from the Assamese, who apprehended, and rightly, that this step would create a precedent and that her remaining tribes would follow the example of the Nagas and demand separation from the parent body.[4] This fear of the Assamese did come true when in 1971-72 more States and Union Territories were granted to the tribal population of the them composite State of Assam. Meghalaya is one such State which initially came into being as an Autonomous State and then from 1972 as a full-fledged State, on the basis of the North-East Reorganisation Act of 1969 and 1971.

II

Jaintia Hills, a district in the eastern part of Meghalaya, was from the 16th November 1869 till 1971 only a Sub-Division. It was, however, on the 22nd of February 1972 inaugurated as one of the districts of the State of Meghalaya. Before the new district for Jaintia Hills came into being, a separate District Council under the provision of the Sixth Schedule to the Constitution of India was created for the people of Jaintia Hills on the Ist of December 1964 but became operative only from the Ist of February 1966, after its bifurcation from the then United Khasi-Jaintia Hills Autonomous District Council on the recommendation of the Jarman Commission set up by the Assam Government.

This district which lies to the eastern part of the State of Meghalaya, covers a land area of approximately 3,900 sq. km. The northern part of the district is a highland area of rolling hills, small bushes in between and towards the eastern most and southern parts covered with thick forests. The southern portion has a highly irregular feature. Further towards the south and closer to the border of Bangladesh, the sudden drops and depressions become more prominent till they abruptly end in sheer precipices. It is in these precipitous slope that a large number of different horti-cultural crops are grown; the most prominent ones are oranges, betel-nuts, betel-leaves and fruits of different varieties.

The Jaintias are among those tribes who lived under the traditional formations of the hills until the area was integrated into the British Indian colonial state, although their economy has already been linked with the markets in the bordering plains of the Sylhet district (now in Bangladesh). The Jaintia economy 'therefore' depended much on the markets along the foothills of the present day international boundary with Bangladesh.

In the southern slopes of Jaintia Hills, the War Jaintias are mostly enged in their economic activities in the cultivation and production of cash crops like oranges, betel-leaves and betel-nuts. The plantations begin from the plains and foothills bordering the Sylhet district of Bangladesh and rise to an elevation of about 1,500 feet above the sea level. In the earlier days, it was upon this small precipitious area of both Khasi and Jaintia Hills that the greater part of Sylhet district and Assam depended for their supply of oranges. The British officials reported that before and after they took over the administration of Jaintia Hills, oranges formed one of the prominent goods exported by the Khasi and Jaintia people to the plains of Assam and Sylhet. A handsome revenue was also reported to have been received annually by the British Government on the export of oranges to Sylhet and Assam side. For example, Hunter estimated that in the year 1874-75, the export in oranges alone valued at Rs. 78,750.[5]

The transfer of power in 1947 and the change of administration thereafter, tremendously upset the economic life and activities of the Jaintia people in general and the War Jaintias in particular, their relations in trade and commerce with their counterparts in the plains led to a setback in exchange of goods and essential commodities.

After the Re-organisation of Assam in 1971 and the creation of the State of Meghalaya, there was an air of expectation for things to improve especially in terms of trade and commerce between India and the newly liberated nation of Bangladesh. The people of Jaintia Hills especially those inhabiting the border areas with Bangladesh eagerly expected that better relationship, at least in trade, would prevail between the two countries and this would lead to the re-opening of the border markets. There was no doubt an attempt between the two governments to channelise the much needed trade between the bordering neighbours and allow them to exchange their normal necessities through official channels, but this was shortlived. Therefore, once again it belied the hopes and expectations of the people when the entire border was sealed off and market across the international border were closed down. The expectations of the affected people for economic prospects came to a near standstill.

However, the re-opening of a few border *hats* for a brief period between December 1970 and March 1971, seemed to suggest the fact that the people living in both sides of the international border shared the same anxieties and sufferings arising out of the closure of the markets. Thus after prolonged negotiations up to the quarter ending March 1971, a few border *hats* were declared open for transaction in listed articles only. Before the other developments ensued, the maintenance of relations was upset by the Bangladesh affairs bringing with it influx of refugees into the State of Meghalaya.[6]

The influx of refugees from Bangladesh during and after the war of liberation of that country in 1970-71 to Meghalaya was alarming. This state of affairs brought immense suffering to the people living in the border areas of Jaintia Hill district. The influx was much beyond the expectation of the newly formed State of Meghalaya. It put the Government of Meghalaya in a precarious situation. It was far beyond its capacity to handle such a sea of human beings within its small territory. But the worst sufferers due to the influx of these refugees were the people living in the border areas with Bangladesh. They suffered a great deal of hardship. The whole economic life of the people was completely disrupted. It was impossible for the people of the area to work in their orchards or to cultivate, plant and harvest as the whole area was almost swamped with refugees. The entire economy of the local people had to undergo severe stress and train owing to this influx from Bangladesh. The socio-economic tension also accompanied such a heavy influx, more particularly when the economy of the border areas of Meghalaya has been badly disrupted ever since the creation of Pakistan and where even in normal times special border upliftment programmes have to be undertaken to rehabilitate the border economy.

After the Re-organisation of Assam, the State of Meghalaya came into being. It now depends on the political leadership of the State to bring upliftment and improvement in socio-economic activities of all the different districts of the State and especially those areas lying in the border with Bangladesh which have been hard hit due to partition of the sub-continent.

Against this background, it may thus be seen that even after the Re-organisation of the North-Eastern region and the coming into existence of the full-fledged State of Meghalaya, village economies in the border areas of the State, particularly that of Jaintia Hills district, which used to thrive trading their local agricultural produces with the people across the international border have been shattered due to restrictions on trade and commerce and the closure of the border markets. The people have felt this suffocation since the partition of 1947 and they still continue to suffer.

Political parties and their leaders have been submitting memoranda and passed a number of resolutions from platforms of various socio-political organisations demanding an improvement of the plight of the people living in the border areas. Some have even demanded a 10 (ten) kilometre free trade zone on either side of the border. Others have demanded from the Bangadesh as it has received a great jolt in the post-independence period.

The urgent need for reviving border trade between Bangladesh and the neighbouring States of North-East India, especially Meghalaya, was felt as this could bring new lease of economic life to the people in both sides of the international border. In these days of libneralisation of global trade, neither India nor Bangladesh can play a role of passive onlooker. This is more so because there was already an earlier accord signed, the Indira-Mujib Accord to facilitate the traditional border trade, particularly between Bangladesh and the state of Meghalaya. According to this Accord, it was agreed that an eight-kilometre free zone all along the border between Meghalaya and Bangladesh be allowed to help grow their border trade. However, due to political changes in Bangladesh following the assasination of Sheikh Mujibur Rehman, the provisions of the accord had been flouted by the subsequent leaders in Bangladesh. This led to the sealing off the border *hats*. The clouser of the border has already affected a sizeable section of the Meghalaya population living in the border area.

The people in the border areas of Jaintia Hills are therefore eagerly expecting some constructive steps to be taken by the State Government of Meghalaya to improve their long plights. The State Government on its part have been trying to prepare various schemes for border area improvement. It has set up the Border Area Development (BAD) Department to look after the problems faced by the people of the border areas. What the people are eagerly looking forward to is not merely the setting up of such a Department but the action that must follow at all levels. Since certain actions involve not only the State and the Central Governments but also agencies at the international level, it is 'therefore' hoped that the State Government should impress upon other agencies at the Central and international level to take up the matter in the right earnest.

REFERENCES

1. Nari Rustaomji, 1983, *Imperilled Frontiers : India's North- Eastern Border Lands*, OUP, Delhi, p. 36
2. *Ibid.*, p. 37
3. *Ibid.*, pp. 37, 51
4. *Ibid.*, p. 54
5. *Report on the Administration of North-East India*, Mittal publications, Delhi, 1984 (Reprint), p. 18.
6. Hamlet Bareh, 1974, *Meghalaya*, Shillong, pp. 209-10.

17

TRIBAL PROBLEMS
A Reorganisational Matter of Assam

JAGADISH KALITA

Once all the states of North-East India were included into Assam. Gradually, due to reorganisation NEFA, Naga Hill district, Khasi-Jayantia Hill district, Garo Hill district and Lushai Hill district were reorganised separtely and named as Arunachal Pradesh, Nagaland, Meghalaya and Mizoram respectively.

In recent time, a threat of reorganisation comes from Barak valley as Barak Land, Karbi Anglong and N.C. Hills districts as Karbi Land and from the Northern part of Assam, where majority of the Bodos are inhabited as Bodoland.

Demand for Bodo Land touches the districts of North Assam, *i.e.*, Dhubri Kokrajhar, Bangaigaon, Barpeta, Nalbari, Kamrupa, Darrang, Sonitpur, Lakhimpur and Dhemaji.

The issue of Bodo Land is raised amongst the Bodo communities due to the restoration of the Bodo cultural identity, due to identity of ethnicity, due to land alienation problems, due to the influx to the region from inside and outside the country, due to poverty and indebtedness, due to exploitation of the poorer and weaker sections of the community, due to upliftment of social and economic conditions and over and above due to hankering after political benefit.

The total population of the above mentioned districts, according to 1991 census comes to 11,238,965 as against 22,294,562 being the entire population of Assam as per 1991 census. Thus it will be seen that the above districts of northern Assam alone constitute 50.4 per cent of Assamese total population. In 1981, no census was conducted in Assam as the law and order situation was unstable during that time. So, this study has to be based on 1971 and 1991 census reports. Table 17.1 shows the districtwise population figure in the northern part of Assam on the basis of 1991 census.

TABLE 17.1: Districtwise Population Figure in North Assam Based on 1991 Census[1]

District		Population	Percentage of total population in Assam
1		2	3
1.	Dhubri	1,325,653	5.95
2.	Kokrajhar	796,880	3.53
3.	Bangaigaon	806,472	3.62
4.	Kamrup	1,987,662	8.92
5.	Barpeta	1,382,715	6.20
6.	Nalbari	1,012,608	4.54
7.	Darrang	1,286,633	5.77
8.	Sonitpur	1,418,484	6.36
9.	Lakhimpur	749,675	3.36
10.	Dhemaji	472,183	2.12

Source : Census Report of Assam, 1991.

After independence, growth rate of population in Assam are as follows:

TABLE 17.2 : Population Growth Rate in Assam.[2]

Year	Population	Decadal growth rate
1	2	3
1951	8,028,856	+19.93
1961	10,837,329	+34.98
1971	14,625,152	+34.95
1991	22,294,562	+52.44

Source : Census Report of 1951, 1961, 1971 and 1991.

During the decade of 1951-61, the population recorded a very high growth rate. It might be attributed due to influx of religious minority groups and others from neighbouring countries during the post-independence period. On the other hand, during the decade of 1961-71, the growth rate decreased by a small percentage. This fall in the growth rate may be due to increase in the death rate during that period. But during 1971-91 a duration of two decades the growth rate was 52.44 per cent.

On the basis of 1971 census, the scheduled tribe population in the North Assam, which Bodos claim as Bodo land was as follows:

TABLE 17.3 : Districtwise Scheduled Tribe Population in Assam Based on 1971 Cencus[3]

District	Scheduled Tribe Population	Percentage to total Schedule Tribe Population	Percentage of Districtwise Scheduled Tribe Population based on Districtwise total population
1.	2	3	4
1. Dhubri	20,601	1.28	2.42
2. Goalpara	84,139	5.24	12.67
3. Kokarajhar	203,547	12.67	28.67
4. Barpeta	77,451	4.82	7.97
5. Nalbari	102,403	6.37	14.63
6. Sonitpur	57,146	3.56	6.34
7. Darrang	128,494	8.00	15.40
8. Lakhimpur	73,053	4.55	18.34
9. Dhemaji	131,758	8.20	46.90

Source : Census Report of S.T. Population Tables, 1971.

According to 1971 census the Scheduled Tribes population as a percentage of total population of Assam was 10.98 per cent. The total number of Scheduled Tribes population in Assam, as per 1971 cencus, was 1,607 thousands.

From Table 14.3, the percentage to total scheduled tribes population in Kokrajhar district is 12.67 per cent which was found to be the highest. Between Darrang and Dhemaji districts, the latter is higher by a small percentage.

If one analyses the districtwise scheduled tribe population, as a per centage to districtwise total population, Dhemaji have the per centage of scheduled tribes population with 46.9 percent, whereas the percentage of scheduled tribe population is 28.67 percent in the Kokrajhar district. In between Darrang and Lakhimpur districts, the per centage of scheduled tribe population is found higher in Lakhimpur i.e., 18.34 than that of Darrang district i.e., 15.40.

TABLE 17.4 : Tribal Structure – Communitywise

District	Bodo (11.07 Lakhs) P.C.	Mishing (3.15 Lakhs) P.C.	Sonowal (1.02 Lakhs) P.C.	Rabha (0.80 lakhs) P.C.
1	2	3	4	5
1. Kokrajhar	28.5	–	–	1.31
2. Darrang	16.4	–	–	3.78
3. Nalbari	12.4	–	2.43	1.95
4. Bangaigaon	12.0	–		7.3
5. Sonitpur	9.4	11.1	–	4.9
6. Barpeta	9.3	–	–	3.5
7. Kamrup (North)	5.1	–	5.2	2.8
8. Dhemaji	–	45.0	20.6	–
9. Lakhimpur	–	43.3	16.7	–
10. Dhubri	–	–	–	1.08

Table 14.4 depicts a vivid picture of tribal structure in Northern part of Assam. The Bodos are a majority group amongst the various tribal communities in Assam. But Bodos are almost 7 per cent amongst all the population of the State of Assam. In Kokrajhar district, Bodos are 28.5 per cent whereas in Darrang, they are only 16.4 per cent.

For tribal development, and to protect tribal land, Chapter X was brought in and added to the Regulation by the Assam Land and Revenue Regulation (Amendment) Act, 1947.[4] This chapter enacts provision for the protection of backward classes. Under this fact, 44 tribal belts have been constituted for the protection of tribal communities in Assam.

The classes of people who are entitled to the protective measures are to be notified by the State Government of Assam in the official Gazette, and accordingly the following classes of people have been notified as persons entitled to protection.

(1) Plains Tribals, (2) Hills Tribals, (3) Tea Garden Tribals, (4) Santhals, (5) Scheduled Castes and (6) Nepali Cultivators.

Grasziers[5] (Notification No. R.S.D. 26/64 PL/15, Dated, the 27th June, 1969, Shillong, the Governor of Assam is pleased to declare that Nepalies who were notified as protected class with this Department notification No. R. D, 28/47/43, dated 24.8.49 are hereby and henceforth excluded from the list of protected classes).

The landed property of the tribal people, nay of all people are not kept fixed for all the time in the history of a family. The problem of land alienation amongst the tribals in Assam may be classified[6] into:

(a) alienation between the tribals–sellers and purchaser being both tribal;
(b) alienation between tribals and non-tribals;

(i) either the seller is tribal or non-tribals.
(ii) or, the buyer is tribal or non-tribals.

In this category of classifications some trouble between tribals and non-tribals may arise, though the actual economic effect may be the same.

Land is the principal form of property of the agrarian society in Assam. For the rural society, about nine-tenth of them depend on agriculture and their mainstay of living is related to land.

Tribals are migratory in nature. and alienation is one of

the major problems amongst the tribal people in Assam. It is a legacy of generations in which the tribals are compelled to transfer their lands to other Tribals and non-tribals as a last resort to survive.

The number of households transferring land to non-tribals during the last 10 years and beyond 10 to 30 years by tribals within the Integrated tribal Development Project. (I.T.D.P.) areas are as follows.

TABLE 17.5 : Transfer of land within Integrated Tribal Development Project areas[7]

Tribals	Total No. of households	No. of households transferring land to non-tribals during the last 10 years.		No. of households transferring land to non-tribals beyond 10 to 30 years last.	
		No. of household	per cent all total	No. of household	per cent to all total
1	2	3	4	5	6
Schduled Tribes	1,79,395	13,029 (7.26)	48.78	10,173 (5.67)	48.33

Source : Bench Mark Survey, Directorate of E & S, Govt. of Assam 1978

Problems of land alienation is possible due to various reasons. Migration may be inter-district, inter-state and international.

Flow of migration into Assam is seen for a long time from Nepal and occasionally from Bhutan and even from Bangladesh. These classes of immigrants are generally, migratory, though permanent settlement have not been uncommon. They are predominant in the Sonitpur, Lakhimpur, Nalbari, Darrang and Kokrajhar districts.

These immigrants are creating the problem of alienation either directly by forcefully occupying vacant land or indirectly by encroaching upon forest, char, V.G.R. P.G.R., or Sarkari Khas lands.

To preserve the cultural and ethnic identity of the tribals, alienation of land must be stopped from the land hungry immigrants. Inner line system should be introduced. To preserve the ethnic identity and culture of the tribals, the tribal blocks and belts have been constituted under the ALRR Act of 1886 as amended in 1947.

The 'Assam Migration Tribals' Census of India, shows the trend and nature of migration. According to these tables, out of a total state population of 146 lakhs, 93.3 per cent are born in India and the rest 6.7 per cent are born outside the country. International migration within the state is as high as 22.41 per cent of the total population of the state, and interstate migration is 3.58 per cent. This clearly shows that international migration to the state is about seven times more than inter-state migration.[8]

Among the rural people of the state, according to the census of 1971, 33.58 per cent were migrants, 7.07 per cent were migrating from other states of the country and 15.75 per cent were migrants from other counties primarily from Bangladesh and Nepal.

A question arises: Why tribals are going to be poor? Generally, when people face financial stringency either to meet their day-to-day necessities, or to observe any religious or social festivities, or to meet the requirements of education and training of the members of the family or to meet any financial obligation or expenditure on medical treatment of family member or on legal actions, they have to meet these additional expenses by borrowings from those sources which are easily available, easy for payment of interest and capital, cheap in nature and trustworthy. Though in recent times certain organised agencies are coming forward to lend the rural masses against various productive schemes, nobody is anxious to lend them for consumptive or other such purposes.

In 1971-72, according to the Debt and Investment Survey, mortgage constituted about 19.98 per cent of the total debt outstanding in Assam against all households and 20.58 per cent against the cultivators.[9]

In 1968-69, Dr. K.C. Sarma has calculated the usufructuary mortgage covered about 37 per cent of the outstanding debt against all rural households in Nalbari District.[10]

Poverty is the main cause of indebtedness. At present in 1986-87, people below the poverty line in the state account for 47.51 per cent of the total.[11]

If one is serious about stopping alienation, poverty must be eradicated from the midst of the people.

TABLE 17.6 : Number of Households indebted to money lenders within the I.T.D.P. areas[12]

Tribals	Total No. of household	No. of Household indebated to		
		Money lenders	Trades	Total
1	2	3	4	5
Schduled Tribes	1,79,395	36,444 (20.31)	29	36.473 (20.33)

Note: Figures in brackets are percentage to totals.
Source: Bench Mark Survey, Government of Assam, 1978, p. 46.

The finding of the B.M.S. reflected that the indebted scheduled tribes households constituted only 20.33 per cent of the total households of the Integrated Tribal Development Project (ITDP) areas of Assam. Almost all the indebted scheduled tribe households, except 29, were indebted to the money lenders who provided loan usually to the inhabitants of the ITDP areas.

But according to Dr. K.C. Sarma, the incidence of indebtedness in Nalbari district in the year 1968 was found to be much higher. The money lenders contributed about 72.42 per cent of their total debt.[13]

The law Research Institute, Gauhati High Court, had surveyed eight villages out of a total of 117 in the Kokarajhar Revenue circle. It is found that in two villages, namely, Monsergaon and Kalaigaon, no protected classes were in majority in 1971. Monsergaon was non-tribal majority even in 1941 and 1961, but Kalaigaon suddenly shot up to be non-tribal majority in 1971, due apparently to immigration. In 1941, two other villages Haltugaon and Anthaibari, were non-tribal majority but they ceased to be so in 1961 and have continued to be tribal majority in 1971. Anthaibari's case is remarkable, because in 1941, it had no tribal population, in 1971, it had only tribal, but no non-tribal population. In 1961, two different villages, Pakeriguri and Rabhapara had non-tribal majority but ceased to be so in 1971. All this shows that there has been a fluctuation of tribal and non-tribal population in these villages even since 1941.[14]

One of the most important reason for demanding the Bodoland, a separate homeland, for the Bodos, is seeking political benefits. All Assam Bodo Students Union (Bisumutiwary ABSU Faction), the Bodo People's Action Committee and the Bodo Security Force (extremist group) demand separate state as Bodoland. According to them, the issue of Bodoland is to preserve the cultural and ethnic identity of the Bodo communities. To maintain these, they prefer political benefit on their part, creating a separate homeland for them.

Recommendations

Some suggestions may be put forward for the solution of the problems particularly among the Bodos, the plain tribals of Assam in the following ways:

(1) The Government of Assam must restore cultural and ethnic identity of the Bodo communities by which the Bodo problem can be solved.

(2) There should be a proper machinery to look after the implementation of the provisions of the Assam Land and Revenue Regulation Act, 1886, as amended up-to-date, in spirit and action for the protection of tribal communities in Assam.

(3) Land transfer from poor tribals to rich tribals and' benami' land transfer in the name of a tribal for the benefit of a non-tribal, be effectively checked.

(4) Those local non-tribals who have been residing permanently in the tribal belts and blocks even before their formation, should be protected by law.

(5) Legal protection of tribals belts and blocks should be given due emphasis by Government.

(6) Expansion of institutional credit agencies is expected to meet the credit needs of the people particularly of the tribals. Establishment of branches by the Nationalised Banks in interior tribal areas should receive priority. Special steps should also be taken by financial institutions to simplify the procedure of advancing loans to the tribal people so as to facilitate rapid investment.

(7) The root cause of deteriorating tribal economy is indebtedness. The idea of small savings be initiated in the minds of the tribals. Cooperatives if properly organised, can play a significant role in ameliorating the poor economic conditions of the tribals and hence in the traditional form if possible the cooperative society or village panchayats be strengthened for the purpose.

(8) The root cause of alienation of land and indebtedness among the tribal people is poverty. Unless the economic conditions of the tribals are improved, it is hardly possible to check alienation of their land and save these people from indebtedness by enacting legislation and similar measures only. The developmental schemes for their economic upliftment, should be implemented sincerely and expeditiously.

(9) To stop the influx of population to the tribal areas will be one of the best measures to remove the recent tribal problems by which the restoration of the identity in Bodo ethnicity will be possible in the state of Assam.

(10) To uplift the economic conditions of the tribals, the society of each village and of community must be alert, vigilant and protect the weaker sections of the tribal people. A vigilant, progressive, educative

and social structure be created in each village and locality to help emerge a new social order of peace, amity, equality and progress.

(11) Due to unemployment amongst the youths of the tribals also, they have been indulging in militant activities. So, the state Government and Union Government must take fruitful steps to solve the unemployment and underemployment problems among the Bodo communities of Assam, by which the Bodo problem can be solved easily.

(12) To secure political benefit, more political facilities must be provided by Panchayati Raj. Some more seats in the panchayat must be reserved for the tribal population Moreover, whese there is maximum ethnicity of tribals, government should form the Panchayati Raj system with the quota reservation to the tribal community. More seats in the Assam Legislative Assembly be reserved for the benefit of the tribals.

Conclusion

To conclude it is suggested that the Bodo Problems be solved at the earliest and the cultural and ethnic identity amongst the Bodo population restored. The States and the Union Government must take steps to protect the land of their own and stop the immigration from outside the region. Steps should also be taken to promote economic development of the tribal community and provide them with the financial, educational, medical and drinking water facilities. The poorer and weaker sections of the Bodo community must be protected from exploitation by the richer sections of the community. To secure political benefits for the Bodos, more facilities for their political participation must be provided by the implementation of Panchayati Raj and by increasing the tribal reservation quota of seats in the Assam Legislative Assembly.

A three-member Expert Committee was constituted by the Government of India under the Chairmanship of Dr. Bhupinder Singh on February 25, 1991, to determine the area of the Bodos and to make recommendations on the powers that may be given to them. Though they submitted its report in March, 1991, unfortunately, the recommendations of the report were rejected by the ABSU and BPAC. From this report, one can get a clear ethnic picture of the area. There are 11.07 lakh Bodos inhabiting the western middle area of the state and 3.15 lakh Mishing population inhabiting the eastern part of the State.[15]

On May 23,1992, the Chief Minister, Sri Hitweswar Saikia held a discussion with the representatives of ABSU and BPAC in the presence of the then Union Defence Minister, Sri Sharad Pawar, where the Bodoland movement leaders submitted their claim for 4,443 villages spread over nine districts and 37 Assembly constituencies.

The Chief Minister also discussed the matter with Bodo leaders in a series of discussions held in July and August, 1992, during with the ABSU and BPAC made an additional demand for 209 villages.

The ABSU and BPAC want to include in all a total of 4,652 villages in the proposed territory. Of these, 1,035 are pure general villages. In almost 835 villages, and 300 villages, the Bodos and the Mishings respectively are in majority. Besides, more than 80 per cent of non-tribal inhabitants are found in 1,500 villages. From 50 to 80 per cent of tribal inhabited villages are almost 513 in number. Besides there are 109 tea gardens where there is no scheduled tribes population.

The Chief Minister of Assam discussed the matter with the opposition parties and most parties advocated the idea of providing an autonomous territory to the Bodos with adequate administrative, legislative and financial powers with villages having more then 50 per cent Bodo population.

Even it the District Council idea is implemented towards solving the Bodoland issue without further reorganisation of Assam, it will be difficult to demarcate the area for that purpose, as such Bodo villages are not found clustered together in particular area of the state, but spreading all over the region disjointedly.

The Prime Minister and the Union Home Minister have declared that Assam cannot be further reorganised. The

Bodo land issue can be solved without further reorganisation of Assam. According to the recommendations of the Expert Committee. The Bodos demand is for the establishment of a Central University in Kokrajhar. To spread the highest educational facilities amongst the tribals the Government can establish a Central University in Kokrajhar, by which, social and educative developmental values can be measured. The Bodo language is the state language in Kokrajhar district and Udalguri sub division. The State Government must take effective steps to uplift the Bodo language and its literature in the state of Assam.

The extremist groups of the Bodo Community have committed arson, bomb explosions and killings, by which it is impossible to create a separate homeland for them.

It is remarkable that the Bodo land Autonomous Council Accord has been signed on 20th February, 1993, in Guwahati with the leaders of ABSU and BPAC in the presence of the Chief Minister of Assam, Sri Hiteswar Saikia and the Union Minister of State for Home, Sri Rajesh Pilot. Besides, a formal declaration of the Bodoland Autonomous Council has been made by arranging an open meeting in Debargaon of Kokrajhar on the 7th of March 1993. The demarcated area of this council is in a portion of northern part of Assam in between the Sonkhosh river in the western side and the Pass-Nai river in the eastern side. Almost 2,000 villages with 25 tea gardens are included in its area. The 40-member Boboland Autonomous Council will be formed with 30 elected members from the scheduled tribe populations and 10 elected member from general populations.

The Bill of Bodoland Autonomous Council was passed in the Budget session of Assam Assembly in March-April of 1993. It is also happy news that the militant group of Bodos would lay down their arms and amunitions to the Government. The surrender of sophisticated arms will continue from the April 25, 1993. It may also be mentioned that the Chief of the Bodo Militant Group alongwith his six colleagues has already surrendered their arms in front of the Chief Minister of Assam, Sri Hiteswar Saikia and the Union Minister of State for Home, Sri Rajesh Pilot in Debargaon on the 7th March 1993.

The Bodo militant group has thus come to the main stream of national integration and they have come forward to maintain peace and harmony amongst all sections of the communities of Assam. Doubtlessly speaking, it will lead to the path of social progress and economic development of the Bodo inhabited areas as well as the state of Assam and the country as a whole.

REFERENCES

1. Cencus of India, 1991, Assam.
2. Cencus Report of 1951, 1961,1971 and 1991 Assam.
3. Cencus Report of S.T.Population Tables, 1971.
4. The Assam Land and Revenue Regulation (Amendment) Act, 1947.
5. Notification No. R.S.D. 26/64 PI/15, dated, Shillong, the 27th June 1969.
6. Problems of Land Alienation amongst the Plain Tribals in Assam with special reference to Nalbari District, A Ph. D. thesis, submitted to Gauhati University, 1991, by Dr. J. Kalita, 91.
7. Bench Mark Survey, Directorate of Economics and Statistics, Government of Assam, 1978.
8. The Migration Tables - Cencus of India, 1971.
9. All India Debt and Investment Survey 1971-72, Statistical Tables relating to cash dues outstanding. p. 157-158.
10. The Role of Rural Credit in the Development of the Peasants a seminar paper read by Dr. K.C. Sarma in the Xth International Congress of Anthropological and Ethnological Science Post Plenary Session, Dec, 1978, Lucknow.
11. Draft Annual Plan, 1990-91, p. A-9.
12. Bench Mark Survey, Govt. of Assam, 1978.
13. K.C. Sarma, Rural Credit in Assam – A Case Study of Nalbari sub-division, an unpublished thesis, p.188, xi-13.
14. A Study of the Land Systems of North Eastern Region, Vol. I, Assam by Law Research Institute, Eastern Region, Gauhati High Court, Guwahati, Dec. 18, 1982, p. 80.
15. Report of the Study Committee, Bodoland Issue, submitted in March 1991.

Supplimentary References

I. *Land Reforms and Peasant Movement*, ed. by Dr. A. Goswami.

II. *Alienation of Tribal Land and indebtedness*, edited by Dr. B. N. Bordoloi.

III. *Statistical Hand Book*, 1982, 1984, Directorate of Economics and Statistics, Govt. of Assam.

IV. *Tribes of Assam*, Part-I, Bordoloi, Sarma Thakur and Saikia.

V. *Statistical Abstract*, Directorate of Economics and Statistics, Government of Assam,1978.

VI. *Tribal Problem*, Dr. J. Kalita, published in the *Assam Tribune* in 16th December 1992.

18

THE REORGANISATION OF ASSAM AND THE BODO MOVEMENT

S.K. MUKHERJEE

The Boro-Kachari, one of the earliest settlers of Assam, are numerically the largest tribal groups in North-East India. They are Indo-Mongoloid people and speak Bodo, a branch of Tibeto-Burman language. The Bodo Kachari inhabit primarily along the northern bank of Brahmaputra, but their concentration is highest in the Kokrajhar district of Assam. Ethnologically, the term Bodo covers a large number of tribes and in fact includes the majority of the Bodo speaking people of Assam. The Bodo speech area spreads over Tripura, Meghalaya and some other parts of North-East India also. The majority of the Bodo speaking people live in Assam. Other segments of the plains tribals are the Rabha, Hojai, Deuri, Mech, Sonwal, Lalung, Barman Kachari and the Mishing. All except the last belong to Bodo group. The concern here is with the Boro-Kacharis.

In the composite state of Assam, the Assamese were politically the most powerful group, consisting of a mass of cultivating families led by a number of educated and landed families who had branched out into government service, the professions and tea and small trade. They had begun a struggle with the Bengali middle class for political and cultural hegemony already in the late ninteenth century and by the 'fifties were powerfully entrenched both in the state administration and in the Congress organisation. Their dream was now to turn Assam into a homogeneous society adopting the Assamese way of life and the Assamese language. This cultural campaign also paid political dividends as it legitimised the Assamese urge to grab the largest share of the cake and acquire a vertical monopoly of power in the state administration. Very naturally it generated resentment and resistence among the non-Assamese tribes. Eventually, the hill tribes got their own states like Meghalaya, Nagaland and Mizoram.

Before Independence, the leaders of the Assam Provincial Congress Committee had entered into an alliance with the tribal leaders guaranteeing limited self-government in the hill areas and certain safeguards in the plains. But most of the hill tribes were not happy with such limited self-government. The last of such tribes remain with the Assamese, the Karbis who are now demanding an autonomous state in a mass movement with wide popular support. The plains tribes too have been more or less restive for a long time because the Bodo peasants, or large proportion of them, had been squeezed out of their land. Secondly, Bodo-inhabited areas had been badly neglected during the successive Congress governments. Thirdly, the Bodos and other tribals resented the campaign of Assamisation and felt they had no chance of preserving their own cultural heritage in that atmosphere.

Initially, a socio-religious movement began under the guidance of Srimat Kalicharan Brahma in the early part of this century. The religious reform movement called 'Brahma Movement' was instrumental in the development of education, cultural and political consciousness among the Boros. Guru Kalicharan represented to the Simon Commission for reservation of seats in the state legislature and Government services for tribals. He also supported the formation of the Tribal language to focus attention on their social, politcal and economic problems. In the late 'sixties the movement assumed a new phase and developed into a socio-political one for a separate state within the Indian Union. The leadership of the movement vested in the Plains Tribal Council of Assam (PTCA) constituted in 1967. The Bodo Sahitya Sabha established in 1952 and Bodo Students Union also played important roles in the organisation of the movement.

Historically, the plains tribal political movement emerged out of the demand for linguistic rights of the Bodo-Kacharis. It has been aptly stated that language is the most favourite political issue in Assam (Chaube, 1973). In fact, most of the similar movements of this region developed from language issues especially after the enactment of the Official Language Act of Assam in 1960. The Bodo Sahitya Sabha moved the State government in 1953 for the use of Bodo language as a medium of instruction in schools in the Boro-Kachari concentrated areas. The demand was recognised for primary education in 1963 and higher secondary schools in 1968.

With the declaration of policy of reorganisation of Assam on federal structure, before the delegation team of Mizo Union in New Delhi on the 13th January 1967, the Bodos warmly welcomed the policy and their political party the Plains Tribal Council of Assam which was formed on 27 February 1967 at Kokrajhar after the fourth General Elections of 1967. Under the banner of Plains Tribal Council of Assam, the young as well as old tribal leaders and workers from all corners of Kokrajhar sub-division met under the chairmanship of Late Padmasri Modoram Brahma, an educationist and social worker. In the meeting they arrived at the conclusion that full autonomy alone could provide the plains tribals with the necessary conditions to preserve their language and culture and help them to develop according to their own choice and genius.

The meeting discussed in particular the Government of India's proposal made that year for the reorganisation of Assam on federal lines. They held that the federal plan was the most suitable one which could at once satisfy the political aspirations of the Hills people and other minority groups, particularly the plain tribals. Thus it can be said that one of the causes of the setting up of the PTCA was the Government of India's proposal to give Assam a federal structure. A PTCA leader published an essay on the reorganisation plan in Assamese. So as to explain its importance to the Bodo people, an action committee was formed in that meeting.

The PTCA for the first time submitted a memorandum

to the President of India on the 20 May 1967 at New Delhi for the creation of an autonomous region for the plains tribal people of Assam. In course of time the demand for autonomous region gradually gained momentum and thus autonomous region was upgraded to the demand for Union Territory which was nomenclated as 'Udayachal 'on 7th January 1973.

The movement has passed through certain stages in its career. The 'event structure' of the movement with the sequences and consequences was not uniform. Sometimes it was very active like in 1974 when they shed blood and agitated for the recognition of Bodo language to establish their separate identity. Afterwards the leadership of the movement became very passive, and on 4 April 1977, the PTCA leaders announced that on the 4th April 1977 PTCA had given up the demand for separate state 'Udayachal' and wanted autonomous region instead. There was a strong reaction from the party hardliners and ABSU formed another political party, the Progressive Political Party on 22 May, 1979. The Progressive PTCA for the first time submitted a memorandum to the then Prime Minister of India, Smt. Indira Gandhi on the 8th July, 1980 demanding a separate homeland MISHING BODOLAND. The ABSU had been taking keen interest for unification of PTCA and PTCA(P) since 1979 and for that they had organised a convention from 17th to 19th April 1984 and a new political party United Tribal Nationalist Liberation Front (UTNLF) was formed on 19 April, 1984 under the chairmanship of B.K. Basumatary, M.L.A.

The ABSU (U) withdrew its support from PTCA leaders belied the hopes of the innocent tribal people for their narrow political gains. Although PTCA still promises to secure 'Udayachal' the ABSU has clearly stolen the thunder from it. A splinter group of the ABSU known as Ramsiary group has parted company with Upen Brahma on the questions of tactics and strategy. The Upen Brahma group which has undoubtedly succeeded in catching the imagination of the Bodo masses over large areas and mobilising thousands for their programmers of action, has demanded that a contiguous stretch of territory extending over the entire northern bank of Brahmaputra should be formed into a separate Bodoland. Every one says the solution can be found only at the negotiation table, but negotiation seem at the moment the most difficult thing to bring off. The ABSU leaders claim that before they launched the movement they had sought a meeting with senior leaders of the AGP government desparately and strenuously, but they are either denied audience or fobbed off with interviews with unimportant leaders of the government. Both the Chief Minister and the Home Minister denied this. It seems that AGP government was willing enough to negotiate but determind not to make any major concessions, whereas the ABSU leaders were staking all on the demand for a separate state and were prepared only to discuss the modalities of its formation. In the meantime every hundred hour or three hundred hour bandh raised the death toll. Entire hamlets were reduced to ashes.

In 1990, when the tripartite talks with the Central Government was delayed and when ABSU had threatened to take a long agitational programme then the Chandrashekhar Government announced and appointed a three-member committee with Dr. Bhupinder Singh, IAS as chairman, Dr. S.K. Singh , IAS and Mr. Gokhle as member to go into the question as to what extent powers, legislative, financial and political could be extended to the Boros who had been demanding Bodoland. The expert committee was set up after the eighth round tripartite talks on Bodo issue. The Committee had been asked to identify the Bodo-dominated areas of North of Brahmaputra river apparently to ascertain if the claim of the ABSU and BPAC that the entire area covering the North of the Brahmaputra is inhabited mostly by the Bodo – based on facts, besides ABSU-BPAC, the Bodo Sahitya Sabha had hailed the move.

The ABSU-BPAC at first decided not to participate in Assam election, Just as in 1985 the people of Assam under the leadership of the youth got together to a regional party to take the regin of power at Disspur, the Bodo people in north bank of Brahmaputra also joined hands under the ABSU-BPAC to send their representatives to the State

Assembly and Lok Sabha to exert their claims. The ABSU-BPAC combine was able to get nine Assembly and the one Lok Sabha seat. The Plains Tribal Council of Assam drew a blank. On 30 June when the Hiteswar Saikia Ministry was formed the ABSU-BPAC had warmly congratulated the newly formed Congress (I) ministry in the State. They hoped that this government would be able to bring an amicable settlement to the Bodoland issue by creating a separate state in north bank and district Councils in the south bank. In the tripartite talk on 6 January 1992, the Bodo leaders expressed their dissatisfaction at the inordinate delay in finding an acceptable solution to their demand. The ABSU-BPAC had set January 31st as the deadline for a concrete formula to evolve a political solution to the Bodo problem. But the Centre made it clear that unless the expert Committee report was available there could not be any formal discussion on the problem and there could not be any tripartite talk till the Government received the report.

The three-member expert Committee submitted their report on 31th March, 1992 but the Bodo leaders rejected it. The ABSU-BPAC combine held several rounds of negotiation with the Chief Minister of Assam, but no solution was found as the Bodo leadership insisted on inclusion of hundreds of villages without any tribal population in the Bodo administration.

But on 21st February, 1993 the seven-year old Bodo agitation came to a dramatic end with the Assam Government and the Bodo leadership signing a Memorandum of Settlement that gives the plains tribals an autonomous council. The accord was signed in the presence of the Union Minister of Home Mr. Rajesh Pilot and the State Chief Minister, Mr. Hiteswar Saikia.

The Council which will began autonomous administrative unit, will have as many as 38 subjects or departments under its jurisdiction. However, police, law and order authority would remain with the State Government.

The council will comprise 40 members, 35 of whom will be elected and five nominated by the State Government. The area of administration of the Council will comprise about 2,000 villages and 25 tea gardens extending from Sankosh river in Dhubri to the Pachnoi river in Darrang district. The movement leaders have undertaken to ensure the surrender of all arms and ammunition by the Boro Security Force and bring the extremists to the national mainstream. As per the settlement the Council will have full control over the socio-economic and cultural development of the area. The Council will have a 'sort of ministry' for the day to day administration, besides special Court and an official language. An interim Bodoland Council consisting of Bodo leaders will function now till the Assam Assembly pass as a bill for election to the Council. The Chief Minister said that the Bodoland Council to which election would be held every five years would not remain under the Sixth Schedule of the Indian Constitution. Union Minister of State for Home Affairs, Rajesh Pilot, who steered the negotiations to a successful and happy conclusion expressed the hope that the settlement would solve the Bodo problems and would bring peace and progress to the state.

REFERENCES

1. S. Chaube, 1973, Plains Tribals in Assam Politics, *North-Eastern Affairs.*
2. H. Gohain, 1989, Bodo Stir in Perspective, In *Economic and Political Weekly,* Vol. XXV, N. 25, June 1989.
3. S. Mukherjee and D.P. Mukherjee, 1982, Contemporary Tribal and Political Movement among the Bodo Kacharies of Assam, in *Tribal Movement in India,* Vol. I, ed. by K.S. Singh, New Delhi Monohar,.

19

SETTLEMENT ON BODOLAND
A Few Points to Ponder

P.S. DATTA

It is indeed with a sense of relief that the news about signing of a tripartite memorandum of settlement on February 20 to create a Bodoland Autonomous Council reached the people of Assam (and not necessarily the Assamese people alone). This is neither the occasion to spread frustrating ideas and ultimate futility of the pious (i) whishes expressed through such type of memorandum of settlement nor it is the time to make any academic forecast about the capability of the proposed 40-member Council (of whom 5 will be nominated by the Assam Government). It is, right at the moment, a victory for Saikia's much repeated claim that something positive is sure to happen on Bodoland soon as also a belated assertion of the Bodoleadership on their people whom they inspired (if not instigated) very often on a very much characteristic anti-Assamese line to fight the discriminatory tactics of Dispur.

The tripartite memorandum of settlement of course spells satisfaction for Saikia and ABSU-BPAC. But no one probably is sure how much hopes are in store for those millions of people who were motivated and then forced to face the brutality of the state-power for over a decade now. It was indeed nice of the ABSU President (as shown in regional news of Guwahati Doordarshan) to express gratitude to the people of Assam in general, after signing the memorandum, for extending help to their cause, but he should not forget, neither should his colleagues, that the words already uttered cannot be exactly taken back and there were hundreds of such expressions from their side which without hurting Dispur actually offended the people of Assam in general and the Assamese people in particular, Memorandum of Settlement is no more any virgin idea so far the people in Assam are concerned. How and when the categorical gestures to neutralise the hurt feelings of Assamese will come from the ABSU-BPAC leadership enjoying a share in the legitimate state power–is to be watched.

History is indeed a funny chronicle of human action-habitual or conscious. The first concrete plains tribal aspiration may be traced back to January 4,1929 when not less than four memoranda were submitted to the (much maligned) Simon Commission. But that was the phase of protectionist behaviour. Autonomy aspiration of the plains-tribals, however, required about four more decades to be articulated and in fact, on February 27, 1967, with the birth of Plains Tribal Council of Assam (PTCA), a more assertive and definitely a more distinct phase began.

Plains Tribal Council of Assam (PTCA), which stood for the Barmans of Cachar, the Bodo-Kachari, the Deoris, the Hojais, the Mishings, the Kacharis including Sonowals, the Lalungs, the Meches and the Rabhas, submitted a memorandum to the Presdient of India on May 20,1967 demanding full autonomy in the predominantly plains tribal areas of the northern tract of Goalpara, Kamrup, Darrang, Lakhimpur and Sibsagar districts including all the *Tribal Belts and Blocks* of those areas so that the tribals can (a) adequately protect their land; (b) give effective check to economic exploitation of tribals by non-tribals; (c) conserve their language, culture, customs and what is best in them; (d) Prevent political domination by non-tribals over tribals and imposition of anything which would disrupt their traditions and customs; and (e) grow according to their own genius and traditions.

PTCA demand for an *Autonomous Region* of 1967 was upgraded to a demand for *Udayachal,* a Union Territory, in 1973. But in 1977 the top layers of their leadership announced withdrawal of the demand for Union Territory in favour of the earlier demand for Autonomous Region. This announcement (by the PTCA leaders who were by then with the Janata Dal after the lifting of national emergency) shocked the diehards and within a short span of about two years these diehards organised themselves under Plains Tribal Council of Assam (Progressive) shortly known as PTCA (P). The demand of PTCA (P) was for a Union Territory called *Mishing-Bodoland* and they submitted a number of memoranda to the Prime Minister between 1980 and 1983.

At the instance of All Bodo Student's Union (ABSU), which has been active all along since 1967, attempts were made to unite PTCA and PTCA(P). But PTCA leaders were reportedly not ammenable and as such, unity efforts did not pay dividends and the move was abandoned. In 1984, PTCA (P) was dissolved and a new organisation was floated with the name of United Tribal Nationalist Liberation Front (UTNLF) which too, in support of its demand for a Union Territory, named *Tribal Land,* submitted a number of memoranda between 1984 and 1990. ABSU too, between 1972 and 1988, submitted a number of memoranda to the Prime Minister, Home Minister, Governor, Chief Minister in support of their demand for a Union Territory. However, the Twentieth Annual Conference of the ABSU held at Bastibari in Dhubri district during December 19-22, 1988 ushered in a very militant phase in the movement when they decided to suspend all other demands except three political demands. This Conference also upgraded their demand for Union Territory to full-fledged statehood for more autonomy and political power and gave the nomenclature *Bodoland to* the proposed state. "However, 'Bodoland' is not meant for only the Bodos, but is merely a nomenclature of a tribal state including all the plains tribals of Assam. The non-tribals would also be guaranteed with all the constitutional rights in the proposed Bodoland" – thus asserted the ABSU communique in December 1988 that was signed by none other than late Upendra Brahma. Since then almost everyday, by masterly utilisation of pressure tactics, ABSU-BPAC continued to remain in the headlines and ultimately the Government of India had to initiate rounds of tripartite talks (at times appearing to be unending rounds) and then the much publicised three member panel on the *Bodoland* was constituted. Much money and Much abuse has already been visibly showered on this much -trumpeted three-member panel. Openly the ABSU-BPAC rejected it. The Government did not think it necessary to make the report public for the consideration of the concerned citizens. But then the back room experts got active openly to arrange for an accommodation for there calcitrant tribals from the plains of north-east. And now Saikia's promise not to allow division of Assam is *prima facie* ful-filled. ABSU-BPAC demand for *autonomy* too is apparently taken care of. And everything now must be 'quiet on the Western front'.

But is it so simple ? What will happen to the demand of the Koch-Rajbangshis ? Where is the guarantee that the questions raised in WHY SEPARATE STATE (November 1987) or the fifty-three questions and answers mentioned in DIVIDE ASSAM FIFTY-FIFTY (August 1987) will be taken care of by the proposed Bodoland Autonomous Council? Where is the political guarantee that the common Bodo youth will have no reason to be frustrated enough after the memorandum to follow and reorganise and reorient BSF on the lines of ULFA as was seen in Assam? The leadership of Bodoland movement have since long been talking about the enemy outside. What about the enemy within? If within the shortest possible time the leadership can not forge ahead with the toiling people cutting across tribal-non-tribal boundaries, the much publicised memorandum of settlement, will be hijacked from within. And neither Dispur nor Delhi, nor the caste Hindu Assamese can be blamed for that. Bodoland is, in fact on the threshold of a much bigger challenge today.

20

REORGANISATION OF THE HILL AREAS OF ASSAM
A Study of Karbi Anglong District

R.P. ATHPARIA

The Karbi Land

The Karbi Anglong District, formerly known as Mikir Hills, is located at the junction of the two geographically undemarcated segments of Assam popularly referred to as Upper Assam and Lower Assam. The district is divided into two parts-eastern and western. In between the eastern and western parts, the territories of Nowgong and North-Cachar intervene.

Till 1884, there was no administrative boundary of the Karbis. The 'Mikir Hills Tract' was constituted with the administrative boundary of Nowgong district by a notification under Assam Frontier Regulations 1884. This included the hilly tract where Karbi population was numerous. In 1893, a part of this tract was transferred to the then Sibsagar district, later adjoining district boundries were slighttly modified; and as a result the Mikir Hills area in 1913-1914 came within the districts of Nowgong and Sibsagar.

In 1935, the Karbis' inhabited areas were included in the provision of 'excluded' and 'partially excluded' areas as per section 92 of the Government of India Act, 1935. The policy of this Act was to keep the tribesmen administratively separate, perpetuating distrust of the non-tribal neighbours. There were some differences between an 'excluded' and partially excluded 'area. In regard to the 'excluded' areas, the Governor was required to exercise his function in his diseretion but in regard to a 'partially excluded' area, the Governor was couldseek the advice of the ministers. A discussion on a subject relating to the 'excluded' area was not possible in the assembly without Governor's permission.

The areas inhabited by the Karbis in the Khasi & Jantia Hills came fully under the provisions of 'excluded' area while the Karbi areas of Nowgong and Sibsagar districts were under the 'Partially Excluded' area (Bhattacharjee, 1986 :1). Mann and Mann (1986: 35) observe that the British felt that administration in far flung and interior tribal areas was difficult and therefore the isolation of the tribesmen became necessary. It resulted in keeping the tribesmen away from the neo-political life brought in by the Britishers.

It is observed that the political aspirations of the Karbis were largely mooted and developed especially in the 'partialy exculded' areas where the Karbis could assemble freely for political activity and discussion. It is to be noted here that the Karbi leaders in the 'thirties had emerged from this particular 'partially excluded' areas. The leaders of the time, namely, Samson Singh Inghti, Seng Bey and Khorsing Terang submitted a memorandum to the then Governor of Assam, Sir Robert Neil Reid in the year 1937 at Mhungdijwa demanding a separate hill district for the Karbis.

To mobilise public opinion for this purpose big conventions were held one at Kathalguri (Nowgong) in 1945 and another at Hawaipur (Diput) in 1947. The Hawaipur convention was largely attended by the Karbis from the then 'Mikir Hills Tract" and the adjoining areas. The Karbi-A-Darbar, a regional political forum, was formed in that meeting to organise and to intensify the movement on beter lines among the Karbis. In spite of all attempts, the Karbis failed to get a district for themselves in the British Government and the Indian national leaders were engaged in the country's freedom setting aside all local and internal political issues.

Karbis in Post-Independence Period

After independence, there was a strong feeling among the

hill people of Assam for regional autonomy and better status within the framework of the Constitution of India. The Government of India realised the critical situation and aspirations of the hill areas of Assam and wanted to look into the grievances and affairs of the tribal people, so that they might be able to participate in decision making processes and run the institutions according to their own genius. At the same time it was realised that these areas required a special type of government and certain degree of protection against the age-old exploitation by the plains people. In pursuance of this, an Advisory Committee was constituted by the Constituent Assembly of India. One of the sub-committee of Gopinath Bordoloi was known as North-East Frontier (Assam) Tribal and Excluded Area Sub-committee. This sub-Committee was popularly known as the Bordoloi Sub-Committee.

The recommendation of the Bordoloi Sub-Committee was incorporated in the Sixth Schedule to the Constitution of India. The idea behind the Sixth Schedule was to provide the tribal people with a simple and inexpensive administration of their own, so that they could safeguard their own customs and traditions and to provide them maximum autonomy in the management of their tribal affairs.

Steps were taken to constitute District Councils in all Autonomous districts of Assam. In 1952, the District Councils were constituted in all the hill districts except Naga Hills where the Naga National Council had boycotted the election and demanded complete independence.

The Karbi Anglong District formally known as Mikir Hills District Council, was set up on 23 June 1952 as per provision of the Sixth Schedule of the Constitution. In the beginning the district was combined with North-Cachar Hills and it was known as the United Mikir and North-Cachar Hill district. The district was formed on 17 November 1951. It was covering the areas of the Mikir Hills Tract and its contiguous portions from the districts of the then Nowgong, Sibsagar, United Khasi and Jaintia Hills and North Cachar Hills with an area of 15,237 sq. kms. Subsequently, the newly created district was divided into two sub-division, namely (i) North-Cachar Hills and (ii) Mikir Hills. By 2

February 1970 the sub-division of North Cachar Hills and Mikir Hills were turned into two separate full-fledged districts. Since then the Mikir Hills District has been a single administrative unit and has come to be called Karbi Anglong instead of Mikir Hills in October 1976. The present district is bounded by Nowgong and Golaghat districts on the north and north-east, on the south by Nagaland and North Cachar, on the west by the Jantia Hills. The total areas of the district is 10,332 sq. km.

Karbi's Attitude towards the Hill State Movement

In 1954, an idea for the formation of a separate hill state came to be mooted by a section of the hill tribals of Assam. The Karbis has also joined the issue for the hill state alongwith other hill leaders of the state. The State Reorganisation Commission under the chairmanship of Fazal Ali did not recommend the formation of the hill state. Since then the hill state movement grew in intensity and by the election of 1957 all the six Autonomous District Councils of Assam were under pressure to achieve the object of a hill states (Mathur, 1982:91). By that time, the Karbi-A-Darbar was in full control of the District Council in Diphu and it generally associated its policy with those of the ruling Congress Party at the national and state levels.

The Karbis did not participate actively in the hill state movement because, first, there was always an apprehension of the Christian domination in the hill state. Secondly, the Karbis felt that they had relatively greater alignment and closer ties with the greater Assamese society and they considered themselves to be basically a part of it. Thirdly, the Karbis had an inferiority complex in prospect of a self-government in the shape of the hill state which they thought might not be intellectually feasible and economically viable.

In this connection, it is worth mentioning the Pataskar Commission's decision on the official language of Assam. The Commission recommended Assamese as the official language of the State. In accordance with this, the Assamese language Act, 1960 came into being. This infuriated the hill leaders barring those of the Mikir Hills and the movement for hill state was intenified.

The Karbi-A-Darbar is a political party of the Karbis that accommodated in the traditional Karbi spirit, dissent of opinions. Accordingly, a section of the Darbaris began to behave in 1964 as opposition spokesmen who stood for, briefly, (i) Nagaland and Mikir Hills merger movements and (ii) Mikir and Khasi and Jaintia Hills merger movement.

To counter the opposition in the Darbar, a new body known as Riso-A-Darbar was formed in 1964. In fact, this new body was the creation of the section of Darbaris other than the dissidents. This was basically an orgnaisation of the youths, a group of people holding academics and modern outlook.

On Ist June, 1970, the State Government of Assam transferred the administrative powers of some development departments of the Karbi Anglong district to the District Council vide Government Notification No.AAP /95/ 70/36 dated 1.6.1970. The main idea of the State Government was to keep the Karbis aloof from the separatist movement of the Hill state which was in full swing in the districts of the United Khasi and Jantia Hills, the Garo Hills and the Mizo Hills. From June 1970, the services of all the district level officers, subordinate officers and staff working in the then Mikir Hills district were placed under the administrative control of the Mikir Hills District Council. The Karbi leaders received the government plan gladly although they disagreed on some points. The Karbis disagreed on the issue of note giving overall authority of the transferred departments to the District Council. The authority of the State Government continued even after the transfer of the departments.

The leaders of the Karbi-A-Darbar thought of improving the socio-economic condition of the people through the District Council, maintaining throughout the *status-quo* with regard to the traditional patterns of life. But they did not attach much importance to the emotional need for establishing a separate socio-ethnic identity felt by the youth. The difference of opinion between the old and the new gave birth to the emerging youth to rule the Karbis in the modern democratic field. The youths feel aggrieved for not being able to manage their own socio-political affairs according to their own will. A section of the youth began to feel a sense of subordination under the present set up of the Government of Assam. In many cases, the youths were not running parallel with the State Government. There was a demand of the youths for a separate state for asserting their political rights and privileges that got strengthened through massive victory of the youth in 1980 District Council election under the banner of the Autonomous State Demand Committee. This issue is a volatile one among the Karbis.

Conclusion

To sum up it can be said that the Karbis have passed through many socio-political changes and are still undergoing various phases of development that have come to be introduced by the District Council from time to time.

REFERENCES

1. Bhattacharjee, T. 1986, *Sociology of the Karbis,* Delhi, B.R Publishing Corporation.
2. P.R.G. Mathur, 1982, The Khasi Solidarity Movement, in K.S. Singh. *Tribal Movement in India,* Vol. I, Delhi, Manohar Publication, 197 p.
3. R.S. Mann. and K. Mann, 1986, Protective Legislations in British Tribal India *Bulletin of the Tribal Research Institute.* Guwahati., I-IV, 34-37.

21

TRIBAL POLICY AND CONSTITUTIONAL DEVELOPMENT OF ARUNACHAL PRADESH

J.N. CHOWDHURY

The twenty-seventh State of the Indian Federal Union, Arunachal Pradesh, provides an unique example of social and political transformation of a backward tribal area and its emergence into the modern world and modern political system within a pace of barely forty years. Indeed, the tranformation is almost breathtaking, if we bear in mind the historical legacy of colonial rule which treated the hinterland of India's extreme north-east as an 'excluded area'. In fact, it meant a non-regulated area ruled by summary legislation in the discretion of the Governor. In terms of summary legislation, the then Lt. Governor of Bengal was authorised to prescribe a line to be called *Inner Line* in each or any of the districts beyond which no British subjects of certain classes or foreign residents can pass without a license'. Thus came into existence the Inner Line Regulation of 1873 which laid down such lines 'in the districts of Kamrup and Goalpara towards Bhutan; in Darrang towards the Bhutiyas, Akas and Dafflas; in Lakhimpur towards the Daflas, Miris, Abors, Mishmis, Khamtis, Singphos and Nagas; in Sibsagar towards the Nagas'. The ostensible purpose of the Inner Line Regulation was to bring 'under stringent control the commercial relations of the British subjects with the Frontier Tribes' and to prevent encroachment 'of tea gardens beyond the fiscal limits of settled areas and lay down rules for the possession of land and property beyond this line'. The ulterior purpose was, however, different, and best expressed in the words of Colonel Shakespeare:

> "The gradual ejection of these people (tribes) from such areas as they had spread into gave the British officials their acquaintance with many tribes, none too easy to keep in subjection ..... the history of this part of the frontier is chequered during the succeeding decades until 1920, with troubles of varying degrees in intensity".

The above passage gives one an insight into the actual state of British relation with the tribes who were apt to consider the British rulers as usurpers, and were suspicious of British intentions towards the hills. Indeed they were in the habit of carrying out occasional raids into British regulated areas contiguous to the hills, which they considered their natural preserves. The British were obliged to despatch puntitive expeditions into the hills as situations demanded, 'with the object of destroying the culprit village' as a former Adviser to the Governor of Assam after Independence, put it.

To revert to the colonial rule, the British predicament has been very candidly expressed by Mr. A.W.H. Bentinck, a former Deputy Commissioner of Lakhimpur, who went along with the Abor Expedition of 1911-12, in the following passage:

> "It may be taken that those who visit a new tribe expecting to find an unpleasant savage will not be disappointed wherever they may go . . . it must be remembered that to the vast bulk of the people whom we visited, we were utter and mysterious strangers, and that our appearance, out habits, our methods, our designs were alike new and unintelligible to them."

The British response to this predicament was a policy

of segregation whereby the hill tribes were left alone insofar as they did not interfere with the peaceful possession of their empire in the plains of Assam. The state of colonial rule so far as it extended to the hills, has been put in a nut-shell by Lancelot Hare in 1910, in the following words:

> "We have an Inner Line and an Outer Line. Upto the Inner Line, we administer in the ordinary way. Between the Inner Line and the Outer Line we only administer politically. That is, our political officer exercises a very loose jurisdiction, and to prevent troubles with frontier tribes, passes are required for our subjects who want to cross the Inner Line."

In view of the situation in the hills as outlined above, however, briefly, it is necessary to take stock of the colonial legacy which the Government of Independent India inherited and very largely retained, in order to understand the full implications of the post-Independence transformation of the former Frontier Tracts, now Arunachal Pradesh.

Colonial Legacy

It shall be the endeavour to show in this paper that rapid and accelerated transformation of the former Frontier Tracts, described as 'The Hidden Land' by Ursula Graham Bower, a Botanist's wife, as late as 1953, was unrelated to any well-defined tribal policy but was entirely brought about by extraneous circumstances and geo-political compulsions. It has to be reckoned that a Communist Government had already been installed in China, which lost no time in reviving all the claims of imperial China to territories beyond her natural geographical borders. The British had neglected developing the frontier regions out of political expediency, though they had enough warning of Chinese threat to India's northern frontiers. In April 1912, Yuan Shikai, the President of the Chinese Republic, issued a declaration placing Tibet on the same footing as that on any other province of China. The British took alarm at the turn of events, and belatedly became aware of the threat posed by China to our northern borders. This precipitated the British into concluding the 1914 Convention with the Chinese and Tibetan plenipotentiaries attending, which defined the Indo-Tibetan boundary from the eastern frontier of Bhutan to the Isu Razi pass on the Irrawady-Salween water parting. This delimitation of the boundary later came to be known as the McMahon Line. The First World War intervened and the matter stood where it was, without the British taking any action to extend its administration into the hills. It was not until March 22, 1951, after the Constitution of India (1950) had come into force, that Indian Trade Agent at Yatung informed the Tibetan Foreign Bureau of the Government of India's intention of taking control of frontier areas right upto the McMahon Line. An Assistant Political Officer was posted at Tawang in 1952 in persuance of this decision. The following Year, the headquarters of the four frontier tracts were shifted from Sadiya to Tezu in the Mishmi Hills; from Pasighat to Along in Abor Hills; from Kimin to Zero in Subansiri; and from Charduar to Rupa in the sela Sub-Agency, later moved on to Bomdila.

Now, to revert to the question of Independent India's tribal policy with special reference to the frontier tracts, without mincing words, one may possibly say that the national Government failed to evolve an independent tribal policy, and practically continued with the colonial legacy. Most, if not all, of the provision of the Government of India Act, 1935, have been kept in place, including of course the Inner Line Act of 1873. The concepts of 'excluded' and 'partially excluded areas', first evolved during the debate on the recomendations of the Indian Statutory Commission (1928) were retained and incorporated in the Constitution *albeit* under different nomenclatures, namely, Part A and Part B Tribal Areas. It is an irony of history that the Indian National Congress which readily attributed the creation of 'the excluded' and 'partially excluded areas' as yet another British attempt to perpetuate segregation of the hills from the plains, did nothing either to do away with, or even partially modify, the concept after coming to power in 1947.

It would be interesting at this distance of time to refer to the reply of Shri Gopinath Bordoloi, Chairman of the Tribal Sub-Committee, appointed by the Constitent Assembly, to the debate on the tribal question. Reacting to the passionate pleas of Shri Brajeswar Prasad, a member from Bihar, Shri Rohini Kumar Choudhury and Shri Kuladhar Chaliha from Assam and Shri B. Das from Orissa for immediate integration of the tribal areas with the rest of the country, Shri Gopinath Bordoloi developed his arguments very much in tune with the British concepts of 'excluded' and 'partially excluded areas'. He sought to categorise the tribal population of the North-East India according to their respective material and social progress. In the first category he included the plains trials who were considered relatively advanced, the second category comprised hill tribals administered directly by the Governor of Assam (marked as 'excluded areas' in Government of India Act, 1935) and the third category related to hill people generally on the southern bank of the Brahmaputra proposed to be brought under the Sixth Schedule 'to be administered as autonomous groups'.

In the upshot of the whole debate, the Governor's discretionary powers in relation to Part Two of the Sixth Schedule (the North-East Frontier Tracts) were retained, though it is on record that Nehru objected to the discretionary power of the Governor to withhold extension of the State laws to the tribal areas within its jurisdiction. Interestingly it was Sir B.N. Rau, a member of the Indian Civil Service and trained in the British school of thought, who was associated with the drafting of the Indian Constitution, pleaded for the retention of the Governor's discretionary powers. Even the much vaunted Sixth Schedule was no innovation. In fact, on the basis of an amendment moved by Sir Samuel Hoars in the British Parliament, the Sixth Schedule was dropped from the final Government of India Act, 1935, on the specious plea that the list of 'excluded' and 'partially excluded areas' proposed to be included in the Sixth Schedule of the Government of India Bill 1935, was not comprehensive enough. Instead, the then British Government of India was authorised to declare any area to be clashed as 'excluded and partially excluded areas by an executive order, subject to approval of the British Parliament within six months of its promulgation. It was this very provision which was taken over, and incorporated in Article 342 of the Indian Constitution 1950, which authorises the President of India to declare certain areas and certain people as Scheduled Areas and Scheduled Tribes on the basis of certain guidelines, as prescribed. The failure of the Constitution to define its own concept of a 'Tribe' left the question wide open, leading to a growing clamour among all kinds of people for the label of 'Tribal'. Dr. Verrier Elwin was to write many years later:

> "We must fight the danger of pauperization, the creation of a special class called 'tribal' which will want to be labelled 'backward' in order to get material benefit from the government. Unintelligent benevolence can be as great a danger as intelligent exploitation."

Nehru and Elwin vis-a-vis Tribal Policy

It is time now to contend and dispel a myth which marked out Nehru and Elvin as the 'architects of India's tribal policy'. It is historically and chronologically wrong to subscribe to, and perpetuate this myth. It is, therefore, necessary and important to discuss the roles played by Nehru and for that matter Verrier Elwin, in the implementation of India's so-called tribal policy. It should be noted, in this connection that Nehru's participation and intervention during the debate on the tribal question in the Constituent. Assembly was very limited, and not of great moment Understanding Nehru's mind was occupied with more momentous policy matters other than tribal policy. Nehru got the time to formulate his idea on tribal administration, for the first time, in his address to the opening session of the Scheduled Tribes and Scheduled Areas Conference held in New Delhi in June 1952, that is after the Constitution had come into being. Nehru's humility was remarkable and very touching. To quote:

> "My ideas were not clear at all, but I felt that we should avoid two extreme course: one was to keep them as anthropoligical specimens for study; and the other was to allow them to be engulfed by the masses of Indian humanity. These reactions were instinctive and not based on any knowledge or experience."

It would be true to say that Nehru's ideas grew in stature with the passage of time, and he was able to enunciate his now famous Five Principles of tribal administration in his Foreword to the second edition of Dr. Verrier Elwin's Book *A Philosophy for NEFA* (1959), the first edition of which, much more slender volume, had been published in 1957. It may be pointed out here that these principles were intended to be guidlines for implementation of the Tribal Policy Frame Work already laid down by the Constitution. As for Dr. Verrier Elwin, he was nowhere in the picture, and as he was not a member of the Constituent Assembly, there never was any question of his influencing the debate on the tribal question. Elwin's association with the working of the Government dates back to sometime in 1953 when he was invited to sit on a Committee to select the candidates for the new cadre of the Indian Frontier Administrative Service. It was not until December 31st 1953, Elwin reached Shillong to take over, for the first time, a government assignment as Honorary Adviser for Tribal Affairs for NEFA at the instance of Prime Minister, Nehru.

Elwin's response to the extravagant charges levelled against him by the redoubtable Dr. Ram Manohar Lohia, should tell its own story:

> "He (Dr Lohia) seems to be under the impression that I was responsible for the Inner Line which encloses a number of hill areas of Assam and cannot be passed without a permit. But the Inner Line was established in 1873, and though I realize that I am getting on a bit in years, I actually was not even born then."

If there were no roads in erstwhile NEFA when the

Chinese mounted their massive attack across our northern borders, why, of course, Dr. Elwin and his policy were to be blamed! It was never reckoned that from 1951 to 1962 was too short a time to wish for a network of roads connecting the remotest parts of the territory. As stated earlier, it was only in 1951 the Government of India notified its intention of taking control of the forward areas. The British left no roads or 'core services' in the interior of the hills. These facts are not mentioned to defend either Nehru or for that matter Dr. Elwin's so-called policy. Indeed, the contention is that the so-called tribal policy was never at stake at any time and that decisions were taken at the centre as dictated by political expediency and extraneous considerations. Dr. Elwin's evidence on this:

> "Many of the matters which we used to debate so eagerly have been put completely out of date as a result of one major circumstances – that the whole of India, including tribal India, will be covered by Community Development Blocks by 1963. This is a decision, this is going to happen, and it is, therefore meaningless to discuss whether it is desirable to bring the tribes into the stream of modern civilization or whether it is good or bad to open up their country."

As would be seen, Dr. Elwin expressed himself against the Central Government's decision to introduce Panchayati Raj in erstwhile NEFA at a later stage. Elwin's policy, if there was one, did not matter at all in the course of government decisions.

So, the question once again is whether the National Government did have a significant tribal policy apart from the colonial legacy. To quote Dr. Sibsanikinkar Chaube here:

> "The Bardoloi Sub-Committee found the level of consciousness among the people very low and did not recommend franchise rights for them, and the Constitution (Removal of Difficulties) Orders VII and VIII withheld from NEFA the right of representation to Assam and Central Legislature"

The Coming of the Constitution (1950) and the March of Events

Since, however, the Constitution (1950) came into force, the Government of India was forced to take political decisions impelled by extraneous considerations, and not in persuance of any tribal policy. But even before the Constitution came into being, the Bardoloi Committee, already referred to, made the following recommendation:

> "We recommend that when the Central Government which now administers these areas (and which consider it should continue to do with the Government of Assam as its agent) is of the view that the administration has been satisfactorily established over a sufficiently wide area, the Government of Assam should take over the area by the strength of a notification."

While the first part of the recommendation was realized by the India Provisional Constitution Order of 1947, the second part of the recommendation, namely, the assumption of the administration of the territory by the Assam Government at a future date, was never to be realised. Two American researchers Dr. Margaret W. Fisher and Dr. Leo E. Rose outlined the political situation as it obtained following the transfer of powers, as follows:

> "The Assam Government, sorely beset by the consequences of the partition of Bengal, which virtually isolated Assam from the rest of India, apparently felt itself in no position to make any basic change in the NEFA administration."

But even more momentous political consideration weighed with the Government of India to retain the administration of the territory under its own care. The precipitate recognition by India of Tibet as an autonomous region of China had entirely changed the geo-political character of our international border in the north of the region. The

Japanese conquest of Burma in the Second World War and its subsequent attempted thrust into Assam across present Nagaland, had already thrown into focus the vulnerability of our northern frontiers. Now the spectre of Communist China with it's extravagant territorial claims loomed ever larger across our northern horizon. The threat of China's invasion of Tibet seemed imminent ever since late 1949. All these considerations apparently prompted the Government of India to appoint the External Affairs Ministry to take over, and act as the agency for administration of the territory, a measure which in itself was highly anomalous. On January 26, 1950 an Adviser to the Governor of Assam was appointed with direct charge of the administration of the North-East Frontier Tracts. After separation of this Secretariat in June 1950 from the Secretariat of the Tribal Affairs Department of the Government of Assam, the civil servants of the Assam cadre were quickly replaced

Though the public opinion in Assam was greatly agitated over the reported appointment of a Special Commissioner for the area early in 1953 as a deliberate attempt at 'dismemberment of Assam' (the frontier tracts constitutionally formed a part of Assam), the more momentous reorganization of the region under the North-East Frontier (Administration) Regulation, 1954 which inaugurated a full-scale and integrated administration of the area under what was called North-East Frontier Agency-NEFA for short – passed off relatively unnoticed. This one measure sealed off forever any future prospect of integration of the region with Assam. As a direct consequence of this Reorganization, the whole area was divided into six frontier divisions, namely, Kameng, Subansiri, Siang, Lohit, Tirap and Tuensang Frontier Divisions. The last named division was however, short-lived as under the State reorganization Commission, the Naga Hills and Tuensang Area (formerly constituting Part 'A' and Part 'B' Tribal Areas respectively) was formed into one unit, and constituted as Part 'B' Tribal Areas within Assam on December 1, 1957.

The narrative of the external compulsions which persuaded the Government of India to take one political decision after another in relation to the frontier tracts is pursued here. India's post-haste recognition of China's suzerainty over Tibat (1950), failed to assuage Communist China's ambitions and expansionist design. The first calculated assault on India by China, was the publication by 'China Pictorial' on July 1958, of a map showing great chunk of Indian territory as within China. But troubles of various kinds were brewing ever since 1956, culminating in the open revolt of Tibetan people and its ruthless suppression by China in 1959. The Dalai Lama was forced to flee the country, and seek asylum in India. The subsequent invasion of Indian territory by China (October 20, 1962) is too recent a history to need recapitulation. But one may profitably fall back on the description of the ominous foreboding of imminent crisis as given by Dr. Fisher and Dr. Rose:

> "A further complication, which quickly grew in importance, was the imminent threat of a Communist Chinese invasion of Tibet, repeatedly forecast by Peking since 1949. The strategic importance of NEFA, which earlier impressed itself upon the British Government of India during World War II, was thus dramatized in unmistakable terms. The Government of India decided, as the British had done in 1943, that it was imperative to bring the entire north-eastern frontier under direct administration. *It was obvious, under existing conditions, that the Central Government was the only agency with resources and capacity to undertake this difficult and delicate task"*............

It will possibly bear repetition here that Chinese incursion was not a sudden development. Reports of Chinese troops movement along the other side of India's northern border were continuously pouring in since 1960. George Patterson announced in New Delhi about this time that China has amased along the frontiers of Sikkim and Bhutan an estimated eight divisions of Chinese troops. The rest, of course, is history.[3]

It may incidentally be mentioned here that in the wake of the Chinese aggression and the discomfiture of the

Indian Army which was caught unawares, the media and political leaders like Ram Monahar Lohia and a Member of Parliament from Assam like Hem Barua, directed their attack against what they called Dr. Elwin's philosophy. The debacle was squarely blamed on his so-called policy of isolation which prompted Prime Minister Nehru to come out in defence of the Inner-Line and the policy in general on December 17, 1963, in the Rajya Sabha. The attack was of course misplaced, as the tribal policy was never seriously at issue at any time. If there was any policy, it could be conveniently superseded by executive order or political decision as expediency demanded.

In the face of fresh clamour for integration of NEFA with Assam, further reorganization of the administrative set-up took place in 1965 marking the independent status of NEFA Administration and as an indication of further move away from its constitutional link with Assam. The North-East Frontier Agency was transferred from the charge of the External Affairs Ministry to that of the Home Ministry on August 1, 1965. On December 1 of the same year the Frontier Divisions were redesignated as districts, namely, Kameng, Subansiri, Siang, Lohit and Tirap districts respectively. Correspondingly, the political officers were redesignated as Deputy Commissioners. The reorganization of the administrative set-up left no doubt as to the direction in which the political development of the territory was moving.

An even more controversial development was in the offing. The appointment of a Commission called Ering Commission after Mr. Daying Ering belonging to the Adi tribe and a Deputy Minister under the Central Government, was announced on April 11, 1964 by the then *Prime Minister Lal Bahadur Shastri.* Curiously enough, the Commission headed by a Tribal himself, recommended a *Panchayati Raj* for the territory, a totally foreign concept, known to have been opposed by Dr. Verrier Elwin who saw in it a departure from the traditional tribal councils. The opposition was however, overruled and North-East Frontier Agency *Panchayati Raj* Regulation of 1967 introduced a four-tier scheme of administration with an Agency

Council at the apex. It is not necessary for this purpose to go into the details of the scheme here.

Events, since the introduction of the *Panchayati Raj*, moved with break-neck speed. Speculations and rumours were already afloat about an early possiblity of reorganization of the entire administrative contour of the North-eastern region as a whole. Nagaland had already broken away, and was constituted into a separate state in 1963. The hill areas of the former united Assam state were in turmoil. The Hill State movement spearheaded by the Khasi & Jaintia leaders with support by the Garos was gathering momentum. The Mizos had already indicated their intention to go their own way. No such movement was, however, evident yet in NEFA except for the fact that a section of students of the Jawahar Lal Nehru College at Pasighat staged a demonstration in favour of Hindi and English in opposition to the Assamese medium. If, however, one is to take the lead of Dr. Shivanikinkar Chaube, high-ups in the NEFA administration were already talking of the prospect of NEFA being converted into an Union Territory in the late sixties in the fact of the commitment of the Government of India to the integration of the territory with Assam. Incidentally note should also be taken here that early in 1971 the Agency Council decided in favour of the change of nomenclature of NEFA to that of Arunachal Pradesh.

Dr. Chaube contends that it was during the fourth meeting of the Agency Council that the members were for the first time taken into confidence about the new thinking of the Central Government on fresh reorganization of the region, hinting at granting of Union Territory status to the North-East Frontier Agency. In support of his contention that the Agency Council was taken by surprise over the proposed change of status, Dr. Chaube extracted the following paragraph from a report published in *NEFA Information* of August, 1971:

> "In the light of the proposal the members had a brief discussion. The consesus of opinion was that the matter being of great importance having political implica-

> tions, the proposal should be discussed thread-bare by the Panchayat institutions at different levels . . . It was accordingly decided that the proposal should be discussed in detail at the earliest opportunity and a decision as to the pattern of administration most suitable to NEFA would be taken . . . To facilitate a fruitful discussion on the proposal the Agency Council members were briefed about the pattern of administration obtaining in Union Territories."

The above passage does reflect on the fact that members of the Agency Council were not yet prepared for a sweeping change of status and that it was a decision not of their own asking, but imposed on them. The rest of the story should not detain one for long, and should be told very briefly.

The North-Eastern Areas (Reorganization) Act, 1971, came handy to the Government of India to convert NEFA into an Union Territory under the Chief Commissioner and the constitutional separation of NEFA from Assam was thus formalized. The Agency Council was converted to a Pradesh Council in 1971, and raised to the status of a Provisional Legislature in 1975. At the instance of the Chief Commissioner, Mr. K.A.A. Raja, a panel of five counsellors appointed previously, was constituted into the provisional council of Ministers with Mr. Prem Khandu Thungon, belonging to the Sherdukpen community from the Kameng district, as the first Chief Minister. The first general election on the basis of adult franchise, to the Union Territory Legislature was held in February 1978. The post of Chief Commissioner was elevated to that of the Lieutenant Governor. The first fully elected government of Arunachal Pradesh was ushered in on 14 March 1978. Interestingly within a short span of hardly two years, the well-known pattern of Indian politics including floor-crossing by members and the political game of topling government, was enacted successfully in the young Union Territory. The first elected government headed by Mr. Thungon bowed out of office within barely a year of assuming power on the 6 September 1979 through defection in the rank. Mr. Tomo

Riba representing the Peoples' Party of Arunachal who took office on 6 September 1979, went the same way, having been deserted by party men, within two months. Arunachal then witnessed a short spell of President's rules until it went to mid-term poll in January 1960 with the rest of the country. A congress (I) Ministry headed by Mr. Geogong Apang was installed in January 1980. Arunachal had since seen change of elected governments in quick succession, the present government being the fourth in the series, also headed by Mr. Geogong Apang. The granduation of the Union Territory to full statehood was only a matter of time and developments across the border centring on a disputed stretch of land quickened the pace of transformation. Arunachal became a full state in 1987 and participated in the general election with the rest of the country in November, 1989. The story of Arunachal Pradesh is thus an unique example of transformation of a backward area treated as an 'excluded area' by the colonial rulers within a little over three decades, solely prompted by political considerations, and not in persuance of any tribal policy.

Conclusion

The unique feature of this trransformation was this, that it was achieved within the parameter of the British policy of segregation as represented by the *Inner Line*. It will possibly bear reiteration that the so-called national tribal policy did not signify any major departure from the colonial legacy. As a result of political and constitutional developments within the precints of a policy of isolation and exclusive ethnic identity, instead of bringing the tribal states closer to the main stream of national polity, has led to greater intolerance of so-called outsiders who are nevertheless Indian citizens. Even the idea of tribal and caste reservation which has developed into a most controversial issue in Indian politics today can be directly traced to the communal award by which the colonial rulers sought to divide Indian people on the basis of caste, creed and ethnicity. All that the national government and the policy makers have succeeded in doing is to improve upon this very concept and widen its scope to include ever increasing areas of Indian masses, instead of looking at the whole problem from the single criterion of national development. Towards the end of his career, Dr. Varrier Elwin was to write as follows:

> "The twenty million semi-civilized aborginals will have to take their chance with the rest of population. It is evident that there is little possiblity of protecting them, although locally it may often be possible to ameliorate their lot by special treatment. It would, however, be deplorable, if yet another minority community which would clamour for special representation, weightage, a percentage of government posts, were to be created. The twenty million aboriginals need what all village India needs – freedom, prosperity, good education, medicine, a new system of agriculture and a fair deal under industrialization."

As another eminent social scientist, A.R. Desai, has pointed out, the policy of reservation and special privileges in the name of protection of minority rights has led to a special type of stratification leading to the emergence of a small 'vocal' 'richer', 'property owning', and 'privileged minority section' and reducing the bulk of population to toiling and exploited classes within their own community.

To conclude here is Dr. Desai's observation which is very much in tune with Dr. Elwin's remarks as quoted above:

> "The fundamental problems of the tribal population are economic-political. They are problems such as security of job, a decent standard of living, easy accessibility to the acquisition of education which can enable them to decide what customs, what rituals and what aesthetic cultural elements they should retain, eliminate or absorb from their culture and various others."

SELECTED READINGS

Bower Ursula Graham, *The Hidden Land* (1953).

Chaube, Shibani K., *Hill Politics in North-East India* (1973).

Dalton E.T., *Descriptive Ethnology of Bengal* (1872).

Desai, A.R., Tribes in Transition (In *Tribe Caste and Religion of India*, ed. by Romesh Thapar, (1977).

Elwin Verrier, *The Tribal World of Verrier Elwin* (1964)

Elwin Verrier, Issue in Tribal Policy Making (in *Tribe Caste and Religion of India*, ed. by Romesh Thapar.

Hansaria B.L., *Sixth Schedule to the Constitution of India - A Study* (1983).

Mackenzie A., *History of the Relations of the Government with the Hill Tribes of the North-East Frontier of Bengal* (1884).

Nehru Jawaharlal, Foreward to *A Philosophy for NEFA* by Verrier Elwin (1957).

Nehru Jawaharlal, *The Tribal Folk (in the Tribal People of India*, Publication Division, (1973).

RoseLeo, E. and Margaret, W. Fisher, *The North-East Frontier Agency* (1967).

Robert, Reid (Sir), *History of the Frontier Areas Bordering on Assam* (1942).

Rustomji N.K., *Adivasis*, 1956, (also vide Leo Ross and Margaret W. Fisher, *The North-East Frontier Agency*, (1967).

Shakespeare, L.W., *History of Assam Rifles* (1929).

Venkata Rao, V., *A Century of Tribal Politics in North-East India*, 1874 - 1947 (1976).

22

REORGANIZATION OF NORTH-EAST INDIA

Process, Problems and Prospects

(An Analysis in the Context of Arunachal Pradesh)

M.C. BEHERA

Conflicts, tensions and separatism are as much internal configurations on mental plane as integration and solidarity. The former sustains on the existence of apparent diversities in the form of divergent ethnic groups and sub-groups, languages/ dialects, beliefs and faiths and environmental conditions; while the latter is an ideological concept of abstract dimension seeking justification in materialistic necessity. At a point of time, the former stands clear and dominant, but the latter, being a latent factor, is beyond mass comprehension. Parochialism exploits apparent diversities to its benefit while latent force of integration remains dormant during the period. to counter-balance the onslaught of separatism. After a time, the need for integration evolves or the movement becomes weak within inconsistent shock waves emanating from separatist forces. But against the backdrop of present global scenario, it would be unwise to allow such movements to roll on unchecked. Foreign hands are more likely to take advantage of it. The situation must be .tackled within the national perspective. Unfortunately, such endeavours mostly prove to be short lasting, because solution is sought on the apparent basis of the movement on the surface without going deep down the problems.

Re-organisation of North-East India as an attept to ease off tension and occurrence of more tensions in later periods may be viewed on the basis of above postulates.

This is unconventional attampt for the study of the problem within the academic premise, without following any guidelines an attempt is made on the basis of observation in the field, to discuss the trend of sporadic occurrences in the hitherto peacefull and of Arunachal Pradesh with reference to factors underlying the reorganisation scenario. Reference is made to the colonial period to trace the development of separatist tendency which magnified in post independence period.

The solution to insurgent activities in the region after independence was most conveniently conceived in the reorganisation of states without giving due consideration to historical perspectives of the problem. The cause for reorganisation was itself wrongly identified in the demands of the interest groups and this has acted as a backdrop to recent insurgencies.

Prior to the British colonial rule, the multitudinous tribal communities of the north-east India were brought within the archaic state process basically through domination, conquest and occupation by more powerful power-centres represented by the Ahoms, the Manipuris, the Burmese, the Ahoms had never incorporated the hill regions into their territory. The region also never succumbed to the pressures of the outside power-centre and the concept of nation state did not develop then, because the pre-condition of it in the form of capitalist mode of production was non-existent in the sub-continent. Before the capitalist mode of production could evolve, the colonial rule was imposed and the history could not take its natural course. The characteristic British colonial policy of exclusion, partial exclusion and non-interference in dealing with the tribals served their very purpose of minimum administrative expense, tribal insulation from people of plains and at the same time their effective control over hill people. The imposed policy of isolation and deliberate intention to encourage continuation of tradition helped maintaining separate entity through existing ethno-lingual diversities within veried environmental conditions though the hill sections were incorporated in the province of Assam. At the same time, the whimsical administrative divisions compartmentalised different major ethnic sub-groups which strengthened their superficial sense of independence.

The economic interest of the British sought its fulfilment through introduction of plantation industries in Assam which resulted into migration of tribal population from the north-east part of Chota Nagpur, Bengal and Orissa (in 1840s) as indentured labour and in the development of transport and communication. Inspite of isolation, the hill people of the periphery were exposed to development taking place in the zone of intensive political and economic activities. Recognition of traditional tribal institutions by the British and colonial administrative measures brought them nearer to the new system in the valleys. Their hopes and aspirations assumed new dimension and different interest groups emerged therefrom. Divergent interests were exposed in different ways in their demands for special status. This development of pre-independence period gathered monentum after independence seeking justification in the ethno-lingual diversities and separate British relations with them. Such attitude sustained on the post-independence liberal attitude towards them especially through the Sixth Schedule of the Constitution.

The benefit of development measures introduced after independence percolated through different layers of socio-economic strata of the region in varying degrees thereby creating inequalities between groups and localities. Newly emerged aspirations got crushed within the then spatial arrangement of administration. The interest groups exploited the ethno-lingual identity for the purpose and gave shape to the movement.

The situation of insurgency was aggravated by the language policy of the then Government of Assam in 1960. Nagaland wrenched away from the Assam Province as a full fledged state in 1963. Meghalaya consisting of Garo, Khasi and Jaintia Hill became an autonomous unit in 1969 and attained statehood in 1972.

The same year Lushai Hills or Mizoram was elevated to the status of Union Territory from a district of Assam. The NEFA was designated as Arunachal Pradesh and became a Union Territory in 1972. Subsequently, Mizoram and Arunachal Pradesh became full-fledged states in 1987. The princely states of Manipur and Tripura which joined Indian Union in 1949 was placed under the administration of the Chief Commissioner, then upgraded to Union Territories and finally attained statehood in 1972.

The region prior to independence was divided into Assam consisting of Garo, Khasi and Jaintia Hills, North Cachar and Mikir Hills, the Naga Hills, the Lushai Hills; the North-Eastern Frontier Tracts and the territories of Manipur and Tripura. But after independence the region had undergone many changes till reorganisation into seven states, namely, Arunachal Pradesh, Assam, Manipur, Meghalaya, Mizoram, Nagaland and Tripura.

Plausible causes advanced in explaining tribal insurgency centre around the orthodox views comprising political domination of the valley over the hills, indifference towards economic development of the tribals and many others floating on the surface. But these are too simplified pursuits of insignificance and are more symptoms. Centuries old isolation, conspicuous absence of socio-economic infrastructure, absence of internal dynamics of change in the tribal society to adopt and appreciate modern line of development, lack of knowledge with regard to initial plan perspectives by the planners of the tribal areas where primitive production relations were predominant, and shortage of human capital acted and interacted to check the diffusion of benefit on an equal scale over the region. And this inevitably was exploited to a large extent by the interest groups to their advantage.

The ethno-lingual divergency should not have been taken as the basis of conferring political status though it has been the yard stick since independence. In the north-east region if this yard-stick is further adopted and used then the whole region will be ramified into a conglomeration of a few households in the name of independent political units, because the area is occupied by many ethno-lingual groups and sub-groups. In Arunachal Pradesh, there are atleast 26 major tribes with more than 100 sub-tribes, each proud of its heritage and culture. Assam state is inhabited by Assamese, both Ahoms and non-Ahoms, Bodo Kachari groups and sub-groups and also immigrants.

When the ethno-lingual identity is to be taken into consideration for conferring independent political status to bring the people nearer to administration and to involve them in the process of development, would it not amount to flaring up the aspirations of the ambitious interest groups, who are deprived of enjoying political power under the existing situation. Besides, these interest groups are bound to exploit the apparent differences and to organise movements thereby reinforcing instability in the region?

Though the movements diplay opposing trends in the form of demands for separate political entities like the Chin unification L.C movement of Manipur under the banner of the Chin Union in 1979, Hmar National Union demand for a separate administrative unit, the Zomi National Congress's plan for Zoram, demand for autonomy by the Karbis, movement of Paite National Council, insurgency in Tripura between Tripurites and immigrants, demand by the All Tribal Student's Union of Manipur; or unification of the region like the movements by the Brachin National Union, the movement for a greater Assam, the motive remains the same; to enjoy more political power by exploiting the existing situation.

The soft stand taken by the Centre, towards such movements in states with opposition Government, aggravates the situation further. Moreover, clandestine support of other political parties or non-chalant attitude to such movements makes the situation worse. What could be even worse is when political status is conferred on such insurgent groups. They face insufficient resource base to fulfil their perceptible aspirations and twist the problem to a different angle and then accuse the Centre of step-motherly treatment. A large portion of the central assistance is spent on establishment rather than on developmental work. Small political units without resource base have to compromise with investment of huge portion of the state revenue on establishment heads and a small portion on development activities thereby perpetuating general backwardness for a longer period. Of course, some achievement is made in the spatial order but inequality accentuates within. This paves roads for frustration and further tension.

II

The creation of Arunachal Pradesh dates back to the introduction of Inner Line in 1875 by the British Government. It acquired an identity of its own for the first time in 1914 when some tribal areas were separated from the then Darrang and Lakhimpur districts of the province of Assam to form the North-East Frontier Tract. In 1954, the North-East Frontier Tract was designated as North-East FrontierAgency and the administrative responsibility was vested with the Ministry of External Affairs which again shifted to the Ministry of Home Affairs of the Government of India in 1965. In 1972, the Agency was elevated to the status of Union Territory and was designated as Arunachal Pradesh. Finally, it attained statehood on 20th February 1987.

The Constitutional development of Arunachal Pradesh after independence has not been the outcome of insurgency by people of the territory as has been in most of other states in the region. Movements and Military insurgency by different ethno-lingual groups in other parts of the region, Nehru's concern about the people of NEFA and its strategic location might have guided the Centre to confer gradual political concessions before the people demanded them. Such timely action has saved the territory from armed insurgency.

Unlike the People of Naga hills and Lushai hills, the people of Arunachal Pradesh are divided many times more into ethno-lingual groups and sub-groups with varied level of problems. Missionary activity had not penetrated into the territory. The existing economic culture type could not develop a common base for demanding more power than conferred. The territory evolved gradually into a full-fledged state peacefully with remarkable progress.

Presently, it is observed that the area is displaying the characteristics of a tension zone. Development activities after independence has brought about socio-economic changes in a spatial order. State Domestic Product at constant prices has increased by about 209 per cent in 1985-86 over the base year prices of 1970-71. Literacy percentage has increased from a negligible figure in 1947 to 41.59 per cent in 1991. Diversification of the economy is noticed in 34.04 per cent (1991 provisional figures) of working population engaged in non-agricultural activities. Production of food grains has been recorded at 201.155 MT in 1988-89. Introduction of plantation industries (Pasighat, Namsai-Chowkham area: Tipinis at Ziro), establishment of forest and agro-based industries, development of tertiary sectors in the area, reflect a positive trend in production relations as compared to pre-independence primitive mode of production.

The pace of development has changed the materialistic outlook of the People. Different interest-groups have been emerging. People have acquired new wants and have nourished new hopes and aspirations. Time is not very far when they will exploit tenaciously apparent diversities in order to fulfil their aspirations. In fact, the sporadic occurrences in a recent years are bearing such under currents which, if not checked judiciously, will more likely create a tension zone as in other parts of the North-East Region.

The developmental activities have not equally benefited the people who had almost an identical socio-economic level before introduction of plan programmes in the territory. Different studies reveal inter and intra tribe inequalities of the area. Presently, people have started perceiving such differences and many have been found expressing the incompatibility of their aspirations with the existing system. Most of the people observe that those who participate in active politics are placed on the higher rung of the ladder of development. Formation of PPA in April 1977, its merging with Janata Dal and then in the ruling party; formation of innumerable organisations and associations at tribe and sub-tribe level, district and block level; reports of violence in Panchayat elections in 1992 even though for the first time secret ballots were used, dissatisfaction among ruling party, M.L.A.'s against present state leadership- all but reflect the motive of immediate material gain through direct involvement in power politics. The mushroom growth of youth and student organisations shows an unhealthy tradition and trend of perpetuating diversities in the name of preserving identity. When their achievement falls short of their aspirations then the only course left for them is to resort to movements of one type or the other, because they are no longer found evincing interest in other fields so tenaciously.

The undertone of regional aspect was felt when Shri K.Krong, after being dropped from Apang Ministry in 1988; changed party loyality and tried to raise the issue of backwardness of Tirap, Changlang, Lohit and Dibang Valley districts as a means to fulfil his aspirations. Of course, the situation was perhaps not ripe to give impetus to the issue but more likely the future may. For such an undercurrent is felt fluttering the dove-cote. Bank robbery in the capital complex, existence of organisations like UPVA and ULVA portend future course of action by youth with unfulfilled aspirations.

The Khampti-Mishmee conflict in February 1984, the Nishi-Apatani violence in November '92 (Tipinis issue) over demarcation of communal land reflect the emergence of ethno-groups in the territory. Nascent unemployment and growing ill-feeling towards the presence of non-Arunachal employees point to another dimension of tension. Within various communities clever persons have been accumulating wealth in the form of landed property by twisting traditional law to their advantage because economic incentives to such persons have grown stronger compared to other members of the community. New elite groups without traditional base have been emerging in the traditional chieftainship communities as an opposing force against those with traditional base. As a result, there is tension brewing between the two groups in such communities.

Plan approach for balanced development with quality improvement in human resources will go a long way in narrowing down the gap of inequalities. Favourable conditions ought to be created for mass participation in the state and national level activities. Spatial arrangement of labour intensive undertakings will play greater role in bringing about inter-tribal co-ordination.

The future peace and prosperity of the territory depend on the present planning to counter emerging divisive forces.

REFERENCES

Arunachal Pradesh, 1980-90. A Decade of Achivements 1980-90. Information and Public Relations Department, Govt. of Arunachal Pradesh Naharlagun.

Behera, M.C. 1992. *A Study of Socio-Economic Development of the Khampti Tribe of Lohit district of Arunachal Pradesh during plan period.* (Thesis submitted to Utkal University on 29th October '92 for the award of Ph.D. degree.

Brass Paul, R. 1992. *Ethnicity and Nationalism : Theory and Comparison,* Sage Publications.

Chaube, S.K. 1975, *Hill Politics in North-East India,* Orient Longman.

Das, G. 1992. Structural Change in the Economy of Arunachal Pradesh in the *Journal of NEICSSR,* Shillong, October, 1992.

Gopal Krishanan R. 1990. *Ideology, Autonomy and Integration in the North-East India* (Issues in Political Geography) Omsons Publication.

Roy, A.K. 1991. Ethnicity and Polity Alternatives: A North-Eastern Experience in the *Journal of NEICSSR,* Shillong, April, 1991.

23

POLITICAL AND CONSTITUTIONAL DEVELOPMENT IN NAGALAND

R.P. SINGH

Introduction

Federal reorganisation in the Indian context has posed two questions at the end of the twentieth century. First, the concept of linguistic states that the fathers of the Indian Constitution had propounded could not go unchallenged.The Assam Official Language Act, 1960 proved to be a necessary evil and the consequent political developments in the Assam hills impelled the Government to soften their stand on language for the tribal areas, so that English, Hindi or even tribal language were accepted as the languages for the hills. The other question was a typical secessionist trend in the hills. Nagaland provided an epic example in this regard. These two questions were faced by Assam in the post-independence period.

So far as the Naga Hills was concerned, the political-administrative issues became quite sensational at the time of Independence in 1947 and after. The Naga Hills became the hot-bed of politics. The political trends were, however, not linear, but the militancy factor in the Naga politics made it a centre of attention not only to the administrators and politicians but also to the academicians.

Against this background, the present study aims to examine in brief the politico-constitutional development in the Naga Hills from 1947 onwards, of course with its background, leading to its emergence as a full-fledged State of the Indian Union. The study also emphasises the geo-economic and strategic viability of the State of Nagaland.

Political Development : Pan Tribal Unification

The Naga resistance to any political change may be traced back to the year 1928, when a small gathering of Naga leaders at the Naga Club, Kohima, conveyed their disinclination for any political reforms to the Simon Commission, which was at that time touring India to gather public opinion on the subject.

With the formation of Lotha Tribal Council in 1923 started the formation of political organisation among the Nagas, of course on the individual tribal basis. Ao Nagas formed a similar council in 1928, and other Naga tribes too organised tribal councils by the mid-forties. Towards the close of British rule in India, the Deputy Commissioner of Naga Hills, C.R. Pawsey, formed Naga Hills District Tribal Council in 1945 with intention of uniting the Nagas, which transformed itself into Naga National Council in 1946, the first and the only political organisation of the Nagas at that time. It aimed to fulfil the social aspirations of the Nagas and their welfare. Later on it emerged as the most powerful political organisation of the Nagas.

At the time of Independence in 1947, the political development in Naga Hills moved into two opposite directions. One was under the control of the militant wing of the Naga National Council, which at one extreme demanded full sovereignty. On the other hand, their moderate section was looking for a viable solution by constitutional means. The nine-point understanding concluded between the Naga National Council and Assam Governor Akbar Hyderi at Kohima in June 1947 came up at this hour as a conflict management mechanism. This understanding stipulated for a 10-year association of the Nagas with India, after which they will be free to decide their own fate. The understanding invited mixed reaction.

After promulgation of the Indian Constitution in 1950,

the provisions of the Hyderi Understanding were inserted in the Sixth Schedule, but the Naga National Council charged the Government its defiance and embarked upon a programme of mass agitation and open rebellion. The armed resurrection erupted in Tuensang in 1954 soon engulfed two other districts of Kohima and Mokokchung. First the police, and later on the army was deployed to put down the risings. The encounter between the hostile Nagas and security forces continued bringing unavailing havoc to the Naga wealth and social fabric. A large body of Naga people decided to rise above considerations of local politics. They felt that peace and progress were of greater significance than any political aims and aspirations. This feeling led to the first Naga people's Convention, held in August 1957 at Kohima which resolved-

(i) That the political future of the Naga people lay within the Union of India–

(ii) That, pending a final solution, a single administrative unit comprising the Naga Hills District of Assam and theTuensang Frontier Division of NEFA be constituted under the Ministry of External Affairs; and

(iii) That the Government of India might consider granting amnesty to the misguided underground elements who realised the futility of their claims,

and submitted the famous 16-point memorandum of their claims, to the Prime Minister, which appeared as a parlimentary alternative to militancy in the strife-torn Naga Hills. The Government agreed to these demands and the Naga Hills Tuensang Area was created on the first of December, 1957.

Back to 1946, there was a demand for the creation of Greater Nagaland comprising contiguous Naga areas. But, the Naga People's Convention memorandum did not press for it, but at the same time kept an open-door policy to include any other Naga area contiguous to it, if they so desire. But the Government did not commit any thing upon integration of the contiguous areas. Accordingly the integration of Mao and Tangkful areas of Manipur with Nagaland was not considered.

The second Naga People's Convention was held in May, 1958 at Ungma, at which the delegates reiterated their previous stand coupled with the necessity of efforts to bring the hostile groups to a saner path.

The third Naga People's Convention, held in October 1959 at Mokokchung, spelt out in concrete terms the settlement of the Naga political impasse. In July 1960, the terms were discussed by the Prime Minister with the Naga People's Convention leaders. This resulted in the 16-point Agreement whereby the Government recognised that the political goal of Nagaland would be a full-fledged state within the Union of India. This State, the sixteenth in the Constitution, was inaugurated by the President on the First of December 1963 at a colourful ceremony at Kohima.

Zeliangrong Movement

The Zeliangrong Nagas, living in the states of Manipur, Nagaland and Assam, started a movement to integrate their areas into one politico-administrative unit, which appears to be a break to the trend of the pan-tribal unification of the Nagas. We find the following points in this regard:

(i) Unification of the three Tribes-Zemi, Liangmei and Rongmei, hitherto known as Kabui and Kacha Nagas, aiming at separate entity from the mainstream of the Naga movement. Thus, the pan-tribal unification of the Nagas and the Zeliangrong movement went in different directions.

(ii) Flexibility and elasticity in their demands for territorial aspirations. The Zeliangrong movement leaders demanded different forms of territorial identity from time to time such as a separate administrative unit, a Union Territory status, and the Sixth Schedule provisions for them.

Electoral Politics

The first general election to the Nagaland Legislative Assembly were held in January 1964, in which the Naga Nationalist Organisation (NNO) got the majority. During 1969 general elections, it transformed into Nagaland Nationalist Organisation, while nine members of the Assembly formed United Front of Nagaland (UFN). During the 1974 general elections, the UFN became United Democratic Front (UDF). A new political party, the National Convention of Nagaland (NCN), also participated in this election.

The subsequent elections to the Assembly and the Lok Sabha have been fought on party lines. The NNO subsequently became the state unit of the Indian National Congress. Some regional parties of the state have become affiliates of the national parties. National political parties like Bhartiya Janata Party and Janata Dal have emerged on the political canvas of the state in 1993 elections. The battle of ballots has brought the much needed political stability to this sensitive state, though there is an undercurrent of insurgency prevalent in some pockets of Nagaland and its neighbourhood.

Constitutional Development

Prior to the occupation of Assam by the British, the Ahom Kings looked upon the Nagas as their subjects. The Raja of Manipur also exercised control over parts of the Naga Hills. The whole of the Naga Hills became part of British India with the conquest of Assam in the early part of the 19th century.

The Naga Hills district was formed in 1866 with headquarters of Samaguting (Now Chumukedima) under the administration of the Lieutenent Governor of Bengal, which was transferred to the province of Assam in 1874. The district headquarter was shifted to Wokha, in the heart of the Hills, in 1876, and two years later it was shifted to Kohima, and Wokha continued to be a subdivision. In 1889, the subdivisional headquarter was shifted from

Wokha to Mokrochung. Thus, the Naga Hills district of Assam under the British administration had two subdivisions– Kohima (Sadar) and Mokokchung. This arrangement was inherited by the Central Government at the time of India's Independence in 1947. With effect from the 26th January 1950, the Constitution of India brought about a change in the administrative set-up of the Naga Hills district. Under the Sixth Schedule (Part A) of the constitution, the Naga district was treated as an Autonomous District and was to have an Autonomous District Council, which could not become a reality as Nagas were dissatisfied with the Sixth Schedule and they, therefore, boycotted the elections for the council. Consequently, the administration of the district was carried on under the transitional provisions Paragraph 19 of the Schedule, by the government of Assam.

Consequent upon the constitution of Naga Hills district in 1866, the residual hill areas of the Naga Hills which lay between the external boundary of the Naga Hills district and the international boundary between India and Burma, continued as an Unadministered Area till 1937 prior to the Government of India Act, 1935 coming into force. Under the provisions of the Act of 1935, it was named as Naga Tribal Area and placed directly under the control of Governor of Assam and the Deputy Commissioner of Naga Hills district on behalf of the Governor-General of India representing the British emperor. After Independence, the Government of India extended the necessary laws, rules and orders to the Naga Tribal area for the Purposes of administration.

After the promulgation of the constitution of India on the 26th January 1950, the Naga Tribal Area was placed under the Sixth Schedule (Part B), and came to be administered by the Governor of Assam as Agent of the President. The North-East Frontier Areas (Administration) Regulation, 1954 created North-East Frontier Agency which also included the Naga Tribal Area, renamed Tuensang Frontier Division under the Regulation.

The Naga Hills Tuensang Area Act, 1957 created a new administrative unit consisting of the existing Naga Hills district, hitherto administered by the Governor of Assam, and Tuensang Frontier Division of North-East Frontier Agency administered by the Governor of Assam as Agent of the President. This new unit was named Naga Hills Tuensang Area, to be administered by the Governor of Assam as the Agent of the Preseent, but was to be distinct from the North-East Frontier Agency Administration. Corresponding amendment to the Sixth Schedule to the Constitution of India was made. By virtue of this amendment, the Naga Hills Tuensang Area shall comprise the areas which at the commencement of the Constitution were known as the Naga Hills district; and Tuensang, which was a frontier division of North-East Frontier Agency, and in Part B of Table 2 of the Sixth Schedule, the Naga Hills Tuensang Area was substituted.

The Naga Hills Tuensang Area (Administration) Regulation, 1957 defined the Naga Hills Tuensang Area in term of three distircts : Kohima and Mokokchung, which were earlier subdivisions of Naga Hills district; and Tuensang, which was a frontier division of the North-East Frontier Agency. Thus, the territorial boundaries of these new distircts remained unchanged.

The Nagaland (Transitional Provision) Regulation, 1961 made certain transitional provisions for the administration of Nagaland. By virtue of this regulation, the Naga Hills Tuensang Area was renamed as Nagaland. The State of Nagaland Act, 1962 granted Statehood to Nagaland without changing its territorial boundaries. With the formation of the state of Nagaland , the areas comprising it have been eliminated from the Sixth Schedule to the Constitution. Under the provisions of the constitution (Thirteenth Amendment) Act, 1962 the Governor has been entrusted with special responsibility in respect of law and order in the state so long as in his opinion internal disturbances continue therein or in any part thereof. This Act *Inter alia* provides that no Act of Parliament in respect of–

(i) religious and social practices of the Nagas,
(ii) Naga customary law and procedure.
(iii) administration of civil and criminal justice involving decisions according to Naga customary law,

(iv) ownership and transfer of land and its resources, shall apply to the State of Nagaland unless the Legislative Assembly of Nagaland by a resolution so decides.

Thus, the constitutional developments in Nagaland from 1947 to 1962 aimed at creating a composite politico-administrative unit for the Nagas living in the State of Assam and the North-East Frontier Agency.

For an effective control of the law and order situation and to accelerate the space of social transformation and economic development, the State of Nagaland was reorganised into seven districts in December, 1973. The Kohima district was divided into Kohima and Phek districts; Mokokchung district into Wokha, Zunheboto and Mokokchung districts; and Tuensang district into Tuensang and Mon districts. The Districts have been divided into subdivisions and circles. The upgradation of subdivisions into districts, and circles into sub-divisions has become a continuous administrative exercise in Nagaland to bring the administration closer to the people.

Nagaland as a Viable State

There are three main criteria for the viability of a state: (a) Financial viability, (b) Strategic Viability, and (c)Territorial viability. Financial Viability of a State, in the district constitutional sense, means the capacity of the state Government to discharge the functions and obligations within the financial resources available to it under the Constitution. The obligations of the State extend to the provision of a reasonably efficient administration, proper facilities for the welfare of the people and an adequate developmental effort. If there is no gap between the resources of the state and its revenue expenditure, it can be regarded as a viable unit. If the revenue is less than the expenditure, it is not. The size of the Central grant indicates the viability of the State or lack of it.

The Fourth Finance Commission determined viability of the states on the basis of per capita deficit. In the case of Nagaland, the per capita deficit was found to be Rs. 191.60, while it was only Re. 0.83 in the case of Madhya

Pradesh and Rs. 1.82 for Andhra Pradesh; Hence from the point of view of financial viability, there is no scope for Nagaland being a viable state. But the Study Team of the Administrative Reforms Commission has observed, "Nagaland is in a class by itself. It was given statehood on purely political grounds without any consideration for financial viability."

An administrative unit or a state can be termed as strategically viable if it does not pose problems for the national security. The State Reorganisation Commission observed the unity of the country as a fundamental prerequisite of national security. the administrative units, therefore, should have the following characteristics:

(a) The administrative units should not have a form which might foster regional, communal and any other narrower loyalties in any section of the Armed Forces;
(b) In strategically sensitive areas, the measure of autonomy given to the people should be governed by considerations of national security; and
(c) Border states should be well-administered, stable and resourceful units capable of meeting the emergency problems arising out of military exigencies.

The grant of statehood to Nagaland was primarily based on strategic considerations to keep the borders peaceful. The people of the state were provided with the self-rule, peace and prosperity to face the emergent needs of national security.

The concept of territorial viability in terms of size and extent is as important as financial and strategic viability. Though there has been no uniform principle in this regard, it is presumed that a State with a medium size of area and population provides an ideal unit for administration and the well-being of its people. In the beginning, the idea of smaller states was not heeded, but after the creation of Haryana, the smaller states are emerging as ideal and viable politico-administrative units in the country. Nagaland, with an area of 16,579 sq.km. and a population of 12.15 lakhs, provides an ideal space for the socio-economic development of the Nagas, the colourful people living on our eastern borders.

Conclusion

The political and constitutional developments were an enextricable part of the whole movement of the Nagas, a people once primitive and self-reliant in the fastness of their jungle habitat on the eastern frontier of India. The chequered history of travail and suffering of Nagaland touched every home and hearth of its territory which presents a record of passionate drama of a people devoted to their land and their way of life. In Nagaland, the sentiments which inspired the people for a special political dispensation were not born of linguistic or religious identity but were inherent in their corporate feeling that as a people they had their own heritage of culture, of local self-government and a sociological distinctness.

The political aspirations of the Nagas culminated into the constitution of a full-fledged state which has proved to be an instrument for them to achieve equal status and partnership with the other constituent states of our country.

NOTES

Ao, M. Alemchiba, 1970 : *A Brief Historical Account of Nagaland,* Naga Institute of Culture, Kohima.

Basic Statistics of North-Eastern Region 1932, North Eastern Council Secretariat, Shillong, 1992.

Bhat, Sudhakar, 1975 : *The Challenge of the Northeast,* Popular Prakashan, Bombay.

Bhattacharjee, A.K. 1973 : *Political Evolution of Nagaland (1945-1965),* The Book Trust, Calcutta.

Chib, Sukhdev Singh, 1980 : *This Beautiful India- Nagaland,* Light and life Publishers, New Delhi.

Ghosh , B.B. 1982 : *History of Nagaland,* S. Chand & Company, New Delhi.

Luthra, P.N. 1974 : *Nagaland From A District to A State,* Director of Information and Public Relations, Arunachal Pradesh, Shillong.

Singh Prakash, 1977 : *Nagaland,* National Book Trust, New Delhi.

24

TERRITORIAL ISSUES AND MANIPUR

ASOK KUMAR RAY

At the pedagogic level, to begin with, the concept of territorial politics is basically an untribal phenomenon in the otherwise tribal dominated societies of the North-Eastern India. A glance at the genesis of the state process in this region unfolds two facts: integration of the tribals in the archaic state process in this region was brought through domination and conquest by the more powerful clans and in this process the kinship base of the tribal societies was hardly touched upon.

In the colony consolidation process, the concept of territoriality was first introduced by the British in the tribal societies. They introduced the concept as a part of empire building and administrative division. In the tribal societies this was out and out an alien concept. And it was erosive of the kinship foundation of the tribal societies. Territorial division and demarcation started to often clash with the transterritorial kinship affinities of the tribes. And so in many cases it assumed international territorial implications. The British policy of Exclusion and Partial Exclusion towards the tribes of Assam and the policy of Least Interference towards many tribes even outside the purview of British India, though never accounted for any political independence of the tribal societies in the real sense of the term, have nevertheless created an impression among them that their pristine freedom was untouched upon. At least a section of the emerging elites of the tribal societies in this region had articulately nurtured this notion. Thus, when the British had left the country the Naga National Council under the leadership of Mr. Phizo had overtly claimed secession. A similar claim was made by the Mizo militant leaders. The Kuki National Assembly also made similar claim in Manipur though it was never made a major public issue. In the sixties the Paite National Council upheld the concept of Chin Unification by rectifying the artificial demarcation of boundary between India and Burma.

On the other hand, there was a moderate integrationist view that was well manageable within the framework of the constitution. It is interesting to note that for both the secessionists and the moderates, the demands of secession and integration served as political bargaining points for the emerging middle class of the tribal societies. Keeping the above point in view the territorial issues in Manipur since the time of Independence of India, are being examined here.

The Official View

The Manipur State Constitution Act of 1947 introduced for the first time a constitutional monarchy in the State. This Act extended to the whole of the state of Manipur *inclusive of the hill areas* saying that it shall not apply in any matter where a specific reservation of power is made to any authority in the hills under the provision of the Manipur State Hill Peoples' (Administration) Regulation, 1947.[1]

The hill areas of Manipur came under the constitutional monarchy and the responsibility for the administration of the hill people was vested in Maharaja-In-Council.[2] Though a dual arrangement was made by the constitution-one for the hills and the other for the valley-officially at least the integration of the hills and the valley was announced by a proclamation of His Highness the Maharaja of Manipur in the first Manipur State Assembly on October 18, 1948. It was proclaimed that "all the time Manipur was in the height of her power, hill and the valley were one, and this oneness defended Manipur against all invasions, and thus, she could maintain her independence upto 1891 . . . Now since the withdrawal of the British paramountcy after 56 years rule we have reinforced the union of the hill and the valley".[3]

The period of constitutional monarchy came to an end

by the Merger Agreement between the Governor-General of India and His Highness the Maharaja of Manipur on the 21st September 1949. By virtue of this agreement the Maharaja of Manipur had ceded to the Union of India. The subsequent Manipur (Administration) order followed on 15th October 1949 from the Minister of State. This order was extended to the whole of the Manipur state, *i.e.*, whole of the area comprising the state of Manipur before the commencement of the order. The era of Constitutional monarchy in Manipur was over and the state of Manipur was taken over by the Chief Commissioner by virtue of the State Merger (Chief Commissioners Province) Order 1950, with effect from the 22nd January 1950. The State of Manipur came to be known as Chief Commissioner's Province thence.

Subsequently, in 1951, Manipur became a Part C State by virtue of the Part C State Act, 1951. In regard to Manipur the State Reorganisation Commission had two opinions:

(a) As a Part C State Manipur should merge with neighbouring Assam;
(b) Alternatively a new state should come up consisting of Manipur, Mizo Hills, Tripura and Cachar.

None of the above opinions was, however acceptable because (i) of the security aspect of the border State, (ii) Manipur had been independent for centuries; (iii) Being relatively backward. Manipur was getting substantial financial assistance from New Delhi and it would have been reduced in case of merger with Assam; (iv) of the cultural and linguistic individuality of Manipur.[4]

Manipur was upgraded as a Central Territory under the State Reorganisation Act of 1956 under the 14th Amendment Act, 1962. A responsible government with a legislature came into existence from July 1963.

In 1972, Manipur was upgraded as full-fledged federal state by virtue of the Manipur Statehood Act 1972. The hill areas *ipso facto* came to form a part of Manipur. Yet there was a separate arrangement for the hills through the introduction of the Autonomous District Councils. The Manipur (Hill Areas) District Council Act was passed in 1971, a year before the Manipur Statehood Act was passed.

The Other View

Though the hill areas of Manipur were always included within the state of Manipur, there were verious problems in the hills relating to the actual future of the hill administration and there arose claims and counterclaims about the actual type of territorial formations in the hill areas of Manipur. As such the time of British departure let loose various stresses and strains in the hill areas. From the time of the British the Political suzerainty of the Rajah of Manipur over the hills was accepted as a fact. (Conditions imposed by the then Rajah of Manipur Gumbeer Singh in 1835). On the other hand there was growing articulation of opinion in the hills to the contrary. But the interesting paradox of the hill politics of Manipur was that none of the hill articulators at that time was well acqainted with the Westminster type of Parliamentary institutions. Hence, it was not possible for them to be too secular in their approach to the territorial problem. There was obvious convergence of tradition and modernity. Whereas the post-Independence political process demanded a territorial solution of the tribal problem (an alien concept), the tribal elites just could not think of territoriality without orienting it to ethnic stereotypes. We can mention here of the Naga National League under the leadership of Mr. Daiho and the Kuki National Assembly the two major para-political organisations of that time. While the Naga National League had the apprehension of Hindu domination in Manipur.[5] the Kuki National Assembly in its famous memorandum to the Prime Minister of India stated that the Kuki inhabited areas were brought under the Manipur territory accidentally. In the same memorandum it was stated that if the British government had left the country, then naturally, the Kukis should be free again, and if they wanted to live in India, it should be on terms agreed upon between the *contracting Parties.*[6]

However both the Kukis and the Nagas had to come within the state of Manipur in different hill districts while the Nagas got a separate territorial status in Nagaland. The Kukis 'however' could not get any compact homeland so far and they are at present distributed not only in Manipur but also in different territorial regions of Assam, Tripura, Nagaland and Mizoram.

There was similar problem with the Mizo people. Though the Mizos could get a territorial status under Assam, the Mizo inhabited areas of Manipur exhibited a note of discontentment with the argument that the Mizo areas came to be merged with Manipur only after the Lushai Expedition in 1891 and that they had never recognised the authority of the Maharaja of Manipur. The plan for Greater Mizoram like that of Greater Nagaland was a very pervasive one in the beginning that cut across the existing state boundaries of Manipur, Assam, Mizoram and Tripura and encompassed all the allied Chin-Kuki-Mizo Allied tribes. It was 'however' too tall a claim to unify all the so-called Mizos in different areas and soon the seeds of dissension were there for all to see on the issue of Mizo integration.

It may be noted that the federal scheme of India was more a legacy of the Government of India Act 1935 than anything else. For the princely state of Manipur accession to the federation of India under the Government of India Act 1935 was thought to be a political necessity on the part of the British. It was the British desire that the Maharaja of Manipur should sign the Instrument of Accession. A discussion was held at the Council House, Calcutta, on 2nd January 1937 between the Maharaja and the Special Representative of the Viceroy. In this discussion it was pointed out that as the hill areas were not administered on behalf of His Majesty but were under the control of the Maharaja, the hill areas would *ipso facto* come under the federation if the state of Manipur is federated. The advent of the Second World War 'however' put the federal scheme and accession plan of Manipur in suspense.[7]

In 1949, the Merger of Manipur with the Union of India was factually a matter of political compulsion backed by the institutionalised state power. But the federal scheme in course of time could not fulfil the aspirations of the hill people of Manipur. The need for political and territorial self-determination of the tribal people was inevitable. But there has often been a conglomeration of divergent demands in the hills. These are: the demand for statehood, demand for separate administrative unit, demand for Union Territory, demand for a separate district, demand for autonomous district council under the Sixth Schedule to the Constitution, demand for Greater Land like the Greater Mizoram and Greater Nagaland affecting the respective tribal groups in Manipur. In another category there appeared trans-territorial (international) political affiliations with the objective of trans-territorial tribal integration. In the third category, there appeared politics of secession which many tribal organisations often resorted to as a means of self-determination.

The task of reorganisation becomes a tough job in this context. It is also difficult to choose which of the demands would be most appropriate for the hill people. This difficulty arises out of two reason: (i) Elasticity and flexibility of the demand: In Manipur the degree of elasticity and flexibility of political demands is quite high. Even the same tribal organisation has made conflicting demands at different times. The Kukis for example voiced the demand with a threat of secession in the 'forties upheld the unity and territorial integrity of the Kukis within Manipur in the 'fifties', demanded a separate state in the 'sixties, a separate Revenue district in the 'seventies endorsed the demand for the 'Sixth Schedule to the Constitution of India in the eighties'. Recently, an organisation called the Kuki National Front is back with the demand for a separate state within the Union of India. The issue of Mizo Unification became the common problem for the Manipur Mizo Integration Council, the Mizo Union, the United Mizo Freedom Organisation, and the Mizo National

Front. The Chin Unification and Zomi Unification movements got the momentum at the instance of the Paite National Council and the Zomi National Congress respectively. These movements had trans-territorial implications often implicating the Burmese territory across the border. But in gradual course these two organisations had to reduce their demands so much so that the trans-territorial implications had gradually toned down. The Mizo National Front in its plan for a Greater Mizoram intended to rally the trains-frontier tribes of Burma and Bangladesh in addition to the Mizo inhabited areas in the North-East India. The MNF too had to tone down its demand for Greater Mizoram at the time of the accord.[8]

(i) Lack of pan-tribal consensus on the actual shape of territorial Reorganisation : though there is an accepted dichotomy between the valley and the hills, there is no consensus also on the actual territorial shape in the course of reorganisation. If we start from the extreme end of secession we find that in the Indian federal system there is no constitutional room for it (unlike the Constitution of the USSR). Hence the former obviously becomes an unconstitutional venture. Politics of secession in this region has become a handy political bargaining point on the part of the tribal middle class that emerged in the pre-and post-Independence period. Next comes the trans-border integration plan. The loose boundary demarcation between India and Burma in the south of Manipur facilitated the Chin-Kuki-Lushai mobility across the mutual borders. Integration with Burma became a very handy political slogan for many para-political groups in this area but in actual practice it has been found that none of these groups could well on the trans-border integration issue for a considerably long time and finally they had to tone down. Thus the Mizo National Front at the time of the Mizo Accord had to shed off the trans-border integration plan.

Ience the choice of reorganisation from the available

constitutional variables. In the last part of the 'eighties there seemed to have emerged a working consensus for the introduction of the Sixth Schedule to the Constitution in the hill areas of Manipur. But I have stated that this consasus is yet to take a final shape.[9] In the National Conference on the Problems of the Scheduled Tribes, held at New Delhi on 31 March 1990, Mr. T.N. Haokip, the then Minister of Tribal Development and District Council, Manipur, voiced his demand for the extension of the Sixth Schedule in the hill areas of Manipur.[10] But Mr. Keishing, Chairperson of Group I, comprising the N.E. States and Sikkim in the above conference, insisted on the introduction of a status similar to that of Jammu and Kashmir as granted under Article 370 of the Constitution of India, for the North-Eastern States through suitable constitutional amendment.[11] Here lies the problem of consensus on the actual course and shape of territorial reorganisation.

Middle-classicism, historically speaking, is relatively a recent phenomenon in the tribal society in this region. But once it has appeared it has become the progenitor of the political elites in the tribal society, who have considered ethnic self-determination as the main task. The entire range of territorial reorganisation in this part has evaded the issue of economic reorganisation which is so vital today. A new light on the basic assumption for the territorial reorganisation is the need of the day. No doubt, after two decades of the N.E. States Reorganisation Act, 1971, many grievances are accumulated that need a practical and thoughtful redressal. The past trend has revealed that if we consider sheer ethnicity (language, race, religion etc.) as the principal base for territorial reorganisation, we may perhaps do the same mistake we did in the past. Because applied ethnicity, in our context, has no end. It creates more problems than it can solve. And hence ultimately a process of nuclearisation sets in to erode the entire system. On the other hand, if we take the hill areas as the Less Development Economic Zones (LDEZ); perhaps there will be a consensus. Over the last four or five decades we have experienced that while the hill politics of Manipur has become diversified and prolified, the hill economy remained relatively stagnant. And if we assume that economic exploitation and relative backwardness in this zone has sensitised the political issues, then reorganisation on the LDEZ lines which may even cut across the ethnic lines, seems to be an effective guideline for the purpose of territorial reorganisation.

REFERENCES

1. The Manipur State Constitution Act, 1947.
2. The Manipur Hill People (Administration) Regulation-1947.
3. Proclamation of H.H. the Maharaja Bodhachandra Singh on the inaugural function of the First Manipur State Assembly, October 18, 1948.
4. Report of the SRC.
5. Ray, A.K. 1992, The Kuki National Assembly – Its social base and working in Manipur, ed. by L.S. Gassah *Regional Political Parties in North-East India,* Omsons Publication, New Delhi.
6. Memorandum of the KNA to the PM of India, 1960.
7. Resistance, June 1, 1976.
8. Ray, A.K. 1990, *Ethnicity and Polity Alternatives. - A North-Eastern Experience,* ed. by Ghosh and Chakraborti *Ethno Nationalism–Indian Experience,* Netaji Institute for Asian Studies Calcutta.
9. Ray, A.K. and Kamkhenthang, The Sixth Schedule and the Manipur Hills, *Van Vandhu,* N.E. Special issue, February 1990, New Delhi.
10. Presentation of T.N. Haokip in the National Conference on the Problem of Scheduled Tribes, Vigyan Bhawan, New Delhi March 31, 1990.
11. Report of the Group I in the above Conference at New Delhi on March 31, 1990.

25

REORGANISATION OF MIZORAM SINCE INDEPENDENCE

M.M. DAS
N.N. SENGUPTA
MRINMAYI BANERJEE

Mizoram, one of the seven sisters of North-East India, is bounded on the north by the Cachar District of Assam and the state of Manipur on the east and south by Chin Hill (Myanmar) on the west by Bangladesh and the state of Tripura, covering an area of 21,063 sq. km. Until 21st January 1972, it was only a district called 'The Lushai Hills District' of Assam, but thereafter it assumed the status of a state through the intermediary of 'Union Territory'.

Although the main focus of this write up is on reorganisation of Mizoram after Independence, *i.e.*, 1947, but it would be a truncated one if the perspective of reorganisation which had its seed in pre-independence era was not discussed.

Pre-Independence Activity

Mr. G.N. Bordoloi, the first Chief Minister of Assam, had a talk with the general secretary of 'Mizo Union Party' about Mizos joining India rather than Pakistan. As a result the Mizo people though wanted full-fledged autonomy after the British rule, decided to join India conditionally. The idea they had behind full autonomy was that in the remote past Mizoram was not under anybody's dictate, then with the British Raj they were ironically ruled by them. So with the exit of British they should get back their earlier status, *i.e.*, 'independent Mizoram'. Lot of meetings and discussions took place regarding the determination of the status of Mizoram after British packed up from India. There was a lot of confusion, charges and counter charges among the 'Mizo Union Party' members regarding the future of Mizoram because annexation by India was also looked upon by them as another form of colonial rule.

Demand for Independence of Mizoram before 1947

The reason for declaring independence for Mizoram by the Mizo Union Party was based on certain principles. Firstly, they had nothing in common with the Indian Vais (as they usually addressed Indians. So they thought that if they were to be a part of India they would loose their identity, thereby they would in no time be turned into a tribe of no importance, as India was vast in size and population. Secondly, they all speak only one language which has no bearing with any other dialects of India, hence they should strive for their own independence and not become a part of Indian territory. Thirdly, Mizoram is a place, rich in resources of deciduous trees, bamboo vines and fruit-trees and many other plants and medicinal herbs, which will impart life line to the Mizo community without bothering about any foreign aid. Moreover, handicrafts and machineries too can be manufactured by them with their own resources. Hence, they are not to depend on others for their necessities. Fourthly, because of their religion also they should be away from Indians who are considered by them as Hindus.

Another reason for putting forward their demand for an independent state was their unique topography. Being surrounded on three sides by foreign countries, Bangladesh and Burma (Myanmar) and having linkage only in north with India, they were not in a position to tolerate Indian presence over their sovereignty. They regard India as Hindu state, hence Mizos being mostly disciples of the Christ were keeping the 'Vais' at an arm's length which made them non-receptive to the rich Indian culture. They were better with the British having been subjected to colonial rule and heavy taxation. So they were apprehensive that they might be subjected to similar tax again, if they were to be in India, which to them was a kind of slavery. Against this backdrop of political scenario they preferred the British Raj for another five to ten years in Mizoram on contractual basis so that they could be trained in the administration of a sovereign country.

However, on the first independence day of India, *i.e.*, 15th August 1947, there was no hoisting of Indian National Flag in Mizoram. Amidst so much uncertainty on the 14th August 1947 the last British superintendent of Mizoram Mr. L.L. Peters called a meeting of all political parties to discuss the perspective of Indian independence and it was unanimous "That the Lushais should have the liberty to come out of the Indian Union whenever they felt so, subject to a minimum period of ten years." A decision which Indian Leaders never liked.

Post Independence Politics

In the post-independence period there was a resurrection of the Hill people of North-East India and Mizoram was no exception. They were all trying to enforce their regional autonomy for a better status in the Indian Union within the framework of the Constitution. Keeping this sentiment in mind, the newly constituted Indian government realised that the tribals required some nursing care to heal the wounds of the age-old exploitation by the British.

Mr. L.L. Peters, the last Superintendent under British rule and the first under the new Indian government, called a meeting of Mizo Union General Assembly on September, 26th 1947. In the Assembly, Mr. Peter's proposed that he was informed by the Governor of Assam to tell the Mizos that it was preferable for them to be a part of India rather than Myanmar or Pakistan. Mr. Peters further added that in near future there would be a district council but the general administration in Mizoram would be totally different from other governing bodies in India even after coming into existence of the District Council. The first Indian

Superintendent of Mizoram in free India was Mr. S.K. Barkatakti. He started building up the infrastructure for Mizoram, constructing highway between two important big cities like Aizawl and Lunglei.

By 1950 India was christened as Republic with the adoption of the Constitution and according to Article 342 of the Constitution the Mizos fell in the category of Scheduled Tribe. As provided in the Constitution, Mizoram was to have a District Council. In the general election of the year 1952 for parliament a non-Mizo representative of Indian Congress from Silchar was elected from both Mizoram and Silchar. For Assam Legislative Assembly, Mizoram was divided into three section: (1) the Aizawl East (2) Aizawl West and (3) the Southern district.

In the late fifties, the Mizo political leaders raised the issue of formation of Hill states. During the Chinese invasion of 1962 in the north-eastern border of Assam there was a difference of opinion whether they should fight for independecne of the hill states or not. But after assurances from the Indian leadership that their grievences would be looked into, they shelved the idea of any movement for statehood of Mizoram at that crucial juncture of Chinese invasion and Mizo National Front agreed to support India. On 9th March 1963, the leaders of MNF (Mizo National Front) adopted the idea of full statehood for Mizoram. In 1965, the Indian government set up Pataskar Commission to look into the grievances of the Mizos. The commission recommended that Mizoram should be accorded the status of 'Union Territory'.

In the year 1960, Mizoram experienced a severe famine and the army was called out to fight the situation. The Indian soldiers immediately went into action distributing the necessities of life in the famine stricken Mizo villages which was the first occasion when the Mizo people came in direct contact with the Indian 'Vais' and that too in such a role that their age-old suspicion of economic exploitation by the Indian 'Vais' started fading out. 'Mizo National Front' was launched in the year 1961. There was a third District Council Election in 1962 but none from the 'Mizo National Front' get elected to the Legislative Assembly. By the year 1963 the District Council was dissolved, the idea being to prevent the Congress Party to come into power in Mizoram. So there was to be byelection in the same year and the Mizo Union Party changed their attitude demanding statehood for Mizoram instead of a Hill State without making any official announcement in the election manifesto. Thus the Mizo National Front, which was always demanding independence for Mizoram had gained an edge over Mizo Union Party and obviously became very close to the Mizo souls. That the Mizo National Front was coming closer to the Mizo electorate was established by the fact that they won the Aizawl West seat with a big margin of 8,737 votes. In the Lunglei seat (another city of Mizoram next in importance to Aizawl the Mizo National Front candidate won hands down, of course it was a very poor turn out by the electorate. The reason for which could be attributed to an editorial in a newspaper called *Zalenna* (meaning Freedom).

Even since India achieved Independence, some group or the other of Mizos has been raising the demand for Independent Mizoram. The document signed by Mr. L. Peters the Deputy Commissioner, on the Independence eve, said that Mizoram should be a part of India just only for 10 years up to 1957. 'Mizo National Front' was baptised in 1961. By 1964-1965 independence alone was the political issue of the party and talk of the Mizo intellectuals, students and professionals. Mizo National Front was capitalizing the very touchy issue under the Presidentship of Mr. Laldenga who was up in arms to bring home independence for the Mizos at any rate.

Mizo Movement Takes Extremist Turn

On February 28th, 1966, the extremists led by Mizo National Front suddenly made an armed attack on important security and government posts all over the Mizo Hills district. On the 1st March 1966, some Mizos resorted to acts of mischief at Lunglei, Aizawl, Earyrangte (Vairengte), Chawngte and Chinluang to disrupt communications and antegonise public servents. A gang of around

500 extremists attacked a camp of security forces and an Assam Rifles post. They abducted sub-divisional officer of Lunglei, attacked the telephone exchange of Aizawl and the district treasury decamping with rifles, some round of ammunitions and cash from the single lock of treasury. A group of mob gheraoed the sub-divisional officer of Eayrangte and forced him to get out of the district. Army was brought into action to deal with the situation in all the important parts of the district. Due to such spate of violence and deterioration in law and order, Mizoram covered a lot of time in radio news and lot of space in newspapers for the first time in history after independence.

It was suspected that Mizos have become rebellions due to military help from China and Pakistan. Mr. Laldenga, President of the 'Mizo National Front', wrote a letter to Indonesian president in January 1966 seeking his help in their struggle for the liberation of Mizoram. Some leading dailies in Pakistan like the Observer and Guardian were trying to fish in troubled water, by magnifying the Mizoram problem which to their rating was an international problem involving suppression of human rights. Of course, Pakistan was trying to take revenge of their defeat in the 1965 war against India through purposeful sympathy to the Mizo Militants.

Back Home, the politicians were trying to find a rational solution to this Mizo insurgency. Dr. Hem Barua, a representative from Guwahati emphasized that the Mizos are "the bone of our bones and the flesh of our flesh". Mr. Basumatari a member from Goalpara commented that the government of India's negligence is the root cause for this Mizo unrest. Had the Central Government given due attention to the development of the Hill district, this unrest of Mizos would have never surfaced.

A team of six experts was sent to Mizoram by the Government of India who suggested some developmental programme for the hill district with emphasis on agriculture and allied matters and on soil conservation. The central team also suggested that a central farm of 1,000 acres should be set up for raising paddy, oil seeds, poultry, livestock and agriculture.

The extremist leader of 'Mizo National Front', Mr. Laldenga so long was carrying on extremist activities from his hideout headquarter in Chittagong hill tract of Bangladesh, but with the return of democratic government in Bangladesh, Awami League came to power who was not indulging in any extremist activity. So Mr. Laldenga had to move out of Chittagong and went to Burma (now Mynamar) and again moved to Yunan Province in China. In the meantime the so-called nationalist movement was divided into two factions. One, hardcore faction under the leadership of Laldenga whose demand was independence and nothing less and the softcore factions who were in a compromising mood with the Central Government.

Finding this divide in the Mizo Nationalist movement the Assam Government of which Mizoram was a part started sending feelers to the Mizo extremists, offering some sort of concessions and incentives if they surrendered their arms to the nearest Police station.

On the 18th March 1971, the Mizo Union Party and Congress Party jointly demanded of; statehood for mizoram, but the Government of India agreed to giving only a territorial status. Although the achievement fell short of the demand, both the Congress Party and Mizo Union Party accepted this as a plank for their ultimate demand of statehood within the framework of Indian constitution. The new status of territory provides for a Legislative Assembly, Council of Ministers and a Council of Advisors. It also imparts power to make laws ralating to State and Concurrent Lists. However, the control over public order, police, municipal committee, improvement trust etc. remained with the centre. The Ministers were incharge of the legislature and the Chief Commissioner was to preside over their meeting. The president of India was authorised to set up a council of advisors.

Amidst unhappiness and dissatisfaction over non-acceptence of territorial status by many Mizo people, the student community of Mizoram started picketing in cities like Shillong and Aizawl renewing their demand for total independence for Mizoram as maximum and nothing less than statehood as minimum but nothing in between.

However, to the likes and dislikes of many Mizos on the 21st January 1972, the then Prime Minister of India, Mrs. Indira Gandhi, came to Mizoram and inaugurated Mizoram as a Union Territory. Thus Mizo Hills District overnight became 'Union Territory' severing relations with Assam.

Union Territory to Statehood.

Violence in Mizoram did not stop here despite its elevation from the status of district to Union Territory. The student along with 'Mizo National Front' chief Mr. Laldenga were not prepared to accept anything less than statehood., Hence to put an end to this crisis a bill was passed in the Parliament in the year 1986 giving Mizoram statehood. The President of India also gave his assent on the Mizoram statehood bill, on the 14th August 1986. The state bill thus became an act, but was not brought into force with immediate effect in anticipation of some political reapproachment between the Central Government and the MNF Chief, Mr. Laldenga. However, the expectation was not belied for long. On the 20th February 1987, Mizoram was declared a full-fledged state and recognised as the 23rd State of India.

Conclusion

Mizoram, even after achievement of statehood, could not breathe peacefully as some of the smaller groups are now demanding autonomy and started agitation at different places. Hmar community even started extremist activities for achieving their goal in this regard.

REFERENCES

Reid, Sir Robert, 1978, :*The Lushai Hills'* Firma KLM Private Ltd. Mizoram.

Samuelson, Ramchuane Sena, 1985, *Love Mizoram*, Goodwill Press, Imphal.

26

REORGANISATION OF NORTH-EAST INDIA
A Study of Mizoram

R.N. PRASAD

I

The dimensions of state politics in India at macro-level are both horizontal and vertical. There is a slow but sure process of changing territorial alignment within the Indian federation with a view to approximation of such boundaries to what the people consider to be their cultural brundaries either through the creation of new states or through boundary adjustment. On the other hand, there is an increasing desire for power at the state level either expressed in terms of better union-state relations or for greater autonomy. Both these trends are mediated by the party system in the country.

II

The demand for autonomy/statehood is the result of many factors and forces which have been shaping and influencing the post-independence politics in this country. Some of the factors/forces may be mentioned here. States in India are the core areas for political activity. The federating units are heterogeneous units both linguistically and culturally. The States Reorganisation Commission has accepted the linguistic demands and the States Reorganisation Act of 1956 has also demarcated state boudaries in conformity with the dominent language of the region which has certainly fostered regional sentiments and stimulated demands for greater autonomy for states. The states created on linguistic basis have stimulated all the divisive movements for protecting local interests especially employment and trading and as a consequence, the theory of "sons of the soil" has emerged. Besides, the bias of the Central Government in dealing with the government of the opposition parties, unprincipled handling of inter-state conflicts or disputes, emergence or contradictions in the system owing to capitalist path of development, emergence of regional parties/ethnic political party consolidating their position by developing protecting the language and culture through the policies of the State Government, failure of the Central Government in not respecting the constitutional provisions and for not honouring the federal spirit, dependence of the states on the centre for financial assistance, inadequate sources of revenue for the states, discrimination in allocation of grants in-aid and central loans, discrimination in the location of heavy industries and centrally sponsored projects and regional economic imbalances or uneven economic development of the region, are also responsible factors for the demand for state autonomy/statehood.

It is significant to note that the demand for state autonomy movement/statehood in India owes its origin largely to the efforts of the regional parties. The frustration, estrangement and feeling of deprivation coupled with the instinct of preserving 'distinct cultures, languages and traditions' on the part of the people of a defined region or particular nationality (or sub-national groups) prove to be the prime motive. That is why, the people of North-Eastern States particularly the Nagas and the Mizos (due to the diversities of culture, religion, race and language) also initiated their movements for autonomous status of different variations. Moreover, the demand for state autonomy/autonomy movement/statehood is raised from a wide spectrum of political commitments. In a political system, which has a written constitution, some of the norms of political system are laid down in the constitutional law itself and the political structures are, to a large extent shaped by the constitution. Likewise, the Constitution of India has also spurred the growth of many new political structures in this country. Taking advantage of the feelings of the Mizo people such as frustration, deprivation and preservation of identity, culture, lands dialects, and customs/traditions and constitutional provisions, the Mizo Union, the first political party in the then Lushai Hills (Now Mizoram) since its inception in April 1946, raised the demand for achieving democratic system of administration for the Mizos and also fighting the vested interests of the Chiefs in the early 'fifties. Since August 1963, the party has carried on its crusade for statehood for the Mizo Hills and later submitted memoranda to the Union Government demanding separation from Assam. The formation of Autonomous Mizo Hills District Council for the Mizos and the Pawi-Lakher Regional Council for the major tribes (Pawis, Lakhers and Chakmas), the elevation of the Mizo Hills District to the status of Union Territory of Mizoram, and subsequently to statehood may be regarded as the result of the Mizo autonomy movement since independence, though strictly speaking, their statehood owes its origin to the emergence of a Mizo solidarity, against what is frequently described as exploitation of the Plainsmen.

The second feature is the changing status of the political units in India. The Indian Constitution created four types of states. The State Reorganisation Commission reduced them to two viz: Union Territories and states. Since 1972, there is a steady tendency for the Union Territories to grow into fullfledged states, because statehood means more autonomy for the government and more power for the ruling elite of a region.

III

The Lushai Hills, the Naga Hills the North Cachar Hills and the North-East frontier tracts were excluded areas under the Government of India Act, 1935. These excluded areas were guarded by the Inner Line which restricted the entry of outsiders without permit. In the Inner Line regulated areas, there was also no administration till the last day of the Raj. So the hills district, thus, developed a special kind of identity and this has remained a crucial factor in political development. But after, India attained independence, the tribes of the hill areas of Assam demanded regional autonomy and better status within the constitutional framework. So the interim Government of India in 1947 realised the political aspirations of the people of the hill areas of Assam against the background of assurances given by the outgoing British rulers.

So the Government in order to look into the grievances and affairs of the hill people, appointed a sub-committee of the Constituent Assembly known as the North-East Frontier (Assam) Tribal and Excluded Areas Committee under the Chairmanship of Gopinath Bardoloi the then Chief Minister of Assam. The Bardoloi Committee made an on the spot study of the demands and aspirations of the hill people and submitted its recommendations for a simple and inexpensive set-up; (District Councils) of the hill areas which were later accepted and incorporated into Article 244 (2) of the Sixth Schedule of the Indian Constitution. The Bardoloi Committee also provided for Regional Council for the tribes other than the main tribes. This scheme was conceived with a view to building up autonomous administration (District Council and Regional Council) in the hill areas of Assam so that the hill people could continue to follow their traditional way of life, preserving identity, cultures, customs and manner with such changes as they themselves might like to introduce. It was also felt that the Central and the State Governments would help them in securing the benefits of a democratic and liberal constitution of the country by promoting their educational and economic interests and protecting them from social injustice and all forms of exploitation as enshrined in the Directive Principles of the State policy.

The Government of Assam framed rules under paragraph 2 of the Sixth Schedule to the Indian Constitution called the Assam autonomous District (Constitutions of the District Councils) Rules 1951 for the autonomous district and the Pawi-Lakher (Constitution of Regional Council) Rules in 1952 for the autonomous region in the Lushai Hills District. According to the said rules, the Mizo Hills District Council the then Lushai Hills District Council) for Mizos and the Pawi-Lakher Regional Council for Pawi,

Lakher and Chakma tribes were constituted on April 25, 1952 and April 23, 1953. Though the Mizos continued to look after their distinctive functions envisaged in the Sixth Schedule with the setting up of the Mizo Hills District Council from 1952-1972, they were not satisfied with the Autonomous District Council, because, there was no provision in the Sixth Schedule to bring the council to participate in the developmental schemes and social welfare programme to the largest extent possible. Besides, the Mizo Union Party had been having control over the administration of the District Council for more than 18 years. So the Mizo Union Party as well as other political parties wanted the status of statehood and advocated peaceful means to achieve this objective.

IV

On April 2, 1960, Vishnu Sahay, the then Governor of Assam, wrote to the Prime Minister that the Mizo Hills District should be elevated to the status of Union Territory. In the meantime, the Mizo National Front insurgency broke out on the midnight of the 28th February 1966. The M.N.F. declared independence. The Government of India adopted military measures to counter the grave anti-national activity. The troops were despatched to the territory to aid the civil authorities. In order to break the backbone of the M.N.F. and as a counter-insurgency measure, the Mizo Leaders emphasised the creation of a separate state of Mizoram. Ultimately, the united efforts, continuous struggles, political skill and great sacrifices of the Mizos compelled the Government of India to agree to political settlement of the Mizo problem.

The Government came out with the proposal to elevate the Mizo Hills District to the status of Union Territory. The Government of India enacted the North-Eastern Areas (Reorganisation) Act, 1971, by amending the Constitution of India (Twenty-Seventh Amendment) under which the Mizo Hills District became the Union Territory of Mizoram with a thirty-three member Legislative Assembly. It was envisaged in the Act that the Mizo Hills District Council would stand dissolved and cease to exist from the date on which the Legislative Assembly of the Union Territory of Mizoram was constituted.

When the Mizos attained the Union Territory of Mizoram with Legislative Assembly to protect their own culture and way of life the Pawis, the Lakhers and the Chakmas wanted to take advantage of the new political status. In fact, they expected more autonomy for their areas. So on September 7, 1971, the leaders of the three tribes submitted a memorandum to the Government of India demanding creation of a separate Union Territory for their areas. The Government could not accede to their demands, but instead agreed to create District Councils for their respective areas, covering the three tribes in the region-The Pawis, the Lakhers and the Chakmas in order to protect their own distinct customs and cultures as envisaged in the Sixth Schedule to the Constitution. After the Union Territory of Mizoram was set-up, the Administrator of Mizoram passed an order as per the provisions of the North-Eastern Areas (Reorganisation) Mizoram adaption of Laws order, 1972 and the Government of Union Territories (Amendment) Act, 1971, creating three autonomous regions for three Regional Councils, one each for the Pawis, the Lakhers and the Chakmas on April 12, 1972 in place of the Pawi-Lakher Regional Council. The Pawi-Lakher Regional Council was dissolved. As provided under paragraph 205 of the Sixth Schedule, every autonomous region existing immediately before the date on which the Mizoram Assembly was constituted, would become the District Council for the corresponding new District. As a result, the three Regional Councils were elevated to the status of the three District Councils such as the Lai District Council, the Mara District Council and the Chakma District Council on April 29, 1972 with headquarters at Lawngtlai, Saiha and Chawngte respectively.

V

Since Union Territory means lesser autonomy for the government and lesser or negligible power for the ruling elite of a region, the ruling peopie's conference party in Mizoram submitted a memorandum to the then Prime Minister, Mrs. Indira Gandhi, on September 17, 1982 and demanded immediate conferment of statehood on the Union Territory of Mizoram to enable the state to have more powers and resources to manage its own affairs and develop itself in accordance with the social, linguistic and cultural needs of the Mizo people. On 30 June, 1986, the Memorandum of Settlement of Political problems was signed by the Home Secretary, R.D. Pradhan, Government of India, and Laldenga, on behalf of the Mizo National Front, and Lalkhama, Chief Secretary to the Government of Mizoram to ensure permanent peace and harmony in Mizoram. As incorporated in the Memorandum of Settlement, the Central Government agreed to confer statehood on the Union Territory of Mizoram to satisfy the desires and aspirations of the Mizo people with a number of special safeguards. The Union Government with a view to elevating the Union Territory to statehood introduced the Mizoram Statehood Bill, 1986 with special safeguards and provisions of fortry elective seats in the Legislative Assembly and the 53rd Constitution (Amendment) Bill, 1986, in the Parliament and got the bill passed by an absolute majority. The President of India also assented the Mizoram Statehood Bill 1986 on 14, August 1986. The state bill, thus, became an act but was not brought into force with immediate effect. On February 20, 1987. Mizoram was inaugurated as the 23rd state of the Indian Union. Thus the adoption of a Democratic Parliamentary form of Government with the goal of planned modernisation has created an impact on the Mizo society to an extent which, of course, may contribute to secularisation and political integration at a rapid rate. All that is necessary is to accelerate the progress and rapid socio-economic transformation of the Mizo people so that the goal of state building and nation-building is achieved soon.

Meghalaya, Mizoram, Manipr, Tripura and Arunachal Pradesh have been given the status of full-fledged statehood by the re-organisation of North-East Region. Nagaland became a state in 1963. Most new states have been carved out of Assam. The process of re-organisation of north-east region was ethno-cultural in a broad sense and anti-linguistic in a special sense, because none of the new states, except Mizoram has a dominent language and all of them had English as their official language. Indeed, the question of official language has stimulated all the divisive movements in north-east India. As a result, the Assamese have paid the price of their language. Most of the hill areas of Assam have left the state. More may still leave. This may only further strengthen the passion for their language. Besides all this, the reorganisation also aims at providing an opportunity to the people of various ethnic and linguistic origins in the region a hand to shape their own destiny as they like; making them free from the fear of domination by others and immunising them from the feeling that they are being exploited, or that the economy is tied to the plain areas of Assam. With this recognition, the administrative set-up of the entire region has been restructured so as to provide adequate opportunities to the people of different parts to associate themselves with the task of development. But these new states are financially dependent on the Union Government quite heavily -and so unable to take up individual developmental projects and the North-Eastern Council does not enjoy the necessary power and resources to do so. Therefore, although such states do not raise the broad issues of Union-State relations, they are quite jittery about the Central Government's interference in their states' politics. It is only in Assam that the broad issues of Union-State relations have come to focus.

VI

As it is, there is no way possible to state that with the reorganisation of north-east India, the region has undergone any qualitative change. Briefly, the reorganisation of states has failed to fulfil the socio-economic aspirations of most hills and plains people. The task of nation-building in the region has not been successful to the desired extent in spite of disintegration of the state of Assam. In a developing country like India, the major thrust has to be socio-economic development to achieve the goal of state-building and nation-building. It has also been experienced that after Meghalaya, Mizoram, Nagaland, Manipur, Tripura and Arunachal Pradesh became states, the Central Government has been generous with its purse and pumped more funds in these fledgling territories than perhaps in any other state with a comparable population. So most people think that the benefits of planned development must be evenly distributed among the masses of the states. But a more serious problem is how one can hope for a non-exploitative development and equitable distribution of benefits within the capitalist society/market economy framework. It is time now to examine the adverse and cumulative effects of fast enlarging economy mainly due to the expansion of development activities in Meghalaya, Mizoram, Manipur, Nagaland, Tripura and Arunachal Pradesh. Since there is a capitalist path of modernisation and development, effects of fast enlarging money economy are bound to create vested interests--the neo-middle rich class of the contractors, the businessmen, the educated/political elites and the bureaucrat in the classless society of the tribesmen as it has happened in other federating units of India, in continued peace and tranquility. As a result, only a few persons in these states, are the beneficiaries who have become very rich in recent years where as the majority of tribesmen people are still on the old standard of living. This socio-economic disparity is widening such a distinction between the rich and the poor and the urban and the rural sections just like classes already existing in other parts of the country. Earlier, there was neither poverty nor middle class in the societies of the Nagas, the Mizos and the Arunachalis. Now the tribal economy has been exposed to the onslaught of capitalist economy during the last few decades despite the restrictive Inner Line Regulation. As regards the exploitation of the tribesmen, the emerging class of neo-middle rich is no less responsible for this phenomenon now than the crafty and the pioneer businessmen or the traders of the plains areas. It is thus clear that the reorganisation of states, the Inner Line Regulation and several restrictive enactments made against the plains people cannot stop prevent the exploitation of the many for tribeman by the neo-rich class, so long, as a differential distribution of property prestige, income, education and authority within the tribal society continue. Because those groups of people, who acquire more property and prestige come to wield more power than others, and thereby help the beginning of exploitation of the poor by those classes/groups controlling the material means of production and the mode of production not only in terms of exchange but also in terms of allocation of the means of livelihood. So economic power is dialectically related to political power. This phenomenon is now very much visible in the tribal society of North-Eastern states.

The gulf between the rich and the poor is widening. So justification about the reorganisation of states on ethno-cultural and linguistic grounds and introduction of the Inner Line Regulation and its continuity in an inherently exploitative system to prevent exploitation of the tribesmen by the plains rich people and businessmen is not at all convincing. It, therefore, becomes absolutely incomprehensible to expect a non-exploitative society from an exploitative system. It is not that there has been no devlopment but its benefits have been largely covered by a small group of well-off-natives. The indigenous working people have been pauperised. Of course, legal safeguards do provide some help. But Article 39, which enjoins upon the state to prevent concentration of wealth has not been able to prevent the development of monopolies in India, which shocked Jawaharlal Nehru leading to the appointment of Monopolies Commission. In the United States, even the passing of Anti-Trust Laws did not stop the development of the monopolies. In another context, it may be noted that even Article 370 has not prevented the increasing integration of Jammu and Kashmir in the market economy of India. The point, which is being made, is that social and economic forces are often too powerful for the wishes and hopes of leaders, howsoever well meaning and powerful they may be. Therefore, the reorganisation of states and policy of leaving the tribesman alone has not prevented either the widespread introduction of modern values in the region or the exploitation of the less educated and economically poor by vested interests.

VII

The point which is being made here, is that the Inner Line Regulation and other protective land regulations, no doubt bar the plains people from owning landed property in the hill areas, but such regulations also generate a process of progressive concentration of vast landed property in the hands of the local middle class or a small group of well-off-natives and tend to aggravate the situation of rural poverty by pushing an icreasingly larger section of the small and marginal farmers to the status of landless peasants. In this process, no fertile land will be retained for the cultivating families. Not only that such grossly unequal distribution of land also perpetuates the existing disparities of wealth as well as land alienation among the extremely poor tribesmen. This will certainly disturb social harmony. Thus social stratification based on private ownership of land has already become a reality. The emerging middle-class is neither opposed to the landed gentry nor to the Indian capitalist class. However, if the situation is to be improved even in a modest way, codification of tribal rights in land/forests, cadastral survey and land reforms will have to be implemented in an effective manner.

One of the provisions of North-East Areas (Reorganisation) Act, 1971 envisages the preservation of cultural identity of the tribesmen in isolation, but every one knows that cultural identity of a people is lost only under an exploitative order and not by the existence of another culture by their side. Besides, the belated emergence of the well-off-native class in these states has failed to displace ethnic identity as a factor in social, political and economic relations.

The reorganisation has failed to create an atmosphere of equanimity among the people of the seven new political units. It has further alienated the hills and plains people, thereby directly and indirectly augmenting mistrust and misunderstanding. The example of this fact is the occasional innocent people losing their lives.

The question to be raised is: Has the reorganisation of states on linguistic basis solved the problems of the states thus created? It has failed to protect the linguistic minorities of their linguistic rights besides giving rise to socio-economic problems. In this regard, S.K. Chaube in his article "Language Politics in Assam" published in *North-Eastern Affairs* (quarterly), October-December, 1972, Shillong, has aptly said that "the demand for a linguistic state is a peculiar middle class aspiration intended to establish its command on defined territories. It also aims at securing a control of the dominant group on the governmental offices. In the British period, most of the offices were shared by the British and the Bengalis. Introduction of Assamese as the medium is intended to complete the 'Assamese' grip on the offices of the state government." Thus the language movement was apparently emotional and cultural in character but there were solid economic reasons behind it. The regional political parties in the state provide leadership to both the state movement and the language movement in the state. From a political point of view, such movements lead to a sort of consolidation of the emerging middle class in the state which is no doubt true. But it is also to be noted that E.M.S. Namboodripad, the then Chief Minister of Kerala state, in a statement on April 14, 1967 said, that "the emergence of new political forces called for the recognition of the multilingual and multi national character of India and the need to make necessary adjustment in the federal character of the constitution". In a multilingual society, ethnic groups would entertain language apppeals or linguistic appeal. Language is one the instruments to consolidate the group. This is considered as a symbol of an ethnic group.

VIII

Thus a deeper analysis of the reasons/causes for state autonomy/statehood and the adverse effects of the reorganisation of north-east region on its ethno-cultural and socio-economic political transition as mentioned in the foregoing pages, reveal that further reorganisation of north-east India cannot be ruled out from the list of possibilities. The ethno-cultural and linguistic problems in Assam still continue. Assam has not been able to settle the perennial problems like political identity of the Bodos demanding the creation of a state on the northern banks of the Brahmaputra valley to be known as Bodoland, the major hill tribes–the Karbis of the Karbi Anglong District and the Dimasa Kacharis of North Cachar Hill District, demanding for an autonomous state and finally the Karbi-Dimasa-Kachari state and Bengali, which seriously threaten the solidarity of the state. Such a new identity seems to have emerged in the wake of both the language controversy and crisis of capitalist path of development. For sometime, the Garos in Meghalaya have identified themselves with the Khasi political aspirations. There is no reason to assume that the identification will remain fixed. Minority groups in Manipur have long been vocal in retaining their identities and having the aspirations for political and economic control within the areas of residence. Bengali percentage in Tripura is now 70 per cent. The result has been that political and administrative powers have passed from the hands of indigenous tribes to immigrant-Bengalis. Despite the fact, Tripura has yet to fully become a Bengali state, in as much as, non-Bengali interests predominate in the political process of that state. Besides, the hills masses of Tripura inspite of having their District Councils recently created under the Sixth Schedule to the Indian Constitution have not yet reconciled themselves with the present administrative set-up. They have their grievances of social and economic exploitation by outsiders (most Bengalis) and the negligent attitude of their state government. Similarly, the state of Mizoram has not yet finally settled the political identity of the Pawis, the Lakhers and the Chakmas inhabiting the Chhimtuipui District. Although the Pawis, the Lakhers and the Chakmas have been continuing to look after their distinictive functions as envisaged in the Sixth Schedule to the Constitution by the formation of the Pawi-Lakher Regional Council from 1953 to 1972 and the Lai District Council, the Mara District Council and the Chakma District Council from 1972 to till date, identifying themselves with the Mizo political aspiration for sometime, yet they seem to be unreconciled with the Autonomous District Councils because there is no provision in the Sixth Schedule to bring the Council to participate in the development schemes and social welfare to the largest extent possible. But it is yet to be seen whether they will continue to maintain their identification keeping in view their distinct identity separate from that of the Mizo clans, However, the glaring example of this fact is the demand for creation of a separate Union Territory made by the leaders of the three tribes in 1971 for their areas. It, thus, signifies that the leaders of the three tribes-Pawi, Lakher, and Chakma have accepted the autonomous District Council only as a stop gap arrangement.

The Hmar identity crisis, a post eighties development, has emerged in Mizoram politics which has a geo-political significance due to strategic location. Hmar is one of the Mizo clans living in the north and north-eastern part of the Mizoram with a population of over thirteen thousand whose agnates are also living in the contiguous areas of Assam (South Cachar) and Manipur (Churachanpur area) having a population of 80,000 only. Both the tribesmen (Hmars and Mizos) worked together for improving the lot of the Mizo people, but recently the relation among them has become strained, because the Hmars' concentrated action plan is presently to establish a distinct ethno-cultural identity separate from the Mizos. A clearly perceptible unrest among the Hmar tribes has surfaced due to growing frustration, estrangement, feeling of deprivation and crisis of development administration. Therefore, the Hmars have found no other alternative but to organise themselves into a clan based political party named the Hmar People's Convention (H.P.C.) one the ehtnic line of the Pawis, the Lakhers and the Chakmas in order to obtain the Autonomous District Council for their areas under the Sixth Schedule to the Constitution, though they are late in projecting their autonomy demand. The problem of the crisis of Hmar identity is, thus, nothing but a great challenge to the ethnic homogeneity of the Mizos in Mizoram.

Nagaland became a state in 1963 with a population of

only five lakhs that is far below the average population of any district in India. The creation of Nagaland signifies that the viability of a state in the country depends not on its population but on the distinctive ethno-cultural identity of the people. This has significantly inspired the other identity-conscious hills people of north-east India to fight for their statehood. Besides, Keeping in view the sociology of politics in India, one cannot be blind to the emerging trends as reflected by the aspirations and behaviour of various nationalities, sub-nationalities and ethnic groups. The disillusionment for not having obtained fair justice and proper accomodation in the political process of our country has been responsible for arousing a feeling of alienation. These feelings are reflected by the regional parties in the form of demand for autonomy to the states and for creation of statehood, though these regional political parties are generally the political front for the protection and consolidation of the interests of the emergent middle class and of their patrons–the landed gentry and the Indian capitalist class. However, in the context of the character of the Indian nation and federal character of the union, the regional parties are necessary elements to hold the heterogeneous country as one unit.

IX

A question arises as to what should be done for containing the possibility of further reorganisation of north-east India in particular and the rest of the country in general? The answer is the removal/eradication of social and economic grievances of both the plains and the hills people at the earliest possible moment so that they have a better and saner understanding of the whole situation. The growing ethno-cultural identity consciousness among the hills people has also been sharpened by the facts of social and economic injustice that has been in existence owing first to the mischievous policy of the colonial rulers and then the negligent attitude of the leaders of free India. The existing socio-economic structure and the capitalist path of development that the country has adopted after independence, has sharpened not only the caste, religious, linguistic, cultural and ethnic distinctions and communal tensions, it has also widened regional economic disparities, frustration, estrangement, feeling of deprivation, socio-economic injustice, negligence and insecurity coupled with the instinct of preserving the distinct cultures and traditions among various nationalities, sub-national groups and ethnic tribal groups. For instance, massive central grants to the north-eastern states have only helped to create a new properties "Middle Class", bereft of values and which thrives on crass opportunism, favouritism nepotism and corruption. The fruits of development in the form of huge central grants have been pocketed by the politician - bureaucrat - contractor lobby and the conditions of the common people have not registered even marginal improvement. It is also felt that no governments of the hills states of whatever political persuasion, have been able to formulate a plan for self-sustaining economic development for a society making the transition from a village based tribal structure to a more modern set-up. Thus the development process itself including the tribal welfare and other programmes of the Central and State Governments has given rise to new economic, political and social forces and institutions that generate the present social and political tensions. Hence it must be ensured that the benefits of development must reach the masses. If the tribesmen and the plains neglected poor people from oppression, deprivation, exploitation, under development, socio-economic injustice, land alienation and dependency are to be liberated, the present socio-economic structure of the country, which at present, increases/disparity, exploitation and injustice of all sorts, social evils, oppression and emergence of middle class, has to be radically restructured. Besides, a relevant point which is being made here is to be noted for future guidance that the "Opposition conclave" which met in Srinagar on October 5-7. 1983 has called for restructuring the Union State relations in their political, economic, legal and constitutional aspect so that the character of our multi-religious, múlti-lingual and multi-culture country is preserved.

27

CONCEPT OF SMALLER STATES AND THE PACE OF DEVELOPMENT
A Case of Mizoram

S. S. MISHRA

There is a growing tendency among various communities inhabited in different parts of India that preservation of the ethnic identity and better development of the region could be made possible by delimiting the territory to the level of ethnicity, uniformity of culture of geography and other such standards. Many on-going ethnic movements for separate states like Jharkhand of Bihar, Uttarakhand of Uttar Pradesh, Bodoland and Karbiland of Assam are equally influenced to a great extent with the notion of "SMALLER THE STATE, HIGHER THE PACE OF DEVELOPMENT." Some political parties and elite groups have also supported this view. The "Bharatiya Janata Party" in its August 1992 meeting held at Bhopal proposed for the reorganisation of Big States like Madhya Pradesh, Rajasthan and Uttar Pradesh for smooth administrative and developmental activities. Similarly, on 5th March 1993 at a Seminar at New Delhi, the Former President of India called for setting up a Commission for reorganisation of the States to tackle the demands for small States in some parts of the country (*Assam Tribune*–March 8, 1993). While initiating any move for the concept of creation of small states, the questions still remain

(i) Whether uniformity of smallness is a prerequisite factor for development of the region?

(ii) Whether such states that are bigger have not registered noticeable pace of development ?
(iii) Whether such states that are small have succeeded in true sense without any lacuna such as political instability.
(iv) Or all these notions are the outcome of later phase designed for different motives least concerned with welfare and development of the region.

This study aims to examine these notions around the concept of smaller states and in its correlationship with development and related consequences, the context of one of the smaller states of North-East India *i.e.* Mizoram.

Mizoram as one of the seven sisters of North-East India is the abode of altogether seventeen main ethnic groups. As per 1991 census the state is having minimum population living in altogether 722 villages against least in number under three districts, namely Aizawl, Lunglei and Chhimtuipui. But in terms of geographical area (21,081 sq. kms) it is next to Tripura and Nagaland. On the other hand, the state registers highest tribal population *i.e.*, 93.58 per cent with equally highest literacy rate. In this way Mizoram represents smallness in terms of population and geograpby while bigness in other aspects.

Emergence of Mizoram

Mizoram a full-fledged state of the nineties has reached the present status after great struggle from its glowing past. The history of the State dates back to an early period of pre-British age, when the Mizos were being ruled by their hereditary chiefs. Earliest contact with the Mizo by the British was made in the year 1826. Later in 1891, the Mizo land was annexed to British India. On 1st April 1889 the South Lushai Hills, which was then the part of Bengal was transferred to the Assam Administration and the united Lushai hills was formed. "This decision was taken in the same proclamation of 1st April 1889 to transfer the tract known as Ruttan Poiay's village in the hill tracts of Chittagong to Assam and to include it in the United Lushai Hills" (Aitchinson 1962 : 276). In 1935 under the provision of the Government of India Act 1935, Lushai Hills District was declared to be excluded from the operations of the provincial legislations. The objective behind this was to encourage the people to develop themselves according to their own competence and genius.

In the post Independence Era, the major development in the territory was the creation of District Council like Mizo District Council in 1952 and Pawi Lakher Regional Council 1953 under the Sixth Schedule to the constitution of India. The Pawi Lakher Regional Council was ultimately superseded by three District Council, namely, Pawi District Council, Lakher District Council and Chakma District Council. The period from 1958 to 1961 was a critical phase in the history of Mizoram when this area experienced acute food shortage due to famine.

In 1959 "The Mizo National Famine Front "was formed to servce the people suffering from the calamity. Later this organization became political in nature under a new name "Mizo National Front" and spearheaded their movement for united Mizoram comprising the areas of Assam, Manipur and Burma inhabited by the Mizo. Soon this organization involved itself in rebellious activities. In order to curb the armed insurrections of the MNF hostiles, misery of the people due to famine and to accelerate the pace of development; the villages were grouped during 1966 to 1970 into four types of group centres. This grouping of villages proved effective in changing the economic backwardness of the people and also in containing the unlawful elements and activities.

Another important change came up in the structural pattern, when the north-eastern region was reorganised by the "Reorganization Act 1971" when the Mizo Hills District was elevated to a Union Territory with the name of Mizoram. The period of violence and disturbances which started in 1966 remained for more than 20 years. Disturbances subsided and peace restored in the region after the peace accord and settlement. After this a major change came up in the territory on 20th February 1987, when the Mizoram was given the status of full-fledged state.

Development Through Ages

The reorganization process in Mizoram dates back to 1898. Since then this area has witnessed many changes both in terms of development on the one hand and in the administrative and organizational set up on the other. The Mizoram as Lushai Hills District during 1898 to 1953 and Mizo Hills District during, 1954 to 1972 experienced substantial development in different social and economic fields. The pace of development gained further momentum during 1972 to 1987 when Mizoram was Union Territory and later during 1987 to 1993 when Mizoram attained the status of full-fledged state. Different social and economic indicators (Table 27.1) indicate substantial pace of development in the different time period especially in urban population, urban areas, number of academic institutes, number of hospitals and health care facilities, irrigation facilities and production of food grains etc. But above all in some areas, such as literacy, religion and economy, the region has registered tremendous pace of development, which needs to be dealt with separately.

TABLE 27.1: Development of Mizoram through Ages

Social and Economic indicators	Mizoram (1951) as Lushai Hills District (1898-1953)	Mizoram (1961) as Mizo Hills District (1954-1972)	Mizoram (1981) as Mizoram U.T. (1972-1987)	Mizoram (1991) as Mizoram State (1987-93)
Population	1,96,202	2,66,063	4,93,757	686,217
Sex Ratio	1000M/1041 F	1000M/1000F	1000M/919F	1000M/924F
Cultivable Area	2,964,596 hec	NA	84,626,20. hec	NA
Irrigation	4,033 hec	5745 hec	7,287,99 hec	8,000 hec
Crime	82 nos	316 nos	979 nos	NA
Hospitals	4 nos	2 nos	5 (1978) nos	14 nos
Literacy	31,14%	44.01 %	59.88%	67.36 %
Primary School	430 (1952)	625 (1962)	654	1109 (Sept. 1990)
Middle School	62 (")	113 (")	303	544(")
High School	5 (")	10(")	136	202 (")
College	Nil	1(")	10 nos	13 (")
Forest	NA	5,029,740 hec.	1,75,824.33 hec .	15.9 Lakh hec (1985).
Production of Food grains	-	30.7 thousnad Tonnes (1983-84).		63.2 thousand Tonnes1988-89)
Town /Urban areas	-	2 (1971)	6(1981)	22 (1991)

Growth of Christianity

The growth of christianity in Mizoram dates back to 1897 when *Welsh Calvinistic Mission* initiated their work at Aizawl. Later in 1903 *London Baptist Mission* joined hands. Again in 1916, two more christian units namely *Salvation Army Corps* and *Roman Catholic* also came forward to work among the Mizos. Apart from these units of missionaries some other denominations like united penticostal church and *Seventh Day Adventist* mission entered and developed their network of activities in the region from 1947 onwards. The number of Christians in 1901 was marginal *i.e.*, 0.05 percent (45 nos). In the subsequent decades, the rise of Christian population was quite phenomenal. "Twenty years ago there were less than 3000 Christians in that district (Mizoram) there are now over 59,000 and christians form very nearly half of the total population" (Census of India; 1931: 194). By the end of 1971 there were 2,86,141 christians constituting 87 per cent of the total population and at present almost entire Mizo population has become christians.

But earlier they were animist having conception of a supreme God "Pathian 'who was considered to be the creator of everything. They did not worship the natural Gods like Sun, Moon but believed different hills, streams, trees etc. to be the abode of various demons (Huai). They had belief of life after death and used to perform sacrifices to pacify spirits for cure of diseases and during economic activities. Now these age old traditions have been replaced by christianity; which has brought not only Western culture and a new class of intellectuals but also substantial changes in socio-cultural values and norms.

Growth of Education

The credit of introducing modern education in this remote and isolated territory goes to the Christian missionaries by whose efforts rapid spread of education could be made. The first formal school was opened here in the year 1894 and by the turn of 1970 almost every village of the area was having a primary school. The first High School came up in 1944 while the first College in 1958. At present there are 1,109 primary schools, 544 Middle School 202 High School and 13 Colleges. Presently, Mizoram registers second highest literacy rate of country. But in the beginning situation was quite different. As per 1901 census, only 761 (0.98%) persons were literate. This percentage became 3.98 in 1911 and 19.48 by the end of 1941. The rate of literacy subsequently increased after every decade and now as per 1991 census 67.36 percent people are literate in the state. The growth of education has influenced their socio-cultural development also. The rapid growth of education gave birth to a new class of elites; which also resulted into creation of some organizations such as UMA (Young Mizo Association) MHIP (Women Association) etc. having enormous influence at the grass root level, which helped to modernize the society, upgrade the status of women and change in the outlook of people towards dress, house pattern, decoration and sensitive towards new trend in cultural growth and integration.

Agriculture is the backbone of the economy of Mizoram. As per 1991 census about 65 per cent of main workers are engaged in agriculture. Though the proportion of agriculture workers in the main workers group has come down (Table 27.2) in the decade yet this sector occupies prominent place in their economy. In the field of industry, the region lacks developed infrastructure despite richness in different natural resources such as deciduous tree, bamboo and medicinal herbs etc. But the economy of the region witnessed considerable upsurge in the early seventies; when government endeavour to encourage new mode of production, expansion of different areas of economy like large and multifarious cottage industries, horticulture, tea plantation and implementation of different rurual development programmes for the upliftment of rural people proved very effective. It was during this period that there has Yeilded positive begun a real thrust for bringing this remote almost cut off and sharply mountainous part of the country into the national stream by exposing it to new technology, (Mahajan : 1986: 9). In addition to this, the five-year plan provision for

TABLE 27.2: Comparative Economic Situation of Mizoram, Assam and Tripura

Selected Economic Indicators	Mizoram	Assam (Bigger State)	Tripura (Smaller State)	All India
Rural (1991)	369,177 (53.80%)	19,823,674 (88.92 %)	2,325,844 (84.74 %)	627,146,597
Urban (1991)	317,040 (46.20 %)	2,470,888 (11.08 %)	418,983 (15.26 %)	217,177,625
Total Workers (1991)	338,724 (49.36 %)	8,108,785 (36.37%)	860752 (31.36 %)	N.A,
Cultivator	176,713 (25.75 %)	3622017 (16.25%)	301856 (11.00%)	N.A.
Agricultural Labourers	10,835 (1.58 %)	919,386 (4.12 %)	186,671 (6.80 %)	N.A.
Forest Area Lakh hec.(1984-85)	15.9	30.7	6.3	751.85
Net Irrigation Area (1988-89) thousand hect.	8	572	45	N.A.
Per Capita Electric Consumption (KWH) 1989-90	57	78	51	236
Per Capita Domestic Product (current) 1985-86	1773	2037	1945	N.A.
Road per 100 Sq.Kms (1989)	22.99	44.79	65.46	47.24.
Per Capita plan outlays (Seven Plan)	Rs. 5200	1014	1913	2608

Mizoram also played vital role in accelerating the pace of economic development. The five year plan provisions while it was a district of Assam were Rs. 63.02 lakhs and Rs. 210.03 lakhs for the First and Second five-year plan respectively. However, the plan provision was allocated almost double Rs. 411.42 lakhs during the third five-year. It was further raised to Rs. 685.27 lakhs during the Fourth Plan to be spent in different spheres of development including agriculture, soil conservation, Education, co-operative, communication and health. Out of different programmes and plans implemented, some substantial economic development took place in the region, the food production, which was 30.7 thousand tonnes in 1983-84 reached 56.6 thousand tonnes by the end of 1987-88. Similarly, the length of fair weather road which was 415 kms in 1972-73 became 1,612 kms by the end of 1980. Not only this, now the state is on the airmap of India and the extension of rail head in the territory. In this way the region has registered substantial economic growth from its early phase yet the region is not free from different socio-economic odds like unemployment, drug abuses, underdeveloped industrial field etc.

Comparison

The Mizoram in its span of about a century has registered tremendous pace of development in some areas of economy and in social dimension; but the overall picture does not symbolise the integrated development due to its specific territorial constraints. In the field of power, road communication and agriculture still much more needs to be done. By the efforts of government and rising awareness of the people substantial development has been achieved in some sectors specially from the early part of the seventies. The reorganization of the territory and its status as Mizoram Union Territory and later as a full-fledged state may be a good reason for such boost in economic and social fields.

When one compares the situation of Mizoram with other north-eastern state, which are smaller (as Tripura) or bigger (as Assam) in geographical area, it becomes apparent that the social and economic indicators give quite diverse impression. Assam is still one of the biggest states among north-eastern states having an area of 78,438 sq. kms while Tripura having 10,487 sq. kms is the smallest state, whereas Mizoram is next to Tripura in terms of area. Agriculture labourers and the area under irrigation show that Mizoram counts less then both the state; which subsequently the agricultural product. The situation becomes, more abvious, when per capita net domestic product at current price (1984-85) is analysed. Here also Mizoram is lagging behind with Rs.1,773 whete Smaller State Tripura Counts move *i.e.* Rs. 1,945 and Assam registers maximum of Rs. 2,037 only. The position of industrial network is equally not very encouraging. Though the number of registered units of small scale industries in the state has increased from 471 in 1980 to 1,866 by the year 1988 but is still less than Assam having 10,210 SSI units and Tripura with 3,523 SSI units. Similarly, lack of power is another big bottleneck in the sustainable development of the state, where per capita electric consumption as well as number of villages electrified are less than both the states (Table 27.2). Despite this there are certain areas where this small state has experienced tremendous pace of development far ahead of both Assam as well as Tripura. The rate of literacy is certainly one, where more than 67 per cent people are literate. Likewise in the field of urban population growth rate, Mizoram has topped all the states and Union Territory with an urban growth rate, of 160.27 per cent during 1981-91 (Census of India-series 1 pp :16).

In addition, the ethnicity has played effective role in coherence and development of Mizoram whereas Tripura and Assam due to various and diverse cultural and linguistic agglomeration lack such a developed coherence. Apart from these, phenomenal changes have come up in the socio-cultural life of the people of Mizoram. Now almost entire population has given up traditional faith and accepted christianity. Different traditional customs and religious festivals are no longer in practice. In this way traditional culture has been replaced by modern western culture, which has made them highly elite and modernized group. The higher rate of literacy has given them ample scope and now most of them are employed in various services inside and outside the state. But complete departure from traditional way of life has created some socio-culural problems also like apathy towards traditional customs, loss of parental control etc. It is why attempts are going on by them to revive some traditional norms and values.

Conclusion

Thus it is quite obvious that development gained momentum in Mizoram by the efforts of all concerned people. The pace of development may be high or slow due to various reasons of a particular territory like socio-economic conditions, geographical situation and ethnicity. Here the management and organisational set-up for the implementation of various socio-economic plans and projects play very important role. In this way a specific territory has little role to play in achieving the desired objective of economic prosperity. Thus smallness or bigness of an area may not be a big factor if things are organised properly and implementing agency come forward with noble goal to attain the objectives. If things are organised and implemented properly a big state can also attain better result than smaller state with loose management and least concern for the people. Thus the concept of smaller area and the pace of development may or may not be a flexible and pragmatic approach depending upon the area concerned and specific problems of the region, which may not be similar in all cases. In addition to this the process of cultural fussion which assimilated many sub-tribes like Pawi, Lakher etc. to identify entire population as a homogeneous unit in Mizoram having common language, religion and territory has helped them in their efforts to preserve their identity. It equally facilitated them to intensify the all round development of Mizoram, which was, in fact, a late starter in the sphere of development.

REFERENCES

Aitchinson, C.U. 1962. *A Collection of Treaties, Engagements and Sanads,* Vol II.

Darchhawna, 1987. *Mizoram District Gazetteers,* Govt. of Mizoram, Tribal Research Institute, Aizawl.

Mahajan, V.S. 1986. Mizoram at the beginning of 21st century, *Mizoram News* pp. 9-11, Aizawl.

Nanda, 1991. Census of India, Series-1, Paper-2 of 1991. *Rural Urban Distribution,* pp. 16.

Pakynthein, E. H. 1961. Census of India, *District Census Hand Book,* Mizo Hills, Assam.

28

REORGANIZATION QUESTION OF TRIPURA (1949-62)
Reactions of Different Political Parties

MAHADEV CHAKRAVARTI

After the sudden death of Maharaja Bir Bikram Kishore Manikya on May 17, 1947, the Regent Maharani Kanchanprave Devi, ruling Tripura on behalf of her minor son, Kirti Bikram Kishore Manikya, signed the instrument of Accession the Indian Union on 13 August, 1947 Princely Tripura was integrated with the Indian Union on 15th October 1949. Following the Agreement of Merger of Tripura with the Indian Union, the Chief Commissioner took over the reins of administration from the Regent Maharani. It is interesting to read that historic message of Sardar Vallabbhai Patel who with consummate skill and diplomacy succeeded in persuading almost all the princely states, except Jammu and Kashmir, Hyderabad and Junagadh:

> "The State of Tripura, with its isolated situation, yet occupying a position of strategic importance on the eastern border of India, has an ancient history and a rich culture. The partition of the country has, however, brought in its train for this State a host of problems which, in the present state of its development, it was impossible for it to solve unaided. The Government of India and Her Highness the Maharani Regent acting on behalf of the minor Ruler, have come to the conclusion that in the interest of the state and its people and of the

> country as a whole, it was essential that the Centre should make itself directly responsible for the administration of the state and the well-being of its people. Tripura thus becomes from today a Centrally administered area......
> To the people of Tripura I would say this-though their State is far remote from the seat of the Government of India, it would always claim our attention and we shall do all that is possible to ensure that the ties that bind us together are strengthened and that the State and its people become in all respects very near to us."[1]

Sri Prakasa, Governor of Assam, on the occasion of taking over of the Tripura State by the Government of India, sent the following message:

> "Today, the Government of India, are taking upon themselves the burden of responsibility for the welfare and the progress of the people of the Tripura State /. . . As the Central Government takes over the states of Manipur and Tripura, that mighty edifice is completed, fulfilling the dream of ages, of the consolidation and unification of the land, the foundation-stone of which was well and truly laid two year ago when the illustrious and far-famed princess of our great land signed the Instrument of Accession on the attainment of our country's Freedom . . .
> May to-day mark the ushering of yet another era of your great and glorious history. You have no need to have any apprehensions about the future."[2]

Thus Tripura became one of the Part 'C' states where, for administrative, strategic and other special reasons, Central Control was considered necessary. It came to be administered by a Chief Commissioner under the direct control of the Union Government. Neither in the activities and speeches of the Chief Commissioner, nor in the goodwill message of Sardar Patel and Sri Prakasa, as quoted above, there was any mention of democratization of administration for which the democratic minded people of Tripura waged a long struggle even during the princely regime. Out of the ten Part 'C' states, Tripura, Manipur, Bilaspur and Kutch were deprived of the representative institutions as provided in other six Part 'C' states. Different political parties of Tripura expressed their grave discontent with rule of the Chief Commissioner and demanded immediate introduction of responsible government in the State.

After the first general election in 1952, a three-member Advisory Council was formed. The function of the nominated Advisory Council was to advise the Chief Commissioner in 19 subjects of administration distributed among the three members. Although the appointment of the Advisory Council was considered by some, as the first step towards democratization, actually it was an open defiance of the popular wish because the majority of the people who were then influenced by the Communist Party (Dasarath Deb as a candidate of the party won the first Lok Sabha election from underground and the then Lok Sabha seat was also won by the Communist Party) and their popular organisations did not find any place either in the Advisory Council or any place of honour anywhere in the administration. Moreover, the powers of even these nominated Advisers were very much limited and the Chief Commissioner had the over-riding authority in almost all matters.

'Purbachal' Concept

In view of the growing demand for linguistic states, the Government of India decided in 1953 to appoint a Commission unde the Chairmanship of Fazal Ali and consisting of Sardar K.M. Pannikar and Pandit H.N. Kunzru a members. A progressive section of people appealed to all political parties and communities of Tripura to observe 15th August 1953 as the Legislative Assembly Demand Day. As the autocratic rule of princely Tripura continued even after 15 October 1949 in one form or the other, some advocate and medical practitioners and other Bengalee elites headed by Swarna Kamal Roy not only advocated immediate introduction of democratic government in Tripura, but also the formation of 'Purbachal'[3] consisting of Tripura, Manipur, Cachar and the Lushai Hills.

That suggestion was submitted to the States Reorganisation Commission (SRC) on 14 August 1953. But ultimately, the dream of some Agartala Bengalee elites regarding the creation of 'Purbachal' came down to the merger of Tripura and Cachar from the linguistic standpoint. The arguments put forward by Swaran Kamal Roy and others for the creation of a bigger States like 'Purbachal' were the following :

1. According to the Census figures of 1951, the area of the proposed 'Purbachal', consisting of Tripura, Cachar, Manipur and the Lushai Hills District with a constitution as provided for Part 'A' or Part 'B' States, would be 25,521 sq. miles and its population 25,28,731. Its revenue would be over Rs. 2 crores. In 1952, at the time of the introduction of passport system about 75,000 displaced persons from East Bengal took shelter in Tripura and a similar number entered into Cachar. If these figures were taken into account then the population of proposed 'Purbachal' in 1953 would have been about 27 lakhs. Again, if the 12 thanas of the Sylhet District which were under dispute at that time between India and Pakistan, were restored to India, then these thanas would also be included in that proposed new State. In that case, the proposed 'Purbachal' would be bigger in size and population than Patiala and East Punjab States Union which was a Part 'B' State.
2. From the cultural and linguistic point of view, Tripura and Cachar were closely connected. Bengali was the court language of the Tripura Durbar and eightly per cent of the people of Tripura could speak or understand Bengali–the language of Cachar. Regarding Manipur, it was pointed out that the Manipuris followed the Vaishnava cult of the Chaitanya school of Bengal and a good many surnames of the Manipuris are the same as Bengalees providing closed cultural affinity. As the Lushai Hills District lies to the east of Tripura and to the south of Cachar and Manipur, hence it was suggested that the Lushai Hills of Assam might be included in the proposed State of Tripura-cum-Cachar-cum-Manipur.
3. Finally, if Manipur did not join the new State, then

> the people of Manipur should have a separate state of their own and the question of inclusion of the Lushai Hills in the proposed 'Purbachal' did not arise. In that event, the proposed 'Purbachal' would consist of Tripura and Cachar only with an area of 8,751sq. miles and a population of 19,00,000 and a revenue of about one an half crore rupees. The proposed new State would be rich in rice, sugarcane, oil-seeds, tea cotton, timber,cane and other forest produce and would be a viable one.

But the above 'Purbachal' concept did not gain any popular ground among the people; rather, the demand for a separate states of Tripura with a Legislative Assembly became most popular after the observance of 15 August 1953 as the Legislative Assembly Demand Day.

The State Reorganisation Commission submitted its report to the Government of India on 30 September 1955 which was made by public on 10 October 1955. Contrary to the above two demands of the people of Tripura, the Commission recomended merger of Tripura with Assam as that would, in the opinion of the Commission, fulfil the aspirations of representative government without prejudicing the linguistic and cultural interests of the people.[4] But barring some tribal elites of Agartala, the majority people- both tribal and non-tribal very sharply reacted against such recommendation of merger with Assam.

With the objective of launching united struggle against the SRC proposals and for demanding 'autonomous and democratic Tripura' a broad-based platform known as the 'Autonomous Tripura Committee' was formed in 1955 with Swarna Kamal Roy (Praja Socialist Party) as the President and Dasarath Deb (Communist Party of India) as the General Secretary. Under the banner of the 'Autonomous Tripura Committee' (ATC) the history of mass movement opened a new chapter where students, teachers and other middle-class intelligentsia participated in large number.

In the face of such tumultuous protests, the States Reorganisation Act, passed on 31 August 1956, undid for the time being the merger proposal and a large portion of the recommendations of the Commission and Tripura became one of the five Union Territories[5] under the above Act, with effect from 1 November 1956. The Council of Advisers which was constituted before the reorganisation of state had been dissolved after 14 August 1957 and the Tripura Territorial Council began to function with effect from 15 August 1957. The Territorial Council was formed with 32 members, of whom 30 were elected by the local people and two were nominated by the President of India. Against the demand for a full-fledged Legislative Assembly, Tripura was granted for the first time on the model of a municipal administration a limited democratic structure where the Territorial Council could deal only with a few local subjects under the supervision of an administrator with the designation of Chief Commissioner. The territorial Council drama could not fulfil the political aspirations of the people and the question of reorganisation of the state and administration remained open for sometime. The political situation of Tripura continued to be restive.

Representations to the Committee on Union Territories

A Committee of Union Territories (CUT) was formed under the Chairmanship of A.K. Sen, the then Union Lain Minister, in pursuance of the statement made by the Minister of Home Affairs in the Lok Sabha on 7 December 1961 on the Administrative set-up of the Union Territories of Himachal Pradesh, Manipur and Tripura. This was the result of big mass agiations, particularly in Manipur and Tripura, where all political parties demanded immediate introduction of full-fledged Legislative by replacing the existing administrative set-up.

Memorandum of the CPI

Biren Dutta, the Secretary of the CPI, Tripura State Council, in his Memorandum dated 27 March 1962, first pointed out why the existing administrative arrangements were unpopular as the entire set-up stood on three legs, namely, (i) The Advisory Committee, (ii) the elected Territorial Council, and (iii) the Administration under the Chief Commissioner.

The Advisory Committee consisted of the Union Home Minister, the Chief Commissioner, the Chairman of the Territorial Council and three M.Ps to advise the Central Government in all important matters from budget to legislation. The Committee usually met three or four times a year with a sitting of not more than two or three hours at a time. On the recommendations of the Committee during the last four year, a number of important legislations were adopted by the Parliament for Tripura. But the Land Reforms and Land Revenue Act was drafted by the Central Government without taking into consideration the peculiar feature of land system in Tripura and the Land Reforms Rules had been drafted by the Tripura Administration totally disregarding the wishes of the people. The Panchayat Raj Act was imported from Uttar Pradesh and the Pachayat Rules had been framed by the Administration to make these institutions a mockery of democracy. The Agartala Municipality Act had been bodily taken from West Bengal, the Money Lenders' Act and the Cooperative Act from Bombay. In fact, a number of Acts, Rules and Codes had been blindly adopted from different states having least regard for local conditions and public opinion as a result of which popular discontent mounted daily.

According to the CPI, the Territorial Council concept was found to be so unworkable a scheme that at every step insurmountable difficulties cropped up.

> "In course of last 4 years, only about one-fourth of the Budget of Tripura was transferred to the Territiorial Council. But this transfer also was done haltingly. Subjects and Departments were also transferred only partily. Departments were transferred by the officers and the staff, the office buildings and the quarters, even the necessary papers were not transferred....... The limitations imposed in the form of "exceptions and conditions" under the provisions of the Act, made the position of the Territorial Council ludicrous in the eyes of the people."[6]

On the top of it remained the Tripura Administration which was responsible only to the Chief Commissioner who wielded unlimited power over a very wide area of the life of the people. In shorts, the prevalent type of bureaucracy in Tripura, according to the CPI, did not fit in any demoicratic pattern of society. To quote:

> "... that a large part of the Plan-money could not be spent during the Second Plan periods, Whatever was spent was mostly wasted in schemes unsuitable for Tripura. Corruption, wastage, bungling and mismanagement was the general feature almost in all departments. This is why the people of Tripura as well as people of other Territories were so vocal in denouncing the present arrangement of things which stood as the biggest hurdle on their way to progress.........
> "It is our considered opinion that this continued experiment with the administrative set-up should stop forever; the three-tier set-up should end once for all........
> "The SRC recommended for a merger of Tripura with Assam. But the people of Tripura turned down that recommendation through innumerable mass demonstrations. Finding Tripura Territorial Council inadequate to fulfil the democratic aspirations of the people-both before and during the last third General Elections our party made demand for Bidhan Sabha its central political slogan."[7]

Memorandum of the Tripura State Congress

The President of the Tripura State Congress in his Memorandum supported the Union Home Minister for his statement on 7 December 1961 that responsible government is a prerequiste for development and that the powers of the Territorial Council should be extended to make it a meaningful institution.[8] To quote the memorandum:

> "... We, are therefore, in full agreement with the Home Minister's view that the basic appproach is to give an opportunity to the people to develop their areas and also to give them a feeling of genuine participation in running the administration.

"It was in consideration of this, amongst many other factors, that were had opposed the State Reorganisation Commission's recommendations for the merger of Tripura with the neighbouring State of Assam. . . .

"The Union Territories cannot remain contended with the territorial Councils in their present form. Creation of these local bodies which are, as mentioned in the 58th Report of the Estimates Committee (1958-59) of the Parliament, more or less like District Boards undoubtedly fell short of the demands for responsible government at the state level.

". . . What we would like to see is that the status of the Territorial Councils be raised from the position of a local board to that of an arm of the Government. . . .

"In conclusion, we would urge upon the Government of India to give shape to the Administrative set-up of the Union Territories in such a way that the representation of the people can exercise control over as large a field as may be possible without, if the Central Government so desire, bringing about any vital change in the constitutional relation between the Central and the Union Territories."[9]

Memorandum of the Praja Socialist Party

Nibaran Chandra Ghosh, the Chairman, Praja Socialist Party, Tripura Branch, in his memorandum to the Chairman of the Committee on Union Territories, dated 28 March 1962, specifically demanded a legislature for Tripura. To quote Ghose:[10]

"1. That though India has achieved independence, Tripura has not, as the people of Tripura are not the masters of their own destiny which is controlled from distant New Delhi......

3. That the people of Tripura are still wallowing in the mire of poverty, ignorance and despondence, though the Government of India is spending a lot of money for the purpose.

4. That this is due to the fact that the people of the soil have not been allowed to participate actively in the

administration and because administration by out-siders, however well-meaning, cannot be a substitute for self-Government.....

8. That the proper remedy is a legislature.

9. That if thought desirable, it may be a controlled legislature.

10. That the people of Tripura do not lag behind those of other states in India in political consciousness and the ratio of lettered people in Tripura is15.5% according to 1951 Census (according to 1961 Census it is 22.3%); whereas it is 10.8 per cent in U.P., 12.2 in Bihar and 13.5 in M.P.

11. That the strategic situation of Tripura, its lacking in transport facilities, its want of road and canals, its lack of industries the hampers staying the progress of agriculture and business here, demand that the destiny of Tripura should be wielded by the representativ sons of the soil, having love and sympathy for the people and direct knowledge of the entire situation . . .

19. That, in short, a fully responsible legislature only may be expected to be the only panacea for all the crowing and threatening evils".

Memorandum of the Eastern Indian Tribal Union

Sneha Kumar Chakma, President, Eastern India Tribal Union, Tripura Branch, in his memorandum to the Committee on Union Territories, dated 24 March 1962, strongly suorted the old proposal of the States Reorganisation Commission, namely, Tripura should be merged with Assam. To read the Memorandum:"

"3. The real problem of Tripura is that it is too much over-populated in comparison with her resources. Refugees are over-proportionate to the indigenous population, defeating all international law and equity......

4. As a result of scarcity of room and resources in Tripura, other ignoble tendencies like communal feeling, partiality, nepotism etc., have already struck root. And as tribals, we have a genuine complaint that we are fast losing ground under the weight of a non-tribal

majority and its administration. Morever, we have a sincere belief that but for the communal obstruction of the Bengalee majority population of Tripura, we still live as half-citizen in a territory instead of becoming full-citizen in a state, in the State of Assam, which was constitutionally offered to us.

5. Politically we should earn citizenship. Economically we should have space. This is what Tripura is in need of, and not an Executive Committee.....

.... We have had a PLAN submitted to the Scheduled Tribes Commission. In case the proposals are proposed to be forced through, we, the Tribals of Tripura, firmly stand for the present, on our minimum demand contained in the said PLAN, i.e.:

(a) Tripura be declared a Tribal Area.
(b) Part of Tripura be immediately formed into a 'Tripura Autonomous District'.

We also stand firm with the Demand of Creation of "The Eastern Frontier State" contained in the PLAN adopted in the 3rd All Party Hill Leaders Conference.

Counter Proposal

Considering, having opposed the proposals contained in the Statement under reference, that it would be more propoer than improper, we wish to open our mind and suggest:

1. That all the Union Territories be merged with adjoining States.
2. That Tripura should immediately be merged with Assam, for :

   (i) They fulfil the intentions of the Constitution,
   (ii) They enjoin due prestige to the citizen and the Republic of India,
   (iii) They help growth of greater National Integrity,
   (iv) They give space to sufforcating Tripura,
   (v) They solve many problems pertaining to these areas, particularly Tripura,

(vi) They simplify matters enormously."

Memorandum of the Jana Sangh of Tripura

The Jana Sangh, though a paper organisation at that time in Tripura, also submitted a memorandum to the Sen Committee on the administration of Tripura under a revised scheme. The President of Jana Sangh of Tripura pointed out that though his party would like to see Tripura as a separate unit under India with a legislature and an executivre responsible to it, still, the special conditions in Tripura put certain limitation in the practice of that ideal in the immediate future, namely rampant corruption, nepotism etc. of the Congress which was a 'majority' party. To quote:

> ". . . Firstly, the Congress Party that has secured a majority of seats in the Territorial Council with the help of a minority of votes is in the grip of less than half a dozen persons who have managed to remain in power for years now by means that are open secret to the people here. And inquiry by an impartial tribunal will reveal starting facts, particularly in regard to their handling of public funds and managements of institutions....
>
> ". . . Fourthly, there is hardly any one among the top men of the Congress now holding and exercising power in the Territorial Council who know anything of administration or possesses the requisite calibre to pick up such knowledge......
> ". . . We of the Jan Sangh, therefore, propose that:
>
> (I) Instead of the present diarchy, there should be an unified administration for Tripura under the superintendence and control of the President of India through the local administration by whatever name he may be called, and covering all the State subjects except law and order and administration of justice. A more transfer of certain other subjects to the present Territorial Council will serve no democratic purpose but will

only spread thepresent ills to a wider field, which is dangerous for a border region like Tripura.

"... we believe that our proposals will go much further towards extending the democratic powers of the territorial Council than has been proposed in the Home Minister statement of 7 December 1961, without making the Council a mere source of profit to a coterie."[12]

Memorandum of the Tripura Bar Association

Monoranjan Chowdhury and some other members of the Tripura Bar Association, Agartala, in their memorandum dated 28 March 1962,[13] not only welcomed the Union Home Minister's statement on 7 December 1961 that all works of development of Tripura should be transferred to the existing Territorial Council but also requested the Home Minister to see that the development of the Forest Department be entrusted to the Territorial Council.

In short, as opposed to the Jana Sangh demand, the Tripura Bar Association pleaded for more power to the Territorial Council and also separation of the judiciary from the Executive.

From the above representations of different political parties and associations of Tripura, it becomes clear that while the undivided Communist Party and the Praja Socialist Party were strongly demanding a Legislative Assembly for Tripura, the Congress Party at that time (later on it revised its decision) and the Tripura Bar Association were rather in favour of extension of power of the existing Territorial Council, which the Jana Sangh opposed tooth and nail; but the Eastern India Tribal Union strongly reiterated the old demand, *i.e.* immediate merger of Tripura with Assam. In spite of such conflicting demands of different political parties, the movement for separate statehood and legislature gained such a momentum in Tripura, that the Union Territories Act which provided Tripura with its first Legislative Assembly consisting of 30 elected members and a Council of Ministers although the authority of the Central Government remained final and supreme over the administration in Tripura. In the face of various movements, the North-Eastern Areas

(Reorganisation) Act, 1971 was ultimately passed in Parliament and according to that Act, Tripura attained full-fledged statehood with 60 member Legislative Assembly with effect from 21 January 1972.

REFERENCES

1. Message of the Hon'ble Sardar Vallabhbhai Patel on the occasion of the merger of Tripura on the 15 October 1949, as published in the *Tripura Gazette*, Special Number,15 October 1949, Agartala p. 4
2 Message of His Excellency Shri Sri Prakasa, Governor of Assam, on the occasion of the taking over of the Tripura State by the Government of India, as published in the Tripura Gazette, Special Number, 15 October 1949, Agartala, pp. 2-4
3. For the concept of 'Purbachal' as submitted by Swarana Kamal Roy, Nagendra Krishna Roy, Nripendra Kr. Chanda and others in their Memorandum to the Minister of State, Govt. of India, dated 14th August 1953, see Banikanta Bhattacharyya 1986, *Tripura Administration : The Era of Modernisation,* Mittal Publications, Delhi, pp. 242-44
4. V.D. Mahajan and Savitri Mahajan, 1967. *Constitutional History of India*, Seventh Edition, pp. 64--42
5. *Loc. Cit.*
6. Memorandum placed by the C.P.I. , Tripura State Council dated 27 March 1962, before A.K. Sen, Chairman of the Committee on Union Territories
7. *Ibid.*
8. Memorandum on the Administrative set-up othe Union Territories submitted by the President, Tripura State Congress in March 1962.
9. *Ibid.*
10. Memorandum to the Chairman, Committee on Union Territories on behalf of the Praja Socialist Party, Tripura Branch, by Nibaran Chandra Ghosh, Chairman, P.S.P., Tripura, dated 28 March 1962
11. A Short Memorandum of the Eastern India Tribal Union, Tripura Branch to the Committee on Union Territories, presented by Sneha Kumar Chakma, President, E.I.T.U. Tripura Branch, dated 24 March 1962 (Printed pamphlet)
12. Memorandum on the Administration of Tripura under a revised scheme as submitted by the President, Jana Sangh of Tripura , to the Sen Committee at Agartala in March 1962
3. Memorandum submitted on behalf of the Tripura Bar Association, Agartala, by Monoranjan Chowdhury and others, to the Chairman, Committee on Union Territories, dated 28 March 1962

29

TRIPURA IN TRANSITION OF POLITICAL REORGANISATION SINCE 1947

JAGAT JYOTI ROY

Since 1947 Land, being the source of development in political superstructure, was almost absent in the princely state of hill Tripura where hillocks and tilla land covered almost the state. Prior to 1947, the state of Tripura had extended up to the Chakla-Roshanabad in the then district of Coomilla in erstwhile East Bengal (now Bangladesh). The resources of plain land was the only source of revenue of the kingdom which felt the necessity to systematise the collection of land revenue through the agents but the Nowab of Bengal has set his eye on Chakla-Roshanabad before the advent of the British in the area. The King Krishna Manikya 1760-1783, experienced great difficulty in collecting the part of land revenue because of the absence of the definite land tenure system which the British introduced in 1793 under the historic Permanent Settlement though the British laws were not extended to the independent princely state.

Before the British rule in the state, there were frequent clashes between the Nowabs of Bengal and the king of Tripura over the collection of land revenue. After 1783, the British culture of administration practically emereged mainly in Chakla Roshanabad. The then Governor of Bengal, Mr. Vancitart, took full advantage to establish British hegemony over the Plain Tripura. And consequently the Plain Tripura came under the yoke of British rule of politics until 1947. For the first time an Englishman, Mr. Ralf Leak, was appointed as British Resident in Tripura. The historians had no occasion to deny the fact that the British did not annex the state of Tripura despite the privilege allowed in Chakla-Roshanabad but sufficient records are available in the historical account that the British reformatory laws enacted from time to time were also applicable in hill Tripura. The British laws of Abolition of Sati Practice under the title of Regulation Act, XVII of 1829 was enforced in Tripura in 1889-60 years long after the official enactment.

The last king of the state was Bir Bikram Kishore Manikya (1923-1947) who before his death had contemplated to accede to the Indian Union. The king himself felt the necessity for various administrative reforms specially in the interest of his tribal subjects who under the royal yoke were the exploited and neglected lot. After the death of king Bir Bikram, a council of regency was formed with the then Queen Kanchan Prava Devi as the Regent Ruler of the state till formal accession to the Indian Union was complete. On 13th August 1948, the Instrument of Accession was signed by the Council of Regency and thus the historic princely state formally acceded to the Indian Union. The Council of Regency was dissolved for further process to the political development within the mainstream of the national politics of the country. The Queen mother on behalf of her minor son signed the merger on 9th September 1949. Soon with the merger of the state with the Indian Union, a Chief Commissioner was appointed as head of the administration.

In 1950, Tripura became Part 'C' state under the Constitution, with no legislative assembly of its own. In the first election held in 1952, the 30-member electoral college was formed to elect their representatives to the Rajya Sabha. The administrative reforms were brought about by the Government of India to give democratic shape to the political set up of the state. An Advisery Council was formed in 1953 to aid, guide and fadvise the Chief Commissioner. The people of the state hardly experienced any democratic functioning for so long and it was no doubt a great privilege for them to see the transition from tribal kingship to modern democracy. Within a few years the re-organisation started with the prime objective of ensuring the democratic functioning.

The State Re-organisation Commission 1955 proposed the merger of Tripura state with the state of Assam. This proposal was highly acclaimed by the Tribal Union and organisation formed with few Tribal intellectuals who considered that merger with Assam would safequard the Tribals against the hegemony of the Bengalees. As opposed to this idea, a section of Bengalees, chauvinistic in character, put forward their demand for merging the state with Cachar district hereby forming a new state, 'Purbachal'. The idea of Purbachal was virulently opposed by the then CPI and other tribal factions. The Communist party all along favoured independent province within the frame work of the Constitution. In 1956, the state was designated as centrally adminsitered Union Territory. The following year as a ferest step towards parliamentary the people were given the right to elect 30 member Assembly in the Territorial Council.

The need for the formation of a separate state or an administrative set up for the tribals was first felt by a section of an elite close to the king when the massive influx of refugees to Tripura caused an acute shrotage of plain land. King Bir Bikram declared 2170 sq. km. area of land as reserved exclusively for the tribals in Khowai sub-division. In 1960, the Government of India constituted a commission under Mr. U.N. Dhebar, the former AICC president, to find political solution to the problem of the tribals. The Chief Commissioner Tripura, Mr. N.M. Patnayak, recommended to the Dhebar Commission to declare certain tribal areas as scheduled areas. According to him, "the influx of displaced persons from East Pakistan To Tripura has been enormous and has upset the local economy. It has greatly affected the tribals and made the land problem acute. The rights of the tribals in land should be safeguarded." A process of administrative change over was started by the then Government by enacting the tribal demarcated areas Act, and the need for introducing the Sixth Schedule to the Constitution was felt.

Prior to various administrative changes, a section of Tripura tribals soon after the partition desired not to mergers with the Indian Union while some non-tribals favoured merger with Pakistan. But interestingly enough a section of tribal leaders desired to remain independent to resist alien politics. The parliamentary system was practically opposed by a section of tribal elites of royal origin. Moreover, the unabated influx of refugees from erstwhile East Pakistan caused grave concern to the tribal elites who told the state Congress Party to check the en masse migration of the plain people in the interest of the tribals as a whole. Meanwhile the Tripura Mandal Act was passed to user in the local self-government. Which the then Congress opposed on the ground that the real authority was confined in the hands of a few tribals leaders of Agartala. The tribal elites and gentry class of Agartala with the royal patronage formed an organisation of Tripura Sangh to protest against the emergence of democracy and settlement of Bengalee refugees. But wit the premature death of the king, the Tripura Sangh could not make much headway into midst of the turmoil. One Dewan of Tripura was appointed to over see the political changes. His policy of keeping the state Congress in isolation and formting Ministry with the representatives of Anjuman Islam and nominated members of Tripura Sangh had made the politics fluid besides giving rise to doubts in the minds of the common people to the possibility of merger of Tripura with Pakistan. This is borne out by the fact that not only the Anjuman leaders were hosnobbing" with the leaders of Muslim League of Tripura District, but they got undue prominence by being invited in the Ministry. On the other hand, the Congress party with the help of the then Communist Party resisted the parochial attitude of the tribal gentry towards the democratic set up and also the plain people. It was Congress and the other left parties is whose initiatives expedited the accession of Tripura to the Indian Union at last. It was seven long years of democratic movement since 1949, – the year of historic ratification of Aggreement of Merger – till the formation of the 30-member Tripura Territorial Council in 1957 that has transformed this hill state from tribal kingship to modern democratic institution. There is still doubt as to whether the people, both tribals and non-tribals, have any fair concept of modern democracy.

In 1959, the TTC was further reorganised as per the TTC Act 1956. According to the Act the 30-member Council was elected on the basis of universal adult suffrage and 2 members were nominated by the Government Mr. S.L. Singh was the first chairman of the Council. After the second election in 1959, the third election was held in February 1962. In the third election, a 20-member Council was formed. In 1967, the 4th general election was held and 30-member Assembly was formed with a 6-member Ministerial Council under the leadership of Mr. Singh. This system with Chief Commissioner as the executive head of the administration continued till 1970.

Since 1970 the process of growth to full-fledged statehood started practically with good many administrative changes brought about to suit the changing circumstances in the country. In the same year the post of Chief Commissioner was upgraded to that Lt. Governor from the point of view of both manpower and resources, the state having a population of more than 16 lakhs before Bangladesh liberation war was just below the status of a district or subdivision in West Bengal. And hence administrative machinery of a district was enough for the state. Even before the formation of the TTC, the state was administered by only one district magistrate and one police superintendent to maintain law and order in the state. Even with this small staff the question of law and order did not pose any serious problem despite the fact that a good number of East Pakistan people had been passing through the border to Tripura territory.

After the introduction of parliamentary system of government in the state through various phases, the politically aspirant few have been looking for more and more political concessions. The situation so arose that the ethnic agiation for autonomy or self-governing institution started almost throughout the North East India under Assamase political set up. Inside Tripura specially in the remote hill areas, the question of ethnicity was a serious issue of their national movement – a movement for national entity.

After one year or so, the adjoining East Pakistan witnessed a great political turmoil over the demand for recession from Pakistan. It was a struggle for independence by East Pakistan from the yoke of the Pakistani Tanashahi and the struggle was actively backed by the Indian Government. India extended both moral and material support to the fighting people of East Pakistan through the adjoining states of Assam, Tripura and Meghalaya etc. Finally, it was liberated and Bangladesh emerged on the world map as an independent nation. It is admitted that a large number of evacuees took shelter in Tripura under the patronage of the Government and finally settled down in this state, even after the liberation was complete. En masse migration of Bangladesh people to Tripura adversely affected the population balance between the tribals and non-tribals. The tribal population came down to 29 % of the total population. The protection of minority posed a very serious problem. The conscious section of Tripura tribals could ventilate their political grievances through a political platform *i.e.* a purely regional party named Tripura Upajati Juba Samity (TUJS), which was born in 1967. The basic aspiration of the tribals was to form a separate state within the state so that the tribals could protect their national entity and cultural identity. The tribal mass organisation of Upajati Ganamukti Parishad led by CPI(M) at the outset sharad the same feelings of TUJS. Regarding the safeguard of tribals against the onslaught of foreigners. The CPI (M) led organisation recorded and confined their feelings only within their paper resolution. Their approach was the least realistic while the TUJS wanted to translate their pledges into action by any means. Later on CPI (M) kept away from TUJS due to differences of opinion on tribal policy and strategy of struggles. On the other hand, the militant section of this tribal organisation later to know as TNV (Tripura National Volunteers) differed with the leadership on the mode of struggle. TNV wanted complete independence, and wanted to realise their demand of 'Free Tripura' as on 1949 through armed struggle. According to them all non-tribals are foreigners and they should be deported from the state. TUJS considered their demand as most unrealistic as well as disruptive.

Tripura attained full statehood on 21st January 1972, under the North East India Areas Re-organisation Act, 1971. It was a landmark in the history of Tripura when the 30-member Council turned to 60-member legislative assembly with full-fledged ministry and a Governor at the head. Tripura as one of the seven states in the N.E. India is now ruled by a full ministry and large administrative organisation consisting of many officers of all India cadres and more than one lakh employees, though Tripura is smaller than a sub-division of any big state like U.P, or West Bengal in respect of population and resources. Notwithstanding the attainment of statehood could not fulfil the basic aspiration of the Tripura tribals who had been fighting for the tribal autonomy within the state as the best political safeguard for their ethnic entity. TUJS launched their incessant movement for further political rights for self determination. The question of national entity and cultural identity was the main point of their struggle. It arose deeply from the problem of alienation of land which the State reorganisation commission could not solve. In 1978, the CPI (M) led Left Front Government came to power with a thumping majority and attepted to restore the tribal lands from unauthorised occupation. It is no denying the fact that the plain people with better agricultural knowledge possessed lands lying uncultivated for long and had the privilege to break the compactness of the tribal inhabitation in two ways--First the plain lands were provided to the East Bengal peasants under the royal patronage and secondly, after the partition the refugees were given the settlement in rehabilitation. There was of course no other way out except such rehabilitation programme. In the course of implementing the rehabilitation programme the tribals were in reality neglected though the CPI did not antagonise the vast section of the refugees by waging the resistance struggle against them in view of their electoral interest. TUJS pledged that the interest of the tribals must be safeguarded first and for this purpose they would go wild. The Left Front Government under the pressure of the tribals went to implement the programme of land restoration but could not succeed due to communal politics by Amra Bangali Organisation that emerged on this very issue. It is worth mentioning that in 1980 Tripura witnessed an awful communal carnage and later on the issue of land restoration was finally dropped. In January 1980, A Tribal Autonomous District Council was formed under the Seventh Schedule of the Constitution. On 18th January 1982, an ADC started functioning with 28 elected members.

With the political and administrative restructure brought

about under the N.E. Area Act, 1971, the state since the attainment of statehood has undertaken various organisational reforms towards self-governing institution. The municipal and panchayatiraj systems were introduced with democratic set up. Tribals being 29 % of the total population were given the limited scope of autonomy to deal with tribal matters relating to their customs and ethnic problems. But this system of autonomy was not enough for the advancement of socio-economic relations. The struggle for better system of autonomy or self-rule continues. On 23rd August 1984, Parliament passed the Tripura Tribal Areas Autonomous District Council Act granting more self-governing power under the Sixth Schedule to the Constitution and accordingly the TAADC came into being on the Ist April 1985 and elections were held on 30th June in the same year. Of all the powers delegated to the ADC, the important subjects relate to: power to bring forth various agricultural reforms relating to tribal method of cultivation (jhum and shiftong cultivation) and collection of taxes etc., animal husbandry, village council, security guard, judiciary system on the basis of tribal customs, marriage and other ethnic festivals. Apart from all the afore-mentioned subjects, the economic advancement and area development were other subjects within the jurisdiction, but are not practicable within the limited scope of finances. Finances emanate from the state exchequer and all the fiscal politics are determined by the State Government. Again ADC have no power to frame its own educational politics to meet the needs of their society.

The Tripura tribals have their own language – KOKBARAK, but the tribal student can not pursue their studies in their own mother tongue, after class VI. After class VI, Kokbarak was not allowed as a medium of instruction and thus the very language became obsolete. As a result, students having Kokbarak as their medium of studies cannot abruptly switch over to Bangla or English because both the languages are foreign to them. Naturally, there has been an increasing number of dropouts from Class VI onwards. This is a problem which can not be dealt with by ADC itself.

The poverty and socio-economic backwardness cannot be eliminated through 'Leave them Alone' theory because the tribals cannot be happier in the mere grandeur and freedom of their hills. Outsiders are still keen to take the advantage of the trading with the tribals. With the knowledge of different trades hitherto unknown to the tribals, the outsiders are getting easy access to the ADC areas. Now a section of tribals are eager to introduce *Inner Line* permit to stop the entry of outsiders while others opposed to them hold – the view that the policy of 'leave them alone' would neither be effective nor a way out for their economic emancipation. Hence the question seriously posed is as to how far the TTAADC can fulfil the basic objectives and the goal. Is it correct to say that the ADC after seven long years of experiences has served as an effective instrument to safeguard the interests of the tribals?

Finally, the ADC system has proved futile to help fulfil the basic aspirations of the tribals and hence the struggle for the fullest development of national entity and cultural identity would have to continue.

APPENDIX

APPENDIX

REPORT OF THE SEMINAR

A.K.NEOG

For the purpose of presentation, the seminar papers are arranged in thematic order *viz.* historical perspective and micro studies. The first paper was presented by Dr. Imdad Hussain, which gives a historical background of the administrative arrangement of the territorial units of Eastern India prior to 1947. The territorial units of the North-Eastern Region, according to Dr. Hussain, were never administratively integrated during the British period due to factors like commercial interest, security concerns and administrative feasibility Since 'history repeats itself' so reorganisation is inevitable. He argues that in the process of reorganisation of Assam after 1947, the Government of India proved to be the true successor of the British. The other background paper is by Dr. D. Syiemlieh which projects a description of the alternative views preoccupying the minds of some British bureaucrats relating to the future destiny of North East India in pre-independence days. These views were expressed through the plans of Hutton, Parry, Reid, Mills, Clow and the likes and commonly known as Crown colony scheme, Coupland plan, etc. which were often conflicting and unfeasible. However, what the bureaucrats proposed, Government of India disposed and these plans were given a burial.

Dr. A.C. Talukdar presents the background of the State Reorganisation Commission (1953) which recommended the creation of States and Union Territories on linguistic and cultural basis. He is of the opinion that though reorganisation could accommodate linguistic conflicts, it however created more than could be settled through regional political arenas and the issue along caste-religion-ethnic axis. Creation of N.E.

region is a product of such issues, that has a demonstrative effect on the rest of the country also. He criticaly deals with the suggestions made by some experts like Prof. Rashidudin Khan's suggestion of 59 sub-cultural regions in India, and is of the opinion that it will open up a Pandora's box. According to Dr. Talukdar, given the experience of the NE. region, a large scale reorganisation will neither be possible nor desirable, nor can it be a panacea for political ills. He observes an all-Indian phenomenon *viz.*, the political leaders when they are out of power tend to support reorganisation and resist it once they are in power. Dr. Talukdar however, recognises that since Indian federation is still in the process of formation of social goal and development strategies are to be examined before reorganisation.

The important observations made by Dr. S.N. Ali in his paper can be summed up as follows : (i) Reorganisation of the N.E. Region is in response to ethnic demands; (ii) ethnic politics is a dynamic tussle between the dominant and non dominant groups; (iii) non-dominant groups have benefited from the colonial policy of isolation, insularity, exclusiveness, conversion and early modernisation; (iv) absence of strong regional leadership in Assam; (v) legitimisation by the Centre of the feeling that it listens to only threats and violence, encouraging other aggrieved and latent group for similar course of action; (vi) birth of Nagaland legitimising ehtnic politics, and (vii) blind adherence to an institutionalist strategy responsible for the N.E. policy crisis. His paper raises some vital issues like Centre's commitment to universal welfare, class character of the state, its response to real problems and its ability to intervene for public good. He opines that reorganisation has offered merely a few political rights, common man's strugle for socio-economic justice remains weak. He asserts that the elites' concern for the mass remains weak in the new states and the Government remains to be of the elites, by the elites an for the elites'. The urban elites and rural oligarchy manipulate ethnic loyality to project itself as the champion of their causes.

Dr. S. K. Agnihotri gives an exhaustive historical account of the administration of the N.E. areas during the pre-independence period and the struggles carried out by the people, and also the strategies adopted by the Government towards the formation of the political units. He has also dealt with Bodo and Karbi movements in Assam. In their joint paper, Mrs, S .Sen Chaudhury and Mr. S. Choudhuri touch upon the factors behind the birth of political nationalism in India along with the North-East. Though the British established a uniform law in the country it was not imposed on the N.E. India due to geographical factors, existence of small communities etc. They observe that on independence the national leaders and administrators lacked a clear perception of the variegated communities living in the region, resulting in the trial of bringing all those communites under the rule of the then Assam province and the provision of district councils for a few communites.

Dr. S. Mazumdar gives an account of the factors behind reorganisation *viz.* exploitation, neglect during the British rule, gap between administration and people, immigration, maintenance of separate identity by some linguistic groups and economic backwardness. Some such factors still continue to haunt the tribal mind and they feel that they are being exploited and not getting their due share. He is of the opinion that the introduction of Panchayati Raj and District Councils has considerably curbed the authority of the chief and tribal leaders. The District Councils have also shown leniency towards particular tribes leading to ethnic differentiation in some states. He recognises that the demand for autonomous states is a 'global' problem and points out that even after full-fledged statehood the disruptive forces are active in the states like Nagaland, Manipur and Mizoram. Dr. Mazumdar does not advocate further reorganisation since it will harm national integration and economic development. He suggests more government intervention for development, better service from the North Eastern Council (NEC), prevention of infiltration and sealing of international borders.

Examining the problem of ethnic assertion in a historical ers-pective from world experience (USSR, UK, etc), Mr. afulla Misra identifies migration, declaration of majority nguag, as the official language, indigenous people's fear of sing political power to the migrants and identity crisis as the iportant factors behind the problem. He mentions that various ethnic groups, which were earlier disunited or at loggerheads, joined the national movement for freedom of the country to have a just society and order. But the concept of freedom and just order were understood by the ethnic groups in their own ways and specifics. Tribes in the N.E. region were having their own rule or autonomy. Fighting for safeguarding the ethnic identity by the various groups of the region, according to Misra, is a natural urge and cannot be solved through economic development. Therefore their demand should be sympathetically considered without delay to avoid tension and strife. He, however, feels that ethnic identity can only be safeguarded by reservation of seats in Assembly and Parliament.

Dr. S. K. Das in his paper attempts an assessment of the impact of the organisationally weak Indian state on the middle class politics in Assam during the period 1979-90. He observes that the ethnically fragmented middle class politics in Assam is not infused with a universal ethos, which of course sounds tautological. He looks at it as an effect rather than a cause of reorganisation, and also deals with the demonstration effect of reorganisation.

The paper by Dr. B. B. Goswami is along ethnic lines. He finds that, in view of ethnic diversity, reorganisation is a continous process. Though there are multiple factors behind reorganisation, the common denominator is the preservation of identity as enshrined in the Constitution. He observes that the feelings of 'we' versus 'they', ethnicity, etc. are becoming toxic factors, leading to the dispossession of those-called outsiders from administrative and political hierarchy besides creating inter-ethnic conflicts. This seems to be against the spirit of inter-state and intranational integration. He anticipates that the N.E. Region will go through a series of reorganisation to attain relative equilibrium in persistence of aspirations and balance of inter-ethnic relationship. The paper is, however, silent on whether such an equilibrium will be dynamically stable or not. Dr. Goswami's paper raises more issues than it has answered. If the current 'disequilibrium' trend in social milieu is not corrected in time, then as a corollary it can be inferred that days are not far for the 'ethnic volcano' to erupt intensively.

The paper by Mr. R.R. Bhattacharjee is along economic

viability. He demonstrates with the help of hypothesis testing how the N. E. states are overdependent on the Centre for their maintenance and development. The states are not viable, hence on a 'posteriori' economic logic reorganisation is not justified. Counterfactually, he suggests that Central investment without reorganisation could have led to stable economic condition of the entire composite state.

Mr. N.N. Das addresses the issue as deorganisation. He observes that as Assam had been a polyglot state so its deorganisation was inevitable. He does not find uniformity of causes behind the same. For instance, while Cachar wanted separation mainly on linguistic issue, the hill districts wanted it on issues like customs, culture, etc., of course alongwith language. The Language Act of 1960 left the use of the language in the hills to be decided by the District Councils. The hill leaders agitation for separate state preceded the introduction of the said Act and would have continued even without it. The argument that the hills were expiolited by the plains is not tenable as the Pataskar Commission found that the progress of hill people was much faster than the plain counterpart. He mentions additional causes like mistakes committed by the Central and State Governments, Centre's 'divide and rule' policy, the Sixth Schedule sowing the seeds of separation, administrative reorganisation (9 e.g. tribal area department) and selfish motive of the politicians. Mr Das asserts that the main beneficiaries of deoraganisation are the urban elites and the politicians. He observes how the hill-plain historical contact among the people was lost and even though the Government has been trying to revive it, the Inner line regulation system stands in the way. The people in the region are facing the dual problem of political separation and economic unification, of which the latter is important. He advocates the preservation and progress of language, territory, culture and tradition of the people of each state

Referring to the pre-independence status of Assam, British conspiracy, the role of Muslim League and Goalpara problem, Mr. P. C. Biswas presents an analysis of the evolution of the N.E. States. According to him, language formed a very important component of state formation even though there were other factors like economic backwardness, influence of foreign power. The hill tribals were aspiring for achieving sub-national status and wanted separate state. To him, the complicated situation of the North-East is a political problem to be dealt with politically. He suggests for giving of autonomy to linguistic and tribal groups without disintegrating Assam. He further suggests a federal structure of the whole region, without however elaborating the same.

Dr. Biman Kar, observes that the resolution of the Congress party in the twenties on formation of provinces on language basis was an opportunistic step since linguistic sub-nationalism has already shown its face elsewhere. The North-East remained unaffected by the state's reorganisation in the late 'fifties. It was only after the language Act of 1960, that trouble started in Assam. According to him the other factors behind tribal non-tribal rift were migration, exploitation and land alienation. The exogenous causes were wrong policies of the Centre, lack of programme implementation and of concern for the poor and deprived among the autochthons. He puts forward a hypothesis *viz.* "myopia and vanity of Assamese and Bengali people who instead of playing a positive role in bringing about an integration of N. E. Iindia had helped its Balkanisation." His hypothesis however misses the role of the state and one may have reservation on the relevance of 'Balkanisation'. The said two communities have a mission to fulfil in the transformation of the regional economy. Dr. Kar however argues for precedence of material advancement through inter-state cooperation as the existing N.E. States are not viable, and the creation of additional state/district is ultimately a burden on the poor tax payers.

Dr. Archana Sharma makes an attempt to evaluate the costs and benefits of reorganisation. Cost listed by her include both real and monetary like cost of coordination among the states, administrative overheads (due to dual system of government *viz.* government machinery and District Councils), service charges for expertise brought from out-side the region, costs of curbing violence and insurgency, burden of immigration etc. Benefits *viz.* growth of literacy (other than technical), proximity of people to the administration, creation of infrastructure are however mergre. Dr. Sharma is of the opinion that costs out-weights benefits. It may be added that costs and benefits of reorganisation cannot be measured solely in terms of economic balance sheet. One must not ignore social, cultural, political and environmental aspects as well.

The second theme of the seminar is on micro studies of reorganisation. The paper by Dr. L. S. Gassah primarily traces the origin of the economic problems of the border areas of Jaintia hills since the days of India's partition till date. However, these problems are yet to be solved even after the creation of Meghalaya twenty years back. He subscribes to the popular demand of creating a free trade zone along Indo-Bangladesh border and legalisation of border trade to uplift the border economy, that requires action at the government level, both national and international.

In his paper on Bodoland issue, Dr. J. Kalita presents data on the tribal population distribution in Assam. Poverty, land alienation, indebtedness, trans-national migration (from Nepal, Bhutan and Bangladesh) are cited to be the main causes behind the issue. Suggestions offered include restriction on land alienation, introduction of Inner Line system, eradication of poverty and unemployment, setting up of a Central University at Kokrajhar and legal protection to non-tribals living in Bodoland areas. The paper by Dr. S. K. Mukherjee gives an account of the Bodo movement right from its birth till date. It may be mentioned that with the announcement of the creation of Bodoland Autonomous Council on 20th February, 1993 by the Government, Bodoland is now fait accompli. Dr. P.S. Datta, in his note on the settlement of Bodoland issue, however, raises a number of questions that await answers and feels that Bodoland is in the threshold of a much bigger challenge. Dr. R.P. Athparia, in his paper presents the background of Karbi movement in Assam. He observes a dualistic attitude of the Karbis towards the movement in so far as theolder generation thought of maintaining the traditional pattern of life while the younger generation felt aggrieved for not being able to manage their socio-political affairs according to their own will.

In his thought provoking paper, Mr. J.N. Choudhury outlines the circumstances as to how the post-independent constitutional development and tribal policy in respect of

Arunachal Pradesh had been within the precincts of colonial policy. It looks like old wine in new bottle'. The policy of isolation (Inner-Line system) of the tribal has led to greater intolerance against the non-tribals instead of bringing integration. He subscribes to the view that the policy of reservation and special privileges has led to the exploitation of the underprivileged 'majority' by the privileged 'minority' within the tribals. Dr. M. C. Behera, in his paper, expresses that the ethno-lingual divergency should no more be used for reorganisation in the North-East as its use maylead to conglomeration of a few households in the name of political units. Arunachal is a potential example in this repect where there are more than 100 number of tribes and sub-trubes. He observes that though Arunachal was not born out of violence, danger signals have already appeared on the horizon with the birth of orgnisations like UPVA, ULVA, and in the form of inter-tribe conflicts. The reasons cited are rising gap between fulfilment and aspiration of the tribal youth, inter and intra-tribal inequalities, accentuating inter-regional imbalance. The measures suggested by Dr. Behera include balanced development, improvement in human resources, reduction in inequalities, mass participation in development programmes, and inter-tribe integration.

The only paper on Nagaland by Dr. R. P. Singh presents a account of the constitutional and political development in that state. Emergence of Nagaland paved the way for the creation of other states. According to him, Nagaland as a state does not satisfy the viability tests of finance, territory and strategic concern. However, his observation on viability is debatable as it ignores the concepts of political and administrative viability. Dr. Singh also deals with the movement by the Naga groups in the region.

There is one paper in which Dr. A.K. Ray raises the territorial issue in Manipur and asserts that as the integration process of the tribals in the state was done through domination and conquests so that kinship basis of the tribal societies was neglected. He observes that the federal scheme of the country could not fulfil the aspiration of the Manipur tribes. Tribal problems of Manipur are complex as there is oft-conflicting separate demands for statehood, union territory, district councils, separate administrative units, district, trans-statal demands like Greater Mizoram, Greater Nagaland and trans Territorial tribal integration including politics of secession. In such a context reorganisation becomes a tough job. An important observation made by him is that politics of secession in the region has become a mere political bargaining strategy on the part of the tribal middle class. The territorial movement has evaded the economic reorganisation issues. The hill politics diversified and proliferated but the hill economy remained stagnant. Hence he suggests that economics rather than ethnicity should form the base for reorganisation. Ethnicity leads to sub-ethnicity.

There are three papers on Mizoram. In their joint paper, Dr. M. M. Das, N. N. Sengupta and M. Banerjee narrate to events in the pre-and post-independence period leading to elevation of Lushai/Mizo hills district to statehood. They have not added supporting evidence to their conclusion that the Mizo National Front's goal of independence still remains. Dr. R. N. Prasad, in his paper, deals more with the other states of the region than Mizoram. According to him reorganisation has failed to fulfil the socio-economic aspirations of the people, to create inter-state friendliness and to protect the linguistic minority. Despite these failures he predicts further reorganisation of the region. He raises the problem of identity crisis being faced by the Pawis, the Lakhers, the Chakmas and the Hmar tribes. Without elaborating the suggests radical restructuring of socio-economic structure and Union-State relations. Dr. S. S. Mishra in his paper attempts to test the hypothesis *viz.* 'smaller the state, higher the pace of development.' To him, though 'Mizoram is small in population and geography, it is big in other aspects like education and literacy. It needs to be pointed out that Mizoram was far ahead of other N.E. States in literacy even prior to reorganisation. He believes that if things are properly organised and implemented and there is cultural fusion and assimilation, then chances of development can be more irrespective of size of the state. In other words, development can be sizes neutral.

There are two papers on Tripura, Dr. Mahadev Chakravarti presents an account of the actions and reactions of the Central Government and various political parties on the issue ranging from merging Tripura with Assam to its statehood, in the perspective of a political metamorphosis . In his paper, Mr Jagat Jyoti Ray deals with the administrative reforms carried out in Tripura during post-accession period, tribal attitude towards merger, changes in political scenario, migration and refugee factors, land alienation and restoration, statehood and district councils. He observes that neither statehood nor district councils could fulfil tribal aspirations. The absolescance in tribal language laisez faire theory (district council) stands in the path of development. Hence the movement for fullest development of national entity and cultural identity of the Tripura tribals goes on.

The above survey and deliberations in the seminar reveal that political, cultural, social and economic factors interacted to reorganise earlier Assam. The Assam Language Act of 1960 acted as a 'blessing in disguise' for the creation of the 'would be' states. There are three streams of thought on the state reorganisation in the N. E. India *viz.* pro-reorganisation, anti-reorganisation and the neutral stream. Some even like to suggest the social boundaries could be elastic; the geographical land economic boundaries are inelastic in the short run, to which there are obvious limits that cannot easily be trespassed. Therefore the degrees of freedom for further marginalisation is not infinite. Hence the crying need, perhaps, is the search for symbiosis rather than 'mutually exclusive' arrangements.

BIBLIOGRAPHY

BIBLIOGRAPHY*

Adimjati Seva Mandal

Vidyarthi, L.P., 1977, The Voluntry Organisation Service of the Tribal Weak : A Case Study of Adimjati Seva Mandal, *Man and Life* 3 (3-4) July-December, p 9-20.

Adult Education

Anon, 1982, Elementary Education and Adult Literacy, *Assam Information,* 34, September, p 16-21.

Baruh, Meera Bala, 1986, Adult Education Libraries of Assam, *Lucknow Librarian* 18(1) January-March, p 23-28.

Bhowmic, Pradip Kumar, 1986, Literacy Drive and Adult Education through Voluntary Organisation : A Case Study in Naibari District, Assam, *Man and Life* 12 (3-4) July-December, p 199-209, bibliography, tables.

Chakravarty, D.N., 1978, Assam Launches Biggest Education Drive, *Assam Information,* 30, November, p 14-16.

Debi, R., 1979, National Adult Education Programme in Assam, *Indian Journal of Adult Education* 40(4) April, p 11-15, bibliography.

Agricultural Credit

Agnihotri, S.K., 1976, Credit for Rural Poor, *Times of India* November 20, p 11, cols 6-8.

Anon, 1976, Weak Co-operatives and Shy Banks, *Commerce* 133 (3406) September 4, p 438-439.

Anon, 1978, The Assam Credit Situation, *Indian Finance* 101 (11) March 25, p 224-225.

Dutta, Poresh Ch., 1972. Credit Requirements of Small Farmers of Assam, *Kurukshetra* 21 (3) November 1, p 10.

Saha, Niranjan and Dutta, Paresh Ch., 1971, The HYV Programme and Problems of Finance for Small Farms in Assam : A Case Study of Goalpara District, *Indian Journal of Agricultural Economics* 26(4) October-December, p 559-560.

Saikia, P.D., 1971, The Role of Land Mortgage Bank in Agricultural Development in Assam, *Indian Journal of Agricultural Economics* 26 (4) October-December, p 574-575.

---

* Select Classified Documentation list based on Periodical Literature, 1886-1995 compiled under the Guidance of and edited by former Director, National Social Science Documentation Centre, ICSSR, New Delhi.

Sarmah, R. and Singh D., 1980, Problems of Small Farmers under Agricultural Credit Programme in Assam, *Indian Cooperative Review* 18(1) October, p 39-43, bibliography, table.

Agricultural Extension Work

Choudhury, S., 1976, Agricultural Extension, *Link* 18 (48) July 11, p. 27-28.

Agricultural Industries

Gogoi, Hara, 1975, Some Agro-Industries Potential of Assam, *Assam Information* 25 (10-12) January-March, p 17-21.

Agricultural Innovations

Saikia, Padma Dhar, 1968, Farmer's Response to Improved Agricultural Practices in Cachar District (Assam), *Man in India* 48 (1) January-March, p 86-90.

Agricultural Labourers

Alam, Mohammad Anwar, 1976, Level of Living of Agricultural Labour in Bihar : Case Study, *Economic Affairs* 21 (12) December, p 454-462, tables.

Anon, 1974, Agricultural Labourers in Assam : Problems and Prospects, *Assam Information* 25 (4-5) July-August, p 34-37.

Anon, 1976, Terror in Champaran, *Link* 19(20) December 26, p 14-15.

Bora, Phani, 1971, Assam : Big Upsurge among Rural Poor, *New Age* 19 (3) January 17, p 11.

Borgohain, Drupad, 1988, Assam Kisan-Khet Mazdoor Movement Forges Ahead, *New Age* 36 (33) August 14, p 8-9.

Das, Arvind Narayan, 1976, In Bonded Freedom, *Economic and Political Weekly* 11 (20) May 15, p 724-726.

Das, Samir Kumar, 1992, Immigration and Agricultural Modernization : The Case of Assam (1979-83), *Socialist Perspective* 20(3) December, p 165-175, bibliography, footnotes, tables.

Das, Samir Kumar, 1993, Immigration and Agricultural Modernization: The Case of Assam (1979-83), *Socialist Perspective* 20 (4) March, p. 165-175, bibliography, footnotes, tables.

Dutta, Poresh Chandra, 1974, Agricultural Labourers in Assam : Problems and Prospects, *Assam Information* 25(1-3) April-June, p 12+.

Goswami, P.C. and Bora, C.K., 1970, Demand for Labour in Rural Areas of Assam : A Case Study in Nowgong District, *Indian Journal of Agricultural Economics* 25(3) July-September, p 46-52, tables.

Kumar, I.C., 1976, Fair Deal to Farm Workers, *Times of India* April 12, p 9, cols 5-8.

Poresh Chandra, 1974, Pattern of Farm Employment in Assam : Case Study, *Yojana* 18(19) November 1, p 19-90.

Ramamurthi, K.S., 1975, Welfare of Farm Labour, *Assam Information* 27(5-6) August-September, p 23-26.

Roy Chaudhury, P.C., 1976, The Agricultural Labourers in Bihar, *Indian Review* 72(1) April, p 30-35.

Sinha, Arun, 1976, Death of a Share-Cropper, *Economic and Political Weekly* 11 (12) March 20, p 445-446.

Sinha, Arun, 1976, A 'Gift' of Barren Land, *Times of India* March 21, p 12, col 5-8.

Sinha, Arun, 1976, A Laboure Goes to court, *Economic and Political Weekly* 11(37) September 11, p 1493-1495.

Social Service Quarterly (Periodical), 1924, Labour Conditions in Assam, *Social Service Quarterly*, 10(1) July, p 31+.

Agricultural Prices

Talukdal, K.C., 1985, Efficiency and Equity of Farms Prices in Assam State : A Case of Small Farmers, *Indian Journal of Agricultural Economics* 40 (4) July-September p 362-369.

Agricultural Research

Hazarika, J., 1973, Need of an Indigenous Farm Technology to Meet the Peculiar Agricultural Problems of Assam, *Assam Information* 24 (8) November, p 5-7.

Agricultural Wages

Phukan, Umananda, 1974, Employment and Earnings of Agricultural Labour in Assam, *Indian Journal of Agricultural Economic* 29(3) July-September, p 72.

Agriculture

See also Land Tenure

Anon, 1978, Green Gold of Assam : A Review, *Assam Information*, 29, April-May, p 1-10, tables.

Anon, 1979, Agro Schemes' Impact Minimal in Assam, *Economic Times* December 8, p 3, cols 1-3.

Anon, 1980 Agriculture in Assam, *Eastern Economist* 74(11) March 14, p 551.

Anon, 1980, Assam : Action Plan for Farm Growth Soon, *Economic Times* April 16, p 1, col 2-4+.

Anon, 1981. Agricultural Growth Plans Yield Poor Results in Assam, *Economic Times* May 29, p 8, col 5-8.

Anon, 1981, Agriculture in 1980-81 and Plan for 1981-82, *Assam Information*, 33, August, p 6-13, tables.

Anon, 1986, Agriculture : Nature Takes Its Toll, *Capital* 197 (4840-4841) November 1, p 25-28.

Anon, 1987, (Book Review), *Social Scientist* 15(3) March, p 77-78.
Review of the Book : Das, M.M., 1984, *Peasant Agriculture in Assam: A Structure Analysis*, Inter-India Pub, New Delhi, 289 p.

Bhadra, Ranajit, K., 1979, Emerging Patterns of Agrarian Classes in Rural Assam, *Eastern Anthropologist* 32 (4) October-December p 273-285, tables, bibliography.

Chutia, B. and Mehrotra, T., 1977, A Note on Certain Aspects relating to Agriculture in Assam, 1950-1970, *Assam Economic Journal* 3(1) March, p 113-122, bibliography.

Das, M.M., 1979, Population Pressure and Intensity of Cropping in Assam, India, *Geographical Review of India* 41(2) June, p 105-114, tables, bibliography.

Das, M.M., 1985, Agricultural Regionalisation of Assam : A Quantitative Analysis, *North Eastern Geographer* 17(1-2), p 28-34, bibliography, figures, tables.

Das, Manmohan, 1978, Problems of Agricultural Growth in Assam, *Geographical Review of India* 40(2) June, p 144-154, bibliography, tables.

Das, Samir Kumar, 1992, Immigration and Agricultural Modernisation: The Case of Assam (1979-1983), *Socialist Perspective* 20(3) December, p 165-175, bibliography, footnotes, tables.

Das, Samir Kumar, 1993, Immigration and Agricultural Modernisation: The Case of Assam (1979-1983) *Socialist Perspective* 20(4) March, p 165-175, bibliography, footnote, tables.

Dubhashi, P.R., 1981, Leading the Central Task Force, *Indian Journal of Public Administration* 27(1) January-March, p 113-118.

Goswami, P.C. 1979, Assam : Need for Better Productivity, *Commerce* (Annual Number) 139 (3577), p 151-157, bibliography, tables.

Goswami, P.C. and Saikia, P.D., 1972, Pattern of Investment in Agriculturally Prosperous Areas of Assam, *Indian Journal of Agricultural Economics* 27(4) October-December, p 89-90.

Goswami, S.N. and Patgiri, A.K., 1993, Optimum Production under Risk and Uncertainly in Rani block of Assam (India), *Indian Journal of Economics* 73(4) April, p 463-472, bibliography, figures.

Neogi, P.C. and Kalita D.R., 1991, Resource Optimisation for Higher Income in Small Farms, in Titabor Block of Assam, *Assam Economic Journal*, 8, p 29-34, tables.

Phukan, Umananda, 1996, Agricultural Growth in Lahoal Development Block : A Case Study, *Indian Journal of Agricultural Economics* 21(4) October-December, p 208-214, tables.

Mazumdar, N.R. and Laskar, S.U., 1977, The Yield Pattern of Agricultural Crops of Assam, 1972-73 : An Application of the Principal Component Analysis Technique, *Assam Economic Journal* March, p 42-47, bibliography, tables.

Mishra, R.S., et al, 1976, Farm Size, Productivity and Returns to Scale, *Eastern Economist* 67(15) October 8, p 729-732, bibliography.

Saikia, P.D. and Bora, 1975, Impact of Modern Agricultural Technology on Samll Farmers : A Case Study in Assam, *Indian Journal of Agricultural Economics* 30(3) July-September, p 224-229.

Shah, Niranjan, 1966, The Growth of Food Production in Assam, *Indian Journal of Agricultural Economics* 21(4) October-December, p 205-207, tables.

Talukdar, K.C. and Goswami, P.C., 1978, Food Accounts for Assam : A Critical Appraisal, *Assam Economic Journal* 4(1) March, p 1-14, bibliography.

Agriculture : Cooperative Credit Societies

Anon, 1979, Assam village Co-ops Hit, *Economic Times* December 26, p 3, cols 1-4.

Agriculture : Economic Aspects

Bora, N.N., 1976, Food Production Goes up, *Link* 18(48) July 11, p 21-22.

Dutta, S.K, 1976, Record Crop in Assam but Acute Problems Persists, *Times of India* 20, p 4, cols 7-8.
Gogoi, K., 1975, Population and Agriculture, *Assam Information* 27(5-6) August-September, p 8-10.

Agriculture : History

Baruah, S.L., 1979-80, Agriculture in Assam in the Ahom Age, *Journal of the Assam Research Society,* 25, p 59-72, footnotes.
Goswami, Homeswar, 1977, Fertility Patterns in the Brahmaputra Valley Districts of Assam, 1881-1931, *Assam Economic Journal* 3(1) March, p 21-41, bibliography.

Ahoms

Barua, Indira, 1979, Some Aspects of Kin Relationship in an Ahom Village, *Eastern Anthropologist* 32(1) January-March, p 1-12, bibliography, figures.
Lakshmi Devi, 1965-66, Ahom and the Assamese Buranji's, *Quarterly Review of Historical Studies* 5(2), p 97-100, bibliography.
Phukan, J.N., 1963, The Khamjang Valley and the Ahoms, *Journal of the University of Gauhati* 14(1) p 13-20, bibliography, footnotes.

All Assam Students Union

Anon, 1964, First All-Assam Youth Conference, *New Age* 12(28) July 12, p 7.
Anon, 1980, AASU Decides to Resume Stir, *Times of India,* October 23, p 1, cols 2-4.
Times of India (Periodical), 1989, Unreasonable Stand, *Times of India,* June 28, p 6, cols 1-2, editorial.
Times of India(Periodical), 1989, A Welcome Pause, *Times of India,* August 30, p 4, cols 1-2, editorial.

Alluvial Fans

Dutta, Lakhsha Hira, 1984, Alluvial Fans in the Northern Brahmaputra, *Transaction of Institute of Indian Geographers* 6(2) July, p 1-14, bibliography, figures, tables.

Animal Husbandry

Buzarbaruah, J.M., 1981, Animal Husbandry and Veterinary in Retrospect, Assam Information, 33, August, p 16-18.

Annual Plans

Anon, 1973, Largest Annual Plan, *Commerce* 126 (3241) June 16, p 1198-1199.
Anon, 1974, Annual Plan Makes No Larger Provision, *Commerce* 128(3296) July 13, p 68.
Anon, 1974, Assam's Endeavour to Catch up Rest of the Country : Rs 56 Crore Annual Plan for *Assam Information* 25(1-3) April-June, p 6-8+
Anon, 1976, Assam Priority to Agriculture, *Link* 18(28) February 22, p 17.

Anon, 1977, Annual Plan Cut to Hit Development, *Commerce* 135(3451) July 23, p 126.

Anon, 1980, Assam's Annual Plan, *Eastern Economist* 74(25) June 20, p 1225-1226.

Anon, 1980, A Slow-Moving Economy, *Commerce* 140(3584) March 1, p 350-352.

Anon, 1981, Rs 210 Cr. for Assam Plan, *Economic Times* April 1, p 5, cols 7-8.

Anthropometry

Bonoshree Devi and Das, Bhuban M., 1969, Anthropometric Chakaclers of Foot of a Rural and an Unban Population of Assam, *Man in India* 49 (1) January-March, p 41-49, references, tables.

Das, Bhuban M., 1960, Somatic Variations among the Hill and Plains Garo of Assam, *Man in India* April-June, p 128-148, tables.

Das, Priya Bala, 1970, Relative Lengths of the First and Second Toes of Different Population of Assam, *Man in India* 50(2) April-June, p 141-148.

Dutta, Bhupendranath, 1938, A Note on the Presence of Light Coloured Eye-iris amongst the Population of North-Eastern India, *Man in India* 18(1) January-March, p 1-8, footnotes.

Mahapatra, Usha Deka, and Das, Priya Bala, 1973, Earlobe Variation in Various Population of Assam, *Man in India* 53(3) July-September, p 256-261, bibliography, tables.

Pakrasi, Kanti and Das, Bhuban H., 1956, An Anthropometric Study of the Plains Mandes (Garos) of Assam, *Man in India* 36 (2) April-June, p 100-109, reference, tables.

Antiquities

See also Neolithic Period; Stone Implements.

Chaudhury, P.D., 1967, Arts and Crafts, *Illustrated Weekly of India* 88 (17) May 28, p 44-46, Illustrations.

Choudhury, R.D., 1977, A Note on the Temple Ruins of Majgaon, Assam, *Journal of Indian History* 55 (3) December, p 15-17, footnotes.

Choudhury, Rabindranath Dev and Chutia, Dharmeswar, 1968, A Note on the Archaeological Finds at the Narakaswar Hill, *Journal of the Assam Research Society*, 18, p 23-34, bibliography, footnotes.

Hutton, J.H., 1928, Prehistory of Assam, *Man in India* 8 (4) October-December, p 229-232.

Saikia, P.C., 1979-80, A Note on Some Archaeological Relics in and around Barpath and Golaghat, Assam : An Appraisal, *Journal of the Assam Research Society*, 25, p 32-39. footnotes.

Sharma, Sri Pratap, 1981-82, Antiquity of the Kamakhya Temples on the Nilacota, *Journal of the Assam Research Society*, 26, p 46-52, footnotes.

Architecture : Islamic

Kamaluddin Ahmed, 1981, Islamic Architecture in Assam, *Assam Information* 33 April-July, p 18-26.

Archives

Sharma, P.C., 1970, Assam Secretariate Record Office, *Indian Architect* 19(2) July-December, p 29-34.

Assam Agricultural University

Assam Agricultural University : Research Operations in North-East India, *Yojana* 19(10) June 15, p 25-26.

Assam Carbon Products Limited : History

Ghatak, Aditi Roy, 1986, Assam Carbon : Blocking All Imports, *Capital* 196 (4825) March 1, p 28-32.

Assam Company Limited : History

Sircar, Kalyan K., 1986, Labour and Management : First Twenty Years of Assam Company Limited, 1839-59, *Economic and Political Weekly* 21 (22) May 31.

Sircar, Kalyan K., 1986, A Tale of Two Boards : Some Early Management Problems of Assam Co Ltd., 1839-1864, *Economic and Political Weekly* 21(10-11) March 8-15, p 453-459.

Assam Financial Corporation

Anon, 1976, Assam Financial Corporation : Overdues Cause Concern, *Commerce* 133 (3398) July 10, p 78-79.

Anon, 1979, Assistance for Tiny Sector, *Commerce* 139 (3556) August 11, p 284-285.

Baisya, K.N., 1985, State Financing for Industrial Growth and Assam Financial Corporation, *Lok Udyog* 19 (9) December, p 31-37, bibliography, tables.

Assam Harijan Sevak Sangh

Anon, 1975, Child Welfare Activities of the Assam Harijan Sevak Sangh, *Social Welfare* 22 (8) November, p 23.

Assam Kisan-Khetmazdoor Movement

Borgohain, Drupad, 1988, Assam Kisan-Khetmazdoor Movement Forges Ahead, *New Age* 36 (33) August 14, p 8-9.

Assam Library Conference, 1964, Gauhati

Kaula, P.N., 1965, Assam Library Conference; Report of Proceedings Held on 24-25 October, 1964, *Herald of Library Science* 4(2) April, 159-164.

Assam Rifles

Anon, 1986, (Book Review), *Indian Quarterly* 42(2) April-June, p 216-217. Review of the Book : Dalit, D.K., 1984, *Sentinal of the North East*: The Assam Rifles, Palit and Palit Pub, New Delhi, 344 p.

Assam Seva Samiti

Das, Ramcharan, 1955, A Report on the Activities of Assam Seva Samiti, *Vanyajati* 3(3) July, p 131-133.

Assam State Transport Corporation

Anon, 1980, ASTC Achieves Record Utilisation Target, *Economic Times* April 6, p 8, cols 5-8.

Assamese Drama

Barkotoki, Munin, 1970-72, Trends in Assamese Dramatungy, *Journal of University of Gauhati* 21-23 (1), p 158-167.

Goswami, Kesavananda Dev, 1985, The Jhumuras in Assamese, *Sangeet Natak*, 76, April-June, p 5-8.

Guha, Seema, 1978, Assamese Theatre's Leap Foreward, *Times of India (Magazine)* October 15, p 13, cols 1-3.

Néog, Maheswar, 1973-74, Assamese Drama and Theatre, *Journal of the University of Gauhati* 24-25 (1), p 1-43.

Sharma, Arobinda Nath, 1969, Assamese Drama of the Last Decade, *Sangeet Natak* 60 p 22-26.

Assamese Fiction

Sarma, Gobinda Prasad, 1970-72, The Assamese Political Novel, *Journal of the University of Gauhati* 21-23 (1), p 184-196, footnotes.

Sarma, Gobinda Prasad, 1979, Assamese Novel : New Horizons, *Littcrit* 5 (2) December, p 38-45.

Assamese Fiction : Translation Into English

Bhattacharyee, Birendra Kumar, 1988, Lyariungam, *Pratibha India* 7 (4) July-September, p 9-12.

Assamese Folk Dancing

Sharma, Arabinda Nath, 1979, Tantric and Cult Dances of Assam, *Sangeet Natak* 52 April-June, p 27-30, bibliography.

Assamese Folklore

Bhattacharjee, Padma Nath, 1930, Flok Custom and Folklore of the Sylhet District of Assam, *Man in India* 10(2-3) April-September, p 116-149.

Goswami Praphulladatta, 1950, Music in Assam : Its Divine Origin, *Man in India*, 30 (1) January-March, p 13-16.

Goswami, Praphulladutta, 1960, Flok-Drama in Assam, *Folklore* 1(3) May-June, p 148-150.

Goswami, Praphulladatta, 1968, Women in Assam's Folklore, *Folklore*, 9(2) February, p 39-45, references.

Pakrasi, Kanti, 1954, The Traditional Story of Areleng (Mikir) Migration, *Man in India*, 34(3) July-September, p 211-219.

Assamese Folk Music

Ali, Tafazzul, 1979, The Enchanted Drums, *Folklore* 20 (11) November, p 264-269, bibliography.

Assamese Folk Songs

Anon, 1977-78, (Book review), *Journal of Assam Research Society* 23, p 69-71.

Review of the Book : Sharma, Hemanta Kumar, ed., n.d., Asamiya Lokagiti Sanchayan : A Collection of Assamese Folk-Songs, The Author, Gauhati, Part 1, 304 p.

Chattophyay, B.M., 1967, Folk Song of Cachar-Rakhal-Aai, *Folklore* 8 (10) October, p 350-369.

Goswami, Prapulladutta, 1949-50, The Bihu Songs of Assam, *Eastern Anthropologist* 3 (2-3) December 49, March 50, p 57-100, footnotes.

Goswami, Praphulladatta, 1964, Spinning and Weaving in Assam, *Folklore* 5 (12) December, p 441-445.

Goswami, Praphulladutta and Dutta, Birendranath, 1974, Folk Songs of Assam, *Sangeet Natak*, 31, January-March, p 60-69, bibliography.

Sarma, Binod, 1979, A Note on the Assamese Jikir and Its Philosophy, *Folklore* 20 (12) December, p 277-280, bibliography.

Assamese Folk Tales

See assamese Tales

Assamese Folk Toys

See Toys

Assamese Language

Barua, B.K., 1963, Change in Meaning of Some O.I.A., Words in Assamese, *Journal of the University of Gauhati* 14(1) p 171-176.

Goswami, Upendranath, 1977-78, A Script for the Tribal Language of Assam, *Journal of the University of Gauhati* (Arts) 28-29, p 195-197.

Nego, Maheswar, 1972, Prakrits and Assamese, *Journal of Ganganath Jha Kendriya Sanskrit Vidyapeetha* 28 (1-2) January-April, p 407-428.

Assam Language : Analogy

Bhattacharya, Pramod Chandra, 1973-74, Analogy in Assamese Language *Journal of the University of Gauhati* 24-25 (1), p 44-47.

Assamese Language : Case Suffixes

Goswami, S.N., 1971, The Case-Suffixes in Assamese, *Indian Linguistics* 32 (2) April-June, p 139-147, bibliography.

Assamese Languages : Dialects

Goswami, Upendranath, 1970-72, The Language of North Bengal and Western Assam, *Journal of the University of Gauhati* 21-23 (1), p 62-70, footnotes.

Assamese Language : Foreign Words and Phrases

Shafer, Robert, 1964, Kakati and Foreign Loans in Assamese, *Journal of the University of Gauhati* 15(1) p 33-34, footnotes.

Assamese Language : Grammar

Biswas, S., 1977-78, Atomic Alternats of Assamese and Bengali, *Journal of the University of Gauhati* (Arts), 28-29, p 198-205.

Hazarika, Bisweshwar, 1968, Negative Formation in Assamese, *Journal of the Assam Re search Society*, 18, p 35-40, bibliography, footnote.

Assamese Language : Nagatives

Baruah, P.N. Dutta, 1975, Negative Formation in Asamiya and Oriya, *Indian Linguistics* 36(2) June, p 144-151.

Goswami, Upendranath, 1976, A Historical Note on the Negative Particle in Asamiya, *Indian Linguistics* 37(2) June, p 143-145, bibliography.

Hazarika, Bisweswar, 1968, Negative Formation in Assamese, Indian Linguistics 29 (1) p 34-39, footnotes.

Assamese Language : Phonology

Mahanta, Rohini Kumar, 1975-76, The Category of Cash in Assamese : A Phonological Study, *Journal of the University of Gauhati (Arts)* 26-27 (1), p 79-94, bibliography.

Assamese Language : Study and Teaching

Rabha, T.K., 1974, Some Problems in Teaching Assamese as a Second Language, *Journal of Lal Bahadur Shastri National Academy of Administration* 19 (1) Spring, p 65-67, bibliography.

Assamese Literature

See also Bezbaroa, Lakshminath; Bhattacharyya, Birendra Kumar; Kandali, Madhava; Raichoudhuri, Aruhi Kagiri.

Barua, Navakanta, 1964, Shakespeare in Assamese, *Indian Literature* 7(1) p 12-15, bibliography.

Barua, Navakanta, 1980, Assamese Literature : A Continuing Tradition, *Illustrated Weekly of India* 101 (22) June 1, p 24-25.

Barua, Navakanta, 1985, Assamese Literature : Its Past and the Emerging Present, *Vivekananda Kendra Patrika* 14 (1) February, p 141-146.

Bhattacharyya, Birendra Kumar, 1973, Assam : One or Two Giants among Crowded Literary Undergrowth, *Link* 16 (1) August 15, p 135-137.

Bhattacharyya, Birendra Kumar, 1979, Assames Writing : 1978, *Indian Literature* 22 (6) November-December, p 197-204.

Biswanarayan Singh, 1977, Nationalism and Patriotism in Assamese Literature, *Indian Literature* 20 (3) May-June, p 42-53.

Boli Narayan, 1974, Growth of Assamese Literature in the Sixteenth Century, *Journal of the Assam Research Society*, 22, p 84-92.

Emdad Ullah, 1980, Assamese : Quest for New Forms, *Indian Literature* 23 (6) November-December, p 155-167.

Goswami, Praphulladata, 1970, Assamese Books That Sell and Others, *Indian Literature* 13 (4) December p 14-19.

Kotoky, Praphulla, 198?, Biographer, *Indian Literature* 30 (5) September-October, p 11-14.

Malik, Syed Abdul, 1964, A Review of Current Indian Writing : Assamese Literature, *Indian Literature* 7 (2) p 27-31.

Malik, Syed Abdul, 1966, Assamese : A Coludy Horizon, *Indian Literature* 9 (4) October-December, p 15-19.

Naog, Maheswar, 1965, Annual Review of Indian Writing in 1964 : Assamese, *Indian Literature* 8 (2) p 38-43.
Sarma, Arabinda Nath, 1987, Neither Rosy, Nor Bleak, *Indian Literature* 30 (6) November-December, p 25-32.
Sarma, S.N., 1977-78, Historical Biographies in Assamese Literature, *Journal of the University of Gauhati (Arts)*, 28-29, p 171-181.
Shastri, Biswanarayan, 1977, Modern Assamese Literature, *Indian Literature* 20 (1) January-February, p 9-18.

Assamese Literature : Persian Influence

Alam, Mohammed Mansoor, 1983 Persian Influence on Assamese Language and Literature, *Indo-Iranica* 36 (1-4), p 160-73.
Goswami, S.N., 1968, Assamese Phonetics : A Historical Study, *Journal of Assam Research Society*, 18, p 68-75, bibliography, footnotes and tables.

Assamese Poetry

See also Barua, Navakanta.

Bhattacharyya, Birendra Kumar, 1980, Poetry : New Realizations, *Indian Literature* 23(5) September-October, p 6-11.
Kulshershtha, C.M., 1979, Navakanta Barua's Poetry, A Reappraisal, *Indian Literature* 22 (3) May-June, p 108-114, bibliography.
Rakshit, Birendranath, 1977-78, Inheritance of Old Tradition in Assamese Verification, *Journal of the University of Gauhati (Arts)* 28-29, p 182-194.

Assamese Poetry : Translation Into English

Anon, 1980, Assamese, *Indian Literature* 23 (1-2) January-April, p 8-37.

Assamese Proverbs

Sharma, Nabin Ch., 1986, Study of a Few Assamese Proverbs, *Folklore* 27 (4) April, p 71-77.
Goswami, P., 1952-53, Riddles in Assamese, *Anthropologist* 6(2) December '52-February '53, p 110-115.

Assamese Shot Stories

Bhattacharyya, Birendra Kumar, 1989, This Creation, *Indian Literature* 32 (2) March-April, p 116-127.
Bora, Mahim, 1980, Three, *Indian Literature* 23 (3-4) May-August, p 156-172.
Goswami, Atulananda, 1980, The Wait, *Indian Literature* 23 (3-4) May-August, p 425-507.
Goswami, Dinesh, 1988, I've Kept My Word, Pal, *Pratibha India* 8 (1) October-December, p 21-26.
Sneha Devi, 1988, The Silent Scheme, *Pratibha India* 7 (4) July-September, p 17-20.

Assamese Short Stories : Translation Into English

Borgohain, Homen, 1987, The Elephant : Assamiya Short Story, *Pratibha India* 6 (3) April-June; 19-22.

Das, Devabrata, 1987, In the Land of Dead, *Indian Horizons* 36 (3-4), p 41-45.

Goswami, Atulananda, 1989, The Bed is Threshing : She, *Pratibha India* 8 (3) April-June, p 9-12.

Goswami, Indira, 1986, The Offspring : A Short Stories from Assamese, *Indian Literature* 29 (2) March-April, p 12-28.

Goswami, Kumud, 1985, Temple of the Lord, *Pratibha India* 4 (4) July-September, p 13-16.

Goswami, Atulananda, 1986, The Potion, *Pratibha India* 5 (4) July-September, p 7-10.

Saikia, Bhabendranath, 1981, The Cavern, *Indian Literature* 24 (1) January-February, p 69-86.

Sarma, Apurbha, 1980, Conversation in the Dark, *Indian Literature* 23 (3-4) May-August, p 282-293.

Assamese Tales

Agnihotri, Malti, 1970, A Mizo Folk Tale : Zawlpala and Tualvungi, *Folklore* 11(2) February, p 51-55, bibliography, footnote.

Anon, 1976, (Book Review), *Times of India (Magazine)* December 12, p 10, cols 7-8.
Review of the Book : Thapar, Raj, *Seventh Daughter of the Sun*, Thomson Press, Rs 6.50.

Goswami. Praphulladatta, 1949, The Folk Tales of Assam, *Eastern Anthropologist* 2 (4) June, p 175-181.

Goswami, Praphulladatta, 1958, Uttimati Litercy Sourcce of Assamese Folktales, *Indian Folklore* 1 (1) January-March, p 57-63, footnotes references.

Goswami, Praphulladatta, 1962, Assam's Folktales, *Folklore* 3 (1) January, p 30-36.

Goswami, Prapulladatta, 1968, Secret Knowledge of Animal Languages, *Journal of the Assam Research Society*, 18, p 41-45, bibliography, footnotes.

Goswami, Praphulladatta, 1968, Folktales of the Mirus, *Folklore* 10 (10) October, p 390-392.

Lambert, E.T.D., 1946, Three Ahom Folk Tales, *Man in India* 26 (3-4) September-December, p 196-201.

Banks and Banking

Anon, 1976, Assam : Accent on Village Development, *Commerce* (Supplement) 133 (3403) August 14, p 15-17.

Bordoloi, U.N., 1973-74, Some Aspects of Banking Development in Assam, *Journal of the University of Gauhati* 24-25 (1), p 101-107, tables.

Khuntia, Natabar, 1987, Bank Branches in Assam : Why Sluggish Growth? *Economic Times* (Supplement) June, p 11, cols 1-4.

Pai, Santosh, 1986, Lead Bank Scheme in Assam : Critical Evaluation, *Indian Journal of Commerce* 39 (3) July-September, p 7-1.

Pai, Santosh V., 1986, Lead Bank Scheme in Assam : Poor Performance, *Commerce* 153 (3925) August 9, p 258-59.

Banks and Banking : Rural

Bezbaruah, R.N., 1980, Rural Bank in Assam, *Yojana* 23 (24) January, p 30.

Barua, Navakanta

Kulshreshtha, C.M., 1979, Navakanta Barua's Poetry : A Reappraisal, *Indian Literature* 22 (3) May-June, p 108-114, bibliography.

Bezbaroa, Lakshminath

Anon, 1981, Bezbaroa : Hugo of Assamese Literature, *Assam Information* 32 January-March, p 35-38.
Roy, Anand Sankar, 1978, Sahityarathi Lakshminath Bezbaroa, *Assam Information* 30, October, p 21-24.

Bhattacharyya, Birendra Kumar

Anon, 1979, Assamese Writing : 1978, *Indian Literature* 22 (6) November-December, p 197-204.
Anon, 1980, Authors Urged to Shun Irresponsible Writing, *Times of India* December 16, p 1, cols 3-4+.
Anon, 1980, Jnanpith Award for Assamese Poet, *Times of India* April 27, p, cols 2-4+.
Anon, 1980, Poetry : New Realization, *Indian Literature* 23 (5) September-October, p 6-11.
Anon, 1980, Yearning for One Ultimate Noval, *Times of India* September 19, p 3, cols 3-5.
Anon, 1988 Lyaruingam, *Pratibha India* 7 (4) July-September, p 9-12.
Anon, 1989, The Creation, *Indian Literature* 32 (2) March-April, p 116-127.
Anon, 1989, A Very Tentative View, *Indian Literature* 32 (2) March- April, p 131-140.
Sharma, Ajit Kumar, 1980, Jnanpith Award Winner; 1979; Birendra Kumar Bhattacharyya *Illustrated Weekly of Inida* 101 (22) June 1, p 19.
Sitesh, Aruna, 1988, Birendra Kumar Bhattacharyya in Conversation with Ranvir Rangra, *Pratibha India* 7 (4) July-September 88, p 3-8.

Bhil Seva Mandal

Gautama, G.D., 1978, Bhil Seva Mandal, *Adminstration* 23 (1) Spring, p 99-102.

Bhils

Bageshwar Singh, 1978, Bhil Ethnography through Years, *Tribe* 10 (4) March, p 23-26.
Banthia, J.K., 1978, Migrational Tendencies in Bhils, *Administration* 23 (1) Spring, p 85-90.
Barman, Asim K., 1978, an Approach to the Development of the Development of the Bhils *Adminstration* 23 (1) Spring, p 103-106.
Gautama, G.D., 1978, Bhil Seva Mandal, *Administration* 23 (1) Spring, p 99-102.
Gupta, Sagar Mal, 1979, The Ethnography of Speaking of the Bhil Tribe in India, *Eastern Anthropology* 32 (2) April-June, p 83-89, bibliography.
Kulkarni, S.D., 1979, Class and Caste in a Trible Movement, *Economic and Political Weekly* (Annual Number) 14 (7-8) February, p 465-468, footnotes.

Bibliography

Review of the Book : Satyaprakash, ed, 1976, *Assam: A Select Bibliography,* 1962-75, IDS, 100p.
Anon, 1977, (Book Review), *Journal of Library and Information Science* 2 (1) June, p 109-112.

Biological Research

Haldane, J.B.S., 1978, Possibilities of Biological research in Assam, *Assam Information,* 30, December, p 32-34.

Bodo Movement

See also All Bodo Students Union

Anon, 1989, Militant Segment Gaining Upper Hand, *Economic Times* September 3, p 1, cols 2-6+.
Anon, 1989, Bodo Agitation : Failure of Democracy, *Link* 31 (41) May 21, p 11-12.
Anon, 1989, Dramatic Shifiting in Mahanta's Stand on Bodo Issue, *Link* 31(44) June 11, p 27-28.
Anon, 1989, Why the Bodo Are Angry, *Link* March 12, p 15-16.
Anon, 1989, Tripartite Talks on Bodo Issue, *Link* 31 (47) July 2, p 10-11.
Anon, 1989, A Summer of Discontent, *Times of India* (Sunday Review) March 26, p 1, col 1-8.
Anon, 1994, Bodoland : Ethnic Cleansing in Assam : Ruban Banarjee's Report in the India Today, 31 August 1994, *Muslim India* 12 (142) October, p 472-73.
Bhupinder Singh, 1993, Bodo Accord Only the First Step, *Times of India* June 8, p 8, cols 7-8.
Bose, Kunal, 1989, Bodo Deadlock Bodes No Good, *Economic Times* February 26, p 3, cols 1-6.
Bose, Kunal, 1989, A State For the Bonds *Economic Times* February, 26 p 3, cols 1-6.
Economic Times (Periodical), 1989, Bodo Agitation, *Economic Times,* March 2, p 5, cols 1-2, editorial.
Economic Times (Periodical), 1989, Bodo Bandh, *Economic Times,* July 26, p 6, cols 7-8.
Gupta, Barun Das, 1989, Bodo Agitation : Background Prospectus, *Mainstream* 27 (39) June 24, p 15-17+.
Hazarika, Sanjoy, 1989, Why is Bodo Land Burning, *Indian Express* (Magazine) July 30, p 1, col 1-8..
Mahapatra, Meera, 1992, Bodo Extremism and Its Mindless Violence, *Link* 35 (11) October 25, p 18-19.
Misra, Profulla, 1993, Accord Ends Six Years of Bodo Insurgency, *New Age* 41 (11) March 14, p 3.
Misra, Profulla, 1989, Bodo Agitation Taking Violent Turn, *New Age* 37(11) March 12, p 6.
Kakati, Satish ch-1, 1993, A Close Look at the Bodo and Accord, *Illustrated Weekly of India* 113 (29) July 3, p 28-29.

Sonwalkar, Prasun, 1989, Land Alienation Is the Main Problem for Bodos, *Times of India* (See II) February 23, p 3, col 3-8.
Times of India (Newspaper), 1989, Eyeless in Assam, *Times of India*, March 4, p 6, cols 1-2, editorial.
Times of India (Newspaper), 1989, Assam on the Brink, *Times of India* March 16, p 6, cols 1-2, editorial.
Times of India (Newspaper), 1989, A Welcome Pause, *Times of India*, August 30, p 4, col 1-2, editorial.

Borbora, Golap

Guha, Seema, 1978, The Little Know Man Who Is Assam's Chief Minister, *Perspectives* 2 (4) NOvember, p 20-22+.

Border Issues

See Boundaries

Boundaries

Anon, 1979, Border Clashes, *Economic and Political Weekly* 14 (2) January 13, p 42.
Anon, 1989, Border Dispute behind Massacre, *Times of India* April 9, p 1, col 2-5.
Misra, Udyon, 1979, After Raid, *Economic and Political Weekly* 14 (9) March 3, p 499-550.
Times of India (Newspaper), 1979, Disputed Borders, *Times of India* April 16, p 6, cols 1-2, editorial.
Times of India (Newspaper), 1989, Strife without End, *Times of India* April 13, p 8, cols 1-2, editorial.

Boundaries : Bengal

Bhattacharjee, K.K., 1982, Transfer of Territory from Bengal to Assam (1892-98) : An Analysis of the Controversy, *Social Research* 2 (2) April-June, p 28-33, bibliography.

Boundaries : Mughalaya

Anon, 1974, Assam-Meghalaya Border Dispute, *Link* 16(37) April 21, p 28.
Anon, 1974, Assam-Meghalaya Dispute to be Probed, *Times of India* April 18, p 5, cols 2-5.

Boundaries : Nagaland

Anon, 1971, Farcical Confrontation, *Economic and Political Weekly* 6 (6) February 6, p 417-418.
Anon, 1972, Histrocial Disputes, *Economic and Political Weekly* 7 (20) May 13, p 968.
Anon, 1972, Naga Belligerences over Border Claim, *Link* 14 (39) May 7, p 12-13.
Anon, 1989, Assam-Nagaland Accord on Border, *Times of India* April 26, p 1, cols 7-8+.

Bhatia, Sudarshan, 1971, Border Tensions in North East : Assam-Nagaland Dispute, *Times of India* May 1, p 6, cols 7-8.

Bhattacharya, M., 1979, Assam-Negaland Border Raid : Some Unanswered Question, *New Age* 27 (5) February in 4, p 3+.

Bhattacharyya, M., 1979, Behind Assam-Nagaland Border Clash, *New Age* 27 (11) March 18, p 5+.

Bhattacharyya, M., 1979, Centre Must Help Settle Assam-Nagaland Dispute, *New Age* 27 (13) April 1, p 11.

Bhattacharya, M., 1979, Chief Minister for Deferring Assam-Nagaland Border Dispute, *New Age* 27 (6) February 11, p 6.

Datta, K.P., 1985, Genesis of Assam-Nagaland Dispute, *Mainstream* 23 (46) July 13, p 31-33.

Times of India (Newspaper), 1972, Deplorable, *Times of India* April 4, p 6, cols 1-2, editorial.

Times of India (Newspaper), 1987, Boundaries of Dispute, *Times of India* November 13, p 6, cols 1-2, editorial.

Budget

See also Annual Plans

Anon, 1964, Fresh Taxation in Assam and Rajasthan, *Capital* 152 (3801) March 12, p 369.

Anon, 1965, Assam in the Red but No Taxes, *Capital* 154 (3851) March 11, p 339.

Anon, 1972, Assam C.M., Presents Interim Budget, *Times of India* March 24, p 9, cols 1-2.

Anon, 1972, State Budgets: Assam, *Commerce* 124 (3819) June 17, p 1568-1569.

Anon, 1973, Largest Annual Plan, *Commerce* 126 (3241) June 16, p 1194-1199.

Anon, 1974, Finance Commission Comes to Rescue, *Commerce* 128 (3280) March 23, p 374.

Anon, 1975, Demand for Upward Revision of Crude Royalty Rates, *Commerce* 130 (3330) March 15, p 370-371.

Anon, 1976, The Growing Burden of Debts, *Commerce* 132 (3338) March 27, p 416-417.

Anon, 1976, No New Taxes in Assam Budget, *Times of India* March 2, p 5, cols 1-2.

Anon, 1977, Assam Budget Shows Surplus, *Times of India* March 24, p 7, cols 1-2.

Anon, 1977, Hike in Land, Jute Purchase Taxes, *Commerce* 134 (3435) April 2, p 522.

Anon, 1978, Assam Interim Budget : Rs 6.5 Cr Uncovered Gap, *Economic Times* March 24' p 1, cols 2-4+.

Anon, 1978, No Fresh Taxes, *Commerce* 136 (3487) April 8, p 550-555.

Anon, 1978, Rs 10.6 Cr Deficit in Assam Budget, *Times of India* March 24, p 5, cols 2-3.

Anon, 1979, Assam Budget : Deficit Remains Uncovered spite New Taxes, *Capital* 182 (4551) March 22, p 284.

Anon, 1979, More Sops for Agriculture, *Commerce* 138 (3535) March 17, p 421-423.
Anon, 1979, Rs 47.49 Cr Deficit in Assam, *Economic Times* March 6, p 1, col 6+.
Anon, 1980, Assam Budget Passed, *Economic Times* November 28, p 4, col -3.
Anon, 1980, Deficit Budget for Assam, *Economic Times* March 15, p 4, col 3.
Anon, 1980, No Hope for Assam's Economic Development *Janata* 35 (19) June 22, p 7-8.
Anon, 1981, Trust in Taimur, *Eastern Economist* 76 (14) April 3, p 906-907.
Anon, 1983, No Taxes in Assam Budget, *Economic Times* September 3, p 1, cols 2-3+.
Bhattacharya, M., 1967, Opposition Pillories Chaliha : Budget Debate in Assam Assembly, *New Age* 15 (26) June 25, p 3.
Eastern Economist (Periodical), 1974, Central Assistances to Assam, *Eastern Economists* 62 (20) March 17, p 975, editorial.

Business Education

Das, N.C., 1985, Commerce Education in the North East India : With Special Reference to Assam, Indian *Journal of Commerce* 28 (4) October-December p 17-21.

Cachar (Silchar)

Anon, 1976, More Areas Flooded in Cachar, *Times of India* July 19, p 1, cols 2-3+.
Anon, 1976, Serious Flood Threat to Cachar, *Times of India* July 12, p 1, cols 7-8+.
Anon, 1977, (Book Review), *International Studies* 16 (4) October-December, p 571-572.
Review of the Book : Bhattacharjee, Jayanta Bhusan 1977, *Cachar under British Rule in North-East India*, Radiant Publication, Delhi, xiv, 353 p.
Bhattacharya, P.C., 1977-78, The Languages and Dialects of Cachar District in Assam, *Journal of Asssam Research Society*, 23, p 12-15.
Chatterjee, Suhas, 1964, Socio-Economic Survey of Cachar (Assam), *Khadi Gramodyog* 10 (12) September, p 803-805.
Mazarbhuiyan, Nazrul Haq, 1979, The Agony of Cachar, *Economic and Political Weekly* 11 (34) August 21, p 1397-1398.
Sinha, Jagannath, 1975, Plantation Labour Act and Its Fate in Cachar, *Indian Worker* 23 (29-30) May 5, p 13.

Cachar (Silchar) : Economic Condition

Chatterjee, Suhas, 1964, Socio-Economic Survey of Cachar (Assam), *Khadi Gramodyog* 10 (12) September, p 803-805.

Cachar (Silchar) History

Bhattacharyya, B.K., 1978, Cachar in History : A Study, *North-East Spectrum* 2 (9-11) March-May, p 31-34.

Caste

Anon, 1982, (Book Review) *Eastern Anthropologist* 35 (4) October-December, p 355-356.

Review of the Book : Chauhan, S.K., 1980, *Caste,Status and Power: Social Stratification in Assam* Classical Publication, New Delhi.

Anon, 1985, (Book Review), *Hindustan Times* (Magazine) January 6, p viii, cols 1-4.

Review of the Book : Dev, J. Bimal and Lahri, K. Bilip, n.d., *Cosmogony of Caste and Social Mobility in Assam*, Mittal Pub. Delhi, 183p.

Chauhan, S.K., 1972, Caste Hierarchy in Three Villages of Upper Assam, *Man in India* 52 (1) January-March, p 39-45, bibliography.

Chauhan, S.K., 1980, Caste Structure in Assam, *Eastern Anthropologist* 33 (2) April-June, p 124-132, bibliography.

Das, Priya Bala and Buragohain, Satyendra Nath, 1971, Taste Sensitivity to Phenylthiourea in Two Caste Group of Assam, *Man in India* 51 (3) July-September, p 252-256, tables, footnotes.

Caste and Occupations

Goswami, M.C., Ratha, S.N; and Nesh, F., 1966, Caste and Occupation in an Assamese Village, *Man in India* 46 (3) July-September, p 191-197.

Rath, S.N., 1968, Caste and Occupation in the Periurban Assamese Village, *Eastern Anthropologist* 21 (2) May-August, p 155-165, reference, tables.

Caste and Politics

Chauhan, S.K., 1972, Party Preferences : A Study of Political Attitudes in Upper Assam, *Man in India* 52 (4) October-December, p 371-378. bibliography, tables.

Cattle

Anon, 1974, Development of Cattle Population in Assam, *Assam Information* 25 (7) October, p 21-24.

Cements Industry and Trade

Anita, Ferdoon P.,1977, How the Cement Industry Can be Lifted from the Morass, *Capital* (Supplement) 179 (4481) September 15, p 69-73.

Anon, 1977, Cement : Emerging Imbalance, *Commerce* 134 (3438) April 23, p 648.

Anon, 1977, Erratic Coal Supplies Hit Cement Output, *Economic Times* October 26, p 1, cols 5-8+.

Anon, 1977, First Big Industrial Venture in Hill Areas, *Commerce* 134 (3430) February 26, p 246-247.

Anon, 1977, Gingerly as ever, *Economic and Political Weekly* 12 (28) July 9, p 1077.

Anon, 1977, Key Role Likeky for State Sector, *Economic Times* December 17, p 1, cols 5-7+.

Anon, 1977, Predictable Tactics, *Economic and Political Weekly* 12 (22) May 28, p 859-860.

Anon, 1977, Why Cement Shortage? *Commerce* 134 (3442) May 21, p 825.

Chakravarty, D.N., 1973, A Modern Industrial Project in a Most Backward District, *Yojana* 17 (9) June 1, p 383-384.

Commerce (Periodical), 1977, Incentives for Cement, *Commerce* 135 (3457) September 3, p 392, editorial.

Economic Times (Newspaper), 1977, Mini-Cement Plants, *Economic Times* December 16, p 5, cols 1-2, editorial.

Gupta, G.S. and Patel, Kirit, 1976, Location of Indian Cement Industry, *Vikalpa* 1 (4) October, p 27-37, tables, appendix, bibliography.

Gurjar, M.N., 1977, Thriving Black Market in Cement, *Commerce* 135 (3471) December 10, p 1098.

Karmakar, C.K., 1975, Bokajan Cement Factory : Fulfilment of Hope and Aspiration of Hill People, *Assam Information* 27 (5-6) August-September, p 18-22.

Cements Research Institute of India

Anon, 1977, Impressive Work in Cement Research, *Yojana* 21 (13-14) August 15, p 31-32.

Census

Anon, 1971, Assam Maghalaya and Nagaland, *Commerce* 123 (3163) December 18, p 1172.

Central Places

Sharma, P. and Sharma, H.N., 1985, Identification, Ranking and Grouping of Service Centres : A Case Study of Nowgong District, *North-Eastern Geographer* 17 (1-2) p 12-20, bibliography, figures, tables.

Chemical Industry and Trade

Anon, 1976, Untapped Resources, *Commerce* 133 (3414) October 30, p 12.

Anon, 1977, Still in Infant Stage, *Commerce (Supplement)* 135 (3469) November 26, p 31.

Cheros

Singh, K.S., 1976, The Cheros : An Anthropo-Historical Approach of Their Study, *Indian Museum Bulletin.* 11 (1) January, p 55-56.

Chief Ministers

See also Borbora, Golap; Mahanta, Prafulla Kumar.

Anon, 1970, Durgapur's Dilemma, *Commerce* 121 (3105) November 7, p 988.

Times of India (Newspaper), 1986, Into the Mainstream, *Times of India* February 10, p 8, cols 1-2, editorial.

Child Welfare

Agnihotri, S.K. and Khan, S.A., 1985, The Status of Children in Assam, *Social Welfare* 31 (10) January, p 17-20.

Anon, 1975, Child Welfare Activities of the Assam Harijan Sevak Sangh, *Social Welfare* 22(8) November, p 23.

Civil Rights

Anon, 1992, Assam : Invoking NSA to Stifle Human Rights, *Economic and Political Weekly* 27 (33) August 15, p 1723-24.

Civilisation

Barua, T.C., 1975, Cultural Heritage, *Link* 17 (21) January 5, p 27-30.
Goswami, Praphulladatta, 1979, Assam's Contribution to Country's Culture and Well-Being, *Times of India* December 3, p 8, cols 1-3+.
Pandey, B.B., 1977, Culture Pattern among the People of Siang and Trends of Development, *Resarun* 3 (4) October, p 13-15, bibliography.

Clans and Clan System

See also Garos; Khasis

Das Gupta, Pranab Kumar, 1968, A Note on Clan among the War Khasi, *Journal of India Anthropological Society* 3 (1-2) March-September, p 131-140, references.

Clear-Cutting

Bose, Lakshmi Nandan, 1981, Deforestation in Assam, *Economic Times* May 23, p 5, cols 7-8.

Coal Mine and Mining

Anon, 1978, Assam Coal, *Link* 20 (38) April 30, p 12.

Coins

Dutta, S., 1983, A Study on the Matak Coins, *Journal of Indian History* 61 (1-3) April-December, p 117-125, footnotes.

Commerce

Bordoloi, P.C., Trade and Commerce in Assam, *Assam Information* 24 (9) December, p 36-39, bibliography.

Communalism

Anon, 1985, Minority Front Politics Leading to Communal Polarisation in Assam, *Organiser* 37 (28) November 24, p 81+.

Communist Parties

Misra, Udayon, 1983, Trends within the Left, *Economic and Political Weekly* 18 (31) July 30, p 1350-1390.

Communist Party of India

Anon, 1971, CPI : A Wrong Understanding, *Link* 14 (7) September 26, p 22-23.
Anon, 1971, CPI Leads Struggle against Galloping Prices in Assam, *New Age* 19(45) November 7, p 13.
Anon, 1976, Assam : Some Stark Fact, *Link* 18 (42) May 30, p 43.
Anon, 1976, CPI Campaign in Assam , *Link* 18 (34) April 4, p 13-14.
Anon, 1977, Two-Month Mass Campaign Planned in Assam, *New Age* 25 (27) July 3, p 11.
Anon, 1978, Communal Forces Halted but Danger Remain, *New Age* 26 (39) September 24, p 14.

Bhatta, Suren, 1971, Assam CPI Congerence : To Bulid Left and Democratic Unit, *New Age* 19 (39) September 26, p 6.

Bora, Phani, 1971, Concactions in Bourgeois Press, *New Age* 19 (49) December 5, p 4.

Community Party of India : Assam Unit

Anon, 1975, Assam CPI Conference, *Link* 17 (22) January 12, p 23.

Anon, 1975, Assam Conferences Notes Party's Growth, *New Age* 23(2) January 12, p 4, col 5.

Anon, 1981, Behind Desertion from CPI in Assam, *New Age* 29 (29) July 19, p 7.

Anon, 1983, CPI : Call to Resume Assam Dialogue, *New Age* 31 (28) July 10, p 13.

Communist Party of India (Marxist)

Anon, 1978, CPM's Crucial Role in Assam, *Times of India* March 11, p 1, cols 2-4+.

Communist Party of India (Marxist) : Assam Unit

Anon, 1979, Assam State Conference of the CPI (M), *People's Democracy* 2 (24) June 11, p 3.

Anon, 1979, CPI (M) Emerges as Leading Party in Gauhati Corporation *People's Democracy* 3 (12) March 25, p 1+.

Anon, 1980, Violence against CPI (M) by Assam Agitators, *People's Democracy* 4 (22) June 1, p 5+.

Anon, 1985, Assam State Conference, *People's Democracy* 9 (51) December 22, p 5.

Anon, 1988, Thirteenth Assam State Conference, *People's Democracy* 12 (50) December 11, p 12.

Community Development

Phukan Umananda, 1966, Agriculture Growth in Lahoal Development Block : A Case Study, Indian *Journal of Agricultural Eonomics* 21 (4) October-December, p 208-214, tables.

Companies

Khanna, K.C., 1964, A Closer Look at the Tax Changes for Compaines, *Capital* 152 (3800) March 5, p 324-325, tables.

Consumptions : Economic Aspects

Borah, K.C., 1977, Consumer Expenditure Patterns in Selected Rural Areas of Assam 1972-1973, *Assam Economic Journal* 3(1) March, p 90-101, bibliography.

Cooperation and Co-operative Societies

Anon, 1973, New Co-operatives and Whole-Sale Trade, *Assam Information* 24 (7) October, p 5-7+.

Anon, 1977, Many Ills Dog Co-operative Movements in Assam, *Times of India* March 18, p 9, cols 1-2.

Anon, 1978, Co-operative in Economic Prosperity, *Assam Information* 29 January-February, p 3-5.
Anon, 1978, New Look in Co-operative for a Vibrants Democracy *Assam Information* 30, June-July, p 9-11.
Awasthi, R.C., 1964, Cooperation in a Developing Economy with Special Referances to Assam, *Journal of the University of Gauhati* 15 (1) p 57-63.
Das, G.P., 1976, Gaon Level Co-ops Do a Good Job, *Times of India* November 20, p 11, col 5+.
Sah, A.K., 1979, Working of Goan-Panchayat Samabay Samiti in Assam. *Indian Cooperative Review* 16 (3) April, p 297-305, tables.

Corruption

Anon, 1977, Assam Chief Minister Accused of Making Crores, *Organiser* 29 (9) July 25, p 4+.
Anon, 1979, Who Is to Guard the Guardians, *Economic and Political Weekly* 14 (25) June 23, p 1028-1029.

Cost and Standard Living

Anon, 1978, (Book Review), *Social Action* 28 (1) January-March, p 99-100, *Times of India* (*Magazine*) April 2, p 10, cols 1-2.
Review of the Book : Ganguli, B.N., and Gupta, Devendra B., 1976, *Levels of Living in India*, S.Chand, New Delhi, vi 273 p.
Anon, 1981, Extensive Malnutrition, *Commerce* (Supplement) 143 (3661) August 15, p 15-17.
Arshad Mahmood, 1978, Poverty Levels of Living in India, *Southern Economist* 17 (8) August 15, p 35-38, bibliography, tables.
Borah, K.C., 1977, Consumer Expenditure Patterns in Selected Rural Areas of Assam 1972-73, *Assam Economic Journal* 3(1) March, p 90-101, bibliography.
Goswami, Atul, 1970-72, Prices and Cost of Living in Assam in the Last Decade (1960-70), *Journal of the University of Gauhati* 21-23 (1), p 142-157, tables.
Muthayya, B.C., 1977, Indicators of Rural Level of Living and Methodological Issues, *Community Development and Panchayati Raj Digest* 9 (1) July, p 1-13, bibliography.

Costume

Bordolov, N., 1975, Costumes and Ornaments of Assam, *Link* 17(21) January 5, p 32-34.

Cottage Industries

Anon, 1979, Unexamined Wisdom, *Gandhi Vigyan* 2 (4) July, p 13-15.
Anon, 1979, Upgraded Cottage Spinning, *Voluntary Action* 21 (3) March, p 12-14.
Sarma, Joy Kanta, 1978, Bell-Metal Workers of Assam, *Economic and Political Weekly* 13 (42) October, 21, p 1764-1765.

Council of Ministers

See also Sarma, Nagen

Anon, 1967, House Trading with Crumbs of Power, *New Age* 15(17) April 23, p 10.

Anon, 1967, New Cabinet, *Eastern Economist* 48 (12) March 24, p 543-544+.

Anon, 1972, A Pattern in Power Distribution : Assam *Commerce* 124 (3178) April 1, p 778-779.

Anon, 1974, 13 New Minister in Assam Sworn in, *Times of India* October 13, p 1, cols 7-8.

Anon, 1977, Assam Portfolios Reallocated, *Times of India* May 14, p 7, col 1.

Anon, 1978, All but Two Assam Ministers Sworn in, *Times of India* March 13, p 7, cols 4-5.

Anon, 1979, Eight-Man Hazarika Ministry Sworn in, *Times of India* September 10, p 1, cols 1-2.

Anon, 1980, 8 Member Cong-1 Govt Installed in Assam, *Times of India* December 7, p 1, cols 7-8+.

Anon, 1980, Ministry Making Blues, *Link* 23 (17) December 7, p 8.

Anon, 1985, Mahanta to Head Submit List of Minister, *Times of India* December 24, p 1, cols 7-8.

Anon, 1985, Mahanta to Head 20-Man Ministry, *Times of India* December 24, p 1, cols 1-3.

Anon, 1988, Mahanta Drop 12, Inducts 7 Minsters, *Times of India* October 23, p 1, cols 7-8.

Bhattacharya, M., 1971, Assam : Balancing Trick in Cabinet, *New Age* 19 (25) June 20, p 3.

Bhattacharya, M., 1972, Old Policies Dominate in Assam Congress Ministry, *New Age* 20 (15) April 9, p 4-5.

Call (Periodical) 1980, Congress-1 Ministry in Assam, *Call* 30 (12) December, p 5-8, editorial.

Dutta, S.K., 1976, Ministerial Changes in Assam : An Action Oriented Cabinet *Times of India* February 13, p 6, cols 7-8.

Times of India (Newspaper), 1980, New Assam Ministry, *Times of India* December 9, p 6, cols 1-2, editorial.

Times of India (Newspaper), 1985, No Easy Exit, *Times of India* December 25, p 8, cols 1-2, editorial.

Times of India (Newspaper), 1988, No Ordinary Reshuffle, *Times of India* October 25, p 4, cols 1-2, editorial.

Cultura Contribution

See Under Civilization.

Dairying

Dutta, Poresh Chandra and Gohain, Debasingh, 1974, Dairying in Assam, *Yojana* 18 (22) December 15, p 27.

Pathak, P.C., 1983, Growth of Diary Development in Assam, *Assam Information*, 34, January-March, p 7-9.

Dancing

See also Folk-Dancing

Dezbarah, Rama, 1975, Dances of Assam, *Link* 17 (21) January 5, p 31-32.

Bhagawati, Anandamohan, 1981, Dances of Assam, *Assam Information* 32, January-March, p 39-46.

Goswami, Kesovananda Deva, 1973, A Peculiar Prayer Service of Assamese Vaisnavas, *Journal of Music Academic* 44 (1-4) p 227-233.

Debit : Rural

Anon, 1975, Liquidation of Rural Indebtedness in Assam, *Assam Information* 27 (5-6) August-September, p 27-28.

Description and Travel

Anon, (Book Review), 1973, *Indian and Foreign Review* 10 (10) March 1, p 22. Review of the Book : Anon, 1972, *Assam*, Publication Division, 67p, State of Our Union Series.

Anon, 1979, Heaven of Loveliness Where Even Gods Once Aspired to Die, *Times of India*, December 3, p 8, cols 6-8.

Anon, 1983, Assam Smiles Again, *Times of India*, September 12, p 10, cols 1-4.

Anon, 1983, The Thrill of Being in Love, *Times of India* September 12, p 10, cols 6-8.

Barua, Hem, 1967, Introducting India-II : Assam, *Illustrated Weekly of India* 88 (37) October 15, p 29-31, illustrations.

Benerji, Anjan Kumar, 1967, Assam : A Look Back, *Illustrated Weekly of India* 88 (16) May 21, p 35.

Bhagavati, B., 1967, Assam : A Brief Sketch, *Illustrated Weekly of India* 88 (17) May 28, p 33+.

Bhattacharyya, Birendra Kumar, 1979, Search for Community uppermost in the Mind of Assamese, *Times of India* December 3, p 8, cols 4-8+.

Borbora, Golap, 1979, A Very Eventful Year for Assam, *Times of India* 29, p 10, cols 1-5.

Chaliha, B.P., 1967, Foreword, *Illustrated Weekly of India* 88 (16) May 21, p 8-9, illustrations.

Gandhi, Mohandas Karamchand, 1979, Lovely Assam, *Times of India* November 20, p 10, cols 1-2, reprint.

Goswami, Radhika Mohan, 1967, Assam : Past and Present, *Illustrated Weekly of India* 88 (17) May 28, p 37+.

Kakati, Satish Ch. 1967, Profile of a Strategic State, *Illustrated Weekly of India* 8 (17) May 28, p 49.

Kar, Biman, 1976, Tal of the Valley, and the Hill, *Times of India* November 20, p 12, cols 1-5.

Malik, Amita, 1967, A Childhood Recollected, *Illustrated Weekly of India* 88 (16) May 21, p 48-49, illustrations.

Raman, A.S., 1967, Impressions of Assam, *Illustratd Weekly of India* 88 (16) May 21, p 40-41+, illustrations; 88 (17) May 28, p 40-43, illustrations.

Dimasa Kachari

Anon, (Book Review) 1973, *Man in India* 53 (1) January-March, p 114. Review of the Book : Roy Burman, B.K., *Census of India*, 1961 : *Dimasa Kachari of Assam* Ministry of Home Affairs, New Delhi, vii, 34p.

District Administration

Singh, B.P., 1977, Evolution of the Office of the Deputy Commisioner in Assam,

Indian Journal of Public Administration 23 (3) October-December, p 890-912, footnotes.

Droughts

Anon, 1979, Assam : Rs 50 Crores Loss, *Commerce* 139 (3562) September 22, p 552.
Dubhashi, P.R., 1981, Leading the Central Task Force, *Indian Journal of Public Administration* 27 (1) January-March, p 113-118.

Economic Conditions

See also Cost and Standard of Living ; Employment and Unemployment; Food Supply; Manpower : Educated Employment : Employment; Prices.
Akhtar, Nawab, 1983, Assam Crises : Economic Roots of Turmoil , *Economic Times* November 11, p 5, cols 3-6, tables.
Anon, 1967, Prices Go Still Up in Assam, *New Age* 15 (20) May 14, p 11.
Anon, 1967, You Can't Buy a Home in Shillong, *Organiser* 20 (38) May 7, p 5+, map.
Anon, 1970, Governor Inaugurates the Budget Session of the Assam Assembly, *Assam Information* 20 (12) March, p 5-12.
Anon, 1970, Wages of Evasion *Economic and Political Weekly* 5 (41) October 10, p 1681.
Anon, 1971, Famine Condition, *Link* 13 (51) August 1, p 25.
Anon, 1973, Divisiveness on Top of Backwardness, *Link* 16 (1) August 15, p 43.
Anon, 1973, Lack of Enterpreneurs Hampers Development, *Commerce* (Supplement) 127 (3250) August 18, p 15-17.
Anon, 1973, The Mount of Difficulties, *Thought* 25 (29) July 21, p 9.
Anon, 1974, Gram Panchayats Introduced, *Commerce* (Supplement) 129 (3301) August 17, p 13-17.
Anon, 1975, "Basic Problems" Comfronting Growth, *Commerce* 131 (3366) November 22, p 852.
Anon, 1975, Call for 'Serious Concerted Effort to Maintain Economic Stability and Progressively Raise the Standered of Living of the Commom People, *Assam Information* 25 (10-12) January-March, p 1-16+.
Anon, 1977, Assam's Hill Districts, *Link* 19 (48) January 10, p 21.
Anon, 1978, Assam : Stagnant Economy, *Commerce* 136 (3478) February 4, p 131.
Anon, 1979, No Significant Change, *Commerce* 138 (3531) February 17, p 209.
Anon, 1980, Agitation Hits Assam Itself, *New Age* 28 (21) May 25, p 10.
Anon, 1980, Economic Cost of Assam Agitation-II : Many Plywood Units to Close Down, *Commerce* 141 (3606) August 2, p 207-208.
Anon, 1980, The Econopmic Dimension, *Janata* 35 (4) May 18, p 9-10.
Anon, 1980, Economics of Assam Unrest, *Capital* 184 (4609) May 26, p 6.
Anon, 1980, No Hope for Assam's Economic Development, *Janata* 35 (19) June 22, p 7-8.
Anon, 1981, Life in Assam : Rich in Rsources, Poor in All Else, *Times of India* November 1, p 12, cols 1-4.
Anon, 1983, Assam : Times for Decisive Moves, *Mainstream* (Annual Number), p 93-97.

Anon, 1983, Poverty Despite Rich Resouraces, *Commerce* 147 (3767) August 13, p 221-223.

Anon, 1985, Politics and Economics of Assam Accord, *Commerce* 151 (3874) August 24, p 360-362.

Anon, 1986, Assam : Miles to Go, *Capital* 197 (4840-4841) November 1, p 23-24.

Barua, A.M., 1979, Assam Needs Infrastructural Support, *Times of India* December 7, p 8, cols 1-5.

Bhatta, Suren, 1966, Assam Govt. Succumbs to Traders and Black Marketers, *New Age* 14 (28) July 10, p 3.

Bhattacharya, M., 1965, Pitiable Plight of Assam : Cholera, Floods Food Scarcity, *New Age* 13 (29) July 18, p 5.

Bhattacharya, M., 1967, Communists Lead Attack on Assam Govt. *New Age* 15 (16) April 16, p 7.

Bhattacharya, M., 1971, Assam : Stunts to Hide Near Bankruptcy, *New Age* 19 (15) April 11, p 4.

Borbora, Golap, 1978, Assam Economy : Stress on Rural Sector : *Economic Times* July 31, p 1, cols 2-5+.

Boruah, N.K., 1976, Step to Remove Poverty, *Link* 18 (48) July 11, p 24-25.

Chatterjee, Suhas, 1964, Socio-Economic Survey of Cachar (Assam), *Khadi Gramodyog* 10 (12) September, p 803-805.

Dutta, Pulakesh, 1987, Socio-Economic Problem of Assam : A Diagnostic Appraisal, *National Geographer* 22 (1) June, p 29-36, bibliography.

Dutta, S.K., 1977, Shattering Quake in Assam : Fear of Experts, *Times of India* October 20, p 6, cols 7-8.

Dubey, S.M., 1980, The Assam Movement : A Preliminary Study in the Sociology of Politics and Development, *Man and Development* 2 (3) September, p 60-75, bibliography.

Ghoain, Hiren, 1980, Assam and Underdevelopment, *Economic and Political Weekly* 15 (37) September 13, p 1533, letter to the editor.

Gohain, Hiren, 1980, Fallout of Underdevelopment, *Economic and Political Weekly* 15 (12) March 22, p 589-590.

Goswami, Biswa, 1982, Problems of Assam, *Janata* 37 (17) June 6, p 15-16.

Gupta, Shekhar, 1982, Assam : Driver to Desperation, *Indian Express* (Magazine) July 25, p 11, cols 1-8.

Hardev Singh, 1978, Assam : Rich Potential Ready for Tapping, *Eastern Economist* (Annual Number), p 1449-1461.

Jansen, G.H., 1983, The Agony of Assam, *Illustrated Weekly of India* 104 (17) may 15, p 6-7.

Kakety, Jadu, 1979, Assam's Plea for Justice, *Times of India* December 7, p 8, cols 6-8+.

Mahanti, P.C., 1980, Economic Cost of Assam Agitation-I : Weapon of Oil, *Commerce* 141 (3606) August 2, p 200-206, tables.

Mishra, Brhmanand, 1980, Rich but Neglected Assam, *Economic Times* June 3, p 9, cols 7-8.

Misra, Tilottoma, 1980, Assam : A Colonial Hinterland, *Economic and Political Weekly* 15 (32) August 9, p 1357-1364, footnotes.

Pathak, Bharat Ch., 1975, Impact of Development after Emergency, *Assam Information* 27 (5-6) August-September, p 13-17.

Prabhakar, M.S., 1975, Visitations, *Economic and Political Weekly* 10(8) February 22, p 349-351.

Sarma, Joy Kanta, 1983, Economy on the Brink, *Economic Times* (Supplement) July 9, p xii, cols 1-5+.

Sharma, Chandar Kumar, 1995, Poverty and Inequality : Case of Assam, *Economic and Political Weekly* 30 (7-80 February 18, p 403-404, bibliography.

Sharma, V.V.R., 1979, Assam Faces Acute Shortages, *Times of India* October 23, p 8, cols 7-8.

Shreevastava, M.P., and Tandon, K.K., 1967, Economy of Small Towns in Assam, *AICC Economic Review* 19 (9) November 15, p 23-25.

Singh. B.P., 1984, Perspectives for Assam, *Mainstrean* 22 (48) July 28, p 27-32.

Tarlok Singh, 1966, The Problems of Development of the Hill Districts of Assam, Vanyajati 14 (2) April, p 61-70.

Economic Development

Anon, 1969, Infrastructure for State-2 : Assam : Miles to Go, *Commerce* (Annual Number) 119 (3061), p 137.

Anon, 1975, New Oil Finds, *Commerce* (Supplement) 131 (3352) August 16, p 13-15.

Anon, 1976, Assam Accent on Village Development, *Commerce* (Supplement) 133 (3403) August 14, p 15-17.

Anon, 1977, Control of Floods Is the Dire Need, *Commerce* (Supplement) 135 (3454) August 13, p 19-21.

Anon, 1978, Beginning of a New Era, *Assam Information* 30, June-July, p 1-3.

Anon, 1978, Towards Tribal Development, *Assam Information* 30, December, p 1-13.

Anon, 1979, Plans for Balanced Economic Growth, *Economic Times* November 3, p 5, cols 7-8.

Anon, 1981, (Book Review), *Yojana* 25 (21) November 16, p 34.
Review of the Book : Medhi, S.B., 1978, Transport System and *Economic Development in Assam*, Publication Board Government of Assam, Gauhati, 424p.

Anon, 1982 (Book Review), *Indian Journal of Public Administration* 28 (4) October-December, p 936-938.
Review of the Book : Medhi, Shyam Bhadra, 1978, *Transport System and Economic Development in Assam* Publication Board, Government of Assam, Gauhati, 424p.

Anon, 1982, Brief Review of the Economic of Assam 1981-82, *Assam Information*, Independence Day Number, 34, August, p 1-8.

Anon, 1982, Govermor's Message to the People of Assam, *Assam Information*, 34, September, p 3-6.

Anon, 1985, Signs of Normalcy, Economic Times (*Supplement*) June 9, p 1, col 1-4+.

Anon, 1986, Rejuvenation of Assam : The AGP Formula, *Capital* 197 (4837) September 15, p 30-35.

Bagchi, J.K., 1982, Development Programmes in Assam Progress and Prospect, *Yojana* 26 (14-15) August 16, p 65-66.

Barbora, Golap, 1978, Assam on Threshold of New Era, *Assam Information*, 30, October, p 28-32.

Barthakur, M., 1972, A Strategy of Industrial and Regional Development of Assam, *Deccan Geographer.* 10 (1) January-June, p 59-64, tables

Bhuyan, Jadav, 1980, Assam : Neglect By Purpose? *Commerce* (Annual Number) 141 (3628) p 221-227.

Bora, Lakshmi Nandan, 1980, State of Assam Economic Development, *Economic Times* October 17, p 5, cols 7-8.

Chakravarty, D.N., 1979, Assam 1978 : In Retrospect, *Assam Information* 30 January p 23-26.

Chopra, S.P., 1978, Assam : Rich in Resources, *Eastern Economist* 71 (14) October 6, p 684-687.

Gogoi, Pradip Kumar, 1980, Hill Areas of Assam Touch New Economic Heights, *Yojana* 24 (23) December 16, p 18-22.

Jagjit Singh, 1967, Railways in Assam, *Illustrated Weekly of India* 88 (16) May 21, p 22-23, map.

Medhi, Bisnurm, 1967, Hills and Plains : Need for Intergration, *Illustrated Weekly of India* 88 (17) May 28, p 23.

Pandey, B.B., 1977, Cultural Pattern among the People of Siang and Trends of Development, *Resarun* 3 (4) October, p 13-15, bibliography.

Raman, A.S., 1967, An Interview with B.P., Chaliha, *Illustrated Weekly of India* 88 (17) May 28, p 10-11, portraits.

Roy Ghatak, Adit, 1986, Assam : the Task Ahead, *Capital* 197 (4837) September 15, p 26-29.

Sarma, J.N., 1966, Problems of Economic Development in Assam, *Economic and Political Weekly* 1 (7) October 1, p 281-286.

Sarma, M.C., and Mehrotra R., 1977, The Growth of Public Expenditures and Levels of Economic Activity in Assam, *Assam Economic Jourrnal* 3 (10) March, p 126-134, bibliography.

Sharma, U.K., 1979, Developmental Problems of Assam, *Janata* 34 (7) March 18, p 8.

Tarlok Singh, 1966, The Development of Hill Districts of Assam *Yajana* 10(5) March 20, p 2-5.

Tarlok Singh, 1966, The Problems of Development of Hill Districts of Assam, *Vanyajati* 14(2) January, p 61-70.

Venkateswaran, R.J., 1972 Assam : Slow Economic Progress, *Eastern Economist* 59 (7) August 18, p 409-412, tables.

Economic History

See also Agriculture : History; Assam Company Limited : History; Land : History; Opium : History.

Jones, Stuart, 1974, "A Big Push Without a Take-off : A Case Study of Assam, 1871-1901 : A Comment (on the Article of Amalendu Guha Published in 1968, of September Issue), *Indian Economic and Social History Review* 11 (4) December, p 472-479.

Economic Planning

Anon, 1967, Between Interim and Uncertainty, *Economic and Political Weekly* 2 (42) October 21, p 1895-1896.

Anon, 1976, Assam : Top Priority for Water and Power, *Commerce* 132 (3379) February 28, p 261.

Anon, 1980, Plan Has No Impact on Rural Assam, *Economic Times* January 29, p 5, cols 7-8.
Anon, 1986, (Book Review), *Tribune* (Magazine) November 16, p 11, cols 1-8. Review of the Book : Tarsem Lal, n.,d., *District Development Planning : A Case Study of Two Districts*, Concept Publishing Company, New Delhi, xix, p 276.
Baruah, Srinath, 1978, An Optimizing Planning Mode for Assam, *Assam Economic Journal* 4 (1) March, p 76-82, bibliography.

Economic Planning : Annual Plans

See Annual Plans

Economic Planning : Five Year Plan

See under the full name of the Plan, e.g., Seventh Five Year Plan

Economoic Policy

Anon, 1972, Assam : New Look At Agriculture, *Link* 14 (40) May 14, p 24-25.
Anon, 1973, Towards Removal of Poverty, *Assam Information* 24 (7) October, p 23-28 +.
Anon, 1974, Development of Hill Areas, *Assam Information* 25 (1-3) April-June, p 38-41.
Anon, 1973, Pledges and Performances, *Assam Information* 24 (7) October, p 12-14; 24 (8) November, p 12-16.
Chakravarty, D.N., 1978, New Approach to Development and a New Strategy to Solve problems of Assam, *Assam Information*, 30, October, p 6-8.
Saikia, Hiteswar, 1976, Changes in Socio-Economic Scene, *Link* 18 (48) July 11, p 17-19.
Sarma, A.K., 1976, In 20-point Programme Lies Country's Future *Times of India* November 20, p 13, cols 7-8.

Education

Anon, 1974, Educational Expansion in Assam, *Assam Information* 25 (4-5) July-August, p 16-28.
Anon, 1976, Assam : Report on Education System, *Link* 19 (2) August 22, p 19.
Anon, 1976, Progress of Education in Assam, *Assam Information*, 27, January-March, p 1-4.
Anon, 1978, Progress of Education in Assam, *Assam Information*, 29, January-February, p 1-2.
Anon, 1979, Dearth of Teachers in Rural Areas, *Commerce* (Supplement) 139 (3557) August 18, p 19-20.

Education : Health

See Health Education

Education : Stage : Elementary

See Elementary Education

Education : Stage : Higher

See Higher Education

Education : Stage : Primary

See Primary Education

Elections

Abraham, A.S, 1985, AGP Triumph in Assam, Need to Heal, Not Inflame Wounds, *Times of India* December 21, p 8, col. 3-5.

Acharya, S.B., 1983, Assam Elections : Democracy vis-a-vis Party Politics, *Radical Humanist* 47 (12) March, p 15-18.

Anandan, Sujata, 1983, A Mockery of Democracy? *Illustrated Weekly of India* 104 (9) February 27, p 23.

Anon, 1971, Communalism Plays a Part, *Link* 13 (31) March 14, p 14.

Anon, 1971, Disruptions at Work, *Link* 13 (24) January 26, p 24.

Anon, 1971, The Voters Are Asking, *Link* 13 (28) February 21, p 22-23.

Anon, 1975, Large-Scale Rigging in Barpeta By-Election, *Janata* 30 (7) March 16, p 6-7.

Anon, 1975, The Meaning of Nuh and Barpeta, *Organiser* 28 (31) March 15, p 5.

Anon, 1975, Real Story behind Barpeta Poll Rigging Charge, *New Age* 23 (14) April 6, p 6.

Anon, 1978, Accord Eludes Janata, CPI (M) on Assam Seats, *Times of India* January 28, p 1, cols 1-2+.

Anon, 1978, Assam : Congress Out, *Commerce* 136 (3482) March 4, p 314.

Anon, 1978, Assam : Majority of Single Party Doubtful, *Commerce* 136 (3480) February 18, p 204-205.

Anon, 1978, Assam and Mahalaya Key Result, *Times of India* March 1, p 2, cols 4-5.

Anon, 1978, Assam Assembly Election Results, *Times of India* March 2, p 9, cols 1-3.

Anon, 1978, CPM's Crucial Role in Assam, *Times of India* March 11, p 1, cols 2-4+.

Anon, 1978, Confusion in Assam Villages, *Times of India* February 27, p 13, cols 2-4.

Anon, 1978, Congress Compose different on Elections Eve, *Secular Democracy* 11 (4) February (ii) p 25-26.

Anon, 1978, Election Prospects in Assam, *Link* 20 (23) January 15, p 17-18.

Anon, 1978, Janata-Led Government in Assam Likely, *Times of India* February 18, p 1, cols 6-8+.

Anon, 1978, Janata List for Assam Assembly Poll, *Times of India* January 29, p 5, cols 4-5.

Anon, 1978, Janata Move for Poll Pact with CPI (M) in Assam, *Times of India* January 15, p 1, cols 1-2+.

Anon, 1978, Keen contests in Assam, *Link* 20 (28) February 19, p 12.

Anon, 1978, M.M, Chowdhury Facing Tough Fight in Dis, *Times of India* February 23, p 5, cols 4-7.

Anon, 1978, No Party Gets Majority in Assam, *Times of India* March 2, p 1, col 3+.

Anon, 1978, No Party May Gain Majority in Assam, *Times of India* February 20, p 1, col 1+.

Anon, 1978, Opportunity for Left in Assam, *Link* 20 (27) February 12, p 13.

Anon, 1978, Uncertainties, Horse-Trading in Assam, *Link* 20 (30) March 5, p 15.

Anon, 1979, Anti-Poll Bandh in Assam, *Times of India* December 4, p 1, cols 2-4.

Anon, 1979, Assam : Postponent of Elections? *Commerce* 139 (3572) December 1, p 1066-1067.

Anon, 1979, Assam for Assamese : Drive aginst Foreigners Takes Anti-Muslim and Separatist Turn, *Link* 22 (16) November 25, p 23.

Anon, 1979, Assam Poll Not To Be Postponed, *Times of India* November 7, p 1, cols 4-5.

Anon, 1979, Constituency Where Only 25% May Cast Votes, *Times of India* December 27, p 9, cols 1-2.

Anon, 1979, Cynical Manipulations, *Economic and Political Weekly* 14 (50) December 15, p 2026-2027.

Anon, 1979, Hopes of Election in Assam Recede, *Times of India* December 12, p 1, cols 7-8.

Anon, 1979, Imponderables of Electoral Set Up, *Secular Democracy* November 12, p 26-27.

Anon, 1979, Janata for Postponing Poll in Assam, *Times of India* November 26, p 1, col 1-2.

Anon, 1979, None Will File Papers in Assam : Janata Leader, *Times of India* December 5, p 1, cols 5-6+.

Anon, 1979, Poll for Three Assam Seats as Scheduled, *Times of India* December 20, p 1, cols 1-3.

Anon, 1979, Assam Poll on Schedule : President, *Times of India* December 1, p 1, cols 1-2.

Anon, 1979, S.O.S. Election Commission : Complete Collapse of Assam Poll Machinary, *Times of India* December 19, p 1, cols 2-4.

Anon, 1979, Shakdher for Assam Poll in Four of 14 Constituencies *Times of India* December 11, p 1, cols 2-3.

Anon, 1980, Polling for Two Seats, *Commerce* 140 (3538) January 19, p 17.

Anon, 1983, Election at Bayonet-Point, *Economic and Political Weekly* 18 (5) January 29, p 136-137.

Anon, 1983, In Assam Her Slogan Was not 'Jai Hind' But 'Khuda Hafiz', *Organiser* 34 (41) February 27, p 1+.

Anon, 1984, Assam Election Putoff, *Janata* (Diwali Number) 39 (23) p 5.

Anon, 1985, 75 Per Cent Voting in Assam, *Times of India* December 17, p 1, cols 1-3.

Anon, 1985, AGP Forges Ahead in Assam, *Times of India* December 18, p 1, cols 1-3.

Anon, 1985, AGP Is in Sight of Majority, *Times of India* December 20, p 1, cols 6-8.

Anon, 1985, Poised to Emerge Single Largest Party, *Economic Times* December 19, p 1, cols 5-8+.

Anon, 1985, AGP to Stake its Clain to Form Govt, *Times of India* December 21, p 1, cols 1-3.

Anon, 1985, Accord to Bring Lasting Peace to Assam : PM, *Times of India* December 12, p 1, cols 1-3.

Anon, 1985, Agitators Turns Rulers in Assam, *Times of India* December 22, p 9, cols 1-4.

Anon, 1985, Assam Elections on December 16, *Times of India* November 7, p 1, cols 1-3+.

Anon, 1985, Assam Minorities Safe, Says PM, *Times of India* December 14, p 1 cols 1-3+.

Anon, 1985, Assam Polls and Beyond : Uncertain Prospects, *Link* 28 (18) December 8, p 9-11.

Anon, 1985, A Confusing Picture in Assam, *Times of India* December 15, p 1, cols 2-5.

Anon, 1985, Congress Leaders Bungled in Assam, *Times of India* December 21, p 9, cols 1-4.

Anon, 1985, Cong List of Assam Candidates Announced, *Times of India* November 22, p 1, cols 1-4.

Anon, 1985, Congress Shaky in Barpeta, *Times of India* December 13, p 6, cols 1-3.

Anon, 1985, List of Congress Candidates for Assam, *Times of India* November 22, p 5, cols 2-4.

Anon, 1985, the Majority Factor in Assam Elections, *Link* 28 (16) November 24, p 9-10.

Anon, 1985, Tough Going for Saikia, *Times of India* December 6, p 5, cols 1-3.

Anon, 1985, Which 'Accord' Has Won in Assam? *Link* 28 (21) December 29, p 4-5.

Anon, 1986, AGP Isn't Ethnic Chauvinist like DMK : Barooah Speaks at Last, *Link* 28 (22) January 5, p 4-7.

Anon, 1986, Assam, Campaigning in Assam, *Times of India,* March 2, p 16, cols 2-4.

Anon, 1986, Assam Election, 1985, : Election Manifesto of United Minorities Front, *Muslim India* 4 (38) February, p 60.

Anon, 1986, A Poll Analysis : Assam Shows the Power of Block Hindu Votes, *Organiser* 37 (36) January 19, p 12.

Bhasin, Prem, 1978, Assam and the North-East, *Janata* 33 (5) March 5, p 3.

Bhatta, Suren, 1966, Assam : Partial Accord between Left Parties, *New Age* 14 (52) December 25, p 9+.

Bhatta, Suren, 1971, Assam : Cong (R) Fights Shy, *New Age* 19 (6) February 7, p 6+.

Bhattacharya, M., 1971, Quickest way to Get Rich in Assam, *New Age* 19 (6) February 7, p 4.

Bhattacharya, M., 1971, CPI-PSP Agreement in Assam, *New Age* 19 (5) January 31, p 4+.

Bhattacharya, M., 1971, Assam Confrontation between Congress and Left, *New Age* 19 (8) February 21, p 4+.

Bhattacharya M., 1971, Assam : CPI Poised for Breakthrough, *New Age* 19 (10) March 7, p 12.

Bhattacharya, M,.1977, Assam : Janata Divided, Congress Consolidates, *New Age* 25, p 4.

Bhattacharya, M., 1978, Assam : Congress and Janata Riven with Factionalism, *New Age* 26 (8) February 19, p 4+.

Bhataacharya, M., 1979, Assam : Congress-CPI-CPI (M) Talks on Adjustments Progress, *New Age* 27 (43) October 28, p 9.

Bhattacharya, M., 1979, Assam :. Possibility of Broad Electoral Alliaance, *New Age* 27 (39) September 30, p 8-9+.

Bhattacharyya, Achintya, 1983, Assam on the Eve of the Poll, *People's Democracy* 7 (8) February 20, p 1+.

Bhattacharyya, Birendra Kumar, 1985, Assam : Another Chance, *Indian Express* (Magazine) December 15, p 1, col 1-8+.

Bhuyan, B.C., 1994, Parlimentary Election in Assam, 1977 : *Study Journal of North East Indian Council* 18 (2) October, p 55-64.

Commerce (Periodical), 1983, Assam : Election of Civil War, *Commerce* 146 (3743) February 26, p 329, editorial.

Das, Kamakhya, 1984, Nature and Causes of Violence in 1983, Assam Elections, *Janata* (Diwali Number) 39 (23), p 27-30.

Dasgupta, Keya and Guha, Amalendu, 1985, 1983, Assembly Poll in Assam : An Analysis of its Background and Implications, *Economic and Political Weekly* 20 (19) May11, p 843-853.

Deka, K.M., 1979, The Shaking of the Congress Monopoly in 1977 Lok Sabha Election : The Case of Assam, *Poltical Science Review* 18 (3) July-September, p 54-75, footnotes, tables.

Dharmarajan, S., 1971, Eve-of-Poll survey-IX : Local and Regional Issues to the Fore in Assam, *Times of India* February 25, p 6, cols 2-5.

Dharmarajan, S., 1971, Neglect of Assam is Common Poll Theme in Gauhati, *Times of India* February 12, p 4, cols 5-6.

Dutta, S.K., 1975, Opposition in Assam Alleges By-Election Was Rigged, *Times of India* March 15, p 4, cols 7-8.

Economic and Political Weekly (Periodical), 1971, Fight for Floating Vote, *Economic and Political Weekly* 6 (10) March 6, p 554-555.

Economic Times (Periodical), 1985, Assam Poll, *Economic Times* December 19, p 5, cols 1-2, editorial.

Gogoi, Promode, 1986, Assam Poll Result Vindicate Accord, *New Age* 34 (5) ebruary 2, p 3+.

Guha, Seema, 1985, No Easy-Going for Mahanta, *Times of India* December 11, p 6, cols 3-5.

Guha, Seema, 1985, Phukan Looks a Winner, *Times of India* December 1, 4, p 6, cols 1-3.

Inder Jit, 1983, Assam Poll : Let Truth Be Thrashed Out? *Economic Times* February 22, p 5, cols 7-8.

Inder Jit, 1983, Can Assam Poll Be Postfoned, *Economic Times* February 8, p 5, cols 7-8.

Mainstream (Periodical), 1983, Assam, *Mainstream* 21 (26) February 26, p 1-3, editorial.

Maitra, Sankar N., 1983, A 'Khaki' Election That Make the World 'Democracy' Stink, *Organiser* 34 (43) March 13, p 6+.

Mishra, Prafulla, 1985, Assam all Set for December Election, *New Age* 33 (46) November 17, p 1+.

Misra, Prafulla, 1985, Peaceful Campaigning in Assam Election, *New Age* 33 (50) December 15, p 16.

Misra, Udayen, 1985, Form Mass Movement to Electoral Politics *Economic and Political Weekly* 20 (50) December 14, p 2190-2191.

Murty, T.S., 1983, Post-Election Scene in Gauhati, *Mainstream* 21 (33) April 16, p 11-12.

People's Democracy (Periodical), 1983, the Agony of Assam, *People's Democracy* 7 (9) February 27, p 1-2, editroial.

Prabhakar, M.S., 1975, Death in Barpeta, *Economic and Political Weekly* 10 (10) March 8, p 423-425.

Sen, Kranti, 1971, Congress Faces Stiff Contests, *Mainstream* 9 (26) February 27, p 11-12+.

Sen, Sumanta, 1985, D.K. Barooah Keeping Low Profile, *Times of India* December 14, p 6, cols 2-4.

Sinha, P.N., 1983, Only 10 Per Cent May Cast Their Votes in Assam, *Organiser* 34 (38) February 6, p 5.

Surjeet, Harkishan Singh, 1983, Welcome Decision on Assam Election, *People's Democracy* 7 (3) January 16,p1+.

Times of India (Newspaper), 1979, Collapse of Authority, *Times of India* December 12, p 6, col 1-2, editorial.

Times of India (Newspaper) 1983, After the Carnage, *Times of India* February 22, p 6, cols 1-2, editorial.

Times of India (Newspaper), 1983, Assam : Act Two, *Times of India* March 3, p 8, cols 1-2, editorial.

Times of India (Newspaper). 1983, A Bad Decision, *Times of India* January 18, p 6, cols 1-2, editorial.

Times of India (Newspaper), 1983, Cruel Choice in Assam, *Times of India* February 11, p 6, cols 1-2.

Times of India (Newspaper), 1983, Violence in Assam, *Times of India* February 5, p 8, cols 1-2, editorial.

Times of India (Newspaper, 1983, Worse Than Defeat, *Times of India* February 26, p 8, cols 1-2, editorial.

Times of India (Newspaper), 1985, Assam after Punjab *Times of India* December 20, p 8, cols 1-2, ediitorial.

Times of India (Newspaper), 1985, Contentious Poll, *Times of India* November 8, p 8, cols 1-2, editorial.

Venkata Tao, V., 1977, Lok Sabha Elections in Assam (1952 to 1977) : A Sociological Study, *Indian Journal of Political Science* 38 (4) October-December 462-475.

Election : States

Anon, 1977, 15,000 Deprived of Votes in Gauhati, *Times of India* March 21, p 4, cols 1-2.

Anon, 1977, Assam : CPI Keeps Option Open, *Link* 19 (28) February 20, p 20-21.

Anon, 1977, Assam : Tide against Congress, *Link* 19 (31) March 13, p 16-17.

Anon, 1977, Bid to Avoid Triangular Fight : Accord among Assam Opposition Parties, *Times of India* February 17, p 1, cols 3-4.

Anon, 1977, Congress Contesting All 14 Assam Seats, *Times of India* March 2, p 11, cols 1-2.
Anon, 1977, Election Scene XVI : Only Few Hard for Cong in Assam, N.E., Region, *Times of India* March 9, p 1, cols 2-4+.
Anon, 1977, Erosion of Congress Influence, *Commercee* 134 (3434) March 26, p 447-448.
Anon, 1977, The Exception of Assam, *Link* 19 (33) March 27, p 17.
Anon, 1977, Last Round of Polling in Assam Today, *Times of India* March 19, p 7, col 4-5.
Anon, 1971, No Challenge in Assam to Congress (R), *Times of India* January 4, p 1, col 4-5.
Anon, 1977, No Left Turn, *Economic and Political Weekly* 12 (27) July 2, p 1043.
Anon, 1977, No Walk-over, *Economic and Political Weekly* (Annual Number) 12 (6-8) February, p 181-182.
Anon, 1977, Paid Worker Main Force of congress, *Link* 19 (32) March 20, p 19-20.

Electric Power

Anon, 1976, Rising shortage in N.E., Region, *Link* 18 (45) June 20, p 28-31.
Anon, 1978, New Power Projects Assam, *Assam Information* 30, August, p 10-12.
Anon, 1979, Power Shortages in Assam, *Commerce* 138 (3528) January 27, p 79-81.
Boar, Lakshmi Nandan, 1980, Assam's Power Potential, *Economic Times* October 30, p 5, col 7-8, tables.
Chakravorty, Nitya, 1985, No Respite for Assam, *Economic Times* May 13, p 1, cols 5-8+.
Dutta, Pulakesh, 1984, Prospects of Power Development in Assam, *National Geographer* 19 (2) December, p 163-171, bibliography, tables.
Dutta S.K., 1978, Assam Earmarks 40 Per Cent of Plan Outlay for Villages, *Times of India* August 29, p 6, cols 7-8.
Mahanta, Trishna, 1981, Thirty Years of Planning in Assam, *Yojana* 24 (24) January 1, p 23-25.
Neog, Jitendra Nath, 1978, Power Generation and Rural Electrification in Assam, *Assam Information* 30, December, p 29-31.
Osmani, A.F., Golam, 1978, And Miles to Go, *Assam Information*, 30 October, p 9-14.
Osmani, A.F., Golam, 1979, And Miles to go, *Indian Worker* 27 (16-17) January 29, p 13-15.
Osmani, A.F., Golam, 1979, Top Priority to Power Production, *Times of India* March 20, p 10, cols 1-4+.
Phukan, B., 1977 Assam : Critical Power Situation, *Commerce* (Annual Number) 135 (3475) p 141-142, tables.

Elementary Education

Barthakur, S.C., 1986, Elementary Education in Assam, *Educational Review* 92 (8) August, p 126-27.

Employment and Unemployment

Anon, 1974, Immigrants Accentuate Unemployment, *Commerce* 128 (3278) March 9, p 288.

Anon, 1975, Employment Position in Assam, *Indian Worker* 23 (20) February 24, p 8.

Anon, 1981, Big Employment Scope in Assam Forests, *Economic Times* May 12, p 3, cols 3-5.

Bordolon, U.N., 1969, Unemployment in Assam, *Journal of the University of Gauhati* 20(1), p 92-101.

Bordolon, U.N., 1969, Unemployment in Incidence in Assam, *New Age* 35 (25) June 21, p 5.

Dutta, Poresh Chandra, 1974, Patten of Farm Employment in Assam : Case Study, *Yojana* 18 (19) November 1, p 19-20.

Endowments : History

Barpujari, H.K., 1964, The Management and Control of the Religious Endowments in Assam (1825-58), *Journal of the University of Gauhati* p 35-44, bibliography, footnotes.

Engineering Industry and Trade

Anon, 1980, Engineering Industry in Assam, *Eastern Economist* 74 (16) April 18, p 799.

Ethnology

Bhandari, J.S., 1984, Ethnohistory, Ethnic Identity and Contemporary Mishing Society, *Indian Anthropologist* 14 (2) December, p 79-103, bibliography.

Sengupta, Sarthak, 1984, Studies of the whole on Head Hair in Two Mongoloid Population of Assam , *Vanyajati* 32 (4) October, p 20-22.

Terwiel, B.J., 1981, The Tai of Assam : Sacrifices and Time Reckoning, *South East Asian Review* 6 (1-2) January-December, p 1-191, bibliography, footnote.

Excavations

Anon, 19744-75 Exolorations and Excavations ; Assam, *Indian Arcaeology* p 7.

Choudhury, Nishipada, 1968, Righ Wells : New Theory, *Journal of the Assam Research Society*, 18, p 59-63.

Choudhury, Ribindranath Dev and Chutia, Dharmeswar, 1968, A Note on the Archaeological finds at the Norakasur Hill, Journal of the *Assam Research Society*, 18, p 23-34, bibliography, footnotes.

Excise

Bhuyan, P.K., 1978, Assam's Share of Union Excise, *Assam Information* 29, April-May, p 32-35.

Expenditures : Public

See also Budget

Anon, 1978, 57% of Central Spending on Development, *Economic Times* July 7, p 1, cols 2-7+.

Anon, 1978, (Book Review), *Economic Times* September 17, p 7, cols 2-4.
Review of the Book : Ahuja, S.P., 1978, *Distibution of Benefits from Government Expenditure : A Case Study in Selected Districts*, IEMR, vii, 164 p.

Anon, 1978, Promoting Savings and curbing Wasteful Expenditure, *Eastern Economist (Budget Number)* 70 (11) March 17, p 511-521, tables.

Anon, 1978, Rapid Rise in Non-Development Expenditure, *Eastern Economist* (Budget Number) 70(11) March 17, p 499-510, tables.

Economic Times (Newspaper), 1978, Expenditures Pattern, *Economic Times* March 3, p 5, col 1-2, editorial.

Khanna, Kailash, 1978, Need to Rationalise Capital and Revenue Express, *Economic Times* January 31, p 5, cols 3-8.

Masood, Hasan, 1978, Need to Review Public Spending, *Economic Times* February 13, p 7, cols 3-8+. tables.

Sarma, M.C., and Mehrotra, R., 1977, The Growth of Public Expenditures and Level of Economic Activity in Assam, *Assam Economic Journal* 3 (1) March, p 126-134,, bibliography.

Shanmugasundaram, V., 1978, Need for Public Expenditure Commission, *Commerce* (Supplement) 136 (3484) March 18, p 49-53.

Times of India (Newspaper), 1978, Whose Benefit, *Times of India* February 8, p 6, cols 1-2, editorial.

Fairs

Sarma, Dimbeswar, 1968, Religious Fairs and Festivals of Assam, *Assam Research Society Journal*, 18, p 22-45, bibliography, footnotes.

Family

Sen, Lalit Kumar, 1965, Family in Four Indian Villages, *Man in India* 45 (1) January-March, p 1-16, bibliography, tables.

Family Welfare

Anon, 1976, Breakthrough in Family Planning, *Yojana* 29 (9) June 1, p 35.

Bora, Koseswar, 1979, Population Explosion ; New Emphasis on Family Welfare Programme, *Assam Information*, 30, January, p 27-28.

Dass, B.M., and Deka, Ranjan, 1982, Cultural Factors in Fertility Regulation, *Indian Anthropologist* 12 (2) December 181-185, tables.

Sadashivaiah, K., 1979, Trend in Age at Marriage, Family Size and Level of Education amongSterilised Cohont in Assam and Kerala *Journal of Family Welfare* 35 (3) March, p 46-56, tables.

Famines

Anon, 1974, Destitute Swarms Pour Into Assam Towns. *Times of India* October 15, p 4-5.

Baishya, Prabir, 1975, Man-Made Famine, *Economic and Political Weekly* 10 (21) May 24, p 821-822.

Bhattacharyya, M., 1965, Assam : Starvation Deaths in Khasi Hills, *New Age* 13 (31) August 1, p 2?

Bhattacharya, M., 1974, Famine Follows Flood in Assam, *New Age* 22 (37) September 15, p 8.

Rangasami, Amrita, 1975, The Paupers of Kholisabhita Hindu-Para : Report on a Famine, *Economic and Political Weekly* (Annual Number) 10 (5-7) February, p 267-282.

Farm Income

Kalita, D.R., An Economic Analysis of Instability in Farm Income on Unirrigated Medium Farms in Gobardhan Block of Assam, *Economic Affairs* 27 (7-9) July-September, p 485-490, tables.

Farmers

Borgohain, Drupad, 1988, Assam Kisan-Khetmazdoor Movement Forges Ahead, *New Age* 36 (33) August 14, p 8-9.

Dutta, P.C., and Gogoi, K., 1973, Achievements of SFDA/MFAL in Assam, *Kurukshetra* 22 (3) November 1, p 8.

Federal and State Relations

Anon, 1987, (Book Review), *Journal of North-East India Council* 11 (1) April, p 45-47.
Review of the Book : Phukon, Girin 1984, *Assam's Attitude to Federalism* Sterling, New Delhi, 27, 171 p.

Fertilizer Industry and Trade

Choudhury, M.C., 1979, Fertilizer Industry : Its Role in Promoting Fertilizer Use in Assam, *Assam Information*, 30, January p 21-22.

Kalia, B.S., 1979, A Decade of Services ; Namrup Fertilizer, *Assam Information*, 30, January, p 16-20.

Kalia, B.S., 1974, Glimpses of Namrup Expansion Project, *Assam Information* 25 (1-3) April-June, p 21-28.

Festivals

Goswami, Praphulladatta, 1987, the Spring-Time Festival of Assam ; Bohag Bihu, *Pratibha India* 6 (3) April-June, p 3-8.

Goswami, S.N., 1971, Bhatheli : A spring Time Festival of Lower Assam, *Folklore* 12 (2) February, p 57-61, bibliography, footnotes.

Saikia J.P., 1980, Bihu : Assam's spring Festivals, *Illustrated Weekly of India* 101 (22) June 1, p 18.

Sarma, Dimbeswar, 1968, Religious Fair and Festivals of Assam, *Assam Research Society Journal*, 18, p 22-45, bibliography, footnotes.

Field Crops

Anon, 1975, Crop Dilemma in Assam, *Link* 18 (11) October 26, p 16-17.

Anon, 1978, Kharif Prospects-IV : Timely Rain Brightens Hopes in Assam, *Times of India* July 24, p 1, cols 2-4.

Anon, 1980, Rabi Prospects-XIII : Aliens Issue Will Hit Assam's Harvest, *Times of India* March 4, p 1, cols 2-5.

Anon, 1981, Normal Paddy Crop Likely in Assam, *Times of India* July 24, p 5, cols 3-5.

Das, M.M., 1984, Crop Combination Regions of Assam ; A Quantitative Analysis, *National Geographical Journal of India* 30 (3) September p 165-72, figures, tables.

Mazumdar, N.R., and Laskar, S.U., 1978, The Yield Pattern of Agricultural Crops of Assam, 1972-73 : An application of the Principal Component Analysis Technique, *Assam Economic Journal* 3 (1) March, p 42-47, bibliography, tables.

Sarma Girish Chandra, 1975, New thinking Cropping Pattern in Assam, *Assam Information* 35 (10-12) January-March, p 32-36.

Film Industry

Hussain, Anower, 1978, Film Industry in Assam, *Assam Information.* 30, October, p 25-27.

Talukdar, Phani, 1980, Film Making in Assam, *Illustrated Weekly of India* 101 (22) June 1, p 26-27.

Finance

See also Public Finance

Fisheries

Anon, 1979, Fish Prices Soar, *Commerce* 132 (3386) April 17, p 542-543.

Fifth Five Year Plan

Anon, 1973, Rs 1,983 Crore Fifth Plan for Assam, *Commerce* 127 (3244) July 7, p 13-15.

Anon, 1975, Minor Irrigation in Fifth Plan, *Assam Information* 27 (5-6) August-September, p 11-12.

Chakravarty, D.N., 1973, Assam's Fifth Plan Proposals, *Yojana* 17 (16) September 15, p 680.

Flood Control

Hanse, Sri Samsing, 1988, Measures to Control Floods, Erosion, *Economic Times* (Supplement) October 7, p 4, cols 1-5.

Kouli, Ramesh Mohan, 1978, Assam's Grim Battle against Flood, *Assam Information* 30, August, p 39-45.

Floods

Anon, 1974, Controlling the Fury of Brahmaputra, *Commerce* 129 (3307) February 28, p 538.

Anon, 1976, Assam Flood Situation Still Grave, *Times of India* June 13, p 1 cols 7-8+.

Anon, 1976, Flood Situation in Assam Still Difficult, *Times of India* July 15, p 1, cols 7-8+.

Anon, 1976, Revages of Floods, *Commerce* 133 (3397) July 3, p 11.

Anon, 1976, Power Relations in Action, *Economic and Political Weekly* 11 (38) September 18, p 1517-1518.

Anon, 1976, More Areas Flooded in Cachar, *Times of India*, July 19, p 1, cols 2-3+.

Anon, 1976, Serious Flood Threat to Cachar, *Times of India* July 12, p 1, cols 7-8+.

Anon, 1978, The Problem of Floods in Assam, *Assam Information* 30, June-July, p 4-5.

Anon, 1979, Agony of Floods, *Seccular Democracy,* 12 November p 27-28.

Anon, 1979, Army Moves Flood-Hit in assam, *Indian Express* July 4, p 1, cols 4-5+.

Anon, 1980, Assam Agitationists Oppose Flood Relief, *New Age* 28 (42) October 19, p 9.

Anon, 1981, 100 Assam Villages under Water, *Times of India* July 3, p 1, cols 4-6.

Anon, 1981, Army Called Out to Combat Assam Floods, *Times of India* July 3, p 1, cols 4-6.

Anon, 1981, Assam Flood Fury Unabated, *Times of India* July 9, p 1, cols 2-4.

Anon, 1983, Rs 1 Crore Loss in First Spell, *Economic Times* July 31, p 4, cols 1-2+.

Bhatia, Suren, 1974, Flood-Hit Assam Needs Urgent Massive Relief *New Age* 22 (34) August 25, p 7.

Bhattacharya, M., 1977, Flood Havoc in Assam : No Relief, *New Age* 25 (37) September 11, p 10.

Bhattacharya, M., 1979, Assam Hit by Floods after Drought, *New Age* 27 (29) July 22, p 6.

Bhattacharya. M., 1979, Second Round of Flood Cripples Assam, *New Age* 27 (43) October 28, p 12.

Bhattacharya, M., 1980, Floods Hit Assam and Meghalaya, *New Age* 28 (37) September 14, p 14.

Bora, Phani, 1974, Flood Ravaged Assam Cries for Relief, *New Age* 22 (38) September 22, p 11.

Bordolai, Kirti, 1965, Floods Hit 50,000 People in Jorhat and Near Areas, *New Age* 13 (30) July 25, p 4.

Borgohani, Drupad, 1988, Brahmaputra Tears of Assam, *New Age* 36 (30) July 24, p 8.

Chakravorty, Nitya, 1983, The 'River of Sorrow' and the Agony of Assam, *Economic Times* July 31, p 4, cols 1-8+.

Das, H.N., 1971, Agency for Relief Operations : A Case Study, *Management in Government* 3 (2) July-September, p 129-133.

Dutta, Poresh Chandra, 1973, Floods in Assam : the Menace and Protection Measures, *Yojana* 17 (16) September 15, p 665-666.

Dutta, Poresh Chandra, 1973, The Problem of Floods in Assam : A Review, *Kurukshetra* 22 (2) October 16, 6-7.

Dutta, S.K., 1976, Silting of Assam River Beds : Yearly Flood Havoc,. *Times of India* June 28, p 6, cols 7-8.

Mazarbhuiyam Nazrul HQ, 1976, the Agony of Cachar, *Economic and Political Weekly* 11 (34) August 21, p 1397-1398.

Pardesh, Ghanshyam, 1987, Assam's Flood Problem : An analysis, *Mainstream* 25 (47) August 8, p 27-29.

A Folk Dancing, Folk Music, etc.

See Assamese Folk Dancing; Assamese Folk Music etc.

Food Supply

Anon, 1966, Grave Food Situation in Assam : Hungry Parents Sell Children, *Organiser* 20 (13) November 6, p 10.

Anon, 1973, Assam : Trading Cliques, *Link* 16 (7) September 23, p 22-23.
Anon, 1975, Procurement Lags behind Target, *Commerce* 130 (3325) February 8, p 138.
Anon, 1979, Assam's SOS For Food, *Commerce* 139 (3569) November 10, p 909-1010.
Bhattacharya, M., 1964, Assam Faces a Food Crisis, *New Age* 12 (26) June 28, p 10-11.
Bhattacharya, M., 1964, Food Situation in Assam, *New Age* 12 (28) July 12, p 4.
Bhattacharya, M., 1964, Hesitancy to Curb Unscrupulous Traders, *New Age* 12 (29) July 19, p 4.
Bhattacharya, M., 1966, Paddy Procurement Only on Paper in Assam, *New Age* 14 (10) March 6, p 2.
Bhattacharya, Madhusudan, 1966, Food is Scarce in Assam but Not Bullets, *New Age* 14 (34) August 21, p 3+.
Bhattacharyya, Madhusudan, 1964, Food Situation in Assam Serious, *New Age* 12 (21) April 24, p 7.
Bhattacharyya, Mudhusudan, 1964, Govt. Food Policy Helps Millowners, *New Age* 12 (23) May 31, p 7.
Bora, Phani, 1966, Assam is under Policy Raj : People's Struggle for Food, against Repression Still on, *New Age* 14 (53) August 28, p 10.
Khorshed Alam, 1975-76, Food Production and Internal Requirements under the Successives Plans in Assam, *Journal of the University of Gauhati (Arts)* 26-27 (1) 247-253, footnotes, tables.
Sen, Mohit, 1964, While Prices Shoot Up Food Grains Are Scarcer, *New Age* 12 (16) April 19, p 13.
Talukdar, K.C., and Goswami, P.C., 1978, Food Accounts for Assam : A Critical Appraisal, *Assam Economic Journal* 4 (1) March, p 1-14, bibliography.
Trivedi, P.P., 1976, Procurement and Distribution of Essential Commodities, *Times of India* November 20, p 13, cols 1-3.

Forest Fauna

Gogo, P.C., 1981, Flora and Fauna of Assam, *Assam Information* 32 January-March, p 51-57.

Forests and Forestry

Anon, 1974, Assam's Forest Potential : Gold Earner Awaits Proper Harnessing, *Assam Information* 25 (1-3) April-June, p 34-37.
Anon, 1981, Big Employment Scope in Assam Forests, *Economic Times* May 12, p 3, cols 3-5.
Phukan, Bhupen, 1978, the Importance of Forestry, *North-East Spectrum* 3 (1-3) July-September, p 25-27.
Sarma, Parameswar, 1975, Forests in Assam's Economy, *Commerce* 131 (3357) September 20, p 11-15.

Fourth Five Year Plan

Anon, 1973, Study of Plan Achievements and Programme for 1973-74, *Assam Information* 24 (7) October 29-36; 24 (8) November, p 23-25; 24 (9) December, p 19-25.

Funeral Rites and Ceremonies

Ghosh, Dipali, 1964, Post-funeral Ritual in a Dimasa Kachari Village, *Man in India* 44 (3) July-September, p 247-251.

Garos

Das, Bhuban M., 1960, Somatic Variations among the Hill and Plains Garo of Assam. *Man in India* April-June, p 128-148, tables.

Gosami., M.C, and Mazumdar, 1967, Clan Organisation among the Garo of Assam, *Man in India* 47 (4) October-December, p 249-262, references.

Mukherjee, Bhabananda, 1955-56, Machong among the Garo of Assam, *Eastern Anthropologist* 9 (2) December '55-February '56, p 112-116, references.

Pakrasi, Kanti and Das, Bhuban M., 1956, An Anthropometric Study of the Plans Mandes (Garos) of Assam, *Man in India* 36 (2) April-June, p 100-109, references, tables.

Goan-Panchayat Samabay Samiti

Sah, A.K., 1979, Working of Goan-Panchayat Samabay Samiti in Assam, *Indian Cooperative Review* 16 (3) April, p 297-305, tables.

Grant-in-Aid : Central Government

Eastern Economist (Periodical), 1974, Central Assistance to Assam, *Eastern Economist* 62 (20) May 17, p 975.

Hand Weaving

Borthakur, S.K., 1976, Traditional Weaving Implements among the Mikins (The Karbis) of Assam, *Indian Measuem Bulletin* 11 (2) July, p 46-50.

Handicrafts

Bhuayan, Jadav, 1979, Handicrafts of Assam, *Times of India* December 7, p 8, cols 1-3+.

Choudhuri, Alak R., 1980, short Note on Mirijim Tribal Craft of Deshangmukh, Sibsgar Distric, Assam, *Bulletin of the Cultural Research Institute* 14 (3-4), p 5.

Handloom Industry and Trade

Dutta, S.K., 1975, Assam Plans to Rejuvenate Handloom Industry, *Times of India* August 18, p 4, cols 7-8.

Health Education

Sharma, M.K., 1983, A Plan for Health Educational Pyramid in Assam, *EPA Bull* 6 (2) July, p 13-21, bibliography, tables.

High Court : Decisions

Mahmood, Tahir, 1982, An Unreported Judgement on the Islamic Law of Divorce, *Islamic & Comparative Law Quarterly* 2 (1) March, p 38-57, footnotes.

Higher Education

Sutradhar, Samir Kumar, 1980, Higher Education in Assam 1866-1979, *Educational Review* 89 (9) September, p 165-171, bibliography.

Hill Areas

Anon, 1967, Assam Hill Areas, *Link* 9 (51) July 30, p 8-9.

History

See also; Cachar (Silchar) : History, Endowments : History, Local Government : History

Anon, 1969, (Book Reviews), *Journal of Indian History* 47 (3) December, p 591-592.

Review of the Book : Puri, B.N., 1968, *Studies in Early History and Administration in Assam*, Gauhati University, ii, 84 p.

Anon, 1970-71, (Book Review), *Quarterly Review of Historical Studies* 10 (4), p 238-240.

Review of the Book : Lakshmi Devi, 1968, *Ahom-Tribal Relations : A Political Study* Assam Book, ixi, 275 p.

Anon, 1978, (Book Review), *Times of India* (Magazine) July 23, p 10, cols 6-8. Review of the Book : Saikia, J.P., ed. *The Land of Seven Sisters*, Director of Information and Public Relation Government of Assam.

Anon, 1978-79, (Book Review), *Quarterly Review of Historical Studies* 18 (1), p 60- 61.

Review of the Book : Barpujari, H.K., 1977, *Political History of Assam*, Government of Assam, vol xvii, 293 p.

Anon, 1982, Assam : Her Past and Present, *Assam Information*, 34, June-July, p 1-6.

Anon, 1986, (Book Review), *Mysore Economic Review* 71 (2) February, p 23. Review of the Book : Bose, M.L., n.d., *Development of Administration in Assam*, Concept Publishing Company, New Delhi.

Baruah, S.L, 1978, Sadar Minar Atmajivani, *Bengal Past and Present* 97 (1) January-June, p 79-85.

Chatterji, Sunit Kumar, '1986, The Name Assam Ahom, *Journal of Asiatic Society* (Bengal) 28 (3), p 47-56.

Das, Samir Kumar, 1994, Assam Movement, 1979-1985 : A Historiographical Essay, *Journal of North-East India Council* 18 (2) October, p 1-11, bibliography, footnotes.

Gogoi, P., 1974, Tai-Ahom Religion and Customs, *Journal of the Assam Research Society*, 22, p 12-24, appendix.

Goswami, Praphulladatta, 1968, the Dakshinpat Satna, *Journal of the Assam Research Society* 18, p 64-67.

Sankalia, H.D., 1970, From History to Pre-History in Assam, *Assam Information* 20 (11) February, p 27-29.

History : Ancient

See also Inscriptions

Anon, 1970, (Book Review), *Journal of Indian History* 48 (1)April, p 201-202. Review of the Book : Gogoi, P, 1968, *The Tai and the Tai Kingdoms (with a Fuller Treatment of the Tai-Ahom Kingdom in the Brahmaputra Valley)*, Gauhati University, 552 p.

Baruah, U.L., 1968, Gaurana Kunwair and General Turnbak, *Journal of the Research Society*, 18, p 8-13.

Chutia, Dharmeswar, 1981-82, Kuruvabahi (Wagaon) Copper Plate Grant of Harjjar (Verma) Deva, *Journal of the Assam Research Society* 26, p 1-11, footnotes.

Choudhury, P.C., 1976, Historical Material in the Gachtal Grant of Gopaladeva, *Vishveshvaranand Indological Journal* 14 (2) September, p 261-273, footnotes.

Das, Sunil Kumar, 1978, A New Light on the Political History of Kamarupa in the Early Thirteen Century, *Journal of the Indian History* 56 (2) August, p 303-311, footnotes.

Trivedi, Krishna Kant, 1973, Early History and Ancient Sites of Saran District in the Light of Archaeological Finds, *Prajna* 18 (2) March, p 161-168.

History : Medieval

See also Ahoms

Anon, 1970-71, (Book Review), *Quarterly Review of Historical Studies* 10 (2), p 111-114.
Review of the Book : Acharyya, N.N., 1966, *The History of Medieval Assam* (1228-1603 A.D.), Barua, Dutta and Co.

Das, Sunil Kumar, 1973, A Note on Hussain Shah's Assam Expedition, *Journal of Indian History* 51 (20) August, p 337-343, bibliography, footnotes.

Dasgupta, R., 1968, Coins of Mediaeval Assam, *Journal of the Assam Research Society*, 18, p 49-58, bibliography, footnotes, tables.

Guha, Amalendu, 1966, Land Rights and Social Classes in Medieval Assam, *Indian Economic and Social History Review* 3 (3) September p 217-239, bibliography, tables.

Guha, Amalendu, 1983, The Ahom Political System : An Enquiry into the State formation Process in Medieval Assam, 1228-1714, *Social Scientist* 11 (12) December, p 3-34, footnotes.

Guha, Amalendu, 1984, the Pre-Ahom Roots of Medieval Assam : A Reply, *Social Scientist* 12 (6) June, p 70-77, footnote.

Lahiri, nayanjot, 1984, the Pre-Ahom Roots of Medieval Assam; *Social Scientist* 12 (6) June, p 60-69, footnotes.

History : Modern

Anon, 1977, (Book Review), *Journal of Indian History* 55 (1-2) April-August, p 380-381.
Review of the Book : Barpujari, H.K., ed, 1977, *Political History of Assam* 1826-1919, Government of Assam, Vol 1, xvii, 293 p.

Anon, 1978, (Book Review), *Economic and Political Weekly* 13 (13) April 1, p 579-580; *Times of India* (Magazine) March 26, p 12, cols 6-8.
Review of the Book : Guha, Amalendu, 1977, *Planter Raj to Swaraj : Freedom Struggle and Electoral Politics in Assam* 1826-1947, I.C.H.R., New Delhi, xvi, 392 p.

Anon, 1980, (Book Review), *Bengal Past and Present* 99 (1) January-June, p 88-91.
Review of the Book : Guha, Amalendu, 1977, *Planter Raj to Swaraj: Freedom Struggle and Electoral Politics in Assam* 1826-1947, I.C.H.R., New Delhi, 392 p

Anon, 1983, (Book Review), *Tribune* February 19, p 4, cols 5-7. Review of the Book : Venkata Rao, V. and Hazarika, Niru, n.d., *A Century of Government and Politics in North East India*, S. Chand, New Delhi, 28 p.

Barpujari, H.K., 1977, *Political History of Assam* 1826-1919, Government of Assam vol 1, xvii, 293 p.

Bose, M.L., 1977-78, formation of the Chief Commissionership of Assam under the British, 1874, *Journal of Assam Research Society*, 23, p 49-56, footnotes.

Chatterjee, S., 1969-70, The Cause of Lushal Rising 1891-92; An Unknown Episode of Our North East Frontier Review of *Historical Studies* 9 (4), p 215-218, bibliography, footnotes.

De, Amalendu, 1977, The Muslims as a Factor in Assam Politics, 1826-1947, *Bengal Past and Present* 96 (2) July-December, p 114-120, footnotes.

Goswami, Surendra Kumar, 1981-82, Freedom Struggles in the Early Part of the Nineteenth Century in Assam, 1826-1830, *Journal of the Assam Research Society*, 26, p 63-67.

Guha, Amalendu, 1976, East Bengal Immigrants and Maulana Abdul Hamid Khan Bhasani in Assam Politics 1928-47, *Indian Economic and Social History Review* 13 (4) October-December, p 419-453, appendix, footnotes

Talukdar, Nanda, 1979-80, ananda Ram Dhekial Phookan as an Administrator in the Early British Period in Assam, *Journal of the Assam Research Society* 25, p 22-25, footnotes.

History : Sources

Sircar, Kalyan K., 1986, A Note on the Cambridge Archival Material Relating to Assam, *Indian Archives* 35 (1) January-June, p 13-26.

Home Guards

Dey, L.B.K., 1975, Home Guards and Civil Defence Organisation in Assam, *Assam Information* December, p 42-45.

Milli, B., 1980, Assam Home Guard and Border, *Assam Information* 32 December, p 15-18.

Housing

Changkakoti, P.K., 1976, New look at Housing, *Yojana* 20 (22) December 15, p 27-28+.

Das, K.P., 1978, Housing Schemes for the Poor in Assam, *Yojana* 22 (14-15) August 15, p 43-44.

Housing : Rural

Das Gupta, Barun, 1977, Assam Sites But No Homes, *Link* 19(25) January 26, p 31.

Human Population Gentics

Buzarbaruah, P.M., and Phookan, M.N., 1986, Birth Order, Mother's Age and Reproductives Wastages among the Mishing of Disangmukh of Sibsagar, Assam, *Indian Journal of Psysical Anthropology and Human Genetics* 12 (1) January-April, p 43-50, bibliography, tables.

Illumination of Book and Manuscripts

Barkaoti, Kakoli, 1983, A Spurt of Revival than Obscurity : Assam's Vaishnavite Illustrated Manuscripts, *Indian Magazine* 3 (9) August, p 20-33.

Indian National Congress : Assam Unit

Anon, 1972, Assam ; Youth Congress Radicals Come Up, *Link* 14 (23) January 16, p 22-23.

Anon, 1972, Assam Congress Strains, *Link* 14 (52) August 6, p 21-22.

Anon, 1972, Eight Former Minister Dropped in Assam, *Times of India* February 5, p 1, col 8+.

Bhattacharya, M., 1972, Dissidents Gain in Assam Congress Reshuffle, *New Age* 20 (4) January 23, p 13.

Times of India (Newspaper), 1972, A New Look, *Times of India* February 1, p 4, col 1, editorial.

Indian National Congress (I) : Assam Unit

Anon, 1977, Indira Gandhi's Non-Visit, *Link* 20 (17) December 4, p 13.

Anon, 1979, Indira Faction Strong, *Link* 21 (46) June 24, p 12.

Chopra, Sunit, 1978, Assam Indira Congress Fans Chauvinism, *People's Democracy* 2 (46) November 12, p 11.

Misra, Prafulla, 1986, Factional Squabble in Assam Congress (I), *New Age* 34 (34) August 24, p 6.

Indian National Congress (New) : Assam Unit

Anon, 1978, Assam : Backlash of Bossim, *Link* 20 (24) January 22, p 8.

Anon, 1977, Assam Congress Heading for Vertical Split, *Times of India* October 26, p 7, cols 1-2.

Anon, 1974, Assam Congress Infights, *Link* 16 (43) June 2, p 20-21.

Anon, 1977, Assam Leadership : A Mindless Entity, *Link* 19 (35) April 10, p 12.

Anon, 1971, Congress Contesting All 14 Assam Sests, *Times of India* March 2, p 11, cols 1-2.

Anon, 1977, Dilemma for Assam Congress, *Link* 20 (12) October 30, p 18.

Anon, 1977, More Quit Congress in Assam, *Times of India* March 15, p 7, col 1.

Anon, 1978, No End to Congress Confusion, *Link* 21 (20) December 24, p 30.

Industrial Development

Bhattacharyya, Bhupendra Kr. 1966 Industrial Development of Assam, *AICC Economic Review* 18 (6) October 1, p 24-25.

Industrial Estates

Anon, 1985, Assam Industrial Estates in a Mess, *Economic Times* September 20, p 5, cols 7-8.

Anon, 1985, Industrial Estates : Guwahati Lacks Infrastucture, *Economic Times* July 18, p 1, cols 3-6+.

Industry and State

Anon, 1971, Central-State Row, *Link* 13 (50) July 25, p 15-16.

Anon, 1978, Assam Industrial Policy : More Incentives Offered *Economic Times* July 30, p 1, cols 3-5+.

Anon, 1987, Assam Stress on Big Industries, *Economic Times* December 30, p 1, cols 5-8+.

Anon, 1987, Guidelines for New Industrial Policy, *Economic Times* (Supplement) January 20, p 11, cols 1-8.

Sarma, Anil Kumar, 1964, Role of State Entreprenenrship in Assam, *Journal of the University of Gauhati* 15 (1), p 45-56.

Industry and Trade

See also Cement Industry and Trade; Chemical Industry and Trade; Cottages Industries; Engineering Industry and Trade; Fertilizer Industry and Trade; Handloom Industry and State; Industrial Estates; Industry and State; Jute Industry and Trade; Metal Industry and Trade; Paper Industry and Trade; Petroleum Industry and Trade Plywood Industry and Trade; Rural Industries; Silk Manufacture and Trade; Small Scale Industries; Steel Industry and Trade; Sugar Industry and Trade; Tea Industry and Trade.

Anon, 1975, Assam's Industrial Development and Industrial Development Corporation, *Assam Information* 27 (1-2) April-May, p 1-5.

Anon, 1975, The Mirage of Industrialisation, *Commerce*130 (3340) May 24, p 788.

Anon, 1976, Untapped Resources, *Link* 18 (33) March 28, p 39-43.

Anon, 1977, Industries of Assam : Past, Present and future, *Journal of Industry and Trade* 27 (2) February p 12-16.

Anon, 1978, Assam : Lack of Infrastructure, *Commerce* 137 (3503) July 29, p 199.

Anon, 1979, Industrialization Plan for NE Region, *Capital* 182 (4565) July 9, p 5.

Anon, 1981, Industrial Development in Assam : A Story of Neglect, *Capital* 186 (4646) March 2, p 7.

Anon, 1982, Guidelines Framed to Streanline Industrial Strategy, *Economic Times* August 25, p 3, cols 4-6.

Anon, 1983, Industries in Assam; *Assam Information*, 34, January-March, p 4-6.

Barthakur, M., 1972, A Strategy of Industrial and Regional Development of Assam, *Deccan Geographer* 10 (1) January-June, p 59-64, tables

Barus, D.U., 1973, Development of Industries, *Assam Information* 24 (9) December, p 5-8.

Baruah B., 1977, Investment, Employment and Output Relations and Inter-District Variation in Industrial Growth of Assam, 1962-1969, *Assam Economic Journal* 3 (1) March, p 135-145.

Baruah, R.D., 1987, Return to Scale and Elasticity of Substitution of Few Manufacturing Industries of Assam : A Note, *Anvesak* 17 (2) December, p 115-26.

Bezbaruah, K.N., 1982, Industrial Potentiality in Assam Hills Areas, *Yojana* 26 (11) June 16, p 20-21.

Bhatnagar, Y., 1965, Problems of Industrialisation of Assam, *AICC Economic Review* 16 (20) March 25, p 15-18, tables.

Choudhuri, Rabijit, 1986, Assam : Incraesing Joblessness due to Closed Units, *Commerce* 153 (3926) August 16, p 307+.

Gugoi, Hara, 1976 Industrial Potentialities of Goalpara District, *Assam Information* January-March, p 15-18.

Goswami, Atul, 1981, Assam's Industrial Development : Urgency of New Directions, *Economic and Political Weekly* 16 (21) May 23, p 953-956, bibliography.

Hazarika, Jatin, 1983, Industry : A New Surge, *Times of India* September 12, p 13, cols 1-5.

Kalia, B.S., 1976, Namrup Expansion Project, *Assam Information* January-March, p 45-48.

Sarma, C.K., 1981, Impact of District Industries Centres in Goalpara District, *Yojana* 25 (23) December 16, p 27-28.

Sikidar, Sujit, 1984 : Stunted Industrial Growth, *Commerce* 149 (3820) August 18, p 229-230.

Inscriptions

Anon, 1973-74, (Book Review), *Journal of the University of Gauhati* 24-25 (1) p 143-147.

Review of the Book : *Neog, Maheswar, 1974, Pracya Sasanavali : An anthology of Royal Charters and Other Document of Royal Charters and other Documents of the Old Kingdoms of Kamarupa Cooch Behar, Asama (Saumara), Jayantiyapura, etc., Inscribed on Stone, Copper, etc* Gauhati University, 16, 208-225 p.

Anon, 1983, (Book Review), *Journal of Indian History* 61 (1-3) April-December, p 281-284.

Review of the Book : Sharma, Mukunda Madhava, 1978, *Inscriptions of Ancient Assam*, Gauhati University, 329 p.

Choudhury, P.C., 1970, Significance of the Three Stone Inscriptions at the Assam State Museum, Gauhati, *Journal of Indian History* 48 (1) April, p 91-101, bibliography, footnotes.

Choudhury, P.C., 1977, Historical Materials in the Caratbari Copper Plate Grant to Ratnapalavarmadeva, *Journal of Indian History* 55 (1-2) April-August, p 61-69, footnotes.

Choudhury, P.C., 1977-78, Historical Significences of the Stone Inscription from Lanka (Nowong), Assam, *Journal of Assam Research Society* 23, p 57-63.

Sarma, Mukunda Madhava, 1981-1982, On the Nagajari Khanikargaon Fragmentary Stone Inscription, *Journal of Assam Research Society* 26, p 12-21, footnotes.

Sircar, D.C., 1974, On Some Early Inscriptions of Assam, *Journal of the Asssam Research Society* 22, p 1-11.

Internal Revenue

Bhuyan, P.K., 1977, Excise Rvenue in Assam, 1951-52 to 1965-66 and Prohibition Policy, *Assam Economic Journal* 3 (1) March, p 81-90.

Irrigation

Anon, 1975, Minor Irrigation in Fifth Plan, *Assam Information* 27 (5-6) August-September, p 11-12.

Anon, 1976, Irrigation in Development of Agriculture, *Assam Information* January-March, p 11-14.

Anon, 1979, Farm, Irrigation Projects : Assam Expects Big Chunk of World Bank Aid, *Economic Times* October 1, p 6, col 5-8.

Anon, 1980, Tardy Implementation in Eastern States, *Capital* 184 (4610) June 2, p 7.

Anon, 1983, Irrigation in Assam at a Glance, *Assam Information,* 34, January-March, p 1-3.

Anon, 1988, Perspectives Plan for Irrigation, *Economic Times* (Supplements) October 7, p 4, col 6-8.

Irshad Ali, A.N.M., and Phukan, Umananda, 1975, Mayong Lift Irrigation Project ; New Hope for Assam's Farmers, *Yojana* 19 (20) November 15, p 30.

Neog, A.K., 1975, Irrigation in Assam's Agriculture through Plans, *Assam Information* 27 (9-10) October-November, p 5-11.

Saikia, Anuva, 1978, Irrigation in Assam, *Yojana* 22 (9) May 16, p 18.

Janata Party : Assam Unit

Anon, 1977, Defectors Dilemma in Assam Janata, *New Age* 25 (36) September 4, p 10.

Anon, 1978, Janata List for Assam Assembly Poll, *Times of India* January 29, p 5, cols 4-5.

Bhattacharya, M., 1977, Rumblings in Janata's Adhoc Body in Assam, *New Age* 25 (34) August 21, p 11.

Jute Industry and Trade

Baruah, D.N., 1974, Jute Industry in Assam, *Assam Information* 25 (1-3) April-June, p 29-33.

Goswami, P.C,. and Bora, C.K., 1974, Cultivation of Jute vis-a-vis Autumn Paddy in Assam : A Case Study in Nowgon District, India *Journal of Agricultural Economics* 29 (3) July-September, p 147-154, tables.

Mujibur Rehman, A.R., 19, Jute Marketing in Assam, *Economic Affairs* 27 (4-6) April-June, p 410-412.

Khadi and Village Industries Board

Anon, 1979, New Programmes of Assam Khadi and Village Industries Board, *Assam Information,* 30.

Sarma, A.C., 1978, Khadi and Village Industries in Assam, *Khadi Gramodyog* 24 (10) July, p 512-517, bibliography, tables.

Kamakhya Temple

Sarma, Sri Pratap, 1981-82, Antiquity of the Kamakhya Temple on the Nilacola, *Journal of the Assam Research Institute,* 26, p 46-52, footnotes.

Khamjang Valley

Phukan, J.N., 1963, The Khamjang Valley and the Ahoms, *Journal of the University of Gauhati* 14 (1) p 13-20, bibliography, footnotes.

Khamptis

Raikar, Y.A., 1977, Khomong in the History of the Khamptis, *Resarun* 3 (3) July, p 11-26, bibliography.

Khasis

Dixon, Roland B., 1922, The Khasi and the Racial History of Assam, *Man in India* 2 (1-2) March-June, p 1-11, references.

Kamuar, H.I.S., 1959, Folklore of the Khasis of Assam, *Indian Folklore* 2(3) July-September, p 206-212.

Mukherjee, Bhabananda, 1958, Social Groupings among the Khasis of Assam, *Man in India* 38 (3) July-September, p 208-212.

Labour and Labouring Classes

Chakravarty, R.N., 1975, Worker's Problems in Assam Perspective *Indian Worker* 23 (44-45) August 18, p 29-43.

Land

Bhatta, Suren, 1970, Gain of Land Struggle in Assam, *New Age* 18 (42) October 18, p 3.

Chattoraj, Sumanta, 1984, Spatiotemporal Changes in Land Man Rito in Assam, *National Geographer* 19 (1) June, p 73-77, bibliography, figure, tables.

Dutta, Lakhahira, 1985, physiographic Framework and Intensity of Agricultural land-Use in Nowgong District, *North Eastern Geographer* 17 (12), p 51-66, bibliography, figures ,tables.

Jogendra P. Singh, 1977, Residential Use of Land in Shillong *Geographical Review of India* 39 (3) September, p 232-240, bibliography.

Sarma, Madhab Chandra, 1970, Exploration on the Land Utilization of Kamrup, *Deccan Geographer* 8 (1-2) January-December, p 15-25, bibliography, tables.

Land : History

Guha, Amalendu, 1966, Land Rights and Social Classes in Medieval Assam, *Indian Economic and Social History Review* 3 (3) September p 217-239, bibliography, tables

Land Reforms

Anon, 1971, (Book Review), *Indian Journal of Agricultural Economics* 26 (3) July-September, p 268-269.
Review of the Book : Dutta, Narendra Chandra, 1968, *Land Problems and Land Reforms in Assam*, S. Chand, New Delhi, xiv, 159 p.

Anon, 1972, Asam Will Have Three Types of Land Owners, *Times of India* May 30, p 5, cols 2-3.

Anon, 1976, Assam-Official Machinery Geared Up, *Commerce* 133 (3403) August 14, p 323-324.

Anon, 1976, Awareness of Exploitation, *Link* 19 (1) August 15, p 41.

Anon, 1976, Landlord Terror in Rural Assam, *Link* 18 (36) April 18, p 15.

Anon, 1976, Limited Effect Likely in Assam, *Link* 18 (41) May 23, p 14-15.

Anon, 1978, Assam's Land Reforms, *Economic Times* February 17, p 8, cols 5-8.

Anon, 1978, Land Reforms Measures in Assam, *Assam Information* 29, January-February, p 33-34.

Barman, Bhumidhar, 1976, Land Reforms Secure Tenants' Intrests *Times of India* November 20, p 11, cols 1-4.

Bhattacharya, M., 1972, Assam Land Ceiling Bill Passed, What about Implementation? *New Age* 20 (30) July 23, p 13.

Bhattacharya, M., 1972, Kulak Lobby in Assam Wants Higher Land Ceiling, *New Age* 20 (22) May 28, p 7.

Bhattacharya, M., 1972, Land Owners on Warpath in Assam, *New Age* 20 (25) June 18, p 13.

Bhattacharya, M., 1974, Assam : A Start to Land Reform Implementation, *New Age* 22 (35) September 1, p 4.

Bhuyan, H.C., 1976, Land Reform Measures, *Link* 18 (48) July 19-21.

Bora, J.N., 1976, Cooperatives and Land Reform, *Link* 18 (48) July 11, p 23-24.

Changkakoti, P.K., 1976, Big Strides in Land Distribution, *Yojana* 20 (11) July 1, p 50-51.

Sen, Kranti, 1976, Assam : Land Reforms Problems and Prospects, *Mainstream* 14 (38) May 22, p 10-12.

Land Revenue

Behari, Rakesh 1980, A Review of the Mouzadari System of Land Revenue Collection in Assam, *Administrator* 25 (3) Autum, p 389-499, footnotes, tables.

Land Settlements

Bhattacharyya, N.N., 1985, Spatial Characteristics of Rural Settlement System in Barpeta Region, Assam *North Eastern Geographer* 17 (1-2), P 45-50, bibliography, figures, tables.

Land Tenure

Deka, Tarun Sen, 1986, Assam Minister Pleads against Tenants, *New Age* 34 (33) August 17, p 3.

Lynsdoh, Sngli, 1966, The Bhoi Land-Tenure System, *Man in India* 46 (2) April-June, p 95-102.

Sonowal, Harish, 1982, Land Tenure System in Assam, *Administrator* 27 (2) Summer, p 299-308, bibliography.

Language Problem

Anon, 1972, Cool Behind the Noise and Fury, *Economic and Political Weekly* (Special Number) 7 (31-33) August, p 1485-1488.

Anon, 1972, Language Riots in Assam : A Highly Inflammable Sentiment, *Times of India* October 17, p 4, col 3-5.

Anon, 1974, Blood-Bath of Tribals, *People's Democracy* 10 (47) March 24, p 1+.

Barbora, Golap, 1972, Assam : Languages Problem, *Janata* 27 (40) October 22, p 10.

Barua, Sanchya, 1978, Language Problem in Assam, *Social Scientist* 6 (12) July, p 66-74, footnotes.

Bhattacharya, M., 1973, Assam : Language Parleys Shrouded in Uncertainty, *New Age* 21 (11) March 18, p 4.

Bhattacharya, M., 1974, Language Trouble Erputs in Assam, *New Age* 22 (48) December 1, p 5.

Downs, Frederick S., 1977-78, Missionaries and the Languages Controversy in Assam, *Journal of the Univerity of Gauhati (Arts)* 28-29 p 122-159, footnotes,

Guha, Seema, 1986, Assam's Irksome Languages Issue, *Times of India* May 6, p 8, cols 7-8.

Misra, Prafulla, 1986, Assam : Politics behind Language Agitation *New Age* 34 (35) August 31, p 9.

Pardeshi, Ghansyam, 1986, Assam : Language Politics, *Mainstream* 24 (42) June 21, p 8-9.

Roy, Naresh Chandra, 1981, Language : Its Role in Assam Politics Calcutta *Journal of Political Studies* 1 (2) Summer p 1-10, footnotes.

Times of India (Newspaper), 1972, Chauvinistic, *Times of India* November 10, p 8, col 1, editorial.

Times of India (Newspaper) 1973, Assam Tangle, *Times of India* March 28, p 6, col 2, editorial.

Languages and Dialects

Bhattacharya, P.C., 1977-78, The Languages and Dialects of Cachar District in Assam, *Journal of Assam Research Society* 23 p 12-15.

Lexicography

Neog, Maheswar, 1973-74, Lexicography in Assamese, *Journal of the University of Gauhati* 24-25(1), p 88-94.

Libraries

Baruah, Meera Bala, 1986, Adult Education Libraries of Assam, *Lucknow Librarian* 18 (1) January-March, p 23-28.

Goswami, Ram, 1972, A Report on the Working of the Library Services in the State of Assam, *Indian Library Association Bulletin* 8 (1-2) January-June, p 1-9.

Kaula, P.N., 1965, Assam Library Conference ; Report of Proceedings Held on 24-25 October, 1964, *Herald of Library Science* 4 (2) April, p 159-164.

Library and Information Science Schools and Training

Mittal, R.L., 1973-74, Gauhati University's Graduate Library Education Programme : An Evaluation, *Journal of the University of Gauhati* 24-25 (10), p 95-100.

Local Government

Anon, 1977, Panchayati System under Attack, *Commerce* 135 (3473) December 24, p 1204.

Bhattacharjee, K.K., 1979, Constitution of Chief Commissionership in Assam, *Journal of Indian History* 57 (1) April, p 97-128, footnotes.

Local Government : History

Venkata Rao, V., 1963, Beginnings of Local Self-Government in Assam, *Journal of the University of Gauhati* 14 (1) p 1-12, bibliography, footnote.

Mahanta, Prafulla Kumar

Anon, 1986, (Book Review) *Organiser* 38 (2) May, p 6; *Hindustan Times* (Magazine) April 20, p 8, cols 1-8.
Review of the Book : Mahanta Prafulla Kumar, n.d., The Tussle between the Citizen and Foreigners in Assam, Vikas Pub, New Delhi.

Anon, 1986, It Is So difficult to Find Time, *Indian Express* (Magazine) March 30, p 4, cols 3-4.

Guha, Seema, 1986, "Wait and Watch Our Performance : Mahanta", *Times of India* (Sunday Review), February 2, p iv, cols 6-8.

Malarial Fever

Dutta, S.K., 1976, Cerebral Malaria Is again Taking a Heavy Tall of Life in Assam, *Times of India* August 27, p 4, cols 7-8.

Manpower : Educated Persons : Employment

Anon, 1980, Assam : No New Opportunities, *Commerce* (Supplement) 141 (3608) August 16, p 23-25, tables.

Medical Care

Anon, 1981, Improving Public Health Services, *Assam Information*, 33, August, p 14-15+.

Mental Illness

Guha, Seema, 1978, Despondency and Madness, *Economic and Political Weekly* 13 (46) November 18, p 1881-1882.

Metal Industry and Trade

Kapuria, R.S., 1979, The Bell Metal Industry of Assam, *Indian Cooperative Review* 16 (3) April, p 227-235, tables.

Mikirs

Borth, S.K., 1976, Traditional Weaving Implements among the Mikirs (The Karbis) of Assam, *Indian Muscum Bulletin* 11 (2) July, p 46-50.

Moving Picture Industry

See Film Industry.

Municipal Election

Prabhakar, M.S., 1974, More Elections, *Economic and Political Weekly* (Annual Number) 9 (6-8) February, p 181-184.

Venkata Rao, V., 1971, Municipal Administration in Assam, *Journal of* 16 (2) April-June, p 27-34.

Museums

Choudhury, R.D., 1981, Assam State Museum : Treasury Home of History and Culture, *Assam Information* 33 April-July, p 1-5.

Natural Resources

Anon, 1970, Assam : Abundant Power and Oil, *Commerce* (Annual Number) 121 (3113) p 140-147, map.

Native Races

See also Ahoms

Neolithic Period

Goswami, M.C., and Bhagabs, A.C., 1959, A Collection of Neolithic Tool Types from Wastern Assam, *Man in India* 39(4) October-December, p 312-324, references.

Numismatics

Jai Prakash Singh, 1984, On a Gold Coin of Harshapala of Assam, *Journal of Oriental Institute* 34 (1-2) September-December, p 97-102, bibliography.

Occupations

Barua, Indira, 1979, Changing Occupational Structure in Two Villages in Assam, *Man in India* 59 (2) April-June, p 106-119, bibliography, table.

Officials and Employees

Anon, 1980, Assam to Tighten Noose around Errant Employees, *Times of India* November 21, p 1, cols 6-7.

Bhattacharya, M., 1965, Administration at a Standstill in Assam, *New Age* 13 (14) April 4, p 10.

Bhattacharya, M., 1965, Assam Secretariat Staff on Continuous 'No Work' from March 3, *New Age* 13 (12) March 21, p 11.

Bhattacharya, M., 1965, Assam Sectt. Staff Struggle Continues, *New Age* 13 (16) April 18, p 7+.

Bhattacharya, M., 1965, Assam Secretariat Staff Struggle Leaders Arrested Sec. 144 in Shillong, *New Age* 13 (15) April 11, p 6.

Bhattacharya, M., 1965, Assam Sectt. Staff Win Demands, Call off 'No Work' Movement, *New Age* 13 (17) April 28, p 7.

Bhattacharya, M., 1965, 'No Work' Struggle of Sectt. Staff Continues Unabated, *New Age* 13 (13) March 28, p 7.

Officials and Employees : Salaries, Allowances, etc.

Anon, 1964, Resentments against Pay Committee's Report, *New Age* 12 (26) June 28, p 6.

Anon, 1977, Assam Stand on D.A., Demand, *Link* 19 (38) May 8, p 20-21.

Bhattacharya, M., 1965, Assam Govt Employees Demand Pay Revision *New Age* 13 (10) March 7, p 7.

Opium : History

Guha, Amalendu, 1977, Imperialism of Opium in Assam, 1973-1921, *Calcutta Historical Journal* 1 (2) January-June, p 226-245, appendix, bibliography, footnotes.

Opium Trade

Goswami, Shrutidev, 1977, Impact of the Introduction of 'Abkarry' Opium in Assam 1850-1860, *Assam Economic Journal* 3 (1) March, p 48-54, bibliography.

Panchayats

Bardoli, U.N., 1975-76, Reorganisation of Panchayati Raj in Assam, *Journal of the University of Gauhati (Arts)* 26-27 (1), p 236-46.
Barpujari, H.K., 1964, Early Judicial Panchayats in Assam, *Journal of Indian History* 42 (2) August, p 343-349, bibliography, footnotes.
Dasgupta, H.R., 1974, Panchayati Raj in Assam, *Kurukshetra* 22 (9) February 1, p 10.
Dutta, Poresh Chandra, 1973, Panchayati Raj in Assam, *Kurukshetra* 21 (15) May, p 4-7.
Naidu, N.Y., 1980, Community Participation and Socio-Economic Status, *Rural Development Digest* 3 (1) January p 8-18, footnotes, tables.
Sah, A.K., 1979, Working of Gaon-Panchayat Samabuy Samiti in Assam, *Indian Cooperatives Review* 16 (3) April , p 297-305, tables.
Sarma, Anil Kumar and Bhorali, Devdas, 1980, GPLSS in Action : A Case Study of Mangaldoi Sub-Division, *Indian Cooperatives Review* 17 (94) July, p 335-348, bibliography, tables.
Sarma, Parameswar, 1978, The Role of the Community Development Block in Multi-Level Planning : Some Lessons from the Restructuring of the Panchayati System in Assam., *Assam Economic Journal* 4 (1) March p 15-24, bibliography.

Paper Industry and Trade

Anon, 1975, Jogighopa Paper Mill : A Survey, *Assam Information* 27 (1-2) April-May, p 6-10.
Anon, 1979, Assam : Publishing Business Hit, *Commerce* 139 (3558) August 25, p 360.

Performing Arts

Rastogi, T.C., 1981, Performing Arts in Assam; *Sangeet Natak*, 60, April-June, p 41-52, bibliography.

Petro-Chemical Industries and Trade

Anon, 1984, Petro-Chemicals Hold the Key, *Economic Times* October 1, p 3, cols 1-4.

Petroleum Industry and Trade

Anon, 1975, Resentment over Diversion of Crude, *Commerce* 130 (34) April 12, p 514.
Eastern Economist (Periodical), 1981, The End of the Oil Blockade, *Eastern Economist* 76 (6) February 6, p 390-391, editorial.
Economic Times (Newspaper), 1980, Assam Oil, *Economic Times* November 6, p 5, cols 1-2, editorial.
Hardev Singh, 1965, Oil in Assam, *Eastern Economist* 44 (6) February 5, p 260-262.

Sinha, R.P., 1973, The Liquid Gold of Assam, *Yojana* 17 (8) May 15, p 329-332+.

Petroleum Refineries

Anon, 1972, Foundation of Assam's Third Oil Refinery Laid, *Times of India* January 20, p 1-8+.
Capital (Periodical), 1972, New Refinery in Assam, *Capital* 168 (4198) January 27, p 117-118, editorial.
Economic Times (Newspaper), 1987, Assam Refinery, *Economic Times* August 10, p 5, cols 1-2.

Pilgrims and Pilrgrimages

Desani, G.V., 1973, Mostly concerning Kama and Her Immortal Lord, *Indian Horizons* 22 (1) January, p 1-14.

Planation Industry

Dasgupta, Key, 1983, Plantation Economy and Land Tenure Systems in Brahmaputra Valley, 1839-1914, *Economic and Political Weekly* 18 (29) July 16, p 1280-1290, bibliography, footnotes.

Plantation Workers

Anon, 1973, ACMS Submits Memo to P.M., *Indian Worker* 22 (5) October 29, p 7.
Baruah, Geetanjali, 1980, Family Structure among Some Tea Garden Labourers of Assam, *Bulletin of the Cultural Research Institute* 14 (1-2) p 73-79, tables.
Economic Times (Newspaper), 1987, Tea Needs Sympathy, *Economic Times* December 19, p 5, cols 1-2, editorial.
Kar, R.K., and Baruah, Geetanjali, 1979, Tea-Labour : Preliminary Appraisals of Common Identity in a Multi-Ethinc Community in Assam, *Man in India* 59 (1) January-March, p 33-42.
Misra, Udayon, 1983, Bonus Deaths in Tea Gardens, *Economic and Political Weekly* 18 (42) October 15, p 1782-1783.
Phukan, A.C., 1979, A Decade of Employment in the Tea Industry of Assam, *Indian Worker* 27 (14) January 8, p 4-5+.
Saikia, D., 1977, From Planter Raj to Swaraj, *Indian Worker* 25 (31) May 2, p 5+.
Saikia, D., 1977, Pluckers Plight in Plantations, *Indian Worker* 25 (16-17) January 24, p 57-64, tables.
Sinha, Jagannath, 1975, Plantation Labour Act and Its Fate in Cachar *Indian Worker* 23 (29-30) May 5, p 13.

Plywood Industry and Trade

Anon, 1979, Timber : Need to Regulate Use by Plywood Units, *Capital* 182 (4555) April 30, p 7.
Anon, 1979, Wanton Destruction of Forest Wealth, *Commerce* 139 (3555) August 4, p 236-237.
Hardev Singh, 1980, Plywood : A Victim of Blokade, *Eastern Economist* 75 (19) November 7, p 1044.

Sen, B.K., 1993, Capital Structure : Plywood Industry of Assam, *Indian Journal of Economics* 74 (1) July, p 105-123, bibliography, tables.

Police

Anon, 1979, Who Is To Guard the Guardians, *Economic and Political Weekly* 14 (25) June 23, p 1028-1029.

Police Communication Systems

Saikia, B.N., 1978, Role of Police Tele-Communications in Assam, *Assam Information*, 30, November, p 17-18+.

Politics and Government

See also All Assam Students Union; Bodo Movement; Communist Parties; Communist Party of India; Communist Party of India; Assam Unit; Communist Party of India (Marxist); Communist Party of India Marxist; Assam Unit; Elections; Elections : State; Indian National Congress: Assam Unit; Indian National Congress (I): Assam Unit; Indian National Congress (New) : Assam Unit; Janata Party : Assam Unit.

Abraham, A.S., 1983, From Consensus to Conflict : System's Facility Mediatory Powers, *Times of India* January 7, p 6, cols 3-5.

Abraham, A.S., 1983, Massacre of the Innocents : Whose Hands Have Shed this Blood? *Times of India* May 13, p 8, cols 3-5.

Abraham, A.S., 1983, North -Eastern Discontents : Some Unresolved Dilemmas, *Times of India* January 25, p 6, cols 3-5.

Adhikari, Gautam, 1983, Deadlock in Assam : Negotiation Process Breaks Down, *Times of India* February 8, p 6, cols 3-5.

Adhikari, Gautam, 1983, Insanity in Assam, *Times of India* (Sunday Review) February 27 p 1, cols 1-8.

Aggarwal, Yogi, 1980, Left in Waiting *Economic and Political Weekly* 15 (24-25) June 14-21, p 1046-1047.

Ali, Omar A., 1955, Assam Accord Implementation Makes Little Head way, *Economic Times* June 12, p 3, cols 1-6.

Anon, 1970, After Chaliha, *Economic and Political Weekly* 5 (7) February 14, p 324.

Anon, 1970, Promise to One and All, *Link* 13 (13) November 8, p 15-16.

Anon, 1971, Opposition Boycotts Governor's Address to Assam Assembly, *Times of India* March 10, p 7, cols 2-3.

Anon, 1972, All High on High Command, *Thought* 24 (2) January 8, p 9.

Anon, 1972, Assam : Fractional Politics, *Economic and Political Weekly* 7 (44) October 28, p 2170.

Anon, 1972, Assam : Friendships Shuffled, *Link* 14 (43) June 4, p 21-22.

Anon, 1972, Assam CM's Resignation Accepted, *Times of India* January 31, p 1, col 8+.

Anon, 1972, Choudhury's Exit Follows Sustaind Efforts of Dissident Congress Men, *Times of India* February 3, p 4, cols 7-8.

Anon, 1973, Andhra and Assam Imbroglios, *Call* 24 (5) January, p 7-9.

Anon, 1973, Assam : Many Memoranda to the P.M., *Link* 16 (11) October 21, p 20-21.

Anon, 1977, Assam : Waiting for Dismissal, *Link* 19 (49) July 17, p 16.
Anon, 1977, Change in Assam, *Link* 19 (36) April 17, p 20.
Anon, 1977, Congress Squabbles in Assam, *Link* 19 (38) May 1, p 17.
Anon, 1977, Janata Tries Short-Cuts, *Economic and Political Weekly* 12 (35) August 27, p 1535-1536.
Anon, 1977, More Congress MLAs Quit : Demand for Change of Leadership in Assam, *Times of India* May 11, p 1, col 7-8+.
Anon, 1977, Sinha's Burden in Assam, *Link* 19 (40) May 15, p 19.
Anon, 1977, Survial to the Sinha Govt., *Link* 19 (42) May 29, p 12-13.
Anon, 1978, Assam on Threshold of New Era, *Assam Information*, 30, October, p 28-32.
Anon, 1978, Fear of the People, *Link* 20(50) July 23, p 19-20.
Anon, 1978, Political Vacuum, *Link* 21 (21) December 31, p 21-22.
Anon, 1979, 11 Assam Ministers, two Parliamentary Secretaries Resign, *Times of India* December 10, p 1, cols 1-3+.
Anon, 1979, Asom Janata Dol Makes Its Debut, *Link* 22 (5) September 9, p 17-18.
Anon, 1979, Assam : Bleak Prospects, *Link* 22 (21) December 30, p 19.
Anon, 1979, Assam ; CPI (M) Aligns with Jana Sangh, Janata, *New Age* 27 (38) September 23, p 4.
Anon, 1979, Assam : Fall of Borbora Ministry Imminent, *New Age* 27 (35) September 2, p 5+.
Anon, 1979, Assam Cabinet Resigns : Bid by Hazarika to Form Govt., *Times of India* September 5, p 1, cols 2-3+.
Anon, 1979, Assam Congress To Go Ahead with Polls, *Link* 21 (33) March 25, p 28-29.
Anon, 1979, Assam Govt Reduced to Minority, *Indian Express* July 20, p 1, col 8.
Anon, 1979, Assam Govt's Fate Hangs in Balance, *Times of India* November 14, p 1, col 7.
Anon, 1979, Assam Janata Move for Topling Hazarika Ministry, *Times of India* October 30, p 1, cols 1-2.
Anon, 1979, Assam Problem Eludes Solution, *Times of India* November 29, p 1, cols 1-3+.
Anon, 1979, Borbora Losses Majority, *Link* 21 (51) July 29, p 18-19.
Anon, 1979, Borbora Ministry Reduced to Minority, *Indian Express* July 24, p 5, cols 4-5.
Anon, 1979, Borbora Wins First Round, *Link* 21 (38) April 29, p 21+.
Anon, 1979, Borbora's Troubles, *Link* 21 (30) March 4, p 28-29; 21 (47) July 1, p 14-15.
Anon, 1979, Central Rule Imposed in Assam, *Times of India* December 13, p 1, cols 2-3.
Anon, 1979, Congress (U) Executive and Assam Unit on Collision Course, *Times of India* December 27, p 1, cols 2-4.
Anon, 1979, Governmental Crisis in Assam : CPI (M) Stand, *People's Democracy* 3 (36) September 9, p 1+.
Anon, 1979, Gunning for Borbora, *Link* 21 (36) April 15, p 16.
Anon, 1979, Hazarika To Be Sworn in Assam CM Today, *Times of India* September 9, p 1, cols 2-4.

Anon, 1979, Janata against Central Rule in Assam, *Times of India* December 11, p 9, cols 1-2.

Anon, 1979, Last Days of Borbora? *Link* 21 (32) March 18, p 20.

Anon, 1979, More on Infiltrants, *Economic and Political Weekly* 14 (46) November 17, p 1859-1860.

Anon, 1979, Move for Panel on Foreigners' Issue Dropped, *Times of India* December 2, p 1, cols 2-3.

Anon, 1979, Part of the Pattern, *Economic and Political Weekly* 14 (36) September 8, p 1523.

Anon, 1979, Political Situation in Assam, *People's Democracy* 3 (8) February 25, p 10.

Anon, 1979, President's Rule Likely Soon, *Times of India* December, p 1, col 6-8.

Anon, 1979, Real Face of the Assam Agitation, *People's Democracy* 3 (48) December 2, p 1+.

Anon, 1979, Set for Comfrontation, *Economic and Political Weekly* 14 (49) December 8, p 1993-1994.

Anon, 1979, Shared Instability, *Economic and Political Weekly* 14 (28) July 14, p 1138.

Anon, 1979, Shillong Limping Back to Nirmalcy, *New Age* 27 (46) November 18, p 7.

Anon, 1979, Six Party Statement on Assam Situation, *New Age* 27 (47) November 25, p 16.

Anon, 1979, Stop Eviction of Indian Citizens from Assam : Jyoti Basu'u Letter to Assam Chief Minister, *People Democracy* 3 (47) November 25, p 3.

Anon, 1979, Uncertain Beginning, *Link* 22 (6) September 16, p 20.

Anon, 1979, Urs' Advice Ignored ; Assam Cong (U) for Coalition Govt. Now, *Times of India* December 26, p 1, cols 7-8.

Anon, 1979, Vulnerable Government, *Secular Democracy* October 12, p 11-12.

Anon, 1979, Who Is a Foreigner, *Eastern Economist* 73 (15) October 12, p 733.

Anon, 1979, Will Hazarika Be Let Down ? *Commerce* 139 (3564) October 6, p 670-672.

Anon, 1980, 7 Assam MLAs Back Agitator's Stand, *Times of India* October 30, p 1 col 4-5+.

Anon, 1980, 35 Point Plan for 'Total Revolution', *Times of India* May 16, p 1, cols 4-5+.

Anon, 1980, 36 Hour Assam Bandh Planned, *Times of India* November 15, p 15, p 1, cols 1-3.

Anon, 1980, 100 Agitators Injured, 200 Held in Assam, *Times of India* December 28, p 1, cols 1-2.

Anon, 1980, AAGSP, AASU Reject Call to End Agitation, *Times of India* June 2, p 1, cols 2-3+.

Anon, 1980, AAGSP Not to Accept All-Party Formula, *Times of India* June 18, p 1, cols 4-5.

Anon, 1980, AAGSP Wants PM to Spell Out Her 'Offer' *Times of India* June 18, p 1, cols 4-5.

Anon, 1980, AASU, AAGSP Reject Inviation for Talks, *Times of India* November 28, p 1, cols 6-7+.

Anon, 1980, AASU Blames Centre for Stalemate, *Times of India* December 26, p 1, cols 3-4.

Anon, 1980, AASU Call for 7-Day Mass Satyagraha, *Times of India* April 3, p 1, cols 2-3.
Anon, 1980, AASU Decides To Resume Stir, *Times of India* October 23, p 1, cols 2-4.
Anon, 1980, AASU Meet To Review Assam Developments, *Times of India* May 26, p 1, cols 2-3.
Anon, 1980, AASU Not To Let Goods Go out of State, *Times of India* May 8, p 1, cols 4-5.
Anon, 1980, AASU Office Sealed, 525 Held in Swoop, *Times of India* November 29, p 1, cols 2-4+.
Anon, 1980, AASU Ready for Talks If 'Repression' End, *Times of India* 25, p 1, cols 6-7+.
Anon, 1980, AASU Ready for Talks with 'Open Mind', *Times of India* June 14, p 1, cols 6-7+.
Anon, 1980, AASU Rejects P.M.'s Latest Offer for Talks, *Times of India* July 10, p 1, cols 2-3.
Anon, 1980, AASU Remains Firm on Its Stand, *Times of India* July 14, p 1, cols 7-8+.
Anon, 1980, AASU Sees No Ground for Imphal Talks, *Times of India* August 10, p 1, cols 2-3+.
Anon, 1980, AASU Threat Direct Action, *Times of India* May 16, p 1, cols 2-4.
Anon, 1980, AASU To Continue Stir, *Times of India* July 15, p 1, cols 1-3.
Anon, 1980, AASU Warns against Army Development *Times of India* October 25, p 1, cols 5-6+.
Anon, 1980, Accord at Assam Talks on Policy Framework, *Times of India* October p 1, cols 2-4.
Anon, 1980, Act before It's Too Late, *Link* 22 (33) March 23, p 8-9.
Anon, 1980, Action III-Timed, Unwarranted, *Times of India* April 20, p 1, cols 3-5.
Anon, 1980, Agitation Supports Intensify Violence, *People's Democracy* 4 (36) September 7, p 1+.
Anon, 1980, Agitators Firm at Imphal Talks : Sarin Rushes to Delhi Today for Consultations, *Times of India* August 12, p 1, cols 2-3.
Anon, 1980, Agitators Picket Gauhati AIR : Sarin Rushes to Delhi with New Proposals, *Times of India* May 19, p 1, cols 2-3+.
Anon, 1980, Agony of Assam, *Mainstream* 18 (24) February 9, p 27-31.
Anon, 1980, All-Party Plea for End to Assam Stir, *Times of India* March 2, p 1, cols 2-3+.
Anon, 1980, All Set To Call off Assam Stir Today, *Times of India* August 2, p 1, cols 7-8+.
Anon, 1980, Amend the Constitution to Save India from Foregin Infiltration, *Organiser* 1 (50) May 4, p 8-9.
Anon, 1980, An Appeal from Assam : Defend Democratic Values, *People's Democracy* 4 (29) July 20, p 1-2.
Anon, 1980, Army Alerted in Assam : Govt Call To End All Forms of Agitations, *Times of India* March 31, p 1, cols 2-3.
Anon, 1980, Army, BSF Alerted in Assam, *Times of India* October 19, p 1, cols 2-4.
Anon, 1980, Army Called out in Gauhati : Five Killed in Firing, Clashes in Assam Towns, *Times of India* November 25, p 1, cols 2-3.

Anon, 1980, Assam : Dangerous Facets, *Mainstream* 18 (34) April 19, p 6-8+.

Anon, 1980, Assam : A Dangerous Ultimatum, *Link* 22 (41) May 18, p 8.

Anon, 1980, Assam : 'Gherao' A Damp Squib, *Link* 23 (13) November 9, p 33-35.

Anon, 1980, Assam : Hot and the Cold of, *Link* 22 (43) June 1, p 8.

Anon, 1980, Assam again Rocked by a Wave of Volence, *Times of India* July 1, p 1, cols 1-2.

Anon, 1980, Assam Agitation : Basu's Concern, *Eastern Economist* 74 (5) February 1, p 222-223.

Anon, 1980, Assam Agitation Leaders Firm on Cut-Off Year, *Times of India* June 9, p 9 cols 1-2.

Anon, 1980, Assam Agitation To Be Resumed Soon, *Times of India* October 18, p 1, col 3-4.

Anon, 1980, Assam Agitation To Be Withdrawn Today : All Arrested Persons To Be Released : Fresh Talks within a Week, *Times of India* July 26, p 1, col 2-4+.

Anon, 1980, Assam Agitators Agree To Tripartite Talks, *Times of India* January 6, p 1, cols 1-2+.

Anon, 1980, Assam Agitators Agree To Tripartite Talks, *Times of India* January 6, p 1, cols 1-2+.

Anon, 1980, Assam Agitators Attack Communists, *New Age* 28 (23) June 8, p 41.

Anon, 1980, Assam Agitator's Call for Two-Day Protest, *Times of India* May 11, p 1, cols 6-7.

Anon 1980, Assam, Agitators Hold NE Region to Ransom, *New Age* 28 (51) December 21, p 5+.

Anon, 1980, Assam Agitators Move for Violence, *New Age* 28 (44) November 2, p 7.

Anon, 1980, Assam Agitators Plan Two-Day Gherao, *Times of India* May 18, p 1, cols 5-6.

Anon, 1980, Assam Agitators Programme Anti-Minorities, Secessionist, *People's Democracy* 4 (23) June 8, p 1+.

Anon, 1980, Assam and the Janata Party, *Janata* 35 (17) June 8, p 10.

Anon, 1980, Assam Bandh Disrupts Life in Most Areas, *Times of India* October 28, p 1, cols 2-3+; December 30, p 1, cols 2-3.

Anon, 1980, Assam-Bound Trucks Stopped for 5 Hours, *Times of India* March 25, p 1, cols 2-4+.

Anon, 1980, Assam Braces Itself To Face 'Satyagraha' *Times of India* December 18, p 1, cols 3-4.

Anon, 1980, Assam CLP (I) Asks PM To Choose Leader, *Times of India* December 4, p 1, cols 2-4.

Anon, 1980, Assam Cong (I) Confidence of Forming Ministry, *Times of India* December 1, p 1, cols 7-8+.

Anon, 1980, Assam Declared Disturbed Area, *Times of India* April 6, p 1, cols 2-4.

Anon, 1980, Assam Defies Solution, *Link* 22 (37) April 20, p 6-8.

Anon, 1980, Assam Dominates Debate on Opening Days *New Age* 28 (24) June 15, p 9.

Anon, 1981, Assam For a Mrs Gandhi Too, *Organiser* 33 (1) May 24, p 1+.
Anon, 1980, Assam Govt. Braces to Face Bandh Today, *Times of India* December 29, p 1, cols 4-5.
Anon, 1980, Assam Govt-Students on Collision Course, *Times of India* May 30, p 1, cols 2-4+.
Anon, 1980, The Assam Happenings and the Centre, *Janata* 35(8) March 30, p 9-10.
Anon, 1980, Assam Impasse, *Times of India* April 10, p 6 : May 5, p 6, col 6; May 13, p 6, col 6, letter to the editor.
Anon, 1980, Assam Leaders Firm on Not Suspending Stir, *Times of India* November 12, p 7, cols 4-5.
Anon, 1980, Assam Leaders May Come for Talks, *Times of India* September 11, p 1, cols 7-8.
Anon, 1980, Assam Leaders Reject Call for Fresh Tallks, *Times of India* December 25, p 1, cols 6-8.
Anon, 1980, Assam, MLAs' Gherao Begins, *Times of India* October 29, p 1, cols 6-7+.
Anon, 1980, Assam Movement, *Economic and Political Weekly* 15 (30) July 26, p 1246, letter to the editor.
Anon, 1980, Assam Paralysed for Third Day, *Times of India* November 6, p 1, cols 6-7+.
Anon, 1980, Assam People's Agitation, *Economic and Politial Weekly* 15(22) May 31, p 948, letter to the editor.
Anon, 1980, Assam Political Parties Get Wider Response, *New Age* 28 (37) September 14, p 6.
Anon, 1980, The Assam Problem, *Gandhi Marg* 1(12) March, p 793-797.
Anon, 1980, Assam Relaxes after Centre's Declaration, *Times of India* August 1, p 1, cols 2-3+.
Anon, 1980, Assam Remains Cut Off : Fresh Attempt to Resume Negotiations, *Times of India* July 6, p 1, cols 2-3.
Anon, 1980, Assam Satyagrahis Lathi Charged, *Times of Inida* December 27, p 1 cols 1-2.
Anon, 1980, Assam Situation is Very Grave, *New Age* 28 (6) February 10, p 4.
Anon, 1980, Assam Situation Very Tense : People Flee Villages as Mob Fury Continues, *Times of India* May 29, p 1, cols 2-4.
Anon, 1980, Assam Solution Possible If Stir is Withdrawn : PM, *Times of India* June 9, p 1, cols 4-5+.
Anon, 1980, Assam Staff Abstains from Offices, *Times of India* November 5, p 1, cols 7-8+.
Anon, 1980, Asam Stir Hindering Progress : PM, *Times of India* November 5, p 7, col 4-5.
Anon, 1980, Assam Stir is Withdrawn; Detenus Freed, *Times of India* August 3, p 1, cols 2-3+.
Anon, 1980, Assam Stir Leaders Held : Army Swings into Action : Processionists Lathicharged : Picketing Again after Curfew Lifted, *Times of India* April 20, p 1, cols 2-5+.
Anon, 1980, Assam Stir Suspended for Two Weeks, *Times of India* July 21, p 1, cols 2-3.

Anon, 1980, Assam Talks Bogged Down Again, *Times of India* August 20, p 1, cols 6-7.

Anon, 1980, Assam Talks Bogged on Alien's Issue, *Times of India* October 15, p 1, cols 7-8+.

Anon, 1980, Assam Talks Cover "Substantive" Issue, *Times of India* October 16, p 1, cols 6-7.

Anon, 1980, Assam Talks Fail but Door Not Shut, *Times of India* October 17, p 1, cols 2-4.

Anon, 1980, Assam Talks May Be Delayed, *Times of India* August 8, p 1, cols 4-5+.

Anon, 1980, Assam Talks May Be Resumed Soon, *Times of India* October 31, p 1, cols 1-3.

Anon, 1980, Assam Talks Prospects in Jeopardy, *Times of India* August 9, p 1, cols 2-3.

Anon, 1980, Assam Talks Put Off on Optimistic Note, *Times of India* September 25, p 1, cols 1-2+.

Anon, 1980, Fall Out of Opportunism, *Economic and Political Weekly* 15(51) December 20, p 2031.

Anon, 1980, Free Rein for Police, *Economic and Political Weekly* 15 (49) December 6, p 2114.

Anon, 1980, Imperatives for Assam, *Mainstream* 19 (16) December 20, p 3-4.

Anon, 1980, Imphal Talks on Foreigners Off, *Times of India* August 11, p 1, cols 2-4.

Anon, 1980, Intensified Assam Stir from Today, *Times of India* November 17, p 1, col 8+.

Anon, 1980, Janata for Negotiated Settlement in Assam, *Times of India* April 21, p 1, cols 2-3+.

Anon, 1980, Janata Party Eggs on Agitators in Assam, *New Age* 28 (52) December 28, p 16.

Anon, 1980, Joint Appeal by Assam Leaders, Intellectuals, *New Age* 28 (30) July 27, p 4.

Anon, 1980, Leaders Held in morning Swoop : Army Called Out in Assam, *Economic Times* April 20, p 1, cols 6-8+.

Anon, 1980, Let Indira Keep Nehru's Word on Assam, *Organiser* 31 (48) April 20, p 1+.

Anon, 1980, Lok Sabha Spotlight : Cong-I's Game of Disruption behind Assam 'Blockade' *New Age* 28 (14) April 6, p 9.

Anon, 1980, MPs for No New Terms for Assam ~~Talks~~, *Times of India* August 9, p 1, cols 1-2.

Anon, 1980, Magnitude of Assam Disorder : Report of PUCL Team, *Mainstream* 18 (28) March 8, p 18-21.

Anon, 1980, Makwana Feels Assam Issue Will Be Solved Soon, *Times of India* December 26, p 7, cols 4-5.

Anon, 1980, Mass Protest Fast by Assam Students, *Times of India* November 30, p 1, cols 2-3.

Anon, 1980, Mediation Bid Evokes Good Response, *Times of India* May 25, p 1, cols 2-3.

Anon, 1980, Ministry-Making Problems, *Link* 22 (26) February 3, p 23.

Anon, 1980, Most of Assam May be Declared Disturbed Area *Times of India* November 1, p 1, cols 7-8+.

Anon, 1980, Moves, Counter Moves, *Link* 22 (36) April 13, p 17.

Anon, 1980, Mrs Gandhi Hopeful of Amicable Solution, *Times of India* May 14, p 1, cols 1-2+.

Anon, 1980, Mrs Gandhi to Visit Assam on Saturday, *Times of India* April 11, cols 2-3.

Anon, 1980, Mrs Taimur Vows to Restore Peace, *Times of India* December 11, p 1, cols 1-2.

Anon, 1980, Neither Side Willing to Bend in Assam, *Times of India* May 13, p 1, cols 1-2+.

Anon, 1980, New Cut-Off Date for Assam May be Discussed, *Times of India* October 10, p 1, cols 1-2.

Anon, 1980, New Delhi Communalising the Assam Situation, *Organiser* 32 (4) June 15, p 2.

Anon, 1980, New Forfula to Resolve Assam Tangles, *Times of India* June 5, p 1, cols 7-8.

Anon, 1980, New Govt. Proposals on Assam Likely soon, *Times of India* March 14, p 1, cols 5-6.

Anon, 1980, No Accord at Cost of Unity : Says PM, *Times of India* July 2, p 1, cols 1-2+.

Anon, 1980, No Consensus on Assam Cong (I) Leader, *Times of India* December 3, p 1, cols 2-4+.

Anon 1980, No Fresh Stir in Assam Till End of Talks, *Times of India* August 5, p 1, cols 2-3+.

Anon, 1980, No Govt Reaction Yet To AASU Farmula, *Times of India* September 21, p 1, cols 6-7.

Anon, 1980, No Let Up in Assam Blockage : 47 Arrested, *Times of India* March 29, p 1, cols 6-7.

Anon, 1980, No Plan to Visit Assam : Zail Wants Stir Suspended before Talks, *Times of India* November 11, p 1, cols 2-3.

Anon, 1980, No Surrendor To Divisive Forces, *Times of India* June 10, p 1, cols 2-4+.

Anon, 1980, No Talks under Duress : P.M. Denies Dithering on Assam Issue, *Times of India* May 4, p 1, cols 2-3+.

Anon, 1980, Non-Cooperation Stir by Assam Staff Today *Times of India* April 28, p 1, cols 2-4.

Anon, 1980, Options in Assam, *Eastern Economist* 74 (17) April 25, p 822-823.

Anon, 1980, PM Asks Assam Agitators to be Practical, *Times of India* May 16, p 7, cols 4-5.

Anon, 1980, PM Asks Assam Agitators to Resume Talks, *Times of India* May 12, p 1, cols 2-3+.

Anon, 1980, PM not to Insist 1971 as Base Year, *Times of India* June 13, p 1, col 3.

Anon, 1980, PM Rules Out 1951 as Cut-Off Date, *Times of India* March 16, p 1, cols 5-6.

Anon, 1980, PM Sees Foreign Hand in Assam, *Times of India* April 5, p 1, cols 5+.

Anon, 1980, PM Sees RSS Hand in Assam Agitation, *Times of India* March 27, p 1, cols 5-7+.

Anon, 1980, PM Sends Emissaries to Assam, *Times of India* December 2, p 1, cols 1-2+.

Anon, 1980, PM's Statement Welcomed : AASU, AAGSP Hopeful to Early Talks, *Times of India* June 13, p 1, cols 2-3+.

Anon 1980, PM's Talks to End Assam Stir Fail, *Times of India* April 13, p 1, cols 2-4.

Anon, 1980, PM's Talks with Assam Agitators Soon, *Times of India* July 1, p 1, cols 2-3+.

Anon, 1980, PM's Vital Talks with Political Leaders on Assam Today, *Times of India* March 1, p 1, cols 2-3+.

Anon, 1980, Parishad men Detain 14 'Foreigners', *Times of India* May 14, p 1, cols 2-3+.

Anon, 1980, Peculiar RSS Game on Foreigners Issue, *New Age* 28 (17) April 27, p 7.

Anon, 1980, Picketing Paralyses Govt. Offices in Assam, *Times of India* April 23, p 1, cols 6-7+.

Anon, 1980, Planning Is almost Certain : Violence Erupts again in Assam, *New Age* 28 (36) September 7, p 5.

Anon, 1980, Polit Bureau Statement on Assam, *People's Democracy* 4 (3) January 20, p 1+.

Anon, 1980, Polit Bureau : Statement on Assam Situation, *People's Democracy* 4 (16) April 20, p 5.

Anon, 1980, Polit Bureau Statement on Assam, *People's Democracy* 4 (25) June 22, p 7+.

Anon, 1980, Political Parties Hold Meeting in Gauhati, *New Age* 28 (28) July 13, p 4.

Anon, 1980, Political Parties Want Resumption of Talks, *New Age* 28 (47) November 23, p 6.

Anon, 1980, Preparing for a Crack-Down, *Economic and Political Weekly* 15 (1) March 22, p 578.

Anon, 1980, President's Rule for Another 6 Months, *Times of India* June 11, p 1, cols 1-2+

Anon, 1980, 'Quit Assam' Call Soon, *Times of India* May 9, p 1, cols 3-5.

Anon, 1980, Role of the Bureaucracy, *Economic and Political Weekly* 15 (36) September 6, p 1492.

Anon, 1980, A Report on Assam : Cultural Perspectives, *Janata* 35 (11) April 20, p 11-12; 35 (12) April 27, p 13-16.

Anon, 1980, Report on the Assessment of Situation of Assam, *Economic Studies* 20 (11-12) May-June, p 539-545.

Anon, 1980, Sarin Hopeful of Dialogue with Agitators, *Times of India* May 21, p 1, cols 2-3+.

Anon, 1980, Search for an Agent, *Economic and Political Weekly* 15 (47) November 22 , p 1954-1955.

Anon, 1980, Secessionism on the Rise ? *Link* 22 (23) March 23, p 9-11.

Anon, 1980, Secessionists Stir Being Encouraged in Assam : PM, *Times of India* January 21, p 1, cols 2-3.

Anon, 1980, Shillong Talk a Nonstarter, *New Age* 28 (35) August 31, p 5+.

Anon, 1980. A Sinister Design, *Link* 22 (30) March 2, p 17-18.

Anon, 1980, Six-Party Statement on Assam Situation, *New Age* 28 (5) February 3, p 4+.

Anon, 1980, Social Base of Assam Agitation Shrinking, *New Age* 28 (25) June 22, p 5.
Anon, 1980, Stalemate in Assam May End Soon, *Times of India* July 9, p 1, cols 4-5.
Anon, 1980, State-Wide Protest Marches in Assam, *Times of India* May 17, p 1, cols 1-2+.
Anon, 1980, Stern Action To Curb Secessionist Trends, *Times of India* April 20, p 9, cols 1-2.
Anon, 1980, Stir Leaders Adamant on Foreigner's Issue, *Times of India* December 3, p 1, cols 6-7.
Anon, 1980, Stir Paralysis Work in Assam Office, *Times of India* July 8, p 1, cols 2-3+.
Anon, 1980, Student Continue Agitation despite Talks with PM, *New Age* 28 (16) April 20, p 4+.
Anon, 1980, Supreme Court Directive : Centre, Assam Told to Approach High Court, *Times of India* April 17, p 1, cols 2-4+.
Anon, 1980, Talks on Assam Crisis Begin : Early Accord Likely on Foreigners' Dectection, *Times of India* September 18, p 1, cols 2-4.
Anon, 1980, Talks on Assam with Eye on Future, *Times of India* October 11, p 1, cols 2-4+.
Anon, 1980, Talks on Issue of Assam Foreigners Fail, *Times of India* March 13, p 1, cols 2-3.
Anon, 1980, Talks with AASU Leaders Likely Today, *Times of India* April 10, p 1, cols 7-8.
Anon, 1980, Teargassing in Assam Town : 50 Injured, *Times of India* December 12, p 1, cols 7-8.
Anon, 1980, Ten Agitators Hurt in firing Near Gauhati, *Times of India* May 6, p 1, cols 2-3.
Anon, 1980, Tension Grips Many Assam Areas, *Times of India* June 6, p 1, cols 7-8.
Anon, 1980, Testing Ground, *Economic and Political Weekly* 15 (52) December 27, p 2158.
Anon, 1980, Third and Final Phase of Assam, Stir from Today *Times of India* July 7, p 1, cols 2-3.
Anon, 1980,Thousands Court Arrest in Assam, *Times of India* May 7, p 1, cols 6-7.
Anon, 1980, Threat to Resume Stir : Assam Accord Runs into Rough Weather, *Times of India* August 4, p 1, cols 2-3.
Anon, 1980, Three Killed, 100 Injured : Indefinite Curfew in 2 Assam Towns, *Times of India* December 19, p 1, cols 2-4.+.
Anon, 1980, Time Running Out in Assam, Says CPI, *New Age* 28 (20) May 18, p 6.
Anon, 1980, Tough Assam Steps To Deal with Agitators, *Times of India* April 4, p 1, cols 2-3+.
Anon, 1980, Trade Union Joint Call against Agitator, *People's Democracy* 4 (50) December 14, p 3+.
Anon, 1980, Transfer of Cases from Gauhati Court Order, *Times of India* June 10, p 1, cols 1-2+.
Anon, 1980, Treat to Intensify Assam Agitation, *Times of India* May 5, p 1, cols 3-4.

Anon, 1980, Two Refugee Camps and an Unpatriotic Journalist *Economic and Political Weekly* 15 (16) April 19, p 736.

Anon, 1980, United Left, Stand on Assam Situation, *New Age* 28 (10) March 9, p 16.

Anon, 1980, Vorieties of Alienation, *Economic and Political Weekly* 15 (23) June 7, p 997-998.

Anon, 1980, Violence against CPI (M) by Assam Agitators, *People's Democracy* 4 (22) June 1, p 5+.

Anon, 1980, Violence, Firing in Nowgong : SI Injured, *Times of India* December 21, p 1, cols 1-2.

Anon, 1980, Violence Unabated in Assam : Curfew in 3 More Towns : Toll 19, *Times of India* May 28, p 1, cols 2-4.

Anon, 1980, When Cong-I Made a Fool of Itself in Assam Blockade, *Organiser* 31 (49) April 27, p 6.

Anon, 1980, Why the Centre is Avoiding a Meaningful Dialogue on Assam, *Organiser* 31 (51) May 11, p 5.

Anon, 1980, Work at Standstill in Assam Offices, *Times of India* may 22, p 1, cols 1-2.

Anon, 1980, Work in Assam Office Remains Paralysed, *Times of India* April 27, p 1, cols 3-4.

Anon, 1980, Work Remains Paralysed in Assam Office, *Times of India* April 24, p 1, cols 2-3+; May 23, p 21, cols 2-3+; November 26, p 1, cols 2-3.

Anon, 1980, Zail to Consult PM on Cut Off Year, *Times of India* September 19, p 1, cols 6-8+.

Anon, 1980, Ail Singh Wants Talks without Precondition, *Times of India* December 25, p 1, cols 5-6+.

Anon, 1981, 2 Blasts in Assam Assembly Hostel, *Times of India* March 19, p 1, cols 5-7+.

Anon, 1981, AAGSP for 1961, as Cut-Off Year, *Times of India* May 16, p 1, cols 2-3.

Anon, 1981, AASU Concession to Foreigners' Progeny, *Times of India* October 3, p 1, cols 1-2.

Anon, 1981, AASU, AAGSP Dismayed at P.M.'s Directive, *Times of India* April 14, p 11, cols 1-2.

Anon, 1981, AASU-AAGSP Rift Imminent, *Times of India* September 10, p 1, cols 2-4.

Anon, 1981, AASU-AAGSP Stand Rigid : Talks Begin under Cloud of Misgivings, *Times of India* October 30, p 1, cols 7-8.

Anon, 1981, Alliance Hopes to Form Govt. in Assam, *Times of India* November 26, p 1, cols 4-5.

Anon, 1981, Anwara Taimur Has Sinned on Three Different Counts *Organiser* 32 (47) April 12, p 5+.

Anon, 1981, Anwara Taimur Stops All Eviction of Infiltrators, *Organiser* 32 (46) April 5, p 1+.

Anon, 1981, Anwara Taimur to Resign Today, *Times of India* June 28, p 1, cols 4-5.

Anon,1981, Army Alert in Assam on Bandh Eve, *Times of India* November 18, p 1, cols 7-8+.

Anon, 1981, Army to the Fore, *Economic and Political Weekly* 16 (1-2) January 3-10, p 2.

Anon, 1981, Assam : Attempt to Impose Cong-I Minority Ministry *New Age* 29 (44) November1, p 14.
Anon, 1981, Assam : Stalemate again, *Link* 23 (47) July 5, p 7.
Anon, 1981, Assam : the Vicious Circle, *Link* 23 (48) July 12, p 25-27.
Anon, 1981, assam Accord Likely by Sept. 21, *Times of India* September 8, p 1, cols 2-4+.
Anon, 1981, Assam Agitation Leaders Relent, *Times of India* July 5, p 1, cols 2-3; July 7, p 1, cols 2-4.
Anon, 1981, Assam Agitation May Turn to Violence, *New Age* 29 (6) February 8, p 13.
Anon, 1981, Assam Agitationists Resort to Rowdyism, *New Age* 29 (11) March 15, p 4.
Anon, 1981, Assam Agitators Lathi-Charged, *Times of India* December 15, p 1, cols 5-7.
Anon, 1981, Assam Aliens Issue Nearing Solution, *Times of India* May 21, p 1, cols 2-4.
Anon, 1981, Assam Blockade to be Resumed on January 27, *Times of India* January 24, p 1, cols 7-8.
Anon, 1981, Assam Crisis, *Seminar* (Annual Number) 257 January p 76-79.
Anon, 1981, Assam Crisis Depens as Minister Quits, *Times of India* MArch 20, p 1, cols 7-8+.
Anon, 1981, Assam DIG Dimissed from IPS, *Times of India* April 6, p 1, cols 2-4+.
Anon, 1981, Assam Democratic Students under Attack, *People's Democracy* 5 (13) March 29, p 5+.
Anon, 1981, Assam Govt. Quits, *Times of India* June 29, p 1, cols 6-8.
Anon, 1981, Assam Govt. Staff Warned to Penel Action, *Times of India* January 25, p 1, cols 2-3.
Anon, 1981, Assam Govt. Suffers Defeat in Assembly, *Times of India* March 31, p 1, cols 7-8.
Anon, 1981, Assam Govt's Future Hanging in Balance, *Times of India* March 30, p 1, cols 7-8+.
Anon, 1981, The Assam Impasse, *Janata* 36 (38) November 22, p 2+.
Anon, 1981, Assam in Grip of Fresh Constitutional Crisis, *Times of India* April 1, cols 5-6+.
Anon, 1981, Assam Leaders Cling to Negotiations, *Times of India* May 28, p 1, cols 2-4.
Anon, 1981, Assam Leaders Hopeful of Accord with Govt. *Times of India* May 24, p 1, cols 7-8+.
Anon, 1981, Assam Leaders Keep Talks Going, *Times of India* July 3, p 1, cols 2-3.
Anon, 1981, Assam Leaders May be Invited for Talks, *Times of India* February 14, p 1, cols 7-8+.
Anon, 1981, Assam Leaders Relent on Some Points, *Times of India* August 23, p 1, cols 1-2.
Anon, 1981, Assam Leaders Rule out Informal Talks, *Times of India* November 6, p 1, cols 7-8.
Anon, 1981, Assam Leaders Seek Centre's Clarification, *Times of India* May 26, p 1, cols 2-3+.

Anon, 1981, Assam Likely To Have Congress (I) Ministry, *Times of India* December 3, p 1, cols 4-5+.

Anon, 1981, Assam Parleys Deadlocked, *Times of India* July 10, p 1, cols 2-4+.

Anon, 1981, Assam Stire, *Times of India* December 16, p 6, col 6, letter to the editors.

Anon, 1981, Assam Stir Leaders to Join Mini-Panel, *Times of India* July 11, p 7, cols 1-2.

Anon, 1981, Assam Stir Losing Momentum, *Times of India* January 2, p 1, cols 2-4.

Anon, 1981, Assam Talks Adjour for Over a Week, *Times of India* July 16, p 1, col 4-5.

Anon, 1981, Assam Talks Adjourned ; No Accord on Dispersal of Fore Enigners, *Times of India* August 24, p 1, cols 2-3.

Anon, 1981, Assam Talks Bogged again, *Link* 24 (13) November 8, p 10.

Anon, 1981, Assam Talks Continue : Centre Not Yet Decided on Aliens Issue, *Times of India* May 20, p 1, cols 2-3.

Anon, 1981, Assam Talks Enter Final Stage, *Times of India* July 9, p 1, cols 1-2.

Anon, 1981, Assam Talks Enter Vital Phase Today, *Times of India* may 22, p 1, cols 2-4.

Anon, 1981, Assam Talks Heading for Deadlock, *Times of India* July 2, p 1, cols 2-3+.

Anon, 1981, Assam Talks Hinge on Govt. Clarification, *Times of India* June 30, p 1, cols 6-7.

Anon, 1981, Assam Talks May Be Resumed on Feb 7, *Economic Times* January 31, p 1, cols 2-3+.

Anon, 1981, Assam Talks near Breakthrough, *Times of India* May 23, p 1, cols 2-4.

Anon, 1981, Talks on Aliens; Issue Deadlocked, *Times of India* July 14, p 1, cols 2-4.

Anon, 1981, Assam Talks Recessed for Two Weeks, *Times of India* May 29, p 1, cols 2-4.

Anon, 1981, Assam Talks to be Continued, *Times of India* July 15, p 1, cols 1-2.

Anon, 1981, The Assam Tangle, *Janata* 34 (46) January 11, p 4+.

Anon, 1981, Assam Team Insists on Written Clarification, *Times of India* July 1, p 1, cols 7-8.

Anon, 1981, Assam Team Wants it in Writing, *Times of India* May 30, p 1, col 2-4.

Anon, 1981, BJP's Game in Assam, *New Age* 29 (4) January 25, p 5.

Anon, 1981, Bandh Eve Precaution : Ban on Strikes in Assam Vital Services, *Times of India* November 19, p 1, col 2-3+.

Anon, 1981, Bid for Acceptable Solution on Assam, *Times of India* August 3, p 1, cols 5-6.

Anon, 1981, Bid to Avert Showdown in Assam, *Times of India* January 15, p 9, cols 4-5.

Anon, 1981, Breathing Space in Assam, *Mainstream* 19 (30) March 28, p 3.

Anon, 1981, Burden on Geography, *Economic and Political Weekly* 16 (6) February 7, p 166-167.

Anon, 1981, CPI Suggestd solution To Assam Cut-Off Date, *New Age* 29 (40 January 25, p 11.

Anon, 1981, The Challenges before Assam : Past, Present and Future *Capital* 187 (4686) December 28, p 26-27.

Anon, 1981, Chances of Assam Accord Bleak, *Times of India* October 29, p 1, cols 7-8.

Anon, 1981, Cong (I) for Coalition with Janata in Assam, *Times of India* November 8, p 1, cols 6-8.

Anon, 1981, Covention Call for Foreigners' Detection, *Times of India* January 5, p 1, cols 1-2+.

Anon, 1980, The Crisis That Is Assam, *Monthly Commentary on Indian Economic Conditions* 22 (3) October, p 9-10.

Anon, 1981, Date for Assam Talks May be Fixed Soon, *Times of India* January 10, p 1, cols 7-8.

Anon, 1981, Disobedience Stir in Assam on Dec 14, *Times of India* December 4, p 1, cols 2-3.

Anon, 1981, Early Elections in Assam Suggested, *Times of India* January 12, p 9, cols 1-2.

Anon, 1972, Faction Fight in Assam Congress, *Link* 15 (3) August 27, p 21-22.

Anon, 1981, Faith in New Delhi, *Economic and Political Weekly* 16 (42-43) October 17-24, p 1670-1671.

Anon, 1981, Fall Out of Anti Foreigner Agitation, *Economic and Political Weekly* 16 (20) May 16, p 878.

Anon, 1981, GOI's Trap of False Figures for Assam Agitators, *Organiser* 33 (12) August 9, p 5.

Anon, 1981, Govt Offers 1966 as Cut-Off Year, *Times of India* August 4, p 1, cols 2-4.

Anon, 1981, Govt Renews Contact with Assam Leaders, *Times of India* January 9, p 1, cols 4-5.

Anon, 1981, Govt Stand Infexiable : Assam Talks Futile Feel Stir Leaders, *Times of India* May 18, p 1, col 2-4.

Anon, 1981, Hopeful Sign at Assam Talks, *Times of India* July 12, p 1, cols 4-5.

Anon, 1981, Initiative from Top May Untangle Assam. *Times of India* June 25, p 1, cols 7-8+.

Anon, 1981, Janata Rebuffs Cong-I Overtures in Assam, *Times of India* November 9, p 1, cols 4-5.

Anon, 1981, Move to Install Congress-I Govt in Assam, *Times of India* November 9, p 1, cols 2-3.

Anon, 1981, New Assam Ordinance on Govt Spending, *Times of India* April 2, p 1, cols 2-3+.

Anon, 1981, A New Element, *Economic and Political Weekly* 16 (8) February 21, p 255-256.

Anon, 1981, New Proposals on Assam Being Finalised, *Times of India* August 28, p 1, cols 4-5.

Anon, 1981, No Accord on Key Issues in Assam Talks, *Times of India* November 4, p 1, cols 2-3.

Anon, 1981, No Trust Move against Assam Ministry Fails, *Times of India* March 25, p 1, col 4-5+.

Anon, 1981, Normalcy Far Away, *Economic and Political Weekly* 16 (16) April 18, p 686-687.

Anon, 1981, Not Much Progress at Assam Talks, *Times of India* August 22, p 1, cols 4-5+.

Anon, 1981, Offer to Shift 1961-1971 'Unauthorised' DPS, *Times of India* May 25, p 1, cols 7-8+.

Anon, 1981, One Killed in Assam Firing : Bandh Partial, *Times of India* November 20, p 1, cols 1-2+.

Anon, 1981, One Month of Taimur Shahi in Assam, *Organiser* 32 (37) February 1, p 1+.

Anon, 1981, Opposition, Govt Talks ; AASU, AAGSP Told to Reconisder Stand, *Times of India* November 10, p 1, cols 6-7.

Anon, 1981, Opposition to be Associated in Assam Talks, *Times of India* December 11, p 1, col 2-3+.

Anon, 1981, Opposition's Dilemma over Assam, *Times of India* December 22, p 1, cols 2-4+.

Anon, 1981, PM Paves Way for Fresh Assam talks, *Times of India* April 13, p 1, cols 7-8+.

Anon, 1981, Police Lathicharges Mob in Assam, *Times of India* November 21, p 1, cols 4-5+.

Anon, 1981, Prorogation Challenged, *Janata* 36 (11) April 26, p 8.

Anon, 1981, Prospects in Assam Bleak, *Times of India* November 23, p 7, cols 2-4.

Anon, 1981, Protest Satyagraha All over Assam, *Times of India* January 13, p 1, col 1-2+.

Anon, 1981, The Real Issue in Assam, *People's Democracy* 5 (13) March 29, p 1+.

Anon, 1981, The Reincarnation and Taimur Lung in Assam, *Organiser* 32 (33) January 4, p 3.

Anon, 1981, Setback to Efforts for Assam Talks, *Times of India* October 6, p 1, cols 1-2.

Anon, 1981, Solution of Assam Tangle : Tripartite Panel to work Out Formula, *Times of India* May 19, p 1, cols 2-4.

Anon, 1981, Solution to Assam Issue in the Offering, *Times of India* March 27, p 1, cols 6-7+.

Anon, 1981, Stalemate in Assam Talks Averted, *Times of India* May 27, p 1, cols 2-4+.

Anon, 1981, Stir Leaders Seek to Re-Define 'Foreigner', *Times of India* November 3, p 1, cols 2-3+.

Anon, 1981, Tewari to Asses Prospects in Assam, *Times of India* November 29, p 1, cols 7-8+.

Anon, 1981, Twilight over Assam, *Janata* 36 (17) June 14, p 3.

Anon, 1981, Union Govt. for Direct Talks on Assam, *Times of India* January 7, p 1, cols 6-7.

Anon, 1981, Vajpayee for Urgent Assam Assembly Meet, *Times of India* January 19, p 9, cols 4-5.

Anon, 1981, Vajpayee's Seven Point Formula on Assam, *Times of India* January 12, p 1, cols 4-5.

Anon, 1981, Violence Mars Third Phase of Assam Stir, *Times of India* December 1, p 1, col 7-8+.

Anon, 1981, What Is Happening in Assam, *Radical Humanist* 45 (10) January, p 37-39.

Anon, 1981, Zail Singh's Optimism, *Times of India* May 24, p 1, col 7.
Anon, 1982, Assam : CPI Stood against Chauvinism, *New Age* 30 (11) March 14, p 7.
Anon, 1982, Accord Likely on Assam Aliens Issue, *Times of India* September 7, p 1, cols 6-7+.
Anon, 1982, Another Popular Government, *Economic and Political Weekly* 17 (4) January 23, p 87.
Anon, 1982, Assam Leaders Reject New Formula, Talks End, *Times of India* November 10, p 1, col 1-3+.
Anon, 1982, Assam Ministry Faces No-Trust Motion, *Times of India* March 18, p 1, cols 7-8.
Anon, 1982, Assam Put under President's Rule, *Times of India* March 20, p 1, cols 4-5.
Anon, 1982, Assam Talks Again Reach a Deadlock, *Times of India* September 30, p 1, cols 2-3.
Anon, 1982, Assam Talks Fail To Make Headway, *Times of India* April 8, p 1, cols 7-8.
Anon, 1982, (Book Review), *Tribune* June 5, p 4, cols 3-7.
Review of the Book : Das, Amiya Kumar; n.d., *Assam's Agony* : A *Socio-Economic and Political Analysis*, Lancers Pub, New Delhi, p 372.
Anon, 1982, Centre May Not Call Off Assam Talks, *Times of India* June 16, p 7, col 1-2.
Anon, 1982, Central Rule May be Extended in Assam, *Times of India* November 2, p 1, cols 2-5.
Anon, 1982, Assam Talks Have Silver Lining, *Times of India* October 2, p 1, cols 5-6+.
Anon, 1982, Assam Talks Put Off Indefinitely, *Times of India* December 7, p 1, cols 2-3.
Anon, 1982, Assam to Go under President's Rule, *Times of India* March 19, p 1, cols 2-4+.
Anon, 1982, Assam Tripartite Adjourned, *Times of India* September 9, p 1, col 5-6+.
Anon, 1982, Concession to Assam Stir Leaders : Centre May Offer 1967 as Cut-Off Years, *Times of India* November 1, p 1, cols 2-4.
Anon, 1982, Elders Criticise Central Rule in Assam, *Times of India* March 30, p 15, cols 3-8.
Anon, 1982, Govt Firm on Keeping Aliens on Voter's List, *Times of India* September 29, p 1, cols 2-3.
Anon, 1982, GOI Not Interested in Permanent Solution of Assam Problem: AASU, *Organiser* 34 (21) October 10, p 16+.
Anon, 1982, Govt Optimistic about Assam Talks Outcome, *Times of India* September 27, p 1, cols 7-8+.
Anon, 1982, Govt Stand on Assam Aliens May be Modified, *Times of India* September 14, p 1, col 1-2+.
Anon, 1982, Hawks for Snapping Assam Talks, *Times of India* July 14, p 1, cols 2-4+.
Anon, 1982, High-Drama in Assam, *Link* 24 (34) April 4, p 29-30.
Anon, 1982, How GOI is Harassing Assam, *Organiser* 34 (26) November 14, p 3+.

Anon, 1983, The Guilty in Assam, *People's Democracy* 7 (9) February 27, p 1+.

Anon, 1983, Assam Tribunals for Foreigners Has Many Snags, *Radical Humanist* 48 (9) December, p 7-9.

Anon, 1983, (Book Review), *Indian Journal of Political Studies* 6-7, July, p 117-120.

Review of the Book : Murthy, T.S., 1983, *Assam : The Difficult Years,* Himalayan Book, New Delhi, 293 p.

Anon, 1983, Assam Tribunals To Speed Up Work : P.M., *Times of India* November 13, p 1, col 1-3+.

Anon, 1983, Bleeding Assam, *Illustrated Weekly of India* 104 (13) March (27), p 29.

Anon, 1983, (BOok Review), *Hindustan Times* (Magazine) March 22, p 4, col 78.

Review of the Book : Venkat Rao, V. and Hazarika, Nira, *A Century of Government and Politices in North East Asia, Assam,* 1974-80, S.Chand, New Delhi, vol-I, 281 p.

Anon, 1983, C.C. Resolutions on Assam, *People's Democracy,* 7 (16) April 17, p 3+.

Anon, 1983, CPI Call to Resume Assam.Dialogue, *New Age* 31 (28) July 10, p13.

Anon, 1983, Cong-I Conspiracy to Subvert Assam, *Organiser* 35 (30) December 11, p 1+.

Anandan, Sujata, 1983, Assam on Fire, *Illustrated Weekly of India* 104 (11) March 1, p 8-11.

Anon, 1983, Appeal of the Left Parties on the Assam Situation, *Call* 33 (5) June, p 18 -20.

Anon, 1983, Assam : Communalisation Enter AASU, *Mainstream* 21 (36) Many 7, p 9-10.

Anon, 1983, Assam : Danger Rightist Offensive, *Link* 25 (32) March 20, p 13-16.

Anon, 1983, Assam : Politicians Speak Out, *Illustrated Weekly of India* 104 (11) March 13, p 12-13.

Anon, 1983, Assam : Times for decisive Moves, *Mainstream* (Annual Number), p 93-97.

Anon, 1983, Assam Today, *People Democracy* 7 (39) September 25, p 9-10.

Anon, 1983, (Book Review), *Indian Express* May 29, p VI, cols 5-6.

Review of the Book : Murthy, T.S., n.d., *Assam : The Difficult Years,* Himalayan Pub House, Bombay, 293 p.

Anon, 1983, Left Parties Appeal on Assam, *People's Democracy* 7 (24) June 12, p 5+.

Anon, 1983, Left Parties Appeal To Save Assam, *New Age* 31 (24) June 12, p 8.

Anon, 1983, 'Martial Law' in Assam, *Organiser* 34 (43) March 13, p 1.

Anon,1983, The Need of the Hour, *Link* 25 (30) March 5, p 7.

Anon, 1983, Resume Talks : No Decision by Forces of Arms, *New Age* 31 (13) March 27, p 7.

Anon, 1983, Spils for Consolidation, *Economic and Political Weekly* 18 (35) August 27, p 1508.

Anon, 1983, Surrender a Damper to AASU, *Times of India* December 25, p 7, cols 3-5.

Anon, 1983, Thwarting Evil Designs, *Link* 25 (30) March 6, p 15-16.

Anon, 1983, When Will Death Dance Stop ? *Secular Democracy* April p 20-23.
Anon, 1983, The Assam Situation, *Call* 33 (2-3) March-April, p 3-4.
Anon, 1983, The Assam Outrage as Such Demands a Judicial Inquiry as Did Jallianwala, *Organiser* 34 (50) May 1, p 8-9.
Anon, 1983, Assam Movement : Back Ground of History, *Man and Development* 5 (2) June, p 118-125.
Anon, 1983 : Assam, Dirty Hand of RSS, *Illustrated Weekly of India* 104 (17) May, p 8-9.
Anon, 1984, Assam Talks To Begin Next Week, *Times of India* December 30., p 1, col 5-6+.
Anon, 1984, (Book Review), *Patriot* January 29, p 2, cols 5-6.
Review of the Book : Venkata Rao, and Hazarika, Niru, 1983, *A Century of Government and Politices in North East India, Assam* S.Chand, New Delhi, vol 1, 281 p.
Anon, 1984, CEC for Updating of 1971 Assam Rolls, *Times of India* January 29, p 1, cols 7-8+.
Anon, 1984, Showdown in Assam, *Janata* 39 (15) July 22, p 2-3.
Abdi S.N.M., 1985, Assam : A New Dimension, *Illustrated Weekly of India* 106 (26) November 3, p 34-35.
Anon, 1985, (Book Review), *National Herald* March 31, p 7, col 6-8.
Review of the Book : Bakshi, Reka, n.d., *Taming the Tempest* : *Assam Since*, 1983, Allied, New Delhi, 103 p.
Anon, 1985, (Book Review), *Seminar*, 308, April, p 42-45.
Review of the Book : Gupta, Shekhar, n.d., *Assam : A Valley Divided*, Vikas Pub, New Delhi.
Anon, 1985, (Book Review), *Sunday Statesman* February-April 21, p 11, cols 5-8.
Review of the Book : Bhawani Singh, n.d., *Politics of Alienation in Assam*, Ajanta Pub, Delhi, 140 p.
Anon, 1985, (Book Review), *Tribune* August 10, p 4, cols 5-8.
Review of the Book : Gohain, Hirendra Nath, n.d., *Assam : A Burning Question*, Spectrum Pub, Gauhati, 183 p.
Anon, 1985, End of the Assam Discord, *Organiser* 37 (15) August 25, p 1+.
Anon, 1985, Fresh Initiative on Assam Likely Soon, *Times of India* March 25, p 1, cols 2-3+.
Anon, 1985, Text of Assam Agreement, *Commerce* 151 (3874) August 24, p 364+; *Monthly Commentary on Indian Economic Conditions* 27 (1) August p 27-28.
Anon, 1985, Text of Chavan's Statement, *Economic Times* August 17, p 4, cols 5-8.
Anon, 1985, Text of Citizenship Bill, *Times of India* November 19, p 7, cols 1-3.
Anon, 1985, The Unwanted of Assam, *Economic and Political Weekly* 20 (34) August 24, p 1418.
Anon, 1985, Minority Front Leading to Communal Polarisation in Assam, *Organiser* 37 (28) November 24, p 1+.
Anon, 1985, CPI-M Fear Panic among Disenfranchised People, *Link* 28 (3) August 25, p 17.

Anon, 1985, Central Executive on Assam Punjab, *New Age* 33 (35) September 1, p 1+.

Anon, 1985, (Book Review), *India Quarterly* 41 (1) January-March, p 179-181.
Review of the Book : Murty, T.S, 1983, *Assam : The Difficult Years: A Study of Political Development* 1978-83, Himalayan Books, New Delhi, 293 p.

Anon, 1985, Assam Accord, *Times of India* September 4, p 8, col 6, letter to the Editor.

Anon, 1985, Assam Accord Worries Minorities, *Times of India* August 26, p 1, col 2-5.

Anon, 1985, Assam Assembly to be Dissolved, *Organiser* 37 (6) June 23, p 14-15.

Anon, 1985, Assam Citizenship Bill Passed, *Times of India* November 21, p 1, col 4-5.

Anon, 1985, Assam Ready for Poll ; AASU's New Political Ambitions, *Link* 28 (6) september 15, p 19-20.

Anon, 1986, Assam : Yesterday, Today and Tomorrow : A Symposium, *Parlance* 9 (12) September, p 5-34.

Anon, 1986, (Book Review), *Hindustan Times*, April 20, p 8, cols 1-2; *Organiser* 38 (2) May 25, p 6.
Review of the Book : Mahanta, Prafull Kumar, n.d., *The Tussle between the Citizens and Foreiners in Assam*, Vikas, New Delhi.

Anon, 1986, Centre Undermining Assam Accord to Topple AGP Ministry, *Organiser* 38 (8) July 6, p 1+.

Anon, 1987, Onus of Proof, *Times of India* August 22, p 6, col 1-2, editorial.

Anon, 1987, Assam Liberation Front Flirts with Naga Group and China, *Link* 29 (23) January 11, p 4-6.

Ali Omar, A., 1988, Assam Accord Implementation Makes Little Headway, *Economic Times* June 12, p 3, cols 1-6.

Anon, 1988, AASU-AGP Relations Turn Sour *Times of India* (Sec II) July 26, p 1, cols 2-5.

Anon, 1988, Factionalism Eroding the AGP., *Link* 31 (4) September 4, p 31.

Anon 1988, Assam Electoral Rolls Issue Hots Up *Link* 31(2) August 21, p 26-27.

Anon, 1989, Assam : ACP under Pressure, *Economic and Political Weekly* 24(8) February 25, p 399-400.

Anon, 1989, The Elephant Turns White, *Link* 31 (25) January 29, p 6-7.

Anon, 1992 Assam : Invoking NSA to Stifle Human Rights, *Economic and Political Weekly* 27 (33) August 15, p 1723-1724.

Anon, 1992, Autonomy Key to Solution of Assam Problems, *New Age*, 40 (39) September 27, p 7.

Anon, 1994, Winners and Losers, *Frontier* 26 (52) August 6, p 1-2.

Anon 1999, Assam Party Demands Resignation of Saikia Government, *New Age* 42(33) August 14, p 12.

Anon, 1995, Assam : Move for Separate Islami State : MLTA Join Hands with Other Muslim Outfits, *Organiser* 46 (28) February, 6, p 17.

Balasankar, R., 1984, Centre's Talk with AASU An Eyewash, *Organiser* 36 (19) September 23, p 3.

Balasankar, R., 1985, Assam Tribunals Have Detected Just One Foreign National, *Organiser* 36 (36) January 20, p 13.

Banerjee, Subrata, 1980, Assam Distrubances and the Sino-US Threat, *Secutar Democracy* 13(5) May, p 15-17.

Bara, Lily, 1980, The Assam Question : A Historical Perspective : A Comment, *Economic and Political Weekly* 15 (49) December 6, p 2063-2064.

Bargohain, Nirupama, 1980, Incidents in North Kamrup, *Economic and Political Weekly* 15 (20) May 17, p 878.

Barman, Promod, 1981, The Political Identity of Assam under the Indian Constitution, *Janata* 36 (10) April 19, p 3-5.

Borooah, Debo Prasad, 1983, The Assam Problem : An Analysis, *Interdiscipline* 15 (2) October, p 81-93.

Barooah, Debo Prasad, 1981, Mid Term Poll of the Seventh Lok Sabha and Assam, *Man and Development* 3(1) March] p 66-76.

Barua, Indrajit, 1984, Was the Assam Movement Really Necessary ? *Radical Humanist* 48 (6) September, p 16-18.

Baruah, Apurba Kumar, 1983, Assam Movement; Distortions in Analysis, *Man and Development* 5 (4) December, p 162-166.

Basavapunnaiah. M., 1984, On the Assam Electoral Rolls Issue, *People's Democracy* 8 (37) September 9, p 1-2.

Basu, Sajal, 1980, The Assam Question, *Janata* 35 (19) June 22, p 8, letter to the editor.

Bhatia, V.P., 1983, Foreigners in Control of Assam, *Organiser* 34 (50) 1, p 1+.

Bhatta, S., 1980, Assam : A Just Issue Exploited by Chauvinists and Communalists, *New Age* 28 (3) January 20, p 3+.

Bhattacharyya, 1972, Assam : New Chief Minister but Same Old Policies, *New Age* 20 (9) February 27, p 5.

Bhattacharyya, Achintya, 1979, Assam : Reactionary Forces Intensify Disruptionsit Campaigns, *People's Democracy* 3 (28) July 15, p1+.

Bhattacharyya, B.K., 1982, Assam Movement : Background of History, *Man and Development* 4 (3) September, p 9-15.

Bhattacharyya, B.K., 1982, Roots of Assam Movement, *Mainstream* 21 (31) November 27, p 9-11.

Bhattacharyya, M., 1965, Assam : Congress Group Wrangles Worsen, *New Age* 13 (18) May 2, p 2.

Bhattacharya, M., 1966, Assam : Chaliha Faces Rough Weather as Elections Approach, *New Age* 14 (21) May 22, p 8.

Bhattacharyya, M., 1971, Chief Minister Saves Face at Colleague's Expense, *New Age* 19 (23) June 6, p 10.

Bhattacharyya, M., 1972, Assam : Dissidents Pose Threat To New Chief Minister, *New Age* 20 (7) February, p 71.

Bhattacharyya, M., 1973, Joint Man Movement on Agreed Programme, *New Age* 21 (4) January 28, p 4.

Bhattacharyya, M., 1974, Faction-Ridden Assam Congress (I) : Equipped to Meet JP Threat, *New Age* 22 (52) December 29, p 5.

Bhattacharyya, M., 1975, Right Wing Forces Regroup in Assam, *New Age* 23 (13) March 30, p 13.

Bhattacharyya, M., 1978, Ministry Making Game in Assam, *New Age* 26 (15) April 9, p 13.

Bhattacharyya, M., 1979, Gaddi More Important than Humman Lives, *New Age* 27 (29) July 22, p 4.

Bhattacharyya, M., 1979, Assam : Toppling Game is on, *New Age* 27 (31) August 5, p 9.

Bhattacharyya, M., 1980, Undue Thai Interest in Assam, *New Age* 28 (26) June 29, p 8.

Bhattacharyya, M., 1982, 54 Bigger than 65 : Minority Cong-I Govt Foisted on Assam, *New Age* 30 (4) January 24, p 3.

Bhattacharya,Mudhusudan, 1966, Chaliha vs Barua : who will be C.M., *New Age* 14(41) October 9, p 10.

Bhattacharya, Mudhusudan, 1975, Stage Being Set for Rightist Stir in Assam *New Age* 23 (15) April 13, p 5.

Bhattacharya, Saurin, 1980, Agitation in Assam, *Call* 30 (7) March, p 6-8.

Bhaumik, Kirit, 1983, Assam : Agitators Losing Their Grip ? *Illustrated Weekly of India* 104 (4) January 23, p 19-21.

Bidwai, Praful, 1983, Assam on a Short Fuse : Roots of Popular Alienation, *Times of India* March 21, p 8, cols 3-5.

Bidwai, Praful, 1983, Tackling Assam's Real Issues, *Times of India* March 22, p 8, cols 7-8.

Bora, Devanand, 1980, Janata Party and the Assam Movement *Janata* 35 (42) December 14, p 10-11.

Bora, Devanand, 1980, A New Turn in Assam Movement, *Janata* 35 (20) June 29, p 7-8.

Bora, Devanand, 1981, Governing by Terror, *Janata* 36 (13) May 17, p 10.

Bora, Devanand, 1983, Reminiscences of saraighat and Burmese Invasions, *Janata* 38 (9) April 10, p 11-13.

Bora, Somnath, 1981, Assam : Seven Parties Launch Campaign, *New Age* 29 (10) March 8, p 2.

Borgohain, Drupad, 1988, Assam Accord : Both Parties Evade Job, *New Age* 36 (28) July 10, p 7.

Bose, Kunal, 1989, Simmering Discontent among Assam Hill Tribals, *Economic Times* April 2, p 3, col 1-6.

Call (Periodical), 1985, Assam and Punjab Accord, *Call* 1 (2) September-October, p 3-4, editorial.

Capital (Periodical), 1979, Anxiety over assam, *Capital* 183 (4586) December 17, p 1, editroial.

Capital (Periodical), 1980, Aimless in Assam, *Capital* 184 (4610) June 2, p 1, editroial.

Capital (Periodical) (1980), Assam and N.E. Region, *Capital* 185 (4631) November 10, p 1, editorial.

Chakravarty, Basudha, 1980, Moment of Truth in Assam, *Radical Humanist* 45 (7) October p 24-26.

Chakravorti, Rajagopal D., 1980, No Tailor-Made Solution to Assam Problem, *Capital* 185 (4621) August 18, p 6-7.

Chatterji, Dilip, 1980, The Assam Blockade, *Janata* 35 (9) April 6, p 14.

Chattoraj, Sumanta, 1984, Spatio-temporal Changes in Land-Man Ratio's in Assam, *National Geographer* 19 (1) January p 73-77, bibliography, figure, tables.

Choudhury, Shashanka, 1980, Assam : Distorting Facts, *Mainstream* 19 (15) December 13, p 32-33.

Chinal, Rupa, 1984, Assam : A House Divided, *Indian Express* August 19, p 6, cols 1-8.

Chinal, Rupa, 1986, The AGP Want Everyone to Adopt Assamese Culture, *Indian Express* (Magazine) July 13, p 3, cols 1-8.

Chopra, 1978, Assam Indira Congress Fans Chauvinism, *People's Democracy* 2 (46) November 12, p 11.

Chopra, 1982, The Assam Movement and the Left : A Reply to Hiren Gohain, *Social Scientist* 10 (11) November, p 63-70, footnotes.

Choudhury, Ronoo, 1980, the AssamMovement, *Radical Humanist* 44 (1) April, p 11-15.

Choudhury, Ronoo, 1983, Wither the Assam Movement, *Radical Humanist* 48 (1) April, p 31-35.

Choudhury, Sujit, 1985, Election Commission and the Assam Accord, *Economic and Political Weekly* 20 (29) December 7, p 2146-2147.

Choudhury, Sujit, 1986, Assam ; Quest for Homogeneity, *Mainstream* 25 (7) November 1, p 11-14.

Chowdhury, Dilip Ghosh, 1980, Minorities Feel Acute Insecurity, *New Age* 28 (23) June 8, p 4.

Commerce (Periodical), 1980, Assam : No Trial of Strength, *Commerce* 140 (3591) April 19, p 639, editroial.

Dandvate, Madhu, 1983, Assam, The Congress (1) Rule on the Debris of the Dead Bodies, *Janata* 38 (5) March 13, p 4.

Das, Sunil, 1981, The Assam Enigma : whose Identity at Stake ? *Janata* (Annual Number) 36 (1) February 8, p 37-44.

Dasgupta, Ananda, 1984, Assam : the Churning of a Cauldron, *Parlance* 7 (6-7) March-April, p 5-16.

Dasgupta, Barun, 1978, Assam Faces Instability, *Link* (Republic Day Number) 20 (25) January 26, p 57-59.

Dasgupta, Dwaipayan, 1980, Assam Student's Move to Stall Census Operation, *Organiser* 31 (48) April 20, p 5+.

Dasgupta, Prabhat, 1980, Assam Blockade Planned by Indira and Sanjay *New Age* 28 (14) April 6, p 2+.

Dayal, Johan, 1985, Assam Accord : An Era of Peace, Stability, *Link* 28 (8) August 25, p 15-16.

Deoras, Bala Saheb, 1980, Infiltration and Refugges Cannot be Put on Par, *Organiser* 31 (48) April 20, p 7.

Dev Dutta, 1980, Needed : Fresh Initiative in Assam, *Janata* 35 (16) June 1, p 3-4.

Dharma Viram 1980, National Integration : Assam Agitation, *Man and Development* 2 (2) June, p 104-107.

Dubey, S.M., 1980, The Assam Movement : a Preliminary Study in the Sociology of Politics and Development, *Man and Development* 2 (3) September, p 60-75, bibliography.

Dutta, S.K., 1970, the New Ministry in Assam : Stability Not in Doubt, *Times of India* November 23, p 8, cols 7-8.

Eastern Economist (Periodical), 1981, Dark Clouds over Assam; *Eastern Economist* 76 (15) April 10, p 943, editorial.

Economic and Political Weekly (Periodical), 1970, After Chaliha in Assam, *Economic and Political Weekly* 5 (45) November 7, p 1795-1796, editorial.

Economic and Political Weekly (Periodical), 1980, No End in Sight, *Economic and Political Weekly* 15 (35) August 30, p 1457-1458, editorial.

Economic and Political Weekly (Periodical), 1981, Assam Manoeuvres, *Economic and Political Weekly* 16 (13) March 28, p 541, editorial.

Economic and Political (Periodical), 1981 More Evasion, *Economic and Political Weekly* 16 (49) December 5, p 1969-1970, editorial.

Economic and Political Weekly (Periodical), 1981, Number Game, *Economic and Political Weekly* 16 (22) May 30, p 965-966, editorial

Economic and Political Weekly (Periodical), 1982, Escape through Election, *Economic and Political Weekly* 17 (33) August 14, p 1293, editorial.

Economic and Political Weekly (Periodical), 1988, Chance in Assam, *Economic and Political Weekly* 23 (44) October 28, p 2243, editorial.

Economic Times (Newspaper), 1979, The Assam Agitation, *Economic Times* December 9, p 5, col 1-2.

Economic Times (Newspaper), 1979, Confusion in Assam, *Economic Times* September 7, p 5, col 1-2, editorial.

Economic Times (Newspaper), 1979, Unrest in North-East, *Economic Times* Februaty 2, p 5, col 1-2, editorial.

Economic times (Newspaper), 1980, Assam : Bad to Worse, *Economic Times* November 26, p 5, col 1-2, editorial.

Economic Times (Newspaper), 1980, The Assam Blockade, *Economic Times* March 31, p 5, cols 1-2, editorial.

Economic Times (Newspaper), 1980, The Assam Question, *Economic Times* June 14, p 5, cols 1-2, editorial.

Economic Times (Newspaper), 1980, Assam Stalemate, *Economic Times* October 21, p 5, cols 1-2, editorial.

Economic Times (Newspaper), 1980, Assam Talks, *Economic Times* November 19, p 5, cols 1-2, editorial.

Economic Times (Newspaper), 1981, Assam : What Next; *Economic Times* April 2, p 5, cols 1-2, editorial.

Economic Times (Newspaper), 1982, Assam Violence, *Economic Times* January 6, p 5, cols 1-2, editorial.

Economic Times (Newspaper), 1983, Assam after Pollls, *Economic Times* March 8, p 7, cols 1-2, editorial.

Economic Times, 1985, Assam settlement, *Economic Times* August 17, p 5, cols 1-2, editorial.

Economic times (Newspaper) 1986, Times for Caution; *Economic Times* June 19, p 5, cols 1-2, editorial.

Economic Times (Newspaper) 1988, Oil Blockade, *Economic Times* March 2, p 6, col 1-2, editorial.

Economic Times (Newspaper) 1986, Time for Caution, *Economic Times* June 19, p 5, cols 1-2, editorial.

Fernandes, Geogre, 1980, A Spotlight on Assam Today, *Janata* 35 (19) June 22, p 5-7.

Gandhi Marg (Periodical), 1981, The Mulberry Bush, *Gandhi Marg* 3 (5) August, p 253-256, editorial.

Gandhi Marg (Periodical), 1985, Towards Peace in Assam, *Gandhi Marg* 7 (6) September p 323-326.

Gogoi, Promode, 1980, Assam Agitation Enters New Phase, *New Age*, 28 (47) November 23, p 6+.

Gogoi, Promode, 1981, CPI's Struggle for Solution of Assam Problem, *New Age* 29 (3) January 18, p 4+.

Gogoi, Promode, 1983, Assam Situation again Moving to Turmoil, *New Age* 31(36) September 4, p 9.

Gogoi, Promode, 1980, Now Is the Time to Settle Assam 'Foreigners' Agitation, *New Age* 28 (38) September 21,p 3+.

Gogoi, Promode, 1983, Assam Violence Continues, *New Age* 31 (15) April 10, p 5+.

Gogoi, Promode, 1983, Help to End Assam's Agony, *New Age* 31 (10) March 6, p 1-2.

Gogoi, Promode, 1983, Stakes in Assam, *Mainstream* 21 (52) August 27, p 14.

Gogoi, Promode, 1988, AGP Govt. in Crisis, *New Age* 36 (47) November 20, p 8.

Gohain, Hiren, 1977, Need for Democratic Unity, *Economic and Political Weekly* 12 (20) May 14, p 788-789.

Gohain, Hiren, 1980, Resisting Fascist Trend, *Mainstream* 18 (31) March 29, p 28.

Gohain, Hiren, 1982, Once More on the Assam Movement, *Social Scientist* 10 (11) November, p 58-62.

Gohain, Hiren, 1983, Assam Movement and the RSS, *Secular Democracy* (Independence Day Number 16 (7-8), p 73-76.

Gohain, Hiren, 1983, The labyrinth of Chauvinism, *Economic and Political Weekly* 18 (16-17) April 16-23, p 632-635.

Gohain, Hiren, 1980, Tangle Jargonised, *Economic and Political Weekly* 15 (32) August 9, p 1337-1338.

Gohain, Hiren, 1980, Tangled Theories, *Economic and Political Weekly* 15 (16) April 19, p 733-735.

Gohain, Hiren, 1980, Worse Times Ahead, *Economic and Political Weekly* 15 (50) December 21, p 2076-2078.

Goswami, Biswa, 1981, the Confrontation Policy in Assam, *Janata* 35 (43) December21, p 4-6.

Goswami, Biswa, 1982, Administration and People in Assam, *Janata* 36 (46) January 17, p 6..

Goswami, Dharani Dhar, 1985, The Role of the Assam Press in the Eighth Lok Sabha Elections, *Vidura* 22 (3) June, p 165-169.

Goyal, D.R., 1980, Reportage on Assam-4: Indira Gandhi : A Bad Coin, *Secular Democracy* 13 (5) May, p 24-27.

Guha, Amalendu, 1980, Little Nationalism Turned Chauvinist, *Economic and Political Weekly* (Special Number) 15, (41-43) October, p 1699-1720.

Guha, Amalendu, 1981, Little Nationalism turned Chauvinist, *Economic and Political Weekly* (Special Number) 16 (8) February 21, p 290-292; 16 (9) February 28, p 339-340; 16 (14) April 4, p 599-600; 16 (15) April 11, p 676-681; 16 (17) April 25, p 781-784; 16 (20) May 16, p 824; 16 (21) May 23, 957-964, footnotes.

Guha, Amalendu, 1983, Prelude to the Assam Tragedy : The Difficult Years 1979-83, *Link* 25 (33) March 27, p 38-40.

Guha, Seema, 1980, Union Bashing, *Economic and Political Weekly* 15 (33) August 16, p 1388-1389.

Guha, Seema, 1981, Once More unto the Breach, *Economic and Political Weekly* 16 (34) August 22, p 1379.

Guha, Seema, 1982, Contending Chauvinism, *Economic and Political Weekly* 17 (19) May 8, p 765-766.

Guha, Seema, 1956, AGP Still to find its Feet, *Times of India* November 26, p 8, cols 7-8.

Guha, Seema, 1986, Assamese Expect a Lot from AGP Government *Times of India* January 17, p 8, col 7-8.

Guha, Seema, 1987, Assam Imbroglio, *Economic Times* (Supplement) January 20, p 31, col 4-8.

Guha Barun Das, 1989, Assam Government in Crisis, *Mainstream* 27 (18) January 28, p 71-72.

Gupta, Bhupesh, 1980, Assam Imbroglio : Not this Agitation Negotiations Only Way, *New Age* 28 (23) June 8, p 3-4.

Gupta, Pannalal Das, 1983, Stakes in Assam, *Mainstream* 21 (37) May 14, p 6-7.

Gupta, S.K., Pattern and Characteristics of Migrants in Assam, *Journal of Sociological Studies* January 3, p 59-81, bibliography, footnotes, tables.

Gupta, S.N., 1983, Demand of Land from Bangladesh as Solution of the assam Tangle, *Organiser* 35 (2) May 29, p 6+, table.

Gupta, Shekhar, 1982, Assam Driven to Desperation, *Indian Express* (Magazine) July 25, p 11, col 1-8.

Gupta, Shekher, 1983, Battle for the Brahmaputra Valley, *Indian Express* (Magazine) February 13, p 1-8+.

Gupta, Shekher, 1983, On the Assam Beat, *Indian Express* (Magazine) July 3, p 3, col 1-8.

Gupta, Shekher, 1984, Assam's Darkness at Noon, *Indian Express* (Magazine) February 19, p 1, col 1-8+.

Hazarika, Sanjay, 1986, Assam; Full Circle, *Indian Express* (Magazine) January 19, p 2, col 1-5.

Hemendra Narayan, 1985, The Assam Accord Skimming over Troubled Water, *Indian Express* (Magazine) September 1,p 1, cols 6-8.

Hemendra Narayan, 1985, Taking Around in Circles, *Indian Express* May 5, p 8, cols 1-8.

Hemendra Narayan, 1986, The AGP Ministry : Teething Troubles, *Indian Express* (Magazine) March 30, p 1, cols 4-8+.

Hedge, Ramakrishna, 1980, The North-East on Fire, Assam Ablaze, *Janata* 35 (18) June 15, p 7-10.

Hiranyappa, G.S., 1983, Assam Going the Way of Sylhet, *Organiser* 34 (43) March 13, p 13.

Hurdels, 1980, National Consensus, *Link* 22 (44) June 8, p 16.

Inder Jit, 1980, 1980, Assam : Fresh Moves on Aliens, *Economic Times* November 11, p 5, cols 7-8.

Inder Jit, 1980, Assam : No Safety in Weekness, *Economic Times* February 12, p 5, cols 7-8.

Inder Jit, 1980, Assam : Playing with Fire, *Economic Times* May 13, p 5, cols 7-8.

Inder Jit, 1980, New Danger in North-East, *Economic Times* July 15, p 5, cols 7-8.

Inder Jit, 1981, Assam Deserves Better Deal, *Economic Times* January 6, p 5, cols 7-8.

Inder Jit, 1981, New Hurdles in Assam Talks, *Economic Times* July 7, p 5, cols 7-8.

Inder Jit 1981, Political Diary : Fresh Hopes on Assam, *Economic Times* May 12, p 5, cols 7-8.

Inder Jit, 1982, Assam Continues to Bleed, *Economic Times* January 12, p 5, cols 7-8.

Inder Jit, 1983, Assam Stir and Delhi's Apathy, *Economic Times* September 27, p 5, cols 7-8.

Inder Jit, 1983, Parliament Fails on Assam, *Economic Times* March 2, p 5, cols 7-8.

Inder Jit, 1985, Issues beyond the Assam Accord, *Economic Times* September 10, p 5, cols 7-8.

Inder Jit, 1985, People's Power Asserts in Assam *Economic Times* December 27, p 8, cols 7-8.

Inder Jit, 1989, Assam Accord is Not for Trifling, *Economic Times* January 10, p 5, cols 7-8.

Indian Express (Newspaper), 1978, Exit Borbora, *Indian Express* July 21, p 6, cols 1-2, editorial.

Jafa, Jyoti, 1983, Can These Gandhian Provide the Healing Touch ?, *Illustrated Weekly of India* 104 (17) May 15, p 11-13.

Janata (Periodical), 1980, The Assam, *Janata* 35 (410) April 13, p 1-2, editorial.

Janata (Periodical), 1980, In Assam, *Janaya* 35 (41) December 7, p 1, editorial.

Janata (Periodical), 1980, Lest It Be Forgotton, *Janata* 35 (25) August 3, p 1-2.

Janata (Periodical), 1981, A Danger Signal for Jorhat, *Janata* 36 (9), April 12, p 1-2, editorial.

Janata (Periodical), 1981, News from Assam, *Janata* 36 (6) March 22, p 1-2, editorial.

Janata (Periodical), 1982, Assam : The Straws in the Wind, *Janata* 36 (46) January 17, p 2, editorial.

Janata (Periodical), 1983, Assam *Janata* 38 (27) October 2, p 1-3, editorial.

Jansen, G.H., 1983, The Agony of Assam, *Illustrated Weekly of India* 104 (17) May 15, p 6-7.

Jaswant Singh, 1983, Assam : Night without End, *Illustrated Weekly of India* 104 (23) October, p 22-27.

Jaswant Singh, 1986, Assam : Since the Accord : Get Down to Work, *Times of India* August 6, p 8, cols 3-5.

Jatar, S.C.N., 1987, Wages of Fear, *Illustrated Weekly of India* 108 (46) November 29, p 28-29.

Joshi, Mahesh, 1980, Assam, India and Gandhi, *Mainstream* 18 (41) June 7, p 7-8+.

Kamaroopi, 1992, Now There, Now Not There, *Economic and Political Weekly* 27 (30) July 25, p 1593.

Kamath, M.V., 1980, Neglected Assam, *Illustrated Weekly of India* 101 (3) January 20, p 6-11.

Kamath, M.V., 1985, The End of the Assam Struggle, *Organiser* 36 (52) May 12, p 4.

Kamath, M.V., 1985, The Message from Guwahati, *Indian Express* (Magazine) May 12, p 11, cols 1-5.

Kar, M., 1980, Muslim Immigration to Assam, *Social Scientist* 8(7) February, p 67-75, footnotes.

Khanna, K.C., 1980, Renewed Agitation in Assam : Extremists Still Call the Shots, *Times of India* April 29, p 8, col 3-5.

Khanna, K.C., 1980, Sorry Bungling in Assam : Ambivalent Attitude of Authorities, *Times of India* May 13, p 6, cols 3-5.

Khanna, K.C., 1980, The Stalemate in Assam : Students Fighting a Lost Battle, *Times of India* May 13, p 6, cols 3-5.

Khanna, K.C., 1981, Uncertainty in Assam : Critical Role of Leftists, *Times of India* April 7, p 6, cols 3-5.

Khanna, K.C., 1985, Minefield of Uncertainties : The Assam Accord and After, *Times of India* August 20, p 8, cols 3-5.

Koutilya, Mitra, 1980, The Assam Agitation : For a Just Came, *Janata* 35 (28) August 31, p 7-9.

Gopal Krishna, 1983, Assam's Unending Tragedy : Where Do We Go from Here ? *Times of India* March 9, p 8, cols 3-5.

Link (Periodical) 1987, Assam Liberation Front Flirts with Naga Group and China, *Link* 29 (23) January 11, p 4-6.

Madani, Syed Asad, 1980, Assam and Socalled Foreign Nationals, *Secular Democracy* 13 (5) May, p 20-24.

Mahanta, Prafulla Kumar, 1980, Our Movement : Some Truths, *Man and Development* 2 (4) December, p 127-128.

Mahanta, Prafulla Kumar, 1987, Ushering in an Era of Peace, *Economic Times* (Supplement) January 20, p 10, col 1-4.

Mahanta, Prafulla Kumar, 1989, The Forces of Destruction, *Illustrated Weekly of India* 110 (20), May 14, p 26-27.

Mahanta, Prafulla Kumar and Hemendra Narayan, 1984, Saikia and the AASU: At Daggers Drawn, *Indian Express* (Magazine) January 8, p 3, col 1-8.

Mainstream (Periodical), 1980, Assam : Onset of Realism, *Mainstream* 18 (35) April 26, p 1-2.

Mainstream (Periodical), 1980, Trimurti : Dangerous Game, *Mainstream* 18 (31) March 29, p 1-2, editorial.

Mainstream, 1983, Assam : Night Must End, *Mainstream* 21 (31) April 2, p 1-2, editorial.

Maitra, Dilep, 1989, Assam Under Siege, *Business India* 295, June 26, p 52-54.

Maitra, Sankar N., 1980, Three Concrete Suggestions for Solving Assam 'Foreigners' Issue, *Organiser* 32 (15) August 31, p 8-9.

Malhotra, Inder, 1980, Tragic Impasse in Assam : How To Cut Gordian Knot, *Times of India* March 27, p 8, cols 3-5.

Malhotra, Inder, 1981, Running Sore in Assam : Distressing Intransigence, *Times of India* November 19, p 6, cols 3-5.

Malik, K.N., 1979, Regional Roots of Assam, Agitation, *Times of India* December 31, p 6, cols 7-8.

Malik, K.N., 1981, No Formula Yet to End Assam Impasse, *Times of India* August 18, p 9, col 1-2.

Malik, K.N., 1981, Govt Dragging Feet on Assam Meet, *Times of India* December 30, p 1, cols 1-4+.

Manda, Y.A., 1985, Unity, Intégrity and Harmony, *U.S.I. Journal*, 115 (482) October, December, p 293-307.
Mathur, Girish, 1985, Assam Polls and beyond : Uncertain Prospects, *Link* 28 (18) December 8, p 9-11.
Mazumdar, S.K., 1983, A 'Class' Was in Assam, *Link* 25 (46) June 26, p 17-22.
Mishra, Brahmanand, 1980, Sarvodaya Samaj Backs Assam, *Organiser* 32 (2) June 1, p 14.
Mishra, Brahmanand, 1980, Uneasy Calm after the Storm, *Commerce* 141 (3612) September 13, p 498.
Mishra, K.K., 1983, Assam : Return to Normalcy? *Mainstream* 21 (47) July 23, p 5-6.
Mishra, Prafulla, 1985, Assam Settlement Round the Corner, *New Age* 33 (32) August 11, p 1+.
Mishra Prafulla, 1987, Centre's Credibility Being Questioned, *New Age* 35 (22) May 31, p 12.
Misra, Prafulla, 1988, Assam : Mahanta Drops Bigwigs in Cabinet, *New Age* 36 (45) November 6, p 15.
Misra, Tilottoma, 1980, Assam : A Colonial Hinterland, *Economic and Political Weelky* 15 (32) August 9, p 1357-1364, footnotes.
Misra, Udayon, 1980, Worse than Emergency Days, *Economic and Political Weekly* 15 (16) April 19, p 731-732.
Misra, Udayon, 1981, Left Parties to Governments Rescue, *Economic and Political Weekly* 16 (15) April 11, p 651-652.
Misra, Udayon, 1983, Trends within the Left, *Economic and Political Weekly* 18 (31) July 30, p 1349-1350.
Misra, Udayon, 1985, From Mass Movement to Electoral Politics, *Economic and Political Weekly*, 20 (50) December 14, p 2190-91.
Mustafa, Seema, 1983, Neros Fiddle While Assam Burns, *Secular Democracy* March, p 5-7.
Mukherjee, Sadhan, 1982, Cong-I, Agitationist Interests Converge, *New Age* 30 (46) November 14, p 5.
Mukherjee, Sadhan, 1983, Assam Agitators with Mask Off, *New Age* 31 (9) February 27 p 1+.
Namboodiripad, E.M.S., 1980, Assam : Issues That Are Involved, *People's Democracy* 4 (39) September 28, p 1+.
Namboodiripad, E.M.S., 1981, Principled Stand of the Left in Assam, *People's Democracy* 5 (14) April 5, p 3+.
Nandy, Manish, 1980, Twiddling Thumbs while Assam Simmers, *Capital* 184 (4610) June 2, p 5.
New Age (Periodical), 1984, Consensus on Assam, *New Age* 32 (36) September 2, p 2, editorial.
Organiser (Periodical), 1984, Singnals from Assam : *Organiser* 36 (7) July 1, p 3, editorial.
Pal, Subrata, 1980, Total Bandh to Protest Violence on Minorities in Assam, *People's Democracy* 4 (22) June 1, p 9.
Pardesi, Ghanshyam, 1980, Assam Crisis : Dangerous Portents, *Mainstream* 18 (32) April 5, p 7-9.
Pardesi, Ghanshyam, 1980, Internal Colony in a National Exploitative System, *Economic and Political Weekly* 15 (23) June 7, p 1000-1002.

Pardesi, Ghanshyam, 1980, North-East : Issues for Next Round *Mainstream* 19 (6) October 11, p 5.

Pardesi, Ghanshyam, 1985, End of a Nightmore, *Illustrated Weekly of India* 106 (17) September 1, p 14-17.

Pardesi, Ghanshyam, 1986, Assam : Cauldron of Crisis, *Illustrated Weekly of India* 107 (27) July 6, p 40-41.

Pardesi, Ghanshyam, 1986, Assam : Language Politics, *Mainstream* 24 (42) June 21, p 8-9.

Pardesi, Ghanshyam, 1987, The Bubble Bursts, *Illustrated Weekly of India* 108 (5) February 1, p 30-31.

Patil, R.K., 1980, A Separate Kachar State, *Radical Humanist* 45 (6) September p 29-30.

People's Democracy (Periodical), 1980, After Resumption of Assam Agitation, *People's Democracy* 4 (47) November 23, p 1+, editorial.

People's Democracy (Periodical), 1980, Rally to Defeat the Recessionists, *People Democracy* 4 (29) July 20, p 1-2, editorial.

People's Democracy, (Periodical), 1980, Stand by the Minorities in Assam, *People's Democracy* 4 (22) June 1, p 1-2, editorial.

People's Democrat (Periodical), 1981, The Assam Talks, *People Democracy* 5 (21) May 24, p 1-2.

People's Democracy (Periodical), 1982, The Assam Talks, *People's Democracy* 6 (37) September 12, p 1+, editorial.

Phukan, Girin, 1981, Foreign National Issue, 1979-91 in Assam : A Colonial Legacy, *Man and Development* 3 (4) December, p 156-169.

Phukon, Girin, 1981, Assam's Plea for Dual Citizenship : Socio-Political Analysis of Attitude of Assamese Elite to the Question of Dual Citizenship during 1946-50, *Indian Political Science Review* 15 (2) July, p 151-157, footnotes.

Phukon, Girin, 1982, Assamese Demand for Provincial Autonomy, *Journal of State Politics and Administration*, 5 (1-2) January-December, p 33-44, bibliography.

Phukon, Girin, 1982, Assamese Demand for Provincial Autonomy : An Analysis of Constituent Assembly Debates, *Political Science Review* 21 (2-3) April-September, p 195-212, bibliography, footnotes.

Potar, Vibhuti, 1980, Another View of Incidents in North Kamrup, *Economic and Political Weekly* 15 (20) May 17, p 879.

Prabhu, A.N., 1985, One More Feather on Rajiv's Cap, *Economic Times* August 19, p 5, cols 7-8.

Prashant Kumar, 1983, Assam's Blood Bath, *Commerce* 146 (3743) February 26, p 341-342.

Puri, Balraj, 1980, Yet Another Approach to Assam, *Janata* 35 (24) July 27, p 3-5.

Radical Humanist (Pereodical), 1980, The Assam Movement, *Radical Humanist* 45 (4) July, p 2-4, editorial.

Radical Humanist (Periodical), 1981, The Assam Talks, *Radical Humanist* 46 (2) May, p 2-3, editorial.

Radical Humanist, 1983, What Next in Assam, *Radical Humanist* 48 (4) July, p 1-3, editorial.

Rai, Usha, 1981, Life in Assam-I : Surface Calm Hides Undercurrents, *Times of India* October 31, p 5, cols 2-5.

Rajeswara Rao, C., 1980, Situation in Assam is Explosive, *New Age* 28 (20) May 18, p 1-2.

Rajkhowa, Naresh, 1984, Assam : Turn in the Tide ? *Mainstream* 22 (26) February 25, p 33-34.

Ramamurti, P., 1980, Name the Foreign Agencies in Assam, *People's Democracy* 4 (25) June 22, p 5+.

Raman, J. Sri, 1985, Which 'Accord' Has Won in Assam? *Link* 28 (21) December 29, p 4-5.

Ramjee Singh, 1980, The Agony of Assam, *Gandhi Marg* 2 (6) September, p 341-348.

Reddi, P.S., 1981, Electoral Rolls with Special Reference to Assam, *Indian Journal of Political Science* 42 (1) January March, p 27-37, bibliography.

Roy Choudhury, Anil, 1981m National Register of Citizens 1951, *Economic and Political Weekly* 16 (8) February 21, p 267-268.

Roy Burman, B.K., 1983, Assam : A Case for Intellectuals' Intervention, *Mainstream* 21 (32) Aprol 9, p 6+.

Rustomji, K.F., 1982, Assam Agitation : Taking Wrong Turn ?, *Mainstream* 20 (19) January 9, p 5-6+.

Rustomji, Nari, 1983, Assam : The Roots of Discontent, *Indian Express* (Magazine) February 13, p 1, col 1-8+.

Sabherwal, O.P., 1984, Assam : No More Drift, *Mainstream* 22 (44) June 30, p 1-3.

Saksena, N.S., 1983, Many Facets of Assam Carnage, *Times of India* April 20, p 8, col 7-8.

Sardesai, S.G., 1980, Meaning of Assam, *Mainstream* (Annual Number) 19 (1-5), p 29-33.

Sethi, H.S., 1983, Assam Imbroglio : Foreigners Stand between Poll and Peace, *Illustrated Weekly of India* 104 (4) January 23, p 16+.

Sarker, Subhash Chandra, 1983, The Greek Tragedy of Assam, *Commerce* 146 (3743) February 26, p 334-341.

Shamlal, 1980, The National Scene : Has This Sickness a Name? *Times of India* August 30, p 8, col 3-5.

Shamlal, 1980, The National Scene : Limits to Peaceful Protest, *Times of India* May 3, p 6, col 3-5.

Shamlal, 1980, The National Scene : A Touch of the Maniacal, *Times of India* July 12, p 6, col 3-5.

Sharma, K.M., 1980, The Assam Question : A Historical Perspective, *Economic and Political Weekly* 15 (31) August 2, p 1321-1324.

Sharma, Kalpana, 1984, Assam : An Uneasy Calm, *Indian Express* (Magazine) December 16, p 111, col 1-8+.

Sharma, Kalpana, 1985, The Assam Accord : Skimming over Troubled Waters, *Indian Express* (Magazine) September 1, p 1, col 1-5.

Sharma, Kamaleswari Prasad, 1983, When Helicopters Supplied Arms to Foreigners in Assam *Organiser* 34 (44) March 20, p 8.

Shourie, Arun, 1985, New Tasks for a New Situation, *Illustrated Weekly of India* 106 (22) October 6, p 20-23.

Singh, B.R., 1984, Perspectives for Assam, *Mainstream* 22 (48) July 28, p 27-32.

Sinha, Purna Narain, 1980, India Must Save Assam, *Organiser* 32 (1) May 25, p 8-9+.

Sinha, S.C., 1972, Choudhury Resigns as Assam CM : *Times of India* January 30, p 1, cols 1-3.

Sudershan, K.S., 1980, Assam Crisis Culmination of 30 Year Congress Bungling, *Organiser* 31 (47) April 13, p 7-8+.

Suri, Surindar, 1984, Heartbreak in Gauhati : A Challenge to All Indians, *Times of India* February 8, p 8, col 3-5.

Suri, Surindar, 1985, Resolving the Assam Problem : Students' Leaders Are Ready, *Times of India* January 28, p 8, cols 3-5.

Suri, Surindar, 1986, Assam : A New Era or a False Dawn ? *Link* 28 (25) January 26, p 38-40.

Surjeet, Harkishan Singh, 1980, Assam : Find a National Solution : Eschew Narrow Political Ends, *People's Democracy* 4 (7) February 17, p 7.

Surjeet, Harkishan Singh, 1983, What is Going to Happen in Assam, *People's Democracy* 7 (14) April 3, p 1+; 7 (15) April 10, p 5; 7 (16) April 17, p 6; 7 (17) April 24, p 8-9.

Surjeet, Harkishan Singh 1984, A Rational Solution of Assam Problem, *People's Democracy* 8(32) August 5, p1+.

Swell, G.G., Options after Assam Poll, *Times of India* December 27, p 8, cols 7-8.

Taban, Ghulam Rabbani, 1980, RSS Nefarious Game, *Secular Democracy* 13 (6) June, p 37-38.

Thapar, Romesh, 1980, Assam and Delhi, *Economic and Political Weekly* 15 (19) May 10, p 835.

Tharyan, P., 1982, Assam Solving the Jigsaw, *Hindustan Times* (Magazine) March 14, p 1, cols 1-8+.

Times of India (Newspaper), 1972, A New Look, *Times of India* February, 1, p4, col 1 editorial.

Times of India (Newspaper), 1978, Ominous, *Times of India* September 16, p 6, col 1, editorial.

Times of India (Newspaper), 1978, Alines in Assam, *Times of India* October 11, p 8 col 1-2, editorial.

Times of India (Newspaper), 1979, Collapse of Authority, *Times of India* December 12, p 6, col 1-2, editorial.

Times of India (Newspaper) 1979, Confusion in Assam, *Times of India* Septermber 7, p 6, col 1-2, editorial.

Times of India (Newspaper), 1979, End this Agony, *Times of India* November 23, p 8, col 1-2, editorial.

Times of India (Newspaper) 1979, On His Own, *Times of India* April 23, p 6, cols 1-2, editorial.

Times of India (Newspaper 1979, Testing Times in Assam, *Times of India* December 14, p 8, cols 1-2, editorial.

Times of India (Newspaper) 1980, Assam Stalemate, *Times of India* July 12, p 6, cols 1-2, editorial.

Times of India (Newspaper), 1980, Intransigent Still, *Times of India* April 15, p 8, cols 1-2, editorial.

Times of India (Newspaper), 1980, A Minor Setback, *Times of India* Augest, p 6, cols 1-2, editorial.

Times of India (Newspaper), 1980, New Assam Ministry, *Times of India* December 9, p 6, cols 1-2, editorial.

Times of India (Newspaper), 1980, New Danger in Assam, *Times of India* December 25, p 8, cols 1-2 editorial.

Times of India (Newspaper), 1980, On a Collision Course, *Times of India* March 21, p 8, col 1-2, editorial.

Times of India (Newspaper) 1980, Pros and Cons, *Times of India* November 25, p 8, col 1-2, editorial.

Times of India (Newspaper), 1980, Regrettable, *Times of India* October 18, p 6, col 1-2, editorial.

Times of India (Newspaper) 1980, Stalemate in Assam, *Times of India* March 14, p 6, cols 1-2, editorial.

Times of India (Newspaper), 1980, Too Clever by Half, *Times of India* July 22, p 6, cols 1-2, editorial.

Times of India (Newspaper), 1980, Towards a compromic, *Times of India* April 3, p 6, cols 1-2, editorial.

Times of India (Newspaper), 1981, Bipartrian Approach, *Times of India* December 12, p 8, cols 1-2, editorial.

Times of India (Newspaper), 1981, Mrs Taimur Quits, *Times of India* June 30, p 6, cols 1-2, editorial.

Times of India (Newspaper), 1981, No Came for Gloom, *Times of India* July 18, p 6, cols 1-2, editorial.

Times of India (Newspaper), 1981, Not By Confrontation, *Times of India* December 7, p 6, cols 1-2, editorial.

Times of India (Newspaper), 1981, Sense About Assam, *Times of India* January 13, p 8, cols 1-2, editorial.

Times of India (Newspaper), 1981, So Near, Yet So Far, *Times of India* August 26, p 6, cols 1-2.

Times of India (Newspaper), 1981, Still in a Mess, *Times of India* April 4, p 6, cols 1-2, editorial.

Times of India (Newspaper), 1981, Still in the Woods, *Times of India* March 26, p 6, cols 1-2, editorial.

Times of India (Newspaper), 1980, Terror in Assam, *Times of India* May 28, p 6, cols 1-2, editorial.

Times of India (Newspaper) 1982, The Assam Stalemate, *Times of India* November 12, p 8, cols 1-2, editorial.

Times of India (Newspaper) 1982, Continuing Tension, *Times of India* July 2, p 8, cols 1-2, editorial.

Times of India, 1983, Assam's Refugees, *Times of India* March 17, p 8, cols 1-2, editorial.

Times of India, 1983, Explosion in Assam, *Times of India* November 12, p 8, cols 1-2, editorial.

Times of India, 1983, The Image Breakers, *Times of India* May 6, p 8, cols 1-2, editorial.

Times of India, 1983, It's a National Task, *Times of India* April 22, p 8, cols 1-2, editorial.

Times of India, 1983, Next Step in Assam, *Times of India* April 5, p 6, cols 1-2, editorial.

Times of India (Newspaper) 1983, Opportunity in Assam, *Time of India* March 29, p 8, cols 1-2, editorial.

Times of India (Newspaper) 1983, Round One To Mr. Saikia, *Time of India* July 15, p 6, cols 1-2, editorial.

Goswami, Atul, 1970-72, Prices and Cost of Living in Assam in the Last Decade (1960-70), *Journal of University of Gauhati* 21-23 (1), p 142-157, tables.

Goswami, Atul, 1977, Seasonal Variation in Assam's Wholesale Prices, 1954-70, *Assam Economic Journal* 3 (1) March, p 12-20, bibliography.

Kalita, Gobinda, 1980, Prices Jacked Up under Pretext of Agitation, *New Age* 28 (26) June 29, p 9.

Primary Education

Anon, 1981, Primary Education Coverage yet to Make Headway in Assam, *Economic Times* July 7, p 7, cols 5-8.

Prisoners

Anon, 1992, Assam : Invoking NSA to Stifle Human Rights, *Economic and Political Weekly* 27 (33) August 15, p 723-24.

Prohibition

Bhuyan, P.K., 1977, Excise Revenue in Assam, 1951-52 to 1965-66 and Prohibiting Policy, *Assam Economic Journal* 3 (1) March, p 81-90.

Property Tax

Bezborah, 1991, Municipal Property Tax : Some Issue, *Assam Economic Journal* 8, p 65-73, bibliography.

Psyciatric Hoapitals

Anon, 1976, Treating Mental Discorders, *Link* 18 (35) April 11, p 19.

Public Administration

Anon, 1970, First Report of the O and M Division of the Government of Assam, *Journal of National Academy of Adminstration* 15 (1) January-March, p 143-148.

Public Distribution System

Anon, 1978, Towards Checking the Price Hike : A New System of Public Distribution Introduced in *Assam Information*, 30 June-July, p 6-8.

Hazarika, Jatin, 1975, Introduction of New Public Distribution through Co-Operatives : Begining of Economic Revolution in Assam, *Assam Information* 27 (5-6) August-September, p 36-40.

Trivedi, P.P., 1976, Procurement and Distribution of Essential Commodities, *Times of India* November 20, p 13, cols 1-3.

Public Finance

Anon, 1972, Assam : No Clear Plans and Programmes, *Link* 14 (36) April 16, p 15.

Baisya, K.N., 1985, State Financing for Industrial Growth and Assam Financial Corporation, *Lok Udyog* 19 (9) December, p 31-37, bibliography, tables.

Sarangapani, S., 1975, Resource Mobilsation by State (1950-51 to 1974-75), *Commerce* 131 (3357) September 20, p 18-19.

Public Sector Enterprises

Sarmah, S.R., 1988, Personnel Policies Sector of Assam, *Indian Journal of Commerce* (Section II) 41 (1) January-March, p 79-81.

Public Service Commission

Anon, 1985, (Book Review), *Indian Journal of Public Administration* 31 (2) April-June, p 441-442.
Review of the Book : Hazarika, Niru 1979, *Public Service Commission*, Leeladevi Pub, Delhi, 200 p.

Raichoudhuri, Ambikagiri

Sarma, Satyendranath, 1986, Ambikagiri Raichoudhuri : His Life and Work, *Indian Literature* 29 (3) May-June, p 107-114.

Railways

Barua, K.C., 1979, Railways and the People of Assam, *Janata* 34 (10) April 8, p 9-10.

Rationing : Consumer

See Public Distribution System

Regional Planning

Gogoi, Jayanta Kumar, 1977, Construction of Composite Indices to Measure Levels of Development : A Review of the Methods of Analysis, *Assam Economic Journal* 3 (1) March, p 55-61, bibliography.

Refugees

Anon, 1993, Twenty Five Constituencies Show an Increase of 20 Per Cent in One Year, *Organiser* 44 (34) March 28, p 5.

Reorganization

Anon, 1966, Autonomy for the Hills, *Captial* 157 (3921) July 28. p 169-170.

Anon. 1966, Mistrust in the Hills, *Captial* 157 (3926) September 1, p 485-487.

Anon, 1972, Not to be Deserted, *Economic and Political Weekly* (Annual Number) 7 (5-7) February, p 193-199.

Bhatta, Suren, 1964, Nehru Plan for Assam : Hills People Demand Important Charges, *New Age* 12 (5) February 2, p 13.

Bhattacharya,M., 1964, Welcome Relief from Stalemate in Hill Dists., *New Age* 12 (19) May 10, p 8.

Bhattacharya, M., 1966, Background to Disturbances in Mizo District, *New Age* 14 (11) March 13, p 3.

Research

Goswami, A.K., 1978, Effort Does Not Match Challenge, *Commerce* (Annual Number) 137 (3526), P 211-213.

Rice

Anon, 1973, Plans for Machinery for Rice Take-Over, *Commerce* 127 (3255) September 22, p 588-489.

Goswami, Atul, 1970-72, Prices and Cost of Living in Assam in the Last Decade (1960-70), *Journal of University of Gauhati* 21-23 (1), p 142-157, tables.

Goswami, Atul, 1977, Seasonal Variation in Assam's Wholesale Prices, 1954-70, *Assam Economic Journal* 3 (1) March, p 12-20, bibliography.

Kalita, Gobinda, 1980, Prices Jacked Up under Pretext of Agitation, *New Age* 28 (26) June 29, p 9.

Primary Education

Anon, 1981, Primary Education Coverage yet to Make Headway in Assam, *Economic Times* July 7, p 7, cols 5-8.

Prisoners

Anon, 1992, Assam : Invoking NSA to Stifle Human Rights, *Economic and Political Weekly* 27 (33) August 15, p 723-24.

Prohibition

Bhuyan, P.K., 1977, Excise Revenue in Assam, 1951-52 to 1965-66 and Prohibiting Policy, *Assam Economic Journal* 3 (1) March, p 81-90.

Property Tax

Bezborah, 1991, Municipal Property Tax : Some Issue, *Assam Economic Journal* 8, p 65-73, bibliography.

Psyciatric Hoapitals

Anon, 1976, Treating Mental Discorders, *Link* 18 (35) April 11, p 19.

Public Administration

Anon, 1970, First Report of the O and M Division of the Government of Assam, *Journal of National Academy of Adminstration* 15 (1) January-March, p 143-148.

Public Distribution System

Anon, 1978, Towards Checking the Price Hike : A New System of Public Distribution Introduced in *Assam Information*, 30 June-July, p 6-8.

Hazarika, Jatin, 1975, Introduction of New Public Distribution through Co-Operatives : Begining of Economic Revolution in Assam, *Assam Information* 27 (5-6) August-September, p 36-40.

Trivedi, P.P., 1976, Procurement and Distribution of Essential Commodities, *Times of India* November 20, p 13, cols 1-3.

Public Finance

Anon, 1972, Assam : No Clear Plans and Programmes, *Link* 14 (36) April 16, p 15.

Baisya, K.N., 1985, State Financing for Industrial Growth and Assam Financial Corporation, *Lok Udyog* 19 (9) December, p 31-37, bibliography, tables.

Sarangapani, S., 1975, Resource Mobilsation by State (1950-51 to 1974-75), *Commerce* 131 (3357) September 20, p 18-19.

Public Sector Enterprises

Sarmah, S.R., 1988, Personnel Policies Sector of Assam, *Indian Journal of Commerce* (Section II) 41 (1) January-March, p 79-81.

Public Service Commission

Anon, 1985, (Book Review), *Indian Journal of Public Administration* 31 (2) April-June, p 441-442.
Review of the Book : Hazarika, Niru 1979, *Public Service Commission*, Leeladevi Pub, Delhi, 200 p.

Raichoudhuri, Ambikagiri

Sarma, Satyendranath, 1986, Ambikagiri Raichoudhuri : His Life and Work, *Indian Literature* 29 (3) May-June, p 107-114.

Railways

Barua, K.C., 1979, Railways and the People of Assam, *Janata* 34 (10) April 8, p 9-10.

Rationing : Consumer

See Public Distribution System

Regional Planning

Gogoi, Jayanta Kumar, 1977, Construction of Composite Indices to Measure Levels of Development : A Review of the Methods of Analysis, *Assam Economic Journal* 3 (1) March, p 55-61, bibliography.

Refugees

Anon, 1993, Twenty Five Constituencies Show an Increase of 20 Per Cent in One Year, *Organiser* 44 (34) March 28, p 5.

Reorganization

Anon, 1966, Autonomy for the Hills, *Captial* 157 (3921) July 28 p 169-170.
Anon. 1966, Mistrust in the Hills, *Captial* 157 (3926) September 1, p 485-487.
Anon, 1972, Not to be Deserted, *Economic and Political Weekly* (Annual Number) 7 (5-7) February, p 193-199.
Bhatta, Suren, 1964, Nehru Plan for Assam : Hills People Demand Important Charges, *New Age* 12 (5) February 2, p 13.
Bhattacharya,M., 1964, Welcome Relief from Stalemate in Hill Dists., *New Age* 12 (19) May 10, p 8.
Bhattacharya, M., 1966, Background to Disturbances in Mizo District, *New Age* 14 (11) March 13, p 3.

Research

Goswami, A.K., 1978, Effort Does Not Match Challenge, *Commerce* (Annual Number) 137 (3526), P 211-213.

Rice

Anon, 1973, Plans for Machinery for Rice Take-Over, *Commerce* 127 (3255) September 22, p 588-489.

Anon, 1974, Wholesale Take Over the Rice, *Assam Information* 25 (1-3) April-June, p 9-11.

Bhattacharyya, M., 1974, Assam Goes Back on Rice Trade Take-Over, *New Age* 22 (46) November 17, p 12.

Biswas, Rashbihari, 1971, A Study of Operational Cost of Cultivation of Paddy in Assam, *Economic Affairs* 16 (11) November, p 481-484, tables.

Dutta, S.K., 1974, Rice Price Rises in Assam after Take-Over of Wholesale Trade, *Times of India* January 25, p 4, col 7-8+.

Goswami, ATUL, 1978, Public Procurement and Distribution of Rice in Assam : A Critical Review, *Assam Economic Journal* 4(1) March, p 38-58, appendix, bibliography, tables.

Goswami, P.C. and Bora, C.K., 1974, Cultivation of Jute Vis-a-vis Autumn Paddy in Assam : A Case Study in Nowgong District, *Indian Journal of Agriculture Economics* 29 (3) July-September, p 147-154, tables.

Goswami, P.C. and Gogoi, J., 1971, Effect of Price on Cultivation and Disposal of Paddy and Jute (A Case Study of Nowgong District in Assam), *Indian Journal of Agricultural Economics* 26 (4) October-December, p 435-444, tables.

Kakati, N.N. and Borthakur, D.N., 1971, research on Rice in Relation to the Problem of Flood-Affected Areas in Assam, *Indian Farming* 21 (7) October, p 101-103.

Sen, Kranti, 1975, Rice Procurement and State Trading, *Mainstream* 13 (19) January 11, p 15-16.

Riots

Anon, 1972, Diagnosis of Assam Riots, *Link* 15 (11) October 22, p 13-14.

Anon, 1974, Gujarat Type Agitation By Students ? *Commerce* 128 (3289) May 25, p 744

Economics Studies (Periodical), 1972, Red Rivers and Blue Hills, *Economics Studies* 13 (5) November, p 225-226.

Roads

Barua, Dulal, 1979, Gigantic Task of Road Construction, *Times of India* March 29, p 10, cols 5-8+.

Roads : Rural

Anon, 1980, Assam World Bank Assistance or Rural Development, *Commerce* 140 (3588) March 29, p 521-522.

Rural Conditions

See also Debts : Rural

Anon, 1980, Plan Has No Inpact on Rural Assam *Economic Times*, January 29, p 5, cols 7-8.

Bhadra, Ranjit K., 1979, Emerging Patterns of Agrarian Class in Rural Assam, *Eastern Anthropologists* 32 (4) October-December. p 272-285, bibliography, tables.

Bhadra, Ranjit K., 1979, Rural Class Structure in Post Independence Assam, *Economic and Political Weekly* 14 (4) January 27, p 165-167.

Chauhan, S.K., 1972, Status, Power and Institutions : A Test Covergence Hypothesis, *Interdiscipline* 9 (4) Winter, p 27-41, tables.

Dutta, P.C., 1974, Rural Change in Two Decades : A Case Study *Kurukshetra* 22 (8) January 16, p 9-10, tables

Hegde, D.V., 1980, Assam Leads in Rural Inflation, *Economic Times* August 8, p 1, cols 1-5.

Saikia, Abdul Motlib, 1975, Stablising Rural Economy, *Link* 17 (21) January 5, p 35-36.

Sarma, Joykanta, 1979, Barrier to Rural Development, *Economic and Political Weekly* 14 (4) January 27, p 133-135.

Sinha, Sarat Chandra, 1974, New Strategy for Rural Development in Assam, *Assam Information* 25 (1-3) April-June, p 1-5+.

Rural Electrification

Nego, Jiterdra Nath, 1978, Power Generation and Rural Electrification in, *Assam Information*, 30 December, p 29-31.

Rural Industries

Anon, 1978, Government Support to Khadi Board Withdrawn, *Commerce* (Supplement) 137 (3506) August 19, p 23-24.

Anon, 1982, (Book Review), *Yojana* 26 (10) June 1, p 37.
Review of the Book : Dutta, A.K., n.d., *Industrial Potential in Cachar Rural Industrialisation* : A Souvenir, Ramakrishna College, Cachar, 49 p.

Sarma, Nagen

Chinai, Rupa, 1986, Two or Three Murder Cases are Normal in Most States, *Indian Express* (Magazine) March 30, p 4, cols 5-8.

Scheduled Caste and Scheduled Tribes

Anon, 1974, Welfare of Backward Classes in Assam, *Assam Information* 25 (6) September, p 1-7.

Anon, 1977, Assam : Servere Handicaps, *Link* 20 (8) October 2, p 19-20.

Sculpture

Anon, 1985, (Book Review), *Sunday Statesman* September 1, p 13.
Review of the Book : Bhattacharjee, Arun, n.d., *Icons and Sculpturs of Early and Medieval Assam*; Inter-India Pub., New Delhi.

Bhuvan, G.N., 1974, A Survey of the Ahom Sculptures, *Journal of the Assam Research Society*, 22, p 40-48.

Vatsyayan, Kapila, 1981, Some DAnces Sculptures from Assam, *Quarterly Journal of the National Centre of the Performing Arts* 10 (3) September, p 19-35, bibliography, footnotes, illustrations.

Sericulture

Anon, 1981, Reorientation of Sericulture in Assam, *Assam Information* 32 January-March, p 22-31+.

Seventh Five Plan

Anon, 1985, Assam : Seventh Plan Push towards Industry, *Capital* 194 (4801) April 1, p 41-42.

Misra, Prafulla, 1985, Assam : Inadequate Plan Allocation, *New Age* 32 (28) July 14, p 11.

Sikidar, Sujit, 1985, Seventh Plan Fails To Trackle Special Problems, *Commerce* 151 (3873) August 17, p 299-301+.

Shifiting Cultivation

Sharma, Naba, 1988, Clinging to Age-Old Tradition, *Economic Times* (Supplement) October 7, p 7, cols 5-8.

Shrines : Sikh

Anon, 1975, A Short Note about Siri about Takht Harimandir Jie Sahib Patna Sahib, *Punjab Past and Present* 9 (11) April, p 134-136.

Sikhism

Singh, R., 1975, Sikhs and Assam, *Assam Information* 27 (9-10) October-November, p 33-40.

Silk Manufacture and Trade

Sengupta,Ashok, 1979, Sualkuchi's Silky Path to Success *Maharashtra Coorperatives Quarterly* 63 (2) October, p 86-88.

Sixth Five Year Plan

Anon, 1983, Assam Needs More Found Urgently, *Economic Times* July 8, p 8, col 4-8.

Small Scale Industries

Anon, 1976, Development of Small Scale Industries in Assam, *Assam Information* January-March, p 5-10.

Anon, 1979, Ancillary Units in Assam Make No. Headway, *Economic Times* October 25, p 3, cols 1-4.

Anon, 1985, Boosting Assam's Small Scale Industries, *Commerce* 150 (3847) February 16, p 323-324.

Anon, 1985, Langushing Small Sector of the North-East, *Capital* 195 (4813) September 2, p 17-18.

Das, J.C., 1976, Development of Small Scale Industries in the Hill District of Assam, *Assam Information* January-March, p 34-39.

De, Ranabijoy, 1991, Sichness in Small Industry : A Case Study, *Assam Economics Journal* 8, p 54-64, bibliography, tables.

Social Classes

Anon, 1982, (Book Review), *Eastern Anthropologist* 35 (4) October-December, p 355-356.
Review of the Book : Chauhan, S.K., 1980, *Caste-Status and Power Social Stratification in Assam*, New Delhi, Classical Publication

Social Conditions

See also Caste

Anon, 1978, Unscholarly Chauvinist, *Economic and Political Weekly* 13 (45) November 11, p 1843-1845.

Anon, 1985, Why Polls Cannot Answer Assam's Social Question, *Link* 28 (20) December 22, p 8-10.

Anon, 1988, (Book Review), *Sunday Statesman* (Misc) February 7, p 13, cols 1-5.

Review of the Book : Misra, Tillotama, n.d., *Literature and Society in Assam,* Omsons Pub.

Das, J.N., 1976, Social Changes in an Orderly way, *Times of India* November 20, p 10. col 5-8.

Dutta, Pulakesh, 1987, Socio-Economic Problem of Assam : A Diagnostic Appriasal, *National Geographer* 22 (1) June, p 29-36, bibliography.

Goswami, M.C., 1966, Caste and Occupation in an Assamese Village, *Man in India* 46 (3) July-September, p 191-197, tables.

Naidu, N.Y., 1980, Community Participation and Socio-Economic Status, *Rural Devel, Digest* 3 (1) January p 8-18, footnotes.

Social Condition : History

Goswami, Shruti Dev, 1982, The Opium in Nineteenth Century Assam, *Indian Economic and Social History Review* 19 (3-4) July-December, p 365-376.

Sarma, Nabin Ch., 1985, Folk Epic and Its Impact on Early Assamese Life, *Folklore* 26 (9) September, p 161-169.

Sarma, S.N., 1977-78, Social Changes in Assam, 1750-1950, *Journal of the University of Gauhati* (Arts) 28-29, p 109-121, footnotes.

Sarma, Nabis Ch., 1985, Folk Epic and Its Impact on Early Assamese, *Folklore* 26 (9) September, p 161-169.

Times of India (Newspaper), 1978, Academic Bigotry, *Times of India* December 2, p 6, col 1.

Social Education

Anon, 1964, Pattern of a State Programme : Social Education Activities in Assam, Indian *Journal of Adult Education* 25 (4) April, p 6.

Social Mobility

Anon, 1985, (Book Review), *Hindustan Times* (Magazine) January 6, p viii, cols 1-6 .

Review of the Book : Dev, Bimal J., and Lahiri, Dilip K., n.d., *Cosmogony of Caste and Social Mobility on Assam,* Mittal Pub, Delhi, 183 p.

Chauhan, S.K., 1972, Social Mobility in Upper Assam : A Note on Sanskritisation, *Social Action* 22 (3) July-September, p 231-236, bibliography.

Dev, Bimal J., Lahiri, Dilip K., 1981, The Naths of Assam : The Dilemma of Social Mobility, *Social Action* 31 (3) July-September, p 311-324, footnotes.

Social Policy

Saikia, Hiteswar, 1976, Changes in Socio-Economic Scene, *Link* 18 (48) July 11, p 17-19.

Social Service

Anon, 1975, Welfare Activites in Darrang District, *Assam Information* 27 (5-6) August-September, p 29-31.

Soil Conservation

Anon, 1975, Small Project with Big Promise : Soil Conservation in Assam, *Assam Information* 27 (9-10) October-November, p 54-56.

Soils

Sen, T.K., 1992, Satellite Remote Sensing in Soil Resourace Inventroy of Dibrugarh District (Part), Assam, *Photonirvachak* 10 (2-3) June-September, p 95-104, bibliography, tables.

Standered of Living

Anon, 1975, Call for Serious Concerted Efforts to Maintain Economic Stability and Progressively Raise the Standerd of Living of the Common People, *Assam Information* 25 (10-12) January-March, p 1-16+.

State Electricity Board

Anon, 1977, Assam Power Men's Demands, *Link* 19 (50) July 24, p 16.

Barua, R.C., 1979, ASEB : Performance and Prospects, *Times of India* December 7, p 8, cols 7-8+.

Statistics

Anon, 1971, Census 1971 : Assam, Meghalaya and Nagaland, *Commerce* 123 (3163) December 18, p 1182.

Anon, 1976, (Book Review), *Eastern Economist* 66 (9) February 27, p 328-383.
Review of the Book : Hunter, W.W., 1976, *A Statistical Account of Assam*, B.R., Publisher, 2 vols, 420, 490 p.

Statistics : Vital

See Vital Statistics

Steel Industry and Trade

Sen, Mohit, 1965, Andhra Resents Decision on Fifth Steel Plant, *New Age* 13 (26) June 27, p 12.

Steel Plants

Bordoloi. P.C., 1981, Mini steel Plant in Assam, *Assam Information* 32, January-March, p 19-21.

Stone Implement

Goswami, M.C., and Bhagabats, A.C., 1959,

Strikes

Bhattacharya, M., 1964, Life at Standstill in Gauhati, *New Age* 12 (40) October 4, p 2.

Bhattacharya, M., 1978, Assam Government Goes Back on Assurance to Empiyees, *New Age* 26 (5) January 29, p 4.

Student Unrest

Times of India (Newspaper), 1980, Distrust Dispelled, *Times of India* February 7, p 6, col 1-2, editorial

Students

Bhattachary ya, B.K., 1974, Students Fill the Vacuum, *Economic and Political Weekly* 9 (27) July 6, p 1056-1057.
Kar, R.K., 1975, Selection of Spouse : Past and Present Views, *Eastern Anthropologist* 28 (3) July-September, p 241-254, bibliography, tables.

Sugar Industry and Trade

Anon, 1973, Six Sugar Mills Planned, *Commerce* 126 (3221) January 27, p 161.

Taxation

See also Companies

Chartered Accountant (Periodical), 1964, Taxation and Economic Development, *Chartered Accountant* 12 (8) February, p 395-396.
Uppal, J.S., 1964, The Rate, Prices and Level of Output : A Theoretical Approach, *Indian Journal of Economics* 44(4) April, p 327-328.

Tea Industry and Trade

Anon, 1979, Assam : Tea Takes the Brunt, *Eastern Economist* 72 (16) April 20, p 821-822.
Anon, 1979, Occupation of a Tea Estate, *Economic and Political Weekly* 14 (20) May 19, p 873.
Chatterjee, Suranjan and Gupta, Ratan Das, 1981, Tea-Labour in Assam: Recruitment and Govt. Policy, 1840-80, *Economic and Political Weekly* (Speical Number) 16 (44-46) November, p 1861-1868, footnotes.
Kar, R.K., 1981, Tea INdustry in Assam : A Chronological Accounts, *Man in Life* 7 (3-4) July-December , p 131-150, bibliography.
Phukan, A.C., 1979, A Decade of Employment in the Tea Industry of Assam, *Indian Worker* 27 (14) January 8, p 4-5+.
Roy Ghatak, Aditi, 1985, Warren : A New Group Emerges, *Capital* 194 (4806) May 27, p 35-44.
Vohra, Gautam S.G., 1980, Tea Plantations in Assam Undistrubed, *Times of India* July 12, p 6, cols 7-8.

Teachers

Anon, 1975, Assam : Bogeys on Teachers Demands, *Link* 17 (40) May 18, p 16-17.

Telephones

Anon, 1979, Assam : Anything but Unsatisfactory, *Commerce* 139 (3556) August 11, p 277.

Temples

Das Gupta, Baru, 1975, The Temple of Kamakhya, *Link* 17 (21) January 5, p 34-35.

Ghosh, B.K., 1977-78, A Note On the Image and Temple of Jainteswari, *Journal of Assam Research Society*, 23, p 45-48.

Sarma, Sri Pratap 1981-82, Antiquite of the Karnakhya Temples on the Nilacola, *Journal of Assam Research Society* 26, p 46-52, footnotes.

Terracottas

Sen, Sipra and Sharma, T.C., 1968, A Note on Terracotta Objects from Ambari, *Journal of Assam Research Society* 18, p 46-48, bibliography, footnotes.

Theatre

Neog, Maheswar, 1973-74, Assamese Drama and Theatre, *Journal of the University of Gauhati* 24-25 (1), p 1-43.

Tourist Trade

Choudhuri, B.C., 1965, Tourism in Assam, Foreign *Trade of India* August 26, p 42-43.

Phukan, Bhrigu Kumar, 1987, A Paradise for Tourists, *Economic Times* (Supplement) January 20, p 10, col. 5-8.

Das Gupta, H.R., 1986, Assam : A Tourists Paradise, *Capital* 197 (484-841) November 1, p 29-31.

Toys

Datta, Birendranath, 1980, Assamese Folk Toys, *Illustrated Weekly of India* 101 (22) June 1, p 16.

Trade Unions

Anon, 1979, Assam TU Convention Takes United Stand, *New Age* 27 (45) November 11, p 7.

Traffic Accidents

Anon, 1982, Rash Driving Major Contributory Factor, *Commerce* 145 (3731) December 11, p 878-879.

Transportation

Anon, 1982, (Boook Review), *Indian Journal of Public Adminstration* 28 (4), p 936-938.

Review of the Book : Medhi, Shyam, Bhadra, 1978, *Transport System and Economic Development in Assam*, Gauhati Publication Board, p 424. Rs 45.

Bhattacharjee, Bhupendra Kr., 1966, Assam's Transport System, AICC *Economic Review* 17 (18) April 1, p 15-16.

Deka, D., 1985, Distributional Pattern of the Origions and Destinations of Bus Traffic in the Brahmaputra Valley, *North Eastern Geographer* 17 (1-2) bibliography, figures, tables.

Deka, Phani and Deka, Dharitri, 1977, Population as a Factor in the Transport Development in the Brahmaputra Valley, Assam, Geographical Review of India 39 (1) March, p 42-47, bibliography, figure, mapes, tables.

Transporatation : Railways

Jagjit SIngh, 1967, Railways in Assam, *Illustrated Weekly of India* 88 (160 May 21, p 22-23, map.

Transportation : Road

Goswami, Dilip Kumar, 1981, Road Transport and Assam, *Assam Information* 33 April-July, p 6-10.

Tree Worship

Sarma, Binod, 1981, Tree Worship in Assam, *Folklore* 22 (2) Februuary p 34-41, bibliography, footnotes.

Tribal Insurgency

Anon, 1992, (Book Review), *Guru Nanak Journal of Sociology*, 13 (2) October, p 127-129.
Review of the Book : Bhattachaarjee, S.R., 1989, *Tribal Insurgency in Tripura : A Study in Exploration of Cause*, Inter-India Pub. New Delhi, 211p.

Tribes

See also Adimajati seva Mandal; Ahoms, Bils; Cheros; Dimasa Kacharis Mikirs; Scheduled Castes and Scheduled Tribes.

Anon, 1973, Growing Discontents among Assam Plains Tribals, *Link* 15 (41) May 20, p 17.

Anon, 1977, Assam's Hill Districts, *Link* 19 (48) July 10, p 21.

Anon, 1978, Towards Trible Development, *Assam Information*, 30, December, p 1-13.

Chakravarty, L.N., 1977, A Short Notes on' Posa', Resarun 3 (3) July, p 1-10, bibliography.

Chaudhuri, Alak R., 1980, A Short Note on Mirijim Tribal Craft of District, Assam, *Bulletin of the Cultural Research Institute* 14 (3-4), p 59-61.

Mitra, Mrinal K., et al; 1985, Some Observation on Rural Indebtendenss *Rajasthan Economic Journal* 9 (2) July, p 62-74, bibliography.

Tuteja, Usha, 1992, Marketed Surplus in Tribal Village of Assam *Indian Journal of Agricultural Economics* 47 (3), July-September, p 448.

Twenty Point Economic Programme

Anon, 1982, A Short Review on 20 Point Programme in Assam, *Assam Information*, 34, September, p 31-35.

Unemployment

See Employment and Unemployment

Urbanisation

Goswami, Atul and Goswami, Homeswar, 1991, Some Disquieting Trends of

Urbanisation in Asssam, *Assam Economic Journal* 8, p 95-99, bibliography, tables.

Vaisnavism

Anon, 1986, (Book Review), *Annals of Bhandankar Orient Research Institute* 67 (1-4), p 307-308.
Review of the Book : Nego, Maheshwar, 1985, *Early History of the Vaishnav Faith and Movement in Assam,* Motilal Banarsidas, Delhi, 400 p.

Anon, 1987, (Book Review), *Bulletin of Ramakrishna Mission Institute of Culture* 38 (6) June, p 85-86.
Review of the Book : Neog, Maheshwar, 1985, *Early History of the Vaishnav Faith and Movement in Assam,* Motilal Banarsidas, Delhi, 400p

Choudhuri, P.C., 1981-82, Ketekibari Satra : A Vaisnava Institution at Gauhati, *Journal of Assam Research Society* 26, p 68-72.

Goswami, Kesovananda Deva, 1973, A Peculiar Prayer Service of Assamese Vaisnavas, *Journal of Music Academic* 44 (1-4) p 227-233.

Neog, Maheshwar, 1986, Early History of the Vaishnav Faith and Movement in Assam : Sankaradeva and His Time, *Darshana International* 26 (1) January, p 85-86.

Village Defence Organisation

Bora, Phatik, 1978, Rural Policing in India vis-a-vis Role of V.D.O., in Assam, *Assam Information* , 29, January-February, p 28-30.

Vital Statistics

Goswami, H., 1978, Mortality Patterns in the Brahmaputra Valley of Assam, 1881-1931, *Assam Economic Journal* 4 (1) March, p 83-88, bibliography, tables.

Pachal, T.K., 1970, Construction of Life Table for Assam Females (1951-1960), *Sankhya* 32 (1-2) June, p 31-40, bibliography, footnotes, tables.

Voting

Balsara, S.D., 1979, Voting by Post, *Chartered Accountant* 27 (9) March, p 808-810.

Murugess Mudaliar, N., 1979, The List System of Voting : Remedy for Political Instability, *Indian Review* 75 (5) August, p 46-48.

Water Resources Development

Anon, 1975, Assam and Other North Eastern State : Vast Untapped Water Resources, *Commerce* (Annual Number) 131 (3372), p 187-192, figure, map, tables

Water Supply : Rural

Gogoi, K., 1973, Drinking Water in Assam Rural Areas : A Survey, *Kurukshetra* 21 (19) July1, p 9.

Wheat

Gogoi, K., Wheat Cultivation in Assam, *Kurukshetra* 24 (10) February 16, p 13.

Wildlife Convservation

Bhandari, Rakesh, 1982, Manas Wildlife Reserve, *Hindustan Times* (Magazine December 5, p vi, col 4-8.

Women : Education and Training

Das, Lakshahira, 1982, Problem and Priorities in the Education of Women in Assam, *Assam Information*, 34, September, p 7-15; *Education Quarterly* 34 (2) April, p 22-26.

Saikia, Anuva, 1983, Seasonal Variation of Female Participation in Farm Work, *Kurukshetra* 31 (19) July 1, p 15-17.

Women in Agriculture

Phukan, Minati, 1988, Behind the Cup That Cheers, *Indian Farming* 38 (8) November, p 21-22.

Youth

Anon, 1964, First All-Assam Youth Conference, *New Age* 12 (28) July 12, p 7.

INDEX